D0963068

# Cheers for *Cheer!*

"One of the more successful pieces of narrative nonfiction this year, distinguished by Torgovnick's impeccable ear and canny, original choice of subject matter."

—*Kirkus Reviews* (starred)

"Torgovnick spent a year tracking the travails of three teams in pursuit of national championship rings. . . . You'll get sucked into this book."

—Salon.com

"An engaging, voyeuristic narrative that suggests college cheerleaders are as close to real-life superheroes as exist."

—*The Dallas Morning News*

"An engrossing, highly readable narrative."

—*Tucson Citizen*

"Engrossing . . . very close to the kind of hard-edged investigative reporting done by writers like Jessica Mitford."

—*Booklist*

"Readers will learn lots about cheerleading and will find whatever stereotypes they may have about cheerleaders quickly overturned . . . sparkling with energy."

—*Library Journal*

"Torgovnick has clearly done her homework."

—*Publishers Weekly*

"Torgovnick has written an energetic book about the hypercompetitive world of organized college cheerleading, a world that can be crazy fun, disturbing, and quite grueling."

—*The Daytona Beach News-Journal*

"Torgovnick . . . provides a fascinating history of cheerleading."

—*Wilmington Star News*

"Reading *Cheer!* I felt intimately involved in the lives of Tarianne, Chassity, Sierra, Kali, and the rest. Because Kate Torgovnick has captured every voice in this fascinating world verbatim, crack open the book to read just one sentence and you too will be instantly immersed in these characters' riveting ups and downs (pun intended)."

—Jane Pratt, founder of *Jane* and *Sassy* magazines

"Whether you tried out for the Pom squad yourself, or blew off every high school pep rally like Torgovnick did, this suspenseful tale of cheerleading's glorious and addictive highs, and dangerous and pressure-cooked lows, will give you an insight into an ever-growing national phenomenon."

—Lauren Sandler, author of *Righteous: Dispatches from the Evangelical Youth Movement*

"Kate Torgovnick's *Cheer!* is the *Friday Night Lights* of a new generation. Through her painstaking research, compassionate analysis, and uncanny eye for scenes, she offers us a window into the competitive subculture of college cheerleading the way Susan Orlean did for orchid hunters and Stefan Fatsis did for Scrabble players."

—Courtney E. Martin, author of *Perfect Girls, Starving Daughters*

# CHEER!

Inside the Secret World

of College Cheerleaders

## KATE TORGOVNICK

A TOUCHSTONE BOOK

PUBLISHED BY SIMON & SCHUSTER

NEW YORK    LONDON    TORONTO    SYDNEY

*For Lizz, Mom, and Dad,*

*my personal cheerleaders*

Touchstone
A Division of Simon & Schuster, Inc.
1230 Avenue of the Americas
New York, NY 10020

Copyright © 2008 by Kate Torgovnick

All rights reserved, including the right to reproduce this book
or portions thereof in any form whatsoever. For information address Touchstone
Subsidiary Rights Department, 1230 Avenue of the Americas, New York, NY 10020.

First Touchstone trade paperback edition March 2009

TOUCHSTONE and colophon are registered trademarks of Simon & Schuster, Inc.

For information about special discounts for bulk purchases,
please contact Simon & Schuster Special Sales at
1-800-456-6798 or business@simonandschuster.com.

Designed by Mary Austin Speaker

Manufactured in the United States of America

10   9   8   7   6   5   4   3   2   1

The Library of Congress has cataloged the hardcover edition as follows:

Torgovnick, Kate.
   Cheer! : three teams on a quest for college cheerleading's ultimate prize / Kate
Torgovnick.
      p.   cm. — (A Touchstone book)
   1. Cheerleading—United States.   I. Title.
   LB3635.T67  2008
   791.6'4—dc22                                                                2007039277

ISBN-13: 978-1-4165-3596-6
ISBN-10:      1-4165-3596-9
ISBN-13: 978-1-4165-3597-3 (pbk)
ISBN-10:      1-4165-3597-7 (pbk)

Insert photo credits:
Pages 1–5: by Beth Fandal
Pages 6–7: by Gary Bogdon

# CONTENTS

# AUTHOR'S NOTE

I WASN'T ALWAYS FASCINATED by cheerleaders. I grew up in Durham, North Carolina, and in the halls of Jordan High School, I'd see cheerleaders wearing their sky blue skirts—they always seemed to travel in packs and to be laughing about something. I wondered how they never felt discouraged by the fact that the Falcons they so avidly cheered for never won a football game the entire time we were in school.

I was on the opposite end of the high school cliché spectrum. I was the rebel with bright blue streaks in her hair who could usually be found reporting stories for the high school newspaper. In that way that people "stand for things" when they're teens, I thought of myself as an individual, while they stood for conformity. They dutifully cheered on the sidelines of every football game while, truth be told, the only time I ever went to a game was when my friend streaked across the field during halftime. I was one of the occupants of his getaway car.

Pep rallies were held several times a year in the gym, and attendance was mandatory. Still, I skipped every single rally, sneaking across the street to a park. I remember walking back onto campus one day after a rally to meet my ride. As I strolled through the parking lot, there was a lot of commotion—and an ambulance with its lights flashing. "What happened?" I asked a friend. "A cheerleader fell real bad," he said, not at all concerned. "Maybe they should wear helmets."

Others' descriptions weren't as detached. As another friend told me, Courtney, a senior cheerleader with platinum blonde hair, had fallen off the top of a pyramid onto the hardwood floor. The image she described still sticks in my mind—Courtney's head bleeding, the deep red staining her pale yellow hair. A few days later she was back at school, having gotten away with just a concussion.

While I thought of myself as diametrically opposed to the cheerleaders, I recognized their magic. I remember seeing the cheerleaders practicing through the Plexiglas panels of the gym doors. They could all do back handsprings, while I'd practically flunked out of gymnastics class. And of course, there were some cheerleaders I couldn't help but like—Amanda, with her square jaw and baby-doll eyes, the editor-in-chief of my school newspaper who ended harsh edits with a smiley face. And Melissa, with a smattering of freckles across her nose, who whispered jokes in English class and who seemed sincerely annoyed when she was chosen Best Looking for senior superlatives.

When I shipped off to Barnard College in New York City—a part of Columbia University, which is not exactly famous for its athletics—I didn't think cheerleaders would be a fact of life anymore. But lo and behold, a Columbia cheerleader lived next door to me in my dorm sophomore year. I laughed when Evelyn, with her olive skin and exotic features, asked if I wanted to go to a game. Still, there was something admirable about how much enthusiasm she could muster for teams the other students couldn't care less about.

After college, I landed a job as an editor at *Jane* magazine. Among my daily duties of writing and editing, I was assigned a story about how injuries in cheerleading were on the rise. The words instantly made me flash back to high school and the image of the blood in Courtney's blonde hair.

I started doing research, interviewing dozens of college cheerleaders. What they described to me wasn't the happy-go-lucky sport I'd once imagined. They were part of a fervent subculture filled with people willing to take their bodies to the limit. I flew to Daytona Beach, Florida, to watch the National Cheerleaders Association College Cheer Nationals. I was blown away by the gravity-defying women and Herculean men. The glimmer of passion in their eyes was so intense that it was sometimes startling. In a way, I fell in love.

Almost every other sport has had its story told—football in *Friday Night Lights,* basketball in *Season on the Brink,* soccer in *Fever Pitch*—the list could go on and on. I wanted to tell the story of competitive cheerleaders.

What you are about to read is 100 percent real—the drama is authentic and the characters all can be found on their respective college campuses. But I want to give a few caveats. First, in order to construct a gripping narrative, I had to play with time—some scenes may happen out of order, and interviews from one point in time may be transplanted into another. Second, because I was not always present during pivotal moments, several scenes in this book have been re-created based on interviews with people who did witness them. Third, this book is limited by my perception of what is happening around me and by my memory, aided by notebooks and a digital recorder. And finally, as with any good reality TV show, please be aware that a ton of material from my year of research has been left on the cutting room floor.

Now, enjoy. By the end of this book, I hope that you will have a better understanding of college cheerleaders, those daredevils of the sidelines who have been, until now, so often misunderstood.

# INTRODUCTION

**WITH A MASS OF** blonde curls and her eyes coated in purple glitter, Sierra Jenkins looks like she could come in a pink box labeled Bad-Ass Barbie. Every muscle in her body seems crafted out of marble as she hovers seven feet off the ground, balancing in the palm of a hulking guy below her. Sierra curls her right leg behind her and reaches over-head to grab her cheerleading sneaker, the cracking leather held to-gether by masking tape. She yanks her foot up, and the space between her back and leg narrows to almost nothing.

Today is a legendary event for college cheerleaders, known to them by only one word: Nationals. The winner will be determined by mere hun-dredths of a point, yet Sierra beams as if she's never felt an ounce of stress in her life. She opens her mouth like a ventriloquist's dummy and winks at the 5,000-person audience. A Fox Sports Net camera zooms around her.

If you buy into high school mythology, you probably imagine cheerleaders trying out for the squad to cement their vote for home-coming queen or to score a date with a football player. But popularity is the last thing on college cheerleaders' minds. Meet Tarianne Green in her uniform the color of a yellow highlighter—she loves being launched twenty-five feet in the air for basket tosses. Meet Casi Davis, who with-stands more than 250 pounds as her teammates build human pyramids on her shoulders. Meet Kali Rae Seitzer, who pulls off tumbling passes on par with Olympic gymnasts. Meet James Brown, a former college football player and wrestler who says cheerleading is the hardest sport he's ever been a part of.

These cheerleaders spend upwards of twenty hours a week practicing, and that's not including the weight room visits and general conditioning they do on their own. They compete with broken thumbs and twisted ankles, still flashing Vaseline-toothed smiles when they're in pain. Some of them had 4.0 GPAs and high SAT scores but chose legendary cheer colleges like Stephen F. Austin State University, the University of Louisville, and the University of Kentucky rather than the Ivy League, all in the hopes of slipping a National Championship ring on their finger.

Modern cheerleading suffers from a split personality. Spirit cheerleading, where squads step-touch and spell out words from the sidelines, is one variety—the kind most of us think of when we hear the word *cheerleader*. But not as many of us are familiar with competitive cheerleading, where teams perform in intense championships. Some squads do only one of the above. The college cheerleaders you're about to meet do both.

While sports like football and basketball stagnated years ago, cheerleading is attracting new participants by the truckload; last year the four millionth cheerleader joined a squad. The spirit industry has doubled in value over the past five years, to become a $2 billion empire. In 2000, there were 250 gyms around the country that focused exclusively on stunting and tumbling skills for cheerleaders. Today, there are more than 2,000.

"I live for competing," says one college cheerleader. "As soon as I step out on the mat, all eyes are on me—it's straight adrenaline. It's an amazing rush," says another. "Cheerleading is addictive," confirms a third. "It's kind of like a drug," echoes a fourth.

No, these are not just pretty women shaking pom-poms.


## Why Are We All So Fascinated with Cheerleaders?

Cheerleaders are American icons, up there with the Statue of Liberty, the cowboy, and McDonald's arches. Many high-powered people in our society were once cheerleaders. Franklin D. Roosevelt, Dwight Eisenhower, Ronald Reagan, George Bush Sr., and George W. Bush—more presidents were former cheerleaders than members of the Skull and Bones. Other famous former cheerleaders: Madonna, Meryl Streep, Katie Couric, Halle Berry, Reba McEntire, Cameron Diaz. And a few more who will probably surprise you: Samuel L. Jackson, Ruth Bader Ginsburg, Gloria Steinem, and Aaron Spelling.

Anyone who's been to a movie or turned on a television in the past fifty years can list dozens of pop culture images of cheerleaders, from the now-classic movie *Bring It On*, to *Saturday Night Live* sketches, to *Heroes'* telling first season tagline, "Save the cheerleader, save the world." In popular culture, cheerleaders are generally portrayed as the queen bees—the ones at the top of the social pyramid whom everyone admires and/or fears. They have that elusive quality that seemed like the key to happiness when we were young: popularity. In many cases, they are set on high pedestals, objects to be admired from afar. Other times they are airheads without much going on upstairs, vapid and obsessed with how they look. Sometimes they are snotty, even cruel, to the people below them on the totem pole. Often, they are sluts.

We imbue cheerleaders with hundreds of different meanings, but no matter what, we are fascinated by them.

This enthrallment doesn't just play out in fiction. In 1991, we scratched our heads when Wanda Holloway, a Texas cheer mom, was arrested after attempting to hire a hit man to kill the mother of her daughter's cheerleading rival. Holloway was convinced she could secure her daughter a spot on the squad if her daughter's rival was too bereaved to cheer. We were mesmerized.

In March 2005, a twenty-six-year member of the Texas House of Representatives stood on the Senate floor and advocated for a bill to curb "sexually suggestive" cheerleading choreography. "We are telling teenagers not to have sex but are teaching them how to do it on the football field," Al Edwards told the press. He even drew connections between the increase in "overtly sexual" cheerleading dancing and a rise in the number of teen pregnancies, high school dropouts, and HIV cases.

Later that year, two female Carolina Panthers cheerleaders were arrested in Florida after one of them punched a bar patron in a bathroom brawl. The story instantly made the nightly news, and then it got more scandalous—the two women had allegedly been making out before the fight broke out. It became water cooler conversation for weeks.

Similarly, in 2006, a story unraveled out of McKinney, Texas. A group of cheerleaders dubbed the "Fab Five" were running amok at their high school. They harassed their coach, picked on other students, and talked back to teachers (one reported that a Fab Fiver had told her, "Pull your panties out of a wad"). They posted photos on MySpace that showed them drinking and simulating oral sex on penis-shaped candles. As the school district began a $40,000 investigation of the incidents, the story played out on Fox News, ABC News, and *Newsweek*.

In 2007, a batch of letters arrived at television stations and athletic departments across the country—half of them laced with insecticide. The writer's beef? That television networks only gave airtime to modestly dressed cheerleading squads. This crazy person could have written about any topic under the sun—the war in Iraq, gun control, universal healthcare. Instead, he or she wrote about cheerleaders.

In our fascination, we fit cheerleaders neatly into two categories: the chaste A-student in the student council, or the miniskirt-wearing slut most likely to go to third base. Cheerleaders straddle the fault line between the virgin and the whore. They are a group onto which our culture projects its complicated beliefs about women; they can be one extreme or the other, and rarely can we deal with the fact that, in reality, most women fall somewhere in between. It would probably disappoint the people who buy Playboy's video special *Cheerleaders and College Girls* (not the other way around) to learn that there are no pillow fights at cheer competitions. In fact, while I did meet several cheerleader couples and witness a certain level of sexual innuendo on coed teams, there's not nearly as much hooking up as you would think, considering the fact that this is one of the only sports where men and women compete together.

All of this brings me to one of the reasons I was so drawn to writing this book. Our common knowledge of cheerleaders is dramatically at odds with the reality. In American culture, we give athletes the utmost respect. But most of us—even the ones familiar with competitive cheerleading—don't acknowledge that cheerleaders are athletes. It's a rift intricately tied to cheerleading's evolution.

## From Yell Leaders to All-Stars: A Brief History of Cheer

In the beginning, cheerleaders were men. At the first college football game between Princeton and Rutgers, a group of Princeton students began chanting, "Rah rah rah! Tiger tiger tiger! Sis sis sis! Boom boom boom! Ahhhhhh!" It sounds like bad Dr. Seuss, but it caught on. Soon Princeton appointed "yell leaders," whose job was to orchestrate chants and pump up the crowd. The idea spread across the country, and in 1898, at the University of Minnesota, yell leader Jack Campbell darted in front of his fellow students to lead them in a cheer. He had no idea what his random action would inspire.

For the next forty years, male cheerleaders used megaphones, noise-makers, jumps, flips, and chants to get the crowd on its feet. Because cheerleaders were elected, the position became synonymous with popularity, much like homecoming courts and prom queens today.

In the 1930s, Lawrence Herkimer was a Dallas teenager with a stutter. "I couldn't speak worth a darn," he recalls. But, thanks to a gymnastics class, he could do a back flip. It was enough to get him elected as a cheerleader, and something magical happened to him on the sidelines of football games—his stutter disappeared. The whole school applauded as he turned handsprings when his team got a touchdown.

Herkimer went on to cheer at Southern Methodist University, but during his junior year, the country entered World War II. Like many men of his generation, he joined the navy. Just as women were filling the male void in factories, they took over as cheerleaders. At the same time, the president of Kilgore College noticed students drinking in the parking lot during halftime. He asked the now-female cheerleaders to perform during halftime to keep people in their seats. Cheerleaders went from leading a crowd to entertaining them.

In 1949, Lawrence Herkimer was back at Southern Methodist, coaching gymnastics and cheerleading. Other schools began calling him, asking him to work with their cheerleaders. Herkimer had the idea to start a company, the National Cheerleaders Association (NCA).

"That first summer we had fifty-two girls sign up for a summertime course," says Herkimer. "The next summer we had 350." Within a few years, the NCA was running 750 camps around the country.

"I had no idea how big it would become," says Herkimer, who is now in his eighties. His eyes smile behind his glasses, and he touches the pen in the pocket of his collared shirt. "My first wife said, 'You know, Herkie, you can't do back flips all your life. We oughta get into something else.'" Her idea—sell pleated skirts.

The Herkimers were also behind the invention of the spirit stick and the pom-poms. "I always said I had a depression-proof business because if someone's daughter gets elected cheerleader they're going to sell the boat before they tell her she can't have her two pom-poms and sweater," explains Herkimer. Wearing the uniform he created, cheerleaders made the leap to American icons.

In the '70s, Herkimer introduced more gymnastics into the NCA's curriculum and noticed more men joining squads as a result. He began grooming a successor—Jeffrey Webb, a talented cheerleader from the University of Oklahoma. Webb had big ideas. "I wanted to transform the activity. Herkie had taken it to a certain level, but it had pretty much stayed the same," explains Webb. "I had a vision of it being updated, modernized, and made more athletic."

Webb envisioned men lifting women, women sailing to extreme heights, and big, multiple-person pyramids. He started developing techniques to teach these acrobatic skills. In 1974, when he was twenty-four, Webb began running the Universal Cheerleaders Association (UCA) out of his apartment in Memphis, Tennessee. He traveled, giving demonstrations. "We expected resistance, but we got the opposite—it was a stampede," says Webb.

In its first summer, the UCA taught 4,000 cheerleaders. They began offering uniforms that allowed for more movement—the skirts shorter, the tops less bulky. They even came up with a lightweight sneaker to replace saddle shoes. The UCA grew steadily. "But at the five-year mark, we got frustrated because we were still regional and we wanted to be nationwide," says Webb. "Someone said, 'Why don't we create a competition?'"

In 1981, Webb invited twenty teams from around the country to participate in the first-ever National High School Cheerleading Championship. Held at Sea World, it was an instant success. A few years later, Webb added a college championship to the roster. The NCA noticed squads defecting, so Herkimer created an NCA competition, too. Thus began cheerleaders' dual existence: supporting school teams and simultaneously competing in their own right.

In the 1980s, gymnastics found itself in hot water. Stories of poor coaching circulated in the press, and many schools stopped offering the sport because of insurance concerns. A large number of homeless gymnasts channeled their energy into cheerleading, bringing with them their passion for defying gravity and a perfectionist mentality.

Soon, in the mid-to-late '90s, new gyms popped up all over the country specializing in acrobatics for cheerleading. They enrolled girls like ballet schools, and they quickly picked up on the competition model, forming all-star teams. Students could cheer for their school teams as well, but many chose to be all-stars, with no sideline duties whatsoever.

The explosion of all-star gyms fueled a rapid growth in cheerleading, from preschool-aged kids through college. And cheerleading continues to be one of the fastest-growing sports, both within the U.S. and abroad. Today, more than seventy-five organizations regulate cheerleading, many of them holding their own national competitions.

At the college level, because of cheerleading's designation as an "activity" rather than a "sport," it does not fall under the jurisdiction of the National Collegiate Athletic Association (NCAA). Many people in cheerleading would like to see it stay that way, since NCAA governance comes with strict rules. NCAA sports compete during only one season per year, while cheerleading is a year-round activity. In NCAA sports, athletes are eligible to play for only four years. In this book, you'll meet cheerleaders like Doug Daigle, who is beginning his eighth year as a college cheerleader.

For college cheer, Herkimer's NCA and Webb's UCA remain the two largest organizations. They maintain separate identities and national competitions even though they are both now owned by the same parent company, Varsity Brands, Inc. Today, rather ironically, the NCA is known for flashy routines with innovative choreography while the UCA focuses on crowd-leading and more traditional stunting and pyramids. "It's kind of like Coke and Pepsi—you just have a preference," explains Dawn Calitri, the current president of the NCA. Teams may compete at only one, and coaches usually pick whichever they like best. The NCA holds Nationals in April in Daytona Beach, Florida, at an Elizabethan-style amphitheater that has been dubbed "the castle." UCA Nationals take place in January at Walt Disney World's Wide World of Sports.

Jeff Webb, still CEO of the UCA, worries that for school teams, the pendulum has swung too far in favor of competitive cheer. "I think we're going to start to see the emphasis move back to the traditional aspects," he says.

But many of the cheerleaders in this book would predict the opposite—a large chunk would gladly relinquish their sideline duties. Sometime soon, cheerleading may be heading toward a schism.

## And the Trophy for the Most Dangerous Sport Goes To?

In 2006, in the lead-up to the NCAA Men's Basketball Tournament, America witnessed something that hinted cheerleading had changed. Three and a half minutes before the end of a game, the Southern Illinois University cheerleaders ran onto the court to perform during a time-out. As they tossed Kristi Yamaoka onto the top of a pyramid, her foot slipped and she fell backwards. She plummeted, neck and head first, onto the hardwood floor. The television cameras kept rolling, and the game was delayed as Kristi just lay there. Trainers and medics ran onto the court to assess the situation.

As the Southern Illinois squad, 14,000 fans in the arena, and millions of TV viewers held their breath, the medics lifted Kristi onto a stretcher. They began to wheel her off the floor, her cheerleading uniform eerie under the braces holding her neck and head in place.

The band began to play the Southern Illinois fight song. All of a sudden, Kristi's hand shot up, her fingers wiggling. She put one hand to her hip and did a small circle with the other. As she was wheeled out of the arena, Kristi performed her fight song from her stretcher. The crowd roared.

Kristi's fall was replayed on every major news channel. In the hospital, Kristi received phone calls from Diane Sawyer and President Bush. When she left with a concussion and fractured neck vertebrae, she was invited for interviews by dozens of reporters, landing on Katie Couric's couch on the *Today* show. The country was fascinated by this girl who'd shown such determination to keep on cheering.

Cheerleading injuries shock us, and in the past few years the *New York Times, Newsweek, USA Today,* and dozens of other media outlets have written exposés on the topic. The numbers are startling at first glance. In 2007, an estimated 26,786 cheerleaders in the U.S. landed in the emergency room for cheer-related injuries—more than double the number injured in 1991. Over the past twenty-five years, 141 female athletes have been paralyzed or killed as a direct result of a sport in high school and college; almost two-thirds of these catastrophic injuries were in cheerleading. And even though the NCAA does not regulate cheerleading, they announced in 2005 that a quarter of their insurance claims since 1998 came from cheerleaders injured while cheering at NCAA events.

It makes perfect sense why members of the media latch onto this topic. It's dramatic, a slice of tragic Americana, and the people getting hurt are women. Young women. Often attractive young women. But the shock these numbers produce comes from that central misunderstanding of what cheerleaders do. When you see a "flyer"—the cheerleader whose duty it is to do top stunts, pyramids, and basket tosses—soaring through the air at high speeds, it seems almost a given that there are injuries in cheerleading.

And the statistics are misleading when taken out of context of other sports. Cheerleading will never come close to the king of sports injuries: football. All in all, about 6 cheerleaders out of a thousand will visit the emergency room in any given year. For football, it's 42 players out of a thousand. In fact, sledding, bunk beds, volleyball, and television sets all landed more Americans in the hospital last year than cheerleading.

For years, debates have raged about whether cheerleading is an activity or a sport. It is a sport with individual and team components as well as an artistic bent, putting it in the same category as Olympic diving or gymnastics. But it has even more in common with extreme sports like motocross, skateboarding, and skydiving. The intensity is part of the appeal.

Ask any competitive cheerleader, and she or he will rattle off a list of injuries as if it's no big deal. "I've gotten four concussions, broken a rib, knocked my jaw out of place, and of course I've broken fingers," one woman explains. Competitive cheerleaders look at injuries like badges of honor—soldiers recounting war wounds. Their injuries are a symbol of their hard work and sacrifice.

Yes, of course, a single serious injury in any sport is one too many. But competitive cheerleaders, like race car drivers, know there is a risk. Like football players, they know their bodies are put in positions prone to injury. As one woman told me, "Personally, I love the danger of flying high in the air."

Still, as you'll see firsthand, it is no laughing matter when a cheerleader crashes to the ground and must be rushed to the emergency room. Luckily, the injury is catastrophic in far less than 1 percent of these cases.

## Does This Sport Make My Butt Look Big?

In a classic scene from *Bring It On,* a demented choreographer named Sparky Polastri strolls down the line of cheerleaders critiquing their bodies. "You have weak ankles," he says to one. "One of your calves is bigger than the other," he barks to another. "Ah, good tone and general musculature," he says, setting his eyes on a third. "Report those compliments to your ass before it gets so big it forms its own website."

In our society, body dissatisfaction is an epidemic, and cheerleaders feel these same anxieties in a pressure cooker environment. By job description, they wear short skirts and midriff-baring tops—their bodies are constantly on display for public critique. And cheerleading is a sport where human beings lift others in the air, meaning that there is intense pressure on flyers to stay light and tossable. As one cheerleader told me, "People outside the cheerleading world see a normal-sized girl and think, 'This girl is skinny.' That same girl looks huge to cheerleading people."

Listening to cheerleaders talk about their body image is just plain scary. Weight limits are one of the nastiest realities they face. Though many teams have abandoned this system, some teams won't consider taking a cheerleader if she weighs over 120 pounds. Cheerleaders on these teams describe weigh-ins during which they have to step on the scale in front of the whole team—often a traumatic experience. For a college cheerleader, the words *freshman 15* are more frightening than *nuclear war.*

While most coaches are excellent about encouraging proper nutrition and exercise, one cheerleader told me that her coach suggested smoking to keep from packing on pounds. Another alleged that a friend's team used methamphetamines. "In the month before Nationals, the girls on the squad would do a lot of meth and lose like twenty pounds so their rib cages were sticking out," she said. Later on, you'll meet one cheerleader whose weight-loss secret was cocaine.

Diet pills are popular among the cheer set. One former cheerleader told me, "A lot of people do Hydroxycut and all the products that are basically legal speed. It's the number-one subject of locker room talk."

As with all women in their teens and twenties, eating disorders are a huge problem. In the general population 5 percent of women are currently suffering from an eating disorder, but the rate is unquestionably higher for cheerleaders. Soon, you'll meet a cheerleader who's waged a six-year battle with bulimia, and you'll hear from others who find themselves in the gray area between an eating disorder and "watching what I eat."

Being tiny isn't nearly as important as the diet pills and eating disorders would have you believe. Guy after guy cheerleader tells me that they'd rather have a strong partner with a lot of muscle control—making them easy to lift, catch, and hurl about—than one who is simply light. And many coaches tell me that good technique is much more important than the number on the scale.

And it's by no means just female cheerleaders feeling body pressures. In the summer of 2004, a guy cheerleader at the Air Force Academy was court-martialed for using steroids. The story blipped in the media (interestingly, men in cheerleading don't generate nearly as much press as the women), but no one stopped to think that steroids might actually be a problem in cheerleading just as they are in baseball, football, and hockey. When I asked male cheerleaders to estimate the percentage of their peers who take some sort of performance enhancer or steroid to fuel their heavy lifting, the guesses ranged from 50 percent all the way up to 90 percent.

This is an area where not being considered a "sport" hurts college cheerleaders. While the NCAA bans substances and spends millions of dollars a year on drug screening for athletes, it is up to each individual school to determine whether to do expensive testing for cheerleaders. Many don't. Cheerleaders go to these extreme lengths to make themselves better competitors. If there were even a chance of getting caught and kicked off the team, those percentage points would decrease sharply.

While steroid use and extreme dieting are by no means good things, they show just how hard cheerleaders push to be the best, and they hint at the superhuman intensity lurking just underneath the stereotype.

## Meet the Contenders

This is the story of three college cheerleading teams that would give anything to be National Champions. You will follow each team through their 2006–2007 season—beginning at tryouts and culminating in their final, high-stakes performance—as they practice, eat, live, compete, and party together.

The first team is the Stephen F. Austin Lumberjacks from Nacogdoches, Texas. The Lumberjacks are the best of the best—they have eight National titles under their belt. Stephen F. Austin's cheerleaders' hands sparkle with National Championship rings—they have won them the past four years. This year they are gunning for one of the longest winning streaks in cheerleading history—a fifth in a row.

Even though SFA is located in a small East Texas town, it recruits some of the best cheerleaders in the nation. Their tumbling skills are sublime, and they are known for innovating new pyramids. But their bread and butter is killer partner stunting. In addition to the team competition at both UCA and NCA Nationals, there is a Partner Stunt Championship. Under bright spotlights, one guy and one girl perform a crazy array of strength, lifting, and flexibility stunts. At the 2005 NCA Nationals, Stephen F. Austin partner pairs placed first, second, and third. No other school can touch them on this event.

The second squad is the Jaguars from Southern University in Baton Rouge, Louisiana, one of the oldest and most respected historically black colleges in the country. "We're like both squads in *Bring It On* rolled into one," explains their coach, and the description is perfect. This team is known equally for its strong, creative stunting and its heart-pumping, hip-shaking choreography.

The Southern Jaguars have taken home first-place trophies at Black College Nationals five times, but they've shown that they can be competitors in mainstream cheerleading as well. In 2002, they traveled to NCA Nationals and rocked the competition, coming in second in their division, ahead of Stephen F. Austin. To this day, a predominantly black squad has never won a national title at NCA or UCA Nationals. The Southern Jaguars pray that this will be the year.

The final team is the University of Memphis All-Girl Tigers, National Champions of the UCA in 2004. Most teams in college cheerleading are Coed, but All-Girl is a thriving division at both UCA and NCA Nationals. (A college will decide to have an All-Girl squad, a Coed squad, or both based largely on what the coach wants.) In All-Girl cheerleading, two or four women base stunts, the flyer's weight supported by the group rather than by one beefy guy. But at the University of Memphis, the female bases are so strong that many of them can lift a flyer on their own.

In college, All-Girl squads don't get as much respect as Coed teams—they typically have smaller budgets and scholarships, they often get less prestigious cheering assignments (volleyball, anyone?), and their competition gets less television airtime. But the University of Memphis women are hoping to change that.

In most sports, a team's season counts for something. But in college cheerleading, the entire year boils down to the 2 minutes and 15 seconds when a squad performs in the finals at Nationals. All of the teams in this book share one goal: to give the performance of their lives and bring home a National Championship trophy. But before they can even think of competing at Nationals, these men and women will first have to make the team. And that alone is no small feat. . . .

# PART ONE

TRYOUTS
APRIL—MAY

# CHAPTER 1

## The Yale of College Cheerleading

*The Stephen F. Austin Lumberjacks*

BRAD PATTERSON LEANS BACK in his chair. On the blue mat in front of him, more than 150 cheerleaders form an ocean of bodies as they practice. Brad crosses his arms over his chest, his baby face out of place on his bulky body. In his purple SFA polo shirt with sunglasses tucked into the open buttons, he appears laidback. But he's taking careful mental notes. It's the day before tryouts for the Stephen F. Austin cheerleading squad. As head coach, by the end of tomorrow, Brad will have to whittle the 150 people on the mat down to just thirty.

Stephen F. Austin State University is the Yale of college cheerleading. They've won their division, Cheer I at NCA Nationals, eight times. Just three weeks ago, they clinched a fourth set of championship rings in a row. In fact, the squad has won every year since it's been under Brad's direction.

SFA is located in Nacogdoches, Texas, a city that calls itself "The Oldest Town in Texas," although Brad tells me two other cities claim the same thing. As I made the two-hour drive from Houston, I passed logging truck after logging truck, making it obvious how the school chose the Lumberjack as their mascot. Nacogdoches is small—a main drag with the university on one side and strip malls on the other. A water tower looms above the town with the letters SFA emblazoned across it in huge purple letters.

Nacogdoches boasts only 30,000 people, but a third of them routinely show up at SFA football games. There's enough interest in cheerleading here to warrant two all-star gyms. But that shouldn't be surprising. After all, in Texas, football is often referred to as a religion, and cheerleaders are the high priests.

As I watch the SFA hopefuls practice, Newton's theory of gravity seems broken—nearly every woman who goes up stays up. Still, Brad's lips are pursed. "This is one of my smaller tryouts," he says in a smooth Southern twang. "That's how it is the years we win—people get intimidated. In the years we don't win, they come crawling out of the woodwork."

Brad has recruited many of the people on the mat, scoping them out at competitions and swooping down to suggest that they try out. "At this point, I'm seriously looking at fifteen girls and twenty-five guys. But my mind can be changed during tryouts—it always is," he says.

Sierra Jenkins is no doubt one of Brad's top picks. Her über-blonde hair is piled on top of her head in a messy ponytail and a HELLO, MY NAME IS sticker is affixed to her black spandex shorts, dubbing her #48. She hails from Arlington, Texas, and has cheered since elementary school. In the fall, she'll be a junior, and she already wears two National Championship rings around her thin fingers. In fact, in the eight years she's competed at Nationals with school teams, she has *never* lost.

Sierra is used to being the best. As a college freshman, she headed to a top cheer college in Hawaii, where she established herself as a standout. But it wasn't the idyllic year of waterfall hikes and white sand beaches she'd imagined. "I was the biggest girl on the team. I thought I was fine, but my coaches were like, 'You gotta lose weight,' " says Sierra, a just-gargled-gravel roughness to her voice. "My first few weeks in college, all my dreams and aspirations went down the drain."

Sierra developed an eating disorder that brought her weight down to a scary ninety-five pounds. Still, she shone on the mat and was even made a captain. But midway through her sophomore year, Sierra realized she needed help. She headed home to Texas.

Back home, she enrolled in a junior college to keep in shape, and her flexibility and energy quickly made her the team's star. "I'm always trying to be like, 'Look at me. Look at me,' " she says. "My method is just to have more enthusiasm than everyone else. I want to see everyone's eyes going to me."

Today, on the mat, Sierra does a Rewind. It's a move I first saw at last year's Nationals, when a cheerleader explained to me, "Every year, there's a move that's *the* move to try. This year, it's the One-Arm Rewind." The name makes complete sense once you see it—it looks like that old special effects trick where an editor plays the film backwards to make it look like someone is jumping up instead of down.

Sierra stands in front of her partner, her knees bent. His hands are placed on her lower back and she leans back on his wrists. She swings her arms and flips backwards as he grunts and pushes up, like a track and fielder throwing a shot put ball.

Sierra flexes her feet sharply in the air, uncurling her body into a straight line. There's a loud smack as her feet land in her partner's open palm. Her big, brown eyes widen as she smiles. Her brows swoop in thin arches more fitting to a silent movie star.

Along the walls of the women's basketball gymnasium where tryout practice is being held, a mural is painted of women dribbling basketballs. Bleachers run around the perimeter of the room, where a few parents sit, nervously biting their fingernails. Brad admits that parents can be uppity about tryouts. "I'll get phone calls from moms who have kids in the seventh grade. They'll ask, 'What would she need to do to make SFA?' I say, 'Call me in five years,' " he jokes with a dry delivery.

There is no official agenda for today's practice—the cheerleaders are free to rehearse anything they want in preparation for tomorrow. Brad has asked that the cheerleaders find someone new to try out with, rather than auditioning with a regular partner. All day, guys and girls have walked up to each other asking, "Will you stunt with me?" like they're at a middle school dance. By the end of the day, they need to map out the three stunts they'll perform at tryouts.

Most of the cheerleaders in the room are hedging the uncertainty by choosing a partner from last year's SFA team. "Returners spots are not guaranteed," says Brad. "But it's rare that I won't take someone back. I pull kids from all over the country, so if someone uprooted their life and moved here, I'm not gonna replace them with someone who's just a little bit better."

Yvette Quiñones runs up to the table where Brad sits. Her soft belly pokes forward like a little girl unaware that she's supposed to suck in. She is one of the smallest women I've ever seen—4'11" and ninety pounds, a stature she attributes to her Mexican heritage. Her pin-straight hair falls over her rounded cheeks.

Even though she looks young, Yvette will be a senior at SFA. She's one of the few returning flyers from last year's team, and she's already agreed to stunt with four guys at tryouts tomorrow. "I better make captain for this," she jokes, as yet another guy asks to be her partner.

The men flock to Yvette because of her bubbly demeanor and because they assume her small stature will make stunting a breeze. But Yvette knows that isn't always true. "Sometimes guys overtoss me since I'm so light. They can't control it," she explains. "So if it's not working out, I'll tell them, 'I know the perfect girl for you,' and introduce them to someone else."

Yvette strolls back to the mat, and Brad's phone rings for the hundredth time today. "There's a girl on the way now who had to take the SAT this morning," he says. "According to her mom, she's God's gift to cheerleading."

Like academic scholars, cheerleaders have specialties. Men can be stunters or tumblers—a precious few do both well. Occasionally, a woman on a Coed team will be a tumbler, but more often they are flyers. Some flyers are fantastic all-around, while others concentrate on partner stunting, basket tosses, or pyramids. To decide who makes a team, coaches will often factor in what specialties they are currently lacking.

Looking around the room, I see lots of shirts for Navarro College, Trinity Valley Community College, and Kilgore College—three junior colleges located within a few hours' drive of Nacogdoches. These teams have become a minor league feeder system for the Lumberjacks; most team members come to SFA after cheering at a junior college for two years. Because cheerleaders generally start at SFA as juniors, many of them stay on extra years. It's not uncommon to talk to an SFA cheerleader who's in his or her fifth or sixth year as an undergraduate—some even enroll in grad school primarily to cheer. The scholarship means there's no financial burden to staying in school.

"It took me four years after community college because I couldn't pick a major," says Trisha O'Connor, the squad's assistant coach, a quiet woman in her twenties with long, reddish hair. She insists on calling me ma'am even though I am only two years older than her.

Trisha glances at Doug Daigle, whose shaved head and bulging muscles make him look like Mr. Clean squashed down to 5'10". This will be Doug's eighth year in college cheerleading. "I graduated in 2003 and started a career as an insurance agent," he explains. "I was making good money, but I didn't feel prepared for the real world. So I quit my job, applied to grad school at SFA, and came back. Brad was once my captain—now he's my coach."

"Doug's old as dirt," says Brad, shaking his head.

On the mat, Samantha Frazer talks to her partner from the air. Her eyes are lined in kohl, like a Texas Cleopatra, and everything about her is long, from her arms, to her legs, to her narrow face and its steep nose. "Pick it up, pick it up," Samantha commands as her arm bends. With the determination of an Olympic lifter, he powers her back in the air. "Yay," she says as she lifts her chin and smiles.

When Samantha started two years ago at a junior college, she was only a mediocre stunter. Then she saw SFA for the first time. "I was like, 'What are they on?'" she remembers. "They were purebred cheerleaders." Samantha was inspired to join a recreational team with some of them and worked her butt off for the next year and a half to reach their skill level.

Making the SFA squad would be a dream come true for Samantha. The same goes for her boyfriend, Hunter, a petite tumbler with light brown stubble. Both of them are trying out, and they're praying that they both make it so they can move to Nacogdoches together.

"Drop!" bellows Brad, all of a sudden.

On the mat, a girl has fallen straight to the ground, none of the guys having reached her in time to break her fall. All the men stop what they're doing and plunge to the ground for fifty push-ups while the girl slowly stands up and walks it off.

"She's picking mat out of her teeth," someone jokes.

But Brad takes this seriously—hence the push-up punishment. The number-one rule of cheerleading for men is simple: don't let your girl hit the ground.

Practice ends an hour later. The cheerleaders gather around Brad, and he briefs them on what to expect for tomorrow. "We've got good, strong guys," he says as the hopefuls head out the door. "But we need good flyers—I'm losing three of the best in the country."

Almost on cue, Sierra runs back into the gym. Brad's eyes follow her as she picks up a bag and rushes back out the door. "I like her more every day," says Brad.

## "That's a Law of Gravity I Just Don't Understand."

I've never felt so tall. At 5'4", I'm used to being one of the shorter people in any given room. But as I stand at the corner of the mat surrounded by women stretching in the minutes before tryouts, I tower over them. Even the ones who appeared tall from afar, like Samantha, still only reach my nose.

Brad and his wife stroll through the gymnasium holding hands. His wife is half his size, a former college cheerleader herself, with a stylish bob and a balloon for a stomach. She's six months pregnant. Michael Preston, SFA's Director of Student Life and Brad's boss, walks behind them. "This is the worst day for me," he says. "There's all these kids and I don't know their abilities and they're trying all this stuff. I just hope they signed the waiver forms."

Brad, assistant coach Trisha, Michael, and I take seats at the judging table that faces the mat. Trisha neatly arranges stacks of information sheets and judging scorecards, all of which she's printed with matching Lumberjack logos in the corner. "Five minutes until we start," yells Brad, cupping his hands to his mouth.

The women strip off their sweatpants and T-shirts and stand in skimpy sports bras and shorts that barely cover their butt cheeks. A few of them shiver—the air-conditioning is on full blast.

"Everyone move to the right of the mat," says Brad, as all the hopefuls obey. Some of them sit calmly, while others squeeze in a last-minute stunt. Brad begins calling names, the contenders heading to the mat in groups of three in the order of the numbers scrawled on their nametags.

Samantha is one of the first to be summoned. She stands up and claps as she walks to the mat, getting out her nervous energy.

For their tryout, each cheerleader must show Brad three things—their best running tumbling pass, the tumbling they can do from standing, and, finally, the three partner stunts that best show off their skills. For her running tumbling, Samantha will attempt a Full—the Holy Grail of college cheerleading, where a cheerleader flips and twists for one full rotation in the air before landing.

Samantha looks pumped as she runs, and her body whips perfectly into the air. But she stumbles to her knees as she lands. "Oh, man," she says, throwing a fist toward the ground. Brad allows everyone one do-over on each move. She runs again. Handspring, handspring, Full. She lurches forward, her knees dropping to the mat again. It's not the way you want to start a tryout, but Samantha plays it off, turning to the others and pointing her index toward the ceiling.

Samantha is focused on redeeming herself in the partner stunts. But as she and her partner attempt a Rewind, he can't catch her feet. She falls like a defective Weeble. "Ugh," groans Samantha. They move on to a new stunt, and finally they nail it. Samantha kicks her left leg up in a move called a Heel Stretch. Her eyes are focused, unwavering from a point behind me on the wall. She hops down and bows.

Samantha's last stunt has a modest name: the Awesome. Her partner tosses her, catching both of her feet in one palm. Samantha's stomach muscles quiver as she holds the position for several seconds before hopping down.

Samantha takes a seat, her thin lips in a straight line. "I tried out between two other girls—I'm 100 pounds and they're like eighty-five," she says. "Plus I didn't land a single tumbling pass. There's no way I made it." She sighs deeply.

The next group called to the mat is all men. "It's a sausagefest," someone behind me yells. As the guys get into place for their partner stunts, Yvette skips onto the mat, standing in front of guy #1. He throws her in the air like a juggler tossing pins. As she does a trick, Yvette blows kisses to the judging table. She hops down and high-fives her partner.

She moves over to the next guy in line—she'll be stunting with him as well. All in all, Yvette will stunt with five different guys today, her face glowing each time she's up in the air.

We're halfway through tryouts. Everyone is amazing, but it's hard not to feel jaded watching people do the same things over and over again. And then Sierra walks onto the mat.

As she stands before us, it's striking how much darker her tanned skin is than her bleached ponytail. She runs and turns a flawless Full. For her standing tumbling, she looks straight at the judging table and shuffles backwards, bending back toward the ground and flipping over before launching into another Full.

"That's a law of gravity I just don't understand," says Brad as the rest of the cheerleaders clap. "I need more girls with Fulls."

Sierra pauses, her chest heaving as a partner steps behind her.

"Well, are you gonna go?" asks Brad.

"Not yet, my legs hurt too bad," she says.

Brad looks impatient as she takes another minute before flying into a Rewind. As she stands up in midair, she pulls her leg to the point where it appears to bend backwards. Her eyes bug out as she molds her mouth into an O. From here, Sierra does a Double Down, the hardest dismount in cheerleading, where a flyer whips her legs together from whatever position she's in and spins twice like a log rolling in water. Sierra makes it look easy. Whispers arise from around the room.

Sierra gets ready for her next stunt, a Full Up, where a flyer rotates once as her partner throws her into place over his head. As her sneakers land in her partner's hands, Sierra turns to the side and brings her right leg behind her, grabbing her foot over her head in a move called a Scorpion. Her body flattens like a pancake as she pulls her foot higher. I'm prepared for her hip to pop out of its socket at any moment. She sticks out her tongue and Doubles Down.

"That's skills," says Brad quietly as Sierra walks off the mat and sits down, an ear-to-ear grin on her face.

Tryouts are done and a different mood settles over the gym. Nervousness has been replaced by anticipation. "Everyone listen up," yells Brad. "Good job. In two hours, the list will be posted on that bulletin board over there." He points to the corner of the gym at a board with scalloped borders. "If you don't make it, there are coaches from Trinity Valley, Navarro, and Kilgore here if you would like to talk to them."

Everyone starts talking all at once. "Listen up," bellows Sierra in her Southern rasp.

"Go get some food and come back then," says Brad.

## "It's Like She's in an Antigravity Room."

I feel like I'm privy to a meeting of the Joint Chiefs of Staff as I sit in a conference room with Brad, Trisha, three community college coaches, and several SFA cheer alumni who make a point of coming to practices. They act as advisors for the program, and Brad wants their opinions on who should make the squad. The twelve of us sit in cushy black executive chairs, the corporate glamour hindered only by the chalkboards and two-way mirror that takes up one whole wall. One of the alums lays his hand on the table, four fingers sparkling with championship rings. Each one has a different pattern. My favorite has an axe shape beveled on a faux ruby.

The first order of business is to look at videos. Since many cheerleaders can't make the trek to tryouts, they send in a video audition and hope Brad will be dazzled. As the group watches one sent in by a female tumbler, I hear rounds of "Wow," "That's beautiful," "She tumbles like a guy," and "Holy shit."

"It's like she's in an antigravity room," says Brad.

"Sierra is not going to like her—she's used to being the star," someone notes.

"I should also say that she's trying out at Louisville," says Brad.

"Oh, Louisville will take her," moans one of the alumni women.

If SFA is the Yale of college cheerleading, then the University of Louisville is Harvard. In the NCA's Cheer IA division, Louisville is also after their fifth straight title this year. At Nationals, there are many divisions—Cheer IA, Cheer I, Cheer II, All-Girl I, All-Girl II, Small Coed I, Small Coed II, and Junior Colleges. A National Champion will be named in each.

But even though Louisville is Cheer IA and SFA is Cheer I, the two are rivals. At NCA Nationals there is a Grand National Champion—

the team that scores the highest in the competition out of all the divisions. Louisville has been the Grand National Champion four years running. SFA hasn't won since 2000. Still, as Brad told me earlier, Division 1A teams are not better by virtue. "The division you're in is based on how many people attend football games—it doesn't have anything to do with the cheerleaders," he explained. "We can beat everyone, we've done it before."

Brad's interested in two more of the video tryouts. "She's ultra-skinny, which worries me," says Brad, as a girl with limbs the size of pencils stunts on the screen. "But tiny helps, just in the way that big helps when you're playing football." He also likes a tape from a partner pair from Georgia. The rest of the tapes he disperses to the junior college coaches like trading cards.

They move on to the nitty-gritty of judging the cheerleaders from tryouts. "Right now, I'm looking at twenty girls and sixteen guys, but I can only take thirty total," says Brad, blue eyes glued to his list. "I usually take twenty-seven, but I want a few extra because I always lose a few to grades. I'm not dragging ditches again this year." Because the university has stiff academic standards, last summer Brad had several cheerleaders who made the team but did not get admitted to the school itself.

Since there are fewer guys to debate, Brad reads out the names of the definites in his mind as a junior college coach scrawls the names on a chalkboard. "You're taking *him*?" someone asks, as Brad names a tumbler whose GPA was so abysmal last year that he lost his scholarship and had to leave school.

"I'm willing to take a gamble on him," says Brad.

"Can you just have him take an easy schedule?" someone asks.

"If he took underwater basket weaving and sticking his finger up his butt, he still wouldn't show up for class," says Brad, shaking his head. "But he shows up to practice."

In the end, there is one extra name on the list of guys. They debate for a few minutes who to cut and in the end make a surprise decision. Brad axes a current squad member who's been slacking lately. "He'll be mad, but he didn't show up today," says Brad. "He's a no." With that, the men are settled.

The group moves on to discussing the women. Brad takes a minute to look over his list. "We've got six returners. They're all definites," he says, calling Yvette's name along with the others. "And those three from the videos are definites." All nine names are written on the chalkboard.

"I would take Sierra over anyone," says one of the junior college coaches.

"Oh, I'm taking Sierra," says Brad, agreeing. The junior college coach etches her name in bubbly letters at the top of the list.

They've barely mentioned a quarter of the women at tryouts, and already there are twelve names on the board. Brad looks at his score sheets, crossing off the absolute nos. "So there's four women left, but I only have one more spot," says Brad. He reads the four names in the running for the last spot. Samantha is one of them.

Brad rubs his eyes. "What do you think of her?" he asks, referring to a tiny blonde.

"She's got legs like a thoroughbred," snips one of the guys. No one flinches, but it's amazing to me that someone would say this in a room packed with women.

"I like Marly," says someone else. "Her tumbling is better, and she's beautiful in the air."

"I like Samantha," one of the alumni finally says.

"But she's a headcase about her Full," says Brad. "She just can't do it."

Samantha's junior college coach rushes to her defense. "She'll work on it, she'll get it," she says.

Someone at the table has a suggestion. "If you took all four of them, that would only put you at thirty-three people."

Brad shakes his head. "We have twenty-seven full scholarships, so if I take thirty and a few leave, that's perfect," says Brad. Since at Nationals, only twenty people will perform, if Brad takes too many people now, not only will he be over budget but he could also have a morale problem if a third of the squad members are alternates.

"I need to talk to Michael Preston and see if I can take more people," says Brad. Someone passes him his cell, and he dials his boss's number. "Pick up your phone," says Brad. But there's no answer.

Brad stares at the chalkboard and shakes his head. "We gotta cut some people."

"Can some of these girls be alternates?" someone suggests.

"I don't like alternates," says Brad. "I want everyone to be on equal footing, I want everyone to have a scholarship." His scholarship philosophy is unusual—in most sports, coaches don't hesitate to give uneven scholarships based on talent, seniority, and NCAA allotment.

"Some will feel lucky just to make it," nudges a junior college coach. "Maybe give two people a half scholarship? Is anyone rich and won't mind?"

"None of these kids should have to pay to cheer," says Brad. "I'm at a standstill. I don't know what to do."

I glance at my watch—the list was supposed to be posted half an hour ago.

"Take more and hope a few don't show up," someone says.

"But if they all show up, I'm jacked," says Brad. "I've gotta cut someone. Samantha has to be cut."

"I don't understand. Why take those two girls from the videos over Samantha?" asks a former SFA cheerleader, her mouth agape. "Samantha can do those same stunts."

"An itty-bitty girl can just do more. Samantha's tall," says Brad. "It's physics."

"Samantha's like 5'1"," says the alumna, reading my mind.

"Look, she can't be an elite stunter. Whoever gets her for a partner will pout," says Brad. "My partner in college was taller and I didn't mind, but a lot of people don't stunt well with a tall girl. I'm just not that impressed with Samantha. She's gotta be cut."

"She works hard, and she's really developing," her junior college coach protests.

Brad looks at his list. "Shit." He buries his head in his hands. "We gotta get the team posted ASAP. If I post thirty-three names, Michael Preston is gonna have a heart attack," he says. "I've gotta come up with a plan."

The room goes silent, glances shooting across the table. Finally Brad picks up his phone and calls Michael Preston again. This time, he leaves a message. "Remember how I told you I'm gonna take extra cheerleaders this year so we don't have the same situation as last year? Well, I'm gonna take eight extras," he says. Everyone in the room laughs. "We'll probably lose a lot, but if not, then I know I'll have additional fund-raising to do." He hangs up the phone and wipes a bead of sweat off his brow. "Someone come write this list."

## "You're Exploding My Budget."

By the time the list goes up, it's an hour and a half later than Brad had promised. Some of the SFA hopefuls have waited in the bleachers with baited breath, while others have left and come back bearing McDonald's bags. Cheerleaders are not a carrot-stick-and-grilled-chicken-breast kind of crowd.

A stocky alumni cheerleader walks in, holding a sheet of paper. On it are the names of the thirty-three people who will be SFA Lumberjack cheerleaders. All eyes turn to him as he strolls with an air of circumstance. He loosens a pushpin from the bulletin board and secures the list in place.

The cheerleaders surge forward and crane their necks to get a look. Sierra's bleached ponytail is visible at the front of the pack—she quickly finds her name and walks away, a sly grin on her face. Yvette is a few steps behind her and nods as she sees her name at the top. As the others check the list, there are no big, dramatic reactions—no screams of joy or tears of sorrow. I have a feeling they could tell when they walked off the mat whether they made the team. They've had the past few hours to process their fate.

Samantha walks into the auditorium, her fingers interlocked with her boyfriend's. They edge their way to the front of the pack. Samantha uses her index finger to scan the list. At the bottom of the final column is the name she least expected to see: Samantha Frazer. She jumps up and down, clueless to the fact that a half hour of debate went into the decision to give her a chance.

She grasps her boyfriend in a hug. He congratulates her, but his face remains stern. His name is not on the list—he'll have to settle for SFA's less prestigious Small Coed squad. (Many colleges have multiple squads—again, it largely depends on what the coach and school want.)

"When I saw my name, I almost had a heart attack, but at the same time, I saw that he didn't make it," says Samantha, walking away. "I'm a big ball of emotions right now."

Fifteen minutes later the new team meets in a classroom across campus. Plastic chairs have been lined up in exact rows, but as people file in, they pull them into clusters with their friends. People hug and congratulate each other.

Brad walks in, folder in hand. Everyone gets quiet. "Congratulations. You just made the team that is probably the best in the country right now."

"Go Jacks!" screams Yvette in a high pitch.

Brad passes around a packet to each cheerleader. "This is our contract. Our mission is to set the cheer standard for around the country and to be exemplary ambassadors for the school. You must maintain a 2.0 GPA. You must be available for events over the holidays, even winter break. You will have no spring break—that's when we'll be getting everything in line for Nationals," he says, barely looking up.

"Your scholarship will be forfeited if you break the college's drug or alcohol policies," he continues. "Do not do anything in uniform that would be deemed inappropriate—that includes drinking, smoking, and stealing from gas stations." Two guys exchange a glance and crack up. I'm guessing there's a backstory.

"Just don't do stupid stuff," he says. "I'm not your father, I can't tell you what to do, but if you get in trouble, there will be repercussions."

Samantha leans back in her chair, using her knee as a desk to sign her contract. Sierra is perched on the edge of her seat. People stand up and walk toward Brad to hand him their signed contracts. Many of the women have light bruises in the shape of fingerprints on their waists.

Michael Preston walks in the room. Without saying a word, Brad follows him into the hall. All I can hear as they walk away is, "Are you crazy? You're exploding my budget." The cheerleaders don't seem to notice—they continue gabbing.

Michael and Brad return a few minutes later. "From here on out, you guys are Stephen F. Austin cheerleaders," says Michael Preston. "We try to keep it fun around here—that's why we're so good. We just won four National Championships in a row. There's already pressure for the fifth. This year, I wanna score higher than Louisville. I want that Grand National Champion trophy."

"S! F! A!" chants Yvette, the new squad members following her lead. "S! F! A!"

The team forms a circle in the middle of the room, and Brad explains a team cheer. "Put your axes up," he says, sticking out his arm, his thumb holding the pinky and ring finger down. They yell together, "Ohhh . . . Jack, Jack, Jack, L–C–L–M, '07 National Champs," pounding their axes toward the ceiling.

# CHAPTER 2

## Both Teams in *Bring It On* Rolled into One

### *The Southern University Jaguars*

THE FLUORESCENT LIGHTS FLICKER on and off, creating a strobe effect as twenty-two men and women practice on the blue mat in the center of the floor. A woman with creamy brown skin flips backwards over and over again, her hair braided into a million tiny plaits that swish past her face. Near her, a buff woman's feet slip out of her partner's hand as they attempt an Awesome. "Sorry, sorry, sorry," she says as he reaches out to catch her trim waist. In front of her, a guy wearing aviator sunglasses holds a woman like he's carrying her across the threshold after their honeymoon. She places her arms around his neck, and he swings her up, lifting her above his head, both hands wrapping around her white sneakers. "My grip is bad on this right foot," he says.

"Man, you make the woman do all the work," jokes a guy in a tight wife-beater standing nearby.

"You dropped your partner on national TV," Mr. Sunglasses snaps back.

For the past three days, these men and women have spent their afternoons trying out for Southern University's cheerleading squad.

They've learned and performed a cheer full of tongue-twister words and standing tumbling. They've mastered a dance with choreography worthy of a hip-hop music video. They've shown off their tumbling and stunting abilities. Today, they will finally find out who will make the squad.

The cheerleaders seem used to my presence now, but on the first afternoon of tryouts, they were confused. Some would cheer directly toward me, assuming that I was a judge. Others just glanced at me with quizzical expressions; Southern University is a historically black college, and a white face is an unusual sight here.

In 1879, at the Louisiana State Constitutional Convention, Southern University was created "for the education of persons of color." It opened in New Orleans with just twelve students, but, as the student body grew, the university moved to a large bluff overlooking the Mississippi River in Baton Rouge. The land was once a plantation. Rather poetically, today it is one of the largest historically black colleges in the country.

Southern's cheerleaders are phenomenal. They dominated at Black College Nationals through the late '90s, winning five times before the competition was dissolved in the mid-2000s. Every win at Black Nationals earned the team an all-expenses-paid bid to NCA Nationals.

In 2002, when the Southern Jaguars strolled into NCA preliminaries wearing their bright golden uniforms, other teams probably didn't recognize them as a threat. While several historically black colleges regularly send squads to Nationals, a predominantly black team had never won a national title. But at preliminaries, the Southern cheerleaders brought the audience to their feet. At the end of the day, they had the highest score in their division.

Finals day, however, was not so magical. After a pyramid fell in the last seconds of their routine, the team worried that they might be out of medal contention altogether. But the teams that followed them on the stage bobbled and fell, too. In the end, Southern placed second (behind Northeastern University, but ahead of Stephen F. Austin), just two-tenths of a point separating them from what would have been a history-making first-place finish.

Still, theirs was the name on everybody's lips in Daytona Beach that year. But, to the disappointment of every Southern squad since, they've never been back to NCA Nationals. It's not because they lack talent—it's because they just don't have the $17,000 it costs to make the trek.

Cheerleading is an expensive sport. New uniforms run as much as $200 a pop, so the bill for the whole squad can be over $4,000, and that's not including the warm-up suits, shoes, and bags that teams typically provide. Squads also pay for transportation and accommodations when they travel with their basketball and football teams—an expenditure that eats up a huge chunk of a team's budget. Add in the $10,000 it costs for a team to attend spirit camp, and Southern's budget of $37,000 per year is quickly exceeded. When you compare that to SFA's $110,000 a year, the difference is dramatic.

The room on campus where Southern's tryouts are being held doubles as a lecture hall. Desks attached to plastic chairs make a random pattern of tan, blue, and orange around the mat. The high ceilings are covered with water-stained tiles. The women on the mat look taller than the SFA hopefuls, each one of them with clearly defined ab and leg muscles. The men, while larger than the average joe, are half the size of the SFA guys.

At the front of the mat, James Turner takes a break from stunting, his shirt revealing the tattoos that run up and down his bicep muscles. James is one of those rare people who says he wants to be an actor/ model and you actually believe he could make it. Deep dimples punctuate his smile.

James Turner grew up outside of New Orleans and went to a high school where he was the second black drum major and the first black man on the cheerleading squad in more than fifteen years. "I was always the first to do this, the first to do that," he says. "Going to a black college, I see competition from people of my race. It's a good challenge."

Southern University does represent a big first for James—he's the first in his family to go to college. "I've seen how some members of my family struggled, and I don't want that out of life," he explains. "I know for sure when I make something of myself, my parents and grandparents won't have to work another day of their lives."

James will be a senior this year, but when he came to tryouts as a freshman, he did not make the cut. It wasn't until another guy quit that Southern's coach decided to give James a chance on the condition that a friend work with him every day during lunch so he could improve quickly. It worked. Today, James is one of the strongest stunters on the team.

Jasmine Smutherman, a woman with the grace and poise of a beauty queen, saunters toward James. Her almond-shaped eyes take up a large percentage of her classically beautiful face. She stands in front of James, and he sends her sailing into the air. Above his head, Jasmine curls her body into a Scorpion, her expression demure, bordering on bashful.

Jasmine grew up in Dallas, Texas, the daughter of two parents she describes as "Christ-like." She began cheerleading in the fifth grade and knew ever since she was little that she wanted to go to a historically black college. "Growing up, I was always on predominantly white cheerleading squads. Sometimes, I was the only black cheerleader," she told me earlier in a singsong Southern accent. "I wanted to know what it was like to be on an all-black squad."

As Jasmine Doubles Down from the Scorpion, she stands in front of James again. He cups his hands to his mouth and makes a farting sound. Jasmine walks away looking disgusted, returning like a boomerang to hit him on the shoulder.

The door to the lecture hall opens, and in walks James Smith Sr., Southern's coach for the past thirteen years. He is the kind of guy cast as the cool-but-tough dad on a UPN sitcom—he's jovial but has the innate ability to quiet a room with a what-the-heck-are-you-doing stare. He greets everyone in the room, including me, with a hug.

Ironically, in college, James Smith was a star cheerleader at Grambling State University, a fierce rival of Southern. In fact, his becoming coach at Southern happened by accident. After he graduated, he came home to Baton Rouge. "I just happened to see the Southern cheerleaders practicing. Their coach at the time said, 'I remember you. You cheered for Grambling. Can you give us any pointers?' I've been here every day since," says Coach James.

For the past three afternoons, Coach James has watched the hopefuls carefully. "This is the lowest turnout I've ever had," he says. "Normally I bring in judges from out of town, but this year it would be a waste of money."

Hurricane Katrina is in many ways responsible for the low turnout. When it tore through the Gulf region less than a year ago, the devastating effects transformed the area. In addition to the more shocking and immediate damage the hurricane did, college sports throughout the state were canceled. And Coach James relies on traveling for games to recruit. "The further out we go, the more kids see us, think, 'Wow, I like that squad,' and look into the team when they graduate high school," he explains.

On the mat, the line between the cheerleaders who are a possibility and the cheerleaders who aren't quite up to par is clear-cut. Some people are absolute shoo-ins, like James Turner, Jasmine, and several other veteran members of the squad. But nestled among them are a handful of cheerleaders who are obviously new to the sport. My eye goes to a woman in bright pink shorts as she fights to stay up in a stunt. She teeters over like a tree with its trunk chopped. Near her, another woman struggles to do a back handspring, her shoulder colliding with the mat each time.

Coach James takes a clipboard out of his bag. A stack of evaluation sheets sits on top of it, each cheerleader's photo stapled to the front. He begins flipping through them, stopping on a photo of Chassity Crittenden, a Southern sophomore who rocked tryouts with a bubbly smile and tendency to laugh at nothing in particular. Chassity is half Puerto Rican and half black, her caramel skin interrupted by a beauty mark on her cheek.

Because she was a military kid, Chassity was born in Germany and never lived in the same place for long. She didn't go to her first Southern football game until high school, and she remembers being entranced by the cheerleaders. "Ooh, they were all so pretty. I wished I could move like that," she recalls. "I envied them, I really did."

Others on the mat no doubt envy her now. She reminds me of a jack-in-the-box as she soars up in stunts, a goofy grin across her face. She is the best stunter on Southern's squad. Still, four days ago, she was nervous about tryouts. "Last year, there were so many new girls at tryouts that a lot of the old girls didn't make it," she explains. "But once I saw there was only a few new girls, I wasn't worried."

Coach James flips the page, landing on a photo of Jarel Small. I've noticed Jarel over the past few afternoons—he's another person who will easily make the team. He is light-skinned, with dark eyebrows shagging over his eyes and a soul patch resting on his chin. For the past two years, he has been Jasmine's stunt partner. "When I first got here, I looked at her and thought, 'I hope to get to stunt with her.' When coach said we were partners, I was so happy. She's one of the most beautiful girls in the world," says Jarel, a Kansas twang to his voice.

Coach James continues flipping through the stack of tryout sheets. As I look over his shoulder, I notice that almost no one seems to be from Baton Rouge. "You'd think our program along with Louisiana State University's would breed strong cheerleading in Baton Rouge," he says, shaking his head. "Most of these kids, they're from places with stronger cheer traditions, but their parents went to Southern. I also go to competitions in other cities to recruit. If I see a kid who would be great for us, I'll call their coach and ask about them."

He looks at me. "I've never had a white cheerleader before, but I would love to," he says. "Last year there were two twins I was recruiting. I would have put them on each side of the line, like bookends."

A few minutes later, Coach James has the cheerleaders sit down in a clump around him on the mat. "It's just me judging this year, so it didn't take long," he says to the group, his voice tentative. "It's been a rough few days and I'm glad that you want to be a part of this family." The woman in the hot pink shorts already has tears in her eyes.

"When I call your name, come stand over here," says Coach James, pointing to the center of the mat.

"Jarel," he says. Jarel jumps up and walks calmly to the middle of the mat.

"Japaul," says Coach James as the bulky guy still wearing his sunglasses somersaults toward Jarel.

"James." James Turner stands up, his dimples widening like canyons.

"Rishawn." A small guy walks toward the group, giving the others five.

"And the last guy," says Coach James. The three remaining men brace themselves, hoping to hear their name. "Marvin." A big guy with dark skin stands up. The two others' expressions drop. At best, Coach James might take them for the junior varsity squad.

Coach James moves on to the women. "Jasmine," he says. Jasmine picks up the silver purse that sits at her side and hugs James Turner and Jarel.

"Chassity." She claps as she jogs to the center of the mat.

"CJay . . . Tarianne," says Coach James. "Tiffany." The women stand up one at a time, relief rushing over their faces.

"And the last member of the varsity team," he says. Ten women still sit on the mat, the girl in the pink shorts wringing her hands. Another girl buries her face in her palms, and two others lock hands. "Kesha," says Coach James as a girl with long, swingy hair jumps up, a cherry tattoo on her lower back.

The rest of the women look crushed. "For those of you that made it, this is only the beginning," says Coach James. He turns to the others, many already in tears. "For those of you who didn't, if at first you don't succeed, try, try again."

The new squad stands in a clump on the center of the mat, congratulating each other. They look puny in comparison to the thirty-plus people on SFA's team. I count them and am surprised that there are only eleven cheerleaders. To compete at Nationals, they'll need twenty. And that's without alternates in case someone gets hurt or has to leave the team unexpectedly.

Coach James walks to a table, where he gathers his notes to bring to the team's first meeting. "Were you tempted to take anyone else so that you'd have a full squad?" I ask, a little baffled.

"No, I'm not anxious about numbers," he says. "I'm against taking people just to fill positions, because in the long run, they don't work out. I'm an NCA judge, so I'll be out and about all summer, and I can still recruit. And people always call up over the summer and say, 'Hey, I'm coming to Southern, I heard about your cheerleading program.' Each year, it works itself out."

Still, as the rejected cheerleaders grab their bags and head out of the gym with disappointment smacked across their faces, I can't help but wonder if he was just a little too discriminating.

### "Every Year, It's 'This Is *the* Squad.' "

Coach James leads the team outside. The Louisiana night is hot and sticky, and mosquitoes from the nearby ravine swarm as if they've won the lottery. "Congratulations," says Coach James as the new teammates clap around him.

"New cheerleaders, it's going to be a long ride," continues Coach James, waving his hands like he's directing an orchestra. "Old cheerleaders—you are tired, you are out of shape, you got out of breath during your tryout."

Jasmine stares down at her sneakers, while Chassity returns Coach's gaze. "You guys are *college cheerleaders,* which means you have to be a picture of certain things. So get off the sweets. No more Coke—drink water. You gotta start running, and when you're done running, run again." Noticing that a few brows have furrowed, he adds, "I'm your coach now. I don't have to be nice."

Melisha, a petite girl with light brown skin and hair that flips out around her face, asks Coach James, "Can I talk to the girls for a minute?" Melisha is a former Southern cheerleader, a captain of the famous 2002 squad. The women huddle around her—she's obviously someone they admire.

Melisha takes a deep breath. "Tryouts, they were not good. *At all,*" she says, making eye contact with many of the women. "Your stunt sequences need to come up. I know you know tricks," she says, pointing to Jasmine and Chassity. "You better step up your game. I'm twenty-six years old and haven't put on a uniform in years. I should not be able to show you up."

She speaks like a preacher giving a sermon, and the women around her nod as if to say *Amen.*

"You have to fight for these stunts," she continues, motioning to the guys in a huddle with Coach James across the lawn. "Those guys, they're not the strongest. But it doesn't matter if he isn't holding you right, when you fall it's, 'Girl, what happened?' They see *you.* During tryouts, you guys gave up entirely too easily."

Melisha pauses to gather her thoughts. "In 2002, we came in second at NCA Nationals. *Second.* And we haven't been back since. Every year it's 'This is *the* squad.' And every year it just goes poof. You guys have the talent, but it's about what you're able to do with it," she says. The women look at her intensely, fire building in their brown eyes.

"Oh, and you're cute, but learn to put on makeup," she says, addressing the group. "M.A.C. does wonders."

The women start to walk away, but Melisha calls them back. "One more thing. All it takes is three seconds to turn from a lady into a ho. You're not just *you* anymore. The minute you put on the uniform, you're *'that cheerleader.'* " she says. "Don't think you can sneak up into boys' dorms. It won't be, 'There was a girl in the dorm last night.' It'll be, 'Did you see that cheerleader up there?' Don't think it won't get around."

The women walk over to where the men are getting a similar talk. "All right," says Coach, addressing the whole group. "We're gonna finish the week out practicing. Be here at 6:30 p.m. tomorrow."

## "You Look Like You're Having the Worst Day of Your Life."

It's 6:36 p.m. and the Southern Jaguars are standing in the hallway, waiting for the class in their practice room to finish a test. Students trickle out of the room, and when 95 percent of them are gone, the cheerleaders invade. They hook the desks together and push them to the side. In the corner, seven long blue mats are rolled up and standing on their sides like bales of hay. The cheerleaders push them to the center of the room and unroll them. Soon, the mat strips form a solid square of blue. The cheerleaders step on and stretch.

Jasmine smoothes her chin-length hair. She's excited for next year, but nervous about the possibility of switching partners. Coach James will be looking to make partner pairs that are evenly talented, and sometimes that means splitting up a great pair. "Partnerships are like relationships—you have to communicate and build trust," says Jasmine. "Jarel knows me so well, he can tell when it's that time of the month from how heavy I feel. I'm not saying that I wouldn't work with anyone else, but it takes time to build that chemistry."

Across the room, someone turns on a radio, R&B music filling the room. Tarianne Green, her body curving in and out like a cartoon character, begins to dance. Her heavy-hooded eyes light up with each gyration. Tarianne has been James Turner's stunt partner for the past year, and I've heard from several people that she is the class clown who makes practices dissolve into laughter. But during tryouts, she seemed serious, even timid. I feel like I'm seeing the real her for the first time as she dances.

Tarianne hails from New Orleans, and her grandparents, mom, aunts, uncles, sisters, and cousins all went to Southern. "I didn't really have a choice about where I was goin' for college," she jokes.

James Turner walks in and calls practice to order. "Coach is gonna be late," he says, a formality to his voice that makes it hard to imagine him making fart noises just yesterday. "Circle up for jumps."

The team forms a circle, each person a few feet from the next. James jumps high, swinging his legs out in a Toe Touch. The rest follow him in a wave.

They move on to back handsprings, and soon Coach James walks in, dapper in a white linen suit. "Bring your knees together. Point your toes," he says, watching the wave go around.

Next, the team does their Standing Back Tucks. This is the move that separates top cheerleaders from the ones who are simply good. It's a back flip done from standing, zero momentum helping the cheerleader get around. While 90 percent of the cheerleaders who made SFA's squad can do this with no problem, only half the cheerleaders here can land it.

Coach James calls the group into a huddle. "Y'all look like you're having the worst day of your lives," he says. "You have to work on your technique—look in the mirror to see what you're doing. This is *college cheerleading*. This is not the time to teach you the skills. I need you to have them."

The squad begins to work on their stunts. "We're not your typical African American team," Coach James tells me as we watch. "I'll say it politically, but cheerleading has always been a white sport—in every region, you'll get one or two African American kids who can compete with mainstream cheerleaders. It's very hard for me to pull those kids because they want to go to a big cheer school that can offer them lots of money." He rubs his fingers together to underline the word.

His brow furrows as a woman falls from a stunt, legs flailing. "Honey, when you fall, keep your legs still," he yells. "If you're kicking, people can't catch you."

He switches back to his previous thought as if nothing had interrupted him. "I want great skills from the squad when it comes to competing. But the school doesn't want to lose that traditional black college cheerleading style of lots of dancing," he explains. "It's a challenge to make sure the team keeps that but also has the skills."

On the mat, James Turner gives pointers to a younger team member. "In the last few years, it's become much more common for guys to participate in mainstream cheer, but for African American men, it's still not common. We've fought with, 'You should be playing football,'" says Coach James. "We've fought with guys who want to be cheerleaders, but their parents don't agree."

Coach looks at James Turner like a proud father. "He's going to be my captain this year. He's been bad in terms of attitude, but I'm hoping he can step up. I'm going to have a girl captain this year, too," he whispers, pointing to Jasmine. "People genuinely like her, so I think they'll listen to her. It'll be trial by fire, because being a captain changes friendships."

During a pause in the conversation, I ask Coach James what the biggest challenge was for his squad last year. "Katrina," he says. "We were without electricity for two weeks, and two of the team members are from New Orleans, so their families left for Houston. Since Katrina destroyed everything around Baton Rouge, the government pulled a lot of money from the Southern budget to help kick-start those cities. I can't argue with that—but they wiped my budget." NCA Nationals wasn't even an option last year. Coach James had to settle for sending the team to a small competition sponsored by the Southwestern Athletic Conference (SWAC).

For the team's routine, he choreographed a pyramid called "the Katrina," a complex three-layer cake of flips, turns, and lifts. Southern won first place, hands down.

Still, James can't help but think about the castle at NCA Nationals. "When we placed second, we should have won. It would have been *history* for a black school to win," he says. "Second is the worst place to be—I'd rather be tenth. But it was a hell of a performance. We can't beat Louisville or SFA doing what they do—we'll have five Heel Stretches while they have twelve. But we can beat them doing what we do."

Practice is over. "I have a few announcements," says Coach James as the cheerleaders take a seat in the desks at the side of the mat. "As far as partner sets, I'm not promising anybody the same partner—I'm going to be putting together sets that are best for the team." Jasmine and Jarel groan.

Coach James glances at his notes. "I'm gonna go ahead and tell you who your captains are," he says. The squad members give a drum roll. "James Turner and Jasmine Smutherman."

James and Jasmine turn toward each other and lock eyes as the team applauds. They don't seem shocked—it's as if they expected the captainships. "I thought it was gonna be me," says Tarianne, kidding, since she's the one known for goofing off.

"We got our check in from winning SWAC," Coach James continues, ignoring her.

"You should divide it up between us," interjects Tarianne. Coach James stares her down.

"I called the athletic director and said, 'Look, these kids have trophies taller than some buildings on this campus. The one thing they don't have is a ring.'" People gasp.

"Oh my God," squeals Chassity.

"You're gonna get rings," he continues. The team high-fives, and they leave practice hugging and clapping. As they walk out of the building's double doors, many of them flip open their cell phones to tell their family and friends.

In the next few weeks, each of these cheerleaders will also receive a letter in the mail detailing the terms of his or her scholarship. The university gives Coach James $15,000 and six out-of-state fee exemptions to divvy up among the cheerleaders as he sees fit. "The longer they're on the team, the more their scholarship grows," he explains. "Other than that, I look at their skill level and what they need."

James Turner and Jasmine linger in the hallway, talking. It's pouring outside, and James walks Jasmine to her car, holding an umbrella over her head—they seem to have a close friendship. "The girls on the squad are like my younger sisters," he says as he comes back in the building soaking wet. "People always ask, 'Are you holla-ing at 'em?' But I don't even look at them that way."

He glances inside the now-empty gym. "I'm really excited for next year. I hope we can go to NCA—our hopes and dreams can go that far as long as our funding can," he says. "But I'm worried about having enough people. I'm gonna be optimistic because Coach usually comes through, but we *need* more people."

# CHAPTER 3

## The Superwomen

### *The University of Memphis All-Girl Tigers*

CASI DAVIS STABS AT her Caesar salad. "I'm still debating cheering next year," she says, smiling to reveal a Madonna-sized gap between her two front teeth. She's not the stereotypical blonde, cute-as-cute-can-be cheerleader. Casi is tall and muscular, with the café au lait skin of someone whose family is a melting pot in progress (part black, part white, part Hispanic). "I've been trying to quit since the sixth grade," she says. "I just can't get out."

It's the night before the tryouts for the University of Memphis All-Girl squad, and I'm sitting at Chili's with Casi and two of her friends from the team, Ashley Chambers and Courtney Powell. Together, we look like bottles of foundation lined up at a department-store makeup counter—I'm incredibly pale, Casi and Ashley (half black, half Iranian) are in the middle, and Courtney is on the end, with chocolate skin. We laugh constantly. Casi is refreshingly blunt, and Courtney and Ashley—best friends who've reached the finish-each-other's-sentences stage—are the squad's comedians.

We're in a booth, with framed photos of the World's Largest Pickle and Miss Rodeo Texas on the wall behind us. Waitresses scurry past with plates of burgers and Tex-Mex food. When the three suggested this place for dinner, I was expecting a gluttonous feast, but as the waitress went around our table taking orders, they ordered salad, salad, soup. I'm the only one to go all out with a black-bean burger and fries.

Earlier today, Courtney and Ashley spent hours learning a new cheer and fight song, which they'll perform at tomorrow's tryouts. Current members must try out again to keep their spots, but it's just a formality—it's unlikely that their coach would not choose them for the team. Courtney and Ashley are both excited to cheer for their sophomore year.

Casi, who's about to be a senior, isn't so sure that she wants to cheer for her fourth year at Memphis. She skipped practice today and is 90 percent certain that she isn't going to try out tomorrow. If she were to decide over the summer to join the team, her coach would probably take her back. But by skipping tryout practice, she's sent a loud and clear message that she's retiring.

"Please come back," pleads Ashley, her glossy black hair wrestling free from her ponytail. She taps her long acrylic nails on the table.

"I've got a good job, and my grades fell so bad last semester, I almost cried," says Casi, shrugging. "And I just had surgery on my ACL. There's a lot to think about."

"I can't give it up—I'd miss it so bad," says Courtney. She rests her square jaw on her hand. "We're known as cheerleaders. If I quit, I'd be no one. It's shaped my personality. I don't think I'd be at all outgoing without cheerleading."

"Every year I'm like, 'This is the *last* year,' " says Casi as the others laugh in understanding.

"You get sucked back in or you miss Nationals too much," says Courtney.

For competitive cheerleaders, quitting the Memphis All-Girl squad would be like a musician turning down Juilliard. The squad is only four years old, but they've already established themselves as a perennial top All-Girl team. They have one National Championship under their belt. Last year, however, was a big disappointment.

"We got *fourth* place," explains Courtney. "That's *not* good for us."

In the beginning of the routine, five flyers popped into place for a long string of stunts. But one flyer's feet slipped out of her bases' hands, and she plummeted toward the ground. Many people on the squad didn't even realize that she had fallen—they proceeded through what was an otherwise perfect routine. That single mistake took them out of the running. Every year, the All-Girl field of competition gets tougher.

While Coed teams have a one-guy, one-girl setup for stunts, All-Girl teams build stunts using two to four women beneath a flyer. Because stunting is done in groups, All-Girl squads welcome women with a wide range of body types; while someone may be too tall or too heavy to be a flyer on a Coed team, she may have the perfect physical attributes to be a "base." All three women at the table were also drawn to All-Girl cheerleading because it provides a unique bonding experience for women. Many of their closest friends are their teammates.

Too often, All-Girl teams are seen as secondary to Coed teams at the college level. All-Girl teams traditionally cheer for women's sports, while Coed teams get prime assignments like men's basketball. Since most high school cheerleading squads are All-Girl, graduating cheerleaders dream of moving on to college, where strong men can power them higher in the air. Coed teams also sound like the answer for college students who want a sport with a built-in social life.

But this cheer hierarchy is in flux. An amazing All-Girl base, like Casi, can lift a fellow cheerleader on her own for difficult stunts that, until recently, only guys could do. The Tigers are on the forefront of this shift, which would make even the starkest feminist applaud. If only they'd change the division name to *All-Woman.*

Despite their success, many of the All-Girl Tigers see themselves as the neglected stepsisters of the Memphis Coed squad. "For scholarships, we get one thousand dollars a year. We win, we make our grades," says Casi. "Coed gets like fourteenth place, and they get full rides. Mmm."

It reminds me of how WNBA stars typically make less than six figures, while top players in the NBA make millions. But Courtney and Ashley don't seem affected by the lopsided rewards. "Don't get her started," says Courtney.

"We get treated like dirt sometimes," says Casi, her voice rising. "We cheer women's basketball games, and there's nobody there. The players look at you like, 'Why are you happy when we're losing by a hundred points?' One time last year our coaches were like, 'All-Girl gets to cheer a men's basketball game.' We were all excited, but when we get there, nobody's in the stands. The game was at the same time as the Super Bowl. Everyone was home watching."

"I know why I love All-Girl," says Courtney, holding up a French fry she stole off my plate. "We don't have a weight limit."

"What if we had one?" asks Ashley.

"I'd quit," says Courtney. "We'd go on strike, like 'We want food.'" She pounds her fists on the table. I look down again at their skimpy plates. Are they exaggerating the amount of leeway they have, or do they genuinely prefer salads to comfort food?

Our waitress clears our plates, and Courtney asks Casi about her fiancé, Eric. The two have been together for four years—it was love at first sight while working at Wal-Mart. Ten months ago, Eric was sent to Iraq with the Army Reserves, and it's been hard on Casi to have him halfway across the globe in a war zone. She's expecting him home any day, but, as tensions in Iraq continue, she can never be sure.

The table goes silent, the rest of us processing what a different experience it must be to watch the news when someone you love is in Iraq. I grasp to get the lighthearted mood back by asking the girls what they love about cheerleading.

"Lifting one person on your own," says Casi. "It's addictive."

"The football games," says Ashley, smiling.

"All the little girls saying, 'Can I get your autograph?' and taking pictures of you," says Courtney. "The fans are just so into it. One guy dyes his hair blue for the games. And people tailgate. There's the same people there in the RVs in the same spot game after game."

Casi, originally from Georgia, looks up from her plate. "When I joined the squad, I had no idea how big Memphis sports were. I got here and was like, 'Oh God, there are video cameras and the stadium is *full.*'"

We pay our bill and walk to the parking lot. The women laugh as they tell me what to expect at tryouts tomorrow. "You'll be able to tell the freshmen—they'll be the ones who look real nervous," says Courtney. "The rest of us are like, 'Whatever.' Our coaches know what we can do."

"I'll be in the stands," says Casi as she unlocks her car door and hops in the driver's seat.

"Please, please come back," yells Ashley.

Casi rolls down her window and laughs. "I'm gonna wear regular clothes tomorrow so I'm not even tempted to try out," she says. She pulls out of her parking spot and drives off.

## "Welcome to the Jungle."

It's eerie how deserted the University of Memphis campus is on the day of tryouts. Graduation was last week and summer school has yet to start. The campus is all green trees, stately redbrick buildings, and blue sky—the stuff college brochures are made of.

But as I walk into the women's basketball gymnasium, I'm hardly alone. Over a hundred men and women are here hoping to make the Memphis Coed, All-Girl, and Pom squads (the college equivalent of the Laker Girls). Even though it's Mother's Day, the blue and white seats are packed with parents, siblings, and friends. Some people have brought camcorders and binoculars. The gymnasium doors are wide open; unlike the other tryouts, this is a spectator event.

Pennants for the women's basketball team hang from the rafters, and the hoops have been collapsed and moved to the side of the floor. At the far end of the gym is a wall-length banner—a photograph of a tiger's eyes blown up far beyond life-size. The words WELCOME TO THE JUNGLE are printed across the bottom.

I walk across the gym toward Carol Lloyd, the All-Girl squad's thirty-something head coach, who is sitting at the judging table. "Your shirt is cute," she tells me in a fast-paced Southern accent that makes her sound like she's eating her words as she speaks.

Carol's dressed in cropped pants, platform flip-flops, and a hoodie. She has Tammy Faye-ish mascara and a tiny nose ring. If you put her in an evening gown, she could be the spunky Southern girl on every season of *The Bachelor*.

Carol started cheering in the second grade and was on a competitive squad in high school. In 1989, she joined the legendary Memphis Pom squad, who dominated college dance for over a decade. "In the four years I danced, we went to Barcelona, Madrid, Tokyo twice," Carol says. "I remember we were in Kansas about to dance at an NBA game and the announcer said, 'Memphis Pom has now entered the building.' That's how well known we were."

Today, Carol coaches Memphis All-Girl, as well as the Coed and Pom squads. It's a lot of teams for one person to juggle, in addition to the coaching she does at a local cheerleading gym. "Tryout fees, tryout fees," she yells as the cheerleaders hand her their checks. "Oh, you look cute," she says to one girl. "Your top's so cute," to another. It's a compliment she evidently gives a lot.

Frankie Conklin, the University of Memphis Spirit Director, walks in. He stands over six feet tall, dwarfing the cheerleaders. His black-rimmed glasses are perpetually pushed on top of his head. As he walks toward the judging table, mothers come to greet him like metal shavings to a magnet. He gives them all a few calming words and moves on. He is the head honcho when it comes to Memphis cheer.

Frankie started out as a girls' basketball coach at a private school, and he found that his players were as interested in cheerleading as shooting hoops. He met with the school's headmaster and offered to coach cheerleading as well. He had no prior experience and learned as he went along.

One year, Frankie's team came back from spirit camp to find that the school was closing. Not wanting to break up the team, Frankie founded a private cheerleading gym called Memphis Elite in 1992. Even though the members of the squad went to different schools, they could cheer together on evenings and weekends. Memphis Elite was one of the first cheerleading gyms in the country. Frankie had no idea that the trend would explode a few years later.

Frankie took over as the University of Memphis Spirit Director four years ago and appointed Carol head coach. "The first year me and Frankie took over, All-Girl won and Coed got fourth place. It was just like, 'Wow,'" says Carol. "We were so blessed."

Frankie uses Memphis Elite as a training grounds for the college teams, taking the kids he's taught for years and making the University of Memphis squad their goal. Ashley Chambers, for example, has cheered at Memphis Elite since the fifth grade. She does a spot-on imitation of Frankie, nailing the way he walks, leading with his stomach as his legs catch up. "At the gym, Frankie has an intercom," she says. "You think he's not watching, and all of a sudden you hear, 'Chambers, what are you doing?' It's like, 'Yes, God.' " The cheerleaders love Frankie and fear him at the same time.

Frankie sits down and surveys the blue mat on the basketball court. Courtney, Ashley, and a few others from last year's squad run over to give him a hug. "Is Casi trying out?" someone asks.

"Casi's getting married—she's not coming back," says Frankie. It's a different reason than Casi told me, but perhaps this was an easier way for her to break it to Frankie and Carol.

"She's not getting married for a year and her boyfriend can't get back from Iraq," says Ashley, still clinging to the hope that Casi will change her mind. But Casi is nowhere to be found, and All-Girl tryouts are about to start.

Courtney and Ashley run to the mat and warm up. Ashley puts her hands above her head and kicks her leg like a Rockette on speed. Courtney bends down and touches her toes. They throw their arms around each other's shoulders as a friend snaps a photo.

Across the mat, a baby-faced blonde tries to do a Standing Back Tuck. She shakes out her hands and raises her shoulders, like she's fighting off a panic attack. This is what cheerleaders refer to as being "mental"—when you think about something so much that it makes you too terrified to do it. The gymnastics elements of cheerleading, many of the women tell me, rely on being able to chase out of your mind the idea that you could break something.

The blonde girl's mother yells at her from the stands. "I can't," says the blonde. Finally, a friend steps in and spots her, placing a hand on her lower back. She flips, stumbling a little, but lands without a problem. "Yeah, that's right. You can do it," someone yells. They've no doubt watched her struggle with this at tryout practice.

Courtney goes through the cheer she will have to perform in a few minutes. It's relatively easy—simple hand movements and words, though in the middle everyone must do a Toe Touch Back Tuck. Ashley and a few others join her, running through it again and again until everyone has it down perfectly.

Behind the mat, the gym's double doors open. Casi walks in. As promised, she's not in workout clothes—she's wearing a low-cut white top and slouchy black pants. She strolls casually around the edge of the gym floor, waving as people say hello. She heads up the steps of the bleachers and takes a seat next to the squad's captain, Kristen Murdock, a tall blonde with an easygoing Tennessee manner. Kristen will be a second-year senior, so Frankie and Carol aren't making her try out— her spot is guaranteed.

Kristen's roots at the University of Memphis go deep. Her parents met there when they were students, years ago when the school was called Memphis State. In fact, her mom was the school's first Golden Girl baton twirler, swathed in a gold uniform while the other twirlers wore blue and silver. "I've been going to University of Memphis football games since I was born," says Kristen. "When I was little, when people asked what I'd want to be when I grew up, I'd say, 'A Memphis Pom Girl.' They were the greatest things in the world."

While Kristen dreamed of being a Pom girl, many little girls no doubt dreamed of being like her. Kristen was a child actress, singer, and model. She landed parts in Broadway musicals and was in a BP commercial opposite Gary Burghoff of M*A*S*H fame. Most impressive to her friends, Kristen appeared on a billboard, her image high above the traffic on one of Memphis's main strips.

Music blasts from a DJ booth in the back of the gym. It's a recording of the University of Memphis fight song in that heavy-on-the-horns style college bands favor. Everyone on the mat snaps into the dance they learned yesterday. Oddly, the current cheerleaders seem to be having more trouble remembering the motions than the new people are. As Ashley explains later, it's because at games they've performed a different version hundreds of times, so performing the new steps means fighting second nature. The music repeats, and they start over.

At the judging table, Carol tells Frankie about a woman who tried out for the All-Girl squad by video, shaking her head in disbelief. "She's going to be another Casi. Wow," says Carol. "She tossed a girl up, and no one was helping her."

Frankie, who will watch the videos after tryouts, seems impressed. He picks up a microphone. "We're starting in five minutes," he says, his soft voice echoing through the auditorium.

## "You Done Blown It Now."

The judges open their University of Memphis binders, and I peek over one of their shoulders to look at the score sheet. The first category is *Look,* where the judges give up to ten points for the cheerleader's appearance. Next, each cheerleader will do a running tumbling pass of their choice for five points. Then they will do the cheer Carol taught them yesterday. They'll be judged both on the cheer itself (five points), for the Toe Touch Back Tuck in the middle (five points), and the group stunt that comes at the end (five points). Finally, in groups of five, they'll perform the fight song, worth five points for the dance and five points for a stunt on the end. Out of all the things the All-Girl hopefuls will do today, their appearance is the single item that counts for the most points.

Frankie stands up and faces the bleachers, holding the microphone up to his mouth. "I want to welcome you," he says. "Be sure to cheer for everyone—we've got a lot of out-of-towners here who don't have a fan base. We're not going to be announcing anything today. The results will be posted on *GoTigersGo.com* at about 9 p.m."

As he sits down, Carol asks why they aren't announcing this in person. "It's Mother's Day," says Frankie, laughing. "I don't want to make anyone mad—we might get beat up."

The women trying out for the All-Girl squad sit down at the side of the mat. A few are still doing truncated arm motions, like high school students desperately flipping through their notebooks before a test. The returning cheerleaders laugh and joke as Frankie calls the first four women to the mat. Running tumbling pass. Cheer. Toe Touch Back Tuck. Fight song. Just like that, their tryout is done. The audience claps, obeying Frankie's decree.

Frankie calls the next group of four. Courtney pulls up her blue shorts past her navel and steps onto the mat with the other three women. She runs for her tumbling pass, doing two back handsprings to a Back Tuck. "Yeah, Courtney," people yell as she lands.

She lines up with the other three girls horizontally across the mat. "It's cheer time," says Frankie. The women start on the count of four, throwing their arms into quick-paced Vs and their legs into high kicks as they chant, "Go! Tigers! Go!" Courtney nails her Toe Touch Back Tuck while the other women stumble. They do another flourish and walk into a cluster.

In All-Girl stunt groups, the main base does the heaviest of the lifting, the side bases doing their best to absorb some of the weight. The back spot tends to be the tallest person—she reaches from behind to hold the flyer's ankles and stabilize her. All of the members must work together; without perfect timing, they'll trip all over each other.

On the mat, Courtney acts as a side base as her group lifts a woman in a pink shirt into a Liberty—a relatively easy stunt where the flyer lifts her knee like a flamingo. In the air, the girl in pink pumps her fist as everyone, audience included, chants "Yell Blue and White! Fight! Tigers! Fight!" The girl hops down and the audience claps.

Ashley's number is called next, and she adjusts her tie-dyed shirt. "Yeah, Ashley," Courtney yells as Ashley does her favorite movement in the cheer—a hands-on-hip stance she's nicknamed "the superwoman." As Ashley begins the fight song, she beams like a kid whose parents have found her a Tickle Me Elmo for Christmas.

As the judges tally up the All-Girl scores, Frankie picks up his microphone. "Five minutes until Coed tryouts," he says. Men and women flock to the mat to warm up.

Casi walks down the bleacher steps and stops at the judge's table. She bends down and whispers something to Frankie and Carol. "You can still try out if you want to," replies Frankie. They won't give her a hard time about missing yesterday's practice.

"What do I need to do?" asks Casi. They give her a list of moves.

Casi runs to a friend, who plops down on the ground and takes off her cheerleading sneakers. Casi puts them on and saunters to the mat, the Coed cheerleaders clearing a space for her. She has decided to try out after all.

Courtney and Ashley sit down on the bleachers to watch, both of them grinning. "She said that when she saw me and Courtney do our tryouts, she almost started crying," explains Ashley, victorious.

On the mat, Casi launches into a Standing Back Tuck. Her shirt barely holds her chest in as she flips, coming dangerously close to a wardrobe malfunction. Next, she does a Toe Touch Back Tuck, her legs swinging out to the sides, and flipping again. In the bleachers, Courtney and Ashley clap softly for her.

Casi walks toward the judging table, smiling. "The Coed team is probably like, 'What is she doing?'" she says. "My pants are too big—they're fallin' off me."

"Do you want to be on the squad?" Frankie asks her, point blank.

"I still don't know," says Casi.

"Well, call us soon and let us know whether to hold a spot."

Casi nods and heads back to her seat. She looks genuinely torn as she flips open her phone and calls her mom for advice. She only has a few hours to make a final decision.

Courtney and Ashley, sitting together, clap for their friends throughout Coed tryouts. They holler for the tiny blonde struggling with her Back Tuck. For her tumbling pass, this girl runs, does a handspring, and stops herself before getting to the tuck. Her mom yells from across the stands, "Pull! Come on!" As the girl's eyes tear up, her mom shouts, "Smile!" She tries again, but she still can't make herself flip.

When the tryouts are done two hours later, I walk out with Frankie, Carol, and the other three judges. We're heading to a restaurant to discuss who made which team. In the hall, I pass the tiny blonde crying hysterically. Her mom stands beside her. "You done blown it now," she says.


## "The Fatsos Will Be on the Sidelines."

Louie's Italian Restaurant is packed for Mother's Day dinner—families in their Sunday best are squished into the entrance. Frankie squeezes his large body through the crowd, stopping every few seconds as women ranging in age from sixteen to sixty offer him a hug. The man behind the register looks up. "Frankie, you have a reservation, right?" he says, winking. He picks up six menus, ignoring the others who are waiting, and takes us through the crowded restaurant to a corner table. I'm thankful for Frankie's semi-celebrity status here.

The restaurant is lined in dark wood paneling, with Christmas lights hung all around. As we sit down, Frankie, Carol, and the judges get out their binders and look over their score sheets. "This is the first time we've had the luxury of so many eighty-, ninety-pound girls—we normally get 130-pounders," says Frankie, examining the Coed hopefuls. "Everyone wants to be a Coed top, but some of the bigger flyers are going to be shifted to All-Girl. They won't be happy about it—All-Girl has been labeled punishment."

Frankie acknowledges the Coed-first hierarchy of the teams, but he hopes to see it change soon. He explains that while the All-Girl team is higher ranked in competition, the university sees the Coed team as the primary faction since they cheer at men's games. "The university really didn't start this All-Girl team—they kind of formed on their own," he says. "The team wasn't nurtured the way it should have been right off the bat, so it's kind of been put on the back burner."

Since who makes the Coed squad will greatly affect who makes All-Girl, the judges decide to pick that squad first. By the time our salads arrive, they've hashed out the twelve men and twelve women whom they want, and they've even determined which half will get the coveted full scholarships. Unlike Brad Patterson at SFA, they aren't concerned that there will be resentment between the cheerleaders who get a full ride and those who get a partial scholarship.

Everyone flips back to the beginning of their notes to discuss which of the Coed "nos" should be moved to the All-Girl squad. "I like number ten and number fifteen for All-Girl," says Carol in her gritty Southern accent. "They won't like it, but we need more tops." They pick a third small flyer to move as well.

"We compete with twenty people, but in cheerleading you gotta have alternates. Twenty-five is the perfect number," says Carol, reasoning that one or two people might not be admitted to the school. She also needs extras to fill in if someone is hurt during the season. "Right now we've got twenty-three who tried out for All-Girl, not counting these three Coed girls we moved. Plus, we've got Casi, who hasn't decided."

Carol pushes her heavily highlighted hair behind her ear. "I hope Casi cheers. You know she's gonna be able to hold any stunt," she says.

"People always say, 'I can't handle it,' but they'll regret it when every-one's on the football field cheering and they're sitting there with their thumb up their butt."

Our entrées arrive, but everyone still has their noses in their binders, figuring out whom they should cut. "There's only a few who couldn't cut it *at all,*" says Frankie. They eliminate one woman whose Back Tuck had been painful to watch.

They discuss another girl on the borderline. "If she'd come back skinny, she would've made it," says Carol. "We have to take that into consideration, because people blast us. They'll email Frankie after games and say, 'That fat girl was busted.'" Unlike what Casi, Courtney, and Ashley told me, the weight fixation does not seem to be quarantined to Coed flyers.

Frankie nods. "All them fatsos will be on the sidelines. I'd rather look at someone who's cute and boring at a game," he says. He starts to tell a story about a dancer last year who was sidelined because of her weight. "Her mother wrote a letter to the athletic department saying, 'I understand that your Spirit Coordinator is excessively overweight.' I wrote back, 'This is your excessively overweight Spirit Coordinator. The only difference between me and your daughter is that I'm not out there in a skirt.'"

Like a godsend from this unsettling conversation, Carol's phone rings. "It's Casi," she says as she flips it open.

"Have you decided yet?" Carol asks. She pauses, her face ambigu-ously even-keeled. "Okay, well, call Frankie."

Frankie's phone rings almost instantly. "Hello," he says. He nods as Casi talks, but his face is blank. "Well, that's great," he finally says, break-ing the tension.

"Yeah! She's coming back," says Carol.

Carol counts how many women they now have for the All-Girl team. "Twenty-five," she says. "Perfect." With that, all the decisions have been made—Courtney, Ashley, Casi, and Kristen have all solidly made the squad. Everyone at the table digs into their pasta.

Frankie dips a piece of bread in marinara sauce. "This is the time of year when parents start asking me to pull strings. I get calls saying, 'You have to get my kid in,'" says Frankie, laughing. "I'm not admissions, but

I did get someone into nursing school who was on the waiting list. I called and said, 'We need her for the squad. Can you move her up?' "

Carol is still looking at the All-Girl roster to the side of her plate. "I'm scared for tumbling on All-Girl," she says, shrugging. "We didn't have enough tumbling last year."

"Do you think that's why they got fourth at Nationals?" I ask.

Carol brings her hand to her chest. "I fully believe that we would've won if we hit," she says. "The group that fell hit 99 percent of the time in practice—they could do it twenty times in a row. It was a fluke. Afterwards, Kern—the girl who fell—said, 'I let you down.' I told her, 'Honey, you could never let me down. You haven't fallen in the three years I've known you. Shit happens.' "

Carol seems genuinely sad telling the story. "When people come up to you afterwards and say, 'You were awesome,' that means more to me than how many championships we've won." She pauses. "And the squad always works their butts off when they got beat out the year before."

# PART TWO

SPIRIT CAMPS

JULY–AUGUST

# CHAPTER 4

## "Have a Hell of a Good Time."

*The University of Memphis All-Girl Tigers*

"SWEET HOME ALABAMA" BLASTS over the loudspeakers as the University of Memphis All-Girl cheerleaders file into the stands of the University of Alabama's Coleman Coliseum, where their spirit camp is held. Spirit camp is akin to spring training for baseball. Every summer, hundreds of camps are held across the country where teams congregate for three- and four-day cheerleading think tanks. It's where new partners and stunt groups get used to each other, where a fledgling team bonds, and where everyone gets in shape after months of parking it on the couch. It's where coaches get certification and cheerleaders are trained on safety. It's where moves created by top teams the year before are taught to other squads and become part of the cheer lexicon. And, most important, it's where teams assert themselves as major competitors for Nationals.

Naturally, spirit camps are also big business. They are held for cheerleaders of all ages, as well as for Pom squads and mascots. Camps are usually hosted on a college campus—the word on the street is that the colleges with popular camps, like this one, are able to fund their cheer programs for an entire year with the profits. Staff members, culled from the best cheerleaders in the country, can earn a few hundred dollars in three or four days. That's a lot better than scooping ice cream.

Camp days are divided into classes—stunt class, basket toss class, pyramid class, etc. In each class, staff members demonstrate different moves and break down exactly what each cheerleader must do to make the impossible happen. Campers also learn cheers and dances that they'll choreograph into a gameday routine, a fight song, and a spirit routine to perform in an informal competition on the final day of camp. The winner in each category takes home a trophy.

Carol, wearing cropped pants and a hoodie, leads the procession of University of Memphis cheerleaders down the coliseum stairs. I follow her next to Casi, Courtney, and Ashley. The Memphis Coed squad trails behind us. The coliseum is cavernous and dimly lit. The University of Alabama mascot, an elephant that looks ready to eat someone, stares up at us from the center of the court. We pause on the steps as another team walks down a row of seats. "I *hate* camp," whispers Courtney, a contradictory smile on her face.

Monica Moody, a senior flyer on the squad a few steps away, would chew Courtney out for saying that. Like Casi, Monica thought last year would be her final year cheerleading. "I was thinking I needed to get a job and focus on school," she says, her light eyes fixed on me. "I was moping around all summer and I finally started thinking, 'What if cheerleading is what I want to do for the rest of my life? What if I can't live without it?'" Monica called Carol a few weeks ago and asked if she could have a place on the squad. Carol was thrilled to have her back.

Monica waves at friends across the arena, a smile forming each time she sees a new person she knows. She is the queen bee of the room. Every cell of her body seems delighted to be here. She is what most people think of when they hear the word *cheerleader*—long blonde hair, beautiful, upbeat. Her eyes are turquoise, the deep sparkling color of a gem.

The camp attendees fill two entire seating sections of the coliseum. There are about twenty teams here, both All-Girl and Coed, plus about fifteen Pom squads. On the basketball court floor below us, a stage has been erected with a UCA Spirit Camp banner across it. The camp director trots up the stairs of the stage and picks up a microphone. "Welcome. Camp is an important time in determining how successful your program will be next year. You're here, one, to determine how well you're going to work together and, two, to learn as much as you possibly can. And three—to have a hell of a good time," he shouts.

Men and women wearing UCA uniforms run onto the mat in front of the stage. The Memphis women spring to their feet as the UCA staff begins a flashy routine. They look like cheerleading robots as they send up stunts that are smooth and controlled. Since there are more than thirty of them, they build five pyramids and connect them like the latticework of a fence. Women fly high in basket tosses, floating like leaves in the wind. "Woo hoo!" yells the audience, clapping hysterically.

"The staff came in yesterday and put that together for you," says the camp director. "Please give them a big welcome." The staff lines up horizontally across the mat—boy, girl, boy, girl. One by one, the camp director introduces them, and they wave like members of the Mickey Mouse Club. All of them are young—about two-thirds are current college cheerleaders (they'll head to camp with their teams at some point during the summer).

Monica is used to being up there with the staff. This summer, she's taught at eleven camps. It's a rigorous process to join the staff—a cheerleader must be handpicked by a current staffer to even get an application. Then they go through exhaustive tryouts and interviews. "You have to be on at all times, you have to hit your stunts perfectly," explains Monica. "You have to be what cheerleading *is*."

The camp director stops as he introduces an Asian woman in the middle of the staff line. "This is her final year at camp," he says, a note of sadness in his voice. "At some point, all of you will move out of this profession and into another life. After thirteen years, she's going into the real world."

Casi and Monica, both seniors, exchange a mournful glance. "That's so sad," says another Memphis senior.

The camp director invites the teams onto the basketball court for cheer class. The University of Memphis women eagerly pick up their backpacks and walk down the arena stairs. A new staff member strolls on stage and takes the microphone. "Everyone, I want you to turn around and introduce yourself to someone you don't know."

Colored shirts jumble as the cheerleaders go out of their way to talk to someone from another team. "Now, I want you to reintroduce yourself to that person as if they're your best friend you haven't seen in ten years." Some of them look at each other and squeal. Others run dramatically and hug each other. Near me, a woman with a yellow hair ribbon jumps and wraps her arms and legs around the guy whose hand she shook the first time around. I'm surprised that everyone is complying.

"Now, I want you to reintroduce yourself to that person as if they're your best friend you haven't seen for ten years, in *slow motion*." Everyone slow-jogs toward their new friend, "Chariots of Fire" playing in the background. The girl with the yellow ribbon jumps and swings her arms around her partner's neck, slowly bringing her legs around his waist.

"Everyone, shout your mascot's name," says the announcer. "Tigers!" the Memphis women yell, turning up the decibel level. The word excites them. Interestingly, the University of Memphis started out as "the Teachers" back when the school was the West Tennessee Normal School and instructed, go figure, teachers. In 1915 a student chant caught on at football games: "We fight like tigers!" Their new mascot was born.

The truth is that most mascots are equally random, a large number dreamed up by college sports writers (for example, the Georgia Tech Yellow Jackets were named for the yellow jackets they wore—not for the wasp). Mascots began as an unofficial phenomenon, but by the 1970s, colleges realized that they could make a lot of money by marketing their school colors, logos, and mascots. Mascots became licensed and copyrighted.

On the coliseum floor, three female staffers begin cheer class. "T! D! That's right! It's Touchdown! T-D!" the women chant, throwing their fists up like goalposts. As they repeat the cheer, Courtney picks up the words and motions. By repeat number four, almost every arm on the basketball court is moving in unison. Monica's sweet Southern voice floats over the others.

They move on to "Ti-gers got that defense! Dee-fense! Dee-fense!" followed by "Go! Go! C-S-U! C-S-U!" with an accompanying shimmy. The teams peel off and, from around the court, I hear teams altering the chants to include their own mascot and school name. For one team, "Tigers" becomes "Pirates." Memphis morphs "C–S–U" into "U of M." As the Memphis women wait for a staff member to observe their cheers, Casi tightens her polka-dotted hair ribbon, and Ashley swings her mocha arms back and forth.

Two UCA staff members walk toward them, and they turn on their smiles as if a switch has been flicked. They go through the cheers, all of which look and sound good to me. But one staffer puts her hand to her ear. "Louder. And make sure your Ts are out here," she says, sticking her arms out straight to her side. "Not down here." She lowers them a few millimeters.

"Watch your claps," says the guy staffer. He demonstrates a proper clap, bringing his hands together with such force that it ricochets through his body.

As cheer class winds down, the Memphis squad begins the short hike to their next class. "We're not gonna use any of these cheers," says Courtney.

Casi nods. "It's trite."

"But cheer class is my favorite because we don't get hurt in there," says Courtney. "In our other classes, we'll get *hurt*."

Casi laughs. Behind us in the procession, someone blows bubbles that float over our heads like weightless disco balls. Casi reaches up to pop one.

## "Cheerleading As We Know It *Will* Change."

We walk toward a long building with a triangular roof, where many of the camp classes will be held. As we open the doors, I'm surprised to find that it's an indoor football field. I don't know that I've ever seen a room this big—it's sixty yards long, with high-quality AstroTurf covering the ground.

The squads sit down on the faux grass in front of a stage. "I want to talk about the state of cheerleading," says a man in a polo shirt. "The media attention in the last few years hasn't been positive. They don't want to show you out in the community or visiting nursing homes—what they want to talk about is injuries."

Suddenly, I feel like the media enemy. I see a group of UCA staff members whispering and glancing my way. I try to be more discreet about taking notes.

"We all have the responsibility to keep cheerleading at its current athletic state," he says. "If we have *any* more injuries broadcast on national TV, cheerleading as we know it *will* change."

He's referring to Kristi Yamaoka's fall in the lead up to the 2006 NCAA tournament, when she was wheeled off the court still cheering. After the fall, many people in the cheer world feared that the media attention might bring about their worst nightmare—that cheerleading squads around the country would be grounded. Not sent up to their rooms with no phone or TV, but that someone would hand down a ruling that cheerleaders, the fearless acrobats of the air, wouldn't be allowed to leave the floor.

While newspapers and magazines continue to run stories about cheerleading injuries being on the rise, the most recent numbers show the opposite. After years of increase, 2005 began a downward trend with cheerleading emergency room visits *decreasing* by 15 percent. Two things happened that might have started that downward trend. First, the American Association of Cheerleading Coaches and Administrators (AACCA) ramped up efforts to increase safety awareness among both cheerleaders and coaches. Second, the NCAA realized that nearly a quarter of their insurance claims came from cheerleaders injured during NCAA events. So while they do not oversee cheerleading directly, they took back-door action, working with the major cheerleading organizations to require that every college coach is safety certified. It was a great move; a study in the *American Journal of Sports Medicine* shows that coaches with a medium or high level of safety training have *half* the risk of injuries on their teams.

Football history provides an interesting parallel. After years of a steady number of injuries, in 1968, a very scary thirty-six football players died. Most of these deaths occurred because of spinal and brain injuries from helmet-to-helmet contact. Within a few years, blocking or tackling leading with a helmet was outlawed. Injury rates plummeted almost immediately.

The mid-2000s may have been for cheerleading what the late 1960s were for football. Just a few months after Kristi Yamaoka's fall, the AACCA decided on new rules for basketball games and other cheerleading performances on hard surfaces: no pyramids that stack cheerleaders two and a half persons high, no basket tosses, no partner stunts where a base catches a flyer with one hand, and no tumbling passes involving a twist. The only exceptions are during halftime or postgame shows, if a squad rolls out mats. Many cheerleaders feel stifled by the new rules, but they will no doubt prevent injuries.

"Right now, cheerleading attracts athletic people," continues the man on the stage. "Y'all are good-looking, all-American people. If they decide to ground you, they won't see the effects for five years. Then they'll ask, 'Why do games not have the same feel?' Whether they say it or not, they *like* how you represent them now."

He takes a deep breath. "Your coaches know the responsibility, but they can't watch all of you. So think about it next time you're at practice goofing off," he says. "In classes, any time we talk about a stunt, we'll also talk about spotting. It's a skill like anything else. You have to pay attention at *all* times. Stunts fall a certain way, and you have to learn that. Remember, a girl goes down and cheerleading *will* change."

It's a strange way to frame a conversation about safety. First off, it makes it sound like getting hurt is totally within someone's control. If I were giving this speech, the theme would be, "We don't want you to break a bone, get a concussion, or worse." But this guy seems to understand something that I haven't fully grasped yet. Appealing to cheerleaders' allegiance to the sport—to the group—means more to them than their concern for their individual bodies.

Kristen, Memphis's child-star captain, tries to explain it to me before the next class. Her friend Emily Lawrence, a junior on the squad with a perfect button of a nose, joins us. They tell me about the smorgasbord of injuries they've had over the years. "I lost my big toenail last week," says Emily, taking off her shoe and sock to show me that she's not kidding. "I was doing Back Tucks over and over again, and it just popped off."

"One year, I was the back spot in a basket toss and the flyer stopped in the middle of a twist. When she came down, her leg fractured my collarbone," says Kristen, blonde ponytail cascading down her back.

"Then last year, Monica flew into my chest, and I fell backwards on my ankle. I broke it two nights before we left for Nationals, but I still competed on it."

"That just shows how much we *love* cheerleading," says Emily. "We wouldn't keep coming back if we didn't."

Kristen nods heartily. "We're just like football players or baseball players," she says. "We perform no matter what. Hurt, sick, whatever."

"I broke my back in high school—it was from continuous wear-down," explains Emily. "We had our team physicals this year and the same doctor asked, 'Why are you still cheering?' I said, 'I just can't stop.' He was like, 'Obviously, there's nothing I can tell you.'"

All of this helps me understand Kristi Yamaoka a little better. When I first saw the footage of her cheering from the stretcher, I didn't know what to think. Was she conscious? Had she hit her head so hard that her brain was involuntarily doing the last thing it remembered? No. Kristi couldn't stand the idea of her team losing because they were worrying about her. She made a conscious decision to show her squad and the basketball team that she was fine, even if moving her arms could make her injury worse.

As she said later in interviews, her thoughts lying on the basketball floor weren't *How long am I going to be in the hospital?* or even *Will I be able to cheer again?* Kristi explained it best to Katie Couric. "My biggest concern was that I didn't want my squad to be distracted, and I didn't want my team to be distracted from winning the game," she said, a neck brace still around her dainty shoulders. "I'm still a cheerleader—on a stretcher or not."

## "It Feels Like a Billion Pounds."

It's late afternoon, and after sneaking in a nap between classes, the Memphis women are fighting to keep their eyes open through pyramid class. They're exhausted—they've been cheering for hours and still have several classes to go before the day is over.

In front of them, UCA staffers, both male and female, demonstrate how to do a pyramid called a 2-2-1. Step one, two girls stand in front of their guy partners and are tossed onto their shoulders. Step two, the flyer who will be at the top of the pyramid stands between the two Shoulder Stands, a guy in front of her and a guy behind her. The two boost her up so she flies right between the two women on their partners' shoulders. Step three, the middle layer women scoop their arms under the top flyer's feet and hold her in place.

"You'll have half an hour to try this," says a staffer.

The Memphis All-Girl and Coed squads stand up. Kristen rubs her eyes as she walks the All-Girl team to an open area near the twenty-yard line. They huddle around her, and they discuss how they're going to do this pyramid. Behind them, the Memphis Coed team jumps right in, hoisting two women into Shoulder Stands. "It's much harder for an All-Girl team, not just because of strength," explains Kristen. "A guy's shoulder width is three times a girl's. So a flyer can stand there like she's standing on the ground. Ours have to balance on a shoulder which isn't very big."

Ten minutes have gone by, and the women are still in planning mode. Behind them, another All-Girl team morphs the 2-2-1 into a 4-2-1. They lift their middle layer women off the ground in much-easier Elevators, where two bases each hold a foot.

The Memphis huddle finally breaks. Casi and a brunette flyer step to the side of the group. Casi ties her chin-length hair into a stubby ponytail and reaches her arms over her head. She lock hands with the flyer and lunges so that her butt sticks out. The flyer places a foot on the small of Casi's back and scrambles to her shoulders. Casi grunts and pushes up to standing.

Courtney tries the same thing. "Oh shit," she says, her eyes opening wide as her flyer steps up. Lauren Woods, a strong freshman base with dirty-blonde hair that brushes the small of her back, volunteers herself to base a Shoulder Stand, too. Near her, Monica climbs onto yet another base's shoulders. They now have four Shoulder Stands. They're not just building a 2-2-1—they're going to do two of them.

Monica kneels down on the grass next to another middle layer flyer. They bend their inside arms to a 90-degree angle. Their top flyer steps on their forearms and practices balancing. When they feel steady, the top flyer walks over to two more bases, who practice tossing her straight in the air.

The Memphis squad confronts the pyramid like a puzzle, solving the parts first, then putting the pieces together. They're now ready to try the whole 2-2-1. The middle layer women climb onto Casi's and Lauren's shoulders, and the top flyer is tossed in between them. But her legs come apart and the middle layer women can't quite scoop her feet. Spotters reach up to catch her as she falls. They try again. Same thing.

Then finally, it works, the 2-2-1 standing solidly like a three-tiered wedding cake. The top girl swivels her hips ever so slightly to maintain her balance. Casi, on the bottom, grunts. Lauren turns bright red, and tears form in her eyes.

As they hop down, Kristen claps. "We would rather rise to how the guys do it than have someone simplify it for us," she says, her cheeks flushed as they hop down. "Doing it with two people on the bottom frees up other people to tumble in front."

Casi nods. "There's no point baby-stepping it," she explains. "It makes us stand out."

"What does it feel like to be on the bottom?" I ask her.

Casi smiles to reveal the gap between her front teeth. "Like a billion pounds."

## "When People Ask 'What's Your Major?' I Say Cheerleading."

Surreal doesn't begin to cover it. In front of me, a pirate with a plastic head five times too big for his body uses his sword to try to decapitate a fluffy tiger with a perpetual smile. Across the indoor football field, an owl and an elephant, both wearing football jerseys, run in circles, the owl flapping his fake wings. A plush bulldog with a studded collar throws a football right past me, and it sails into the plush hands of a giant brown squirrel.

I'm not going insane. Memphis's camp has ended for the night, and the mascots have come from their classes in the building next door to socialize with the cheerleaders. A tiger walks up to me, leaning back and snapping as he struts. He throws out a huge orange palm. I go to slap him five, but he pulls his hand away before I get there. He points at me, his other hand in front of his face miming laughter. Great, I've been dissed by a guy in a tiger suit.

"Be nice," yells one of the Memphis women, stepping to my defense. The tiger puts his arm around me and pulls me in for a hug.

The Memphis women pick up their backpacks and start the hike to their rooms. I walk with Lauren, the freshman base on the bottom of one of the 2-2-1s. I ask why she volunteered herself for bottom layer duty. "I figured they were going to pull me in anyway. I don't like that stunt," she says, pulling the collar of her shirt over her shoulder to reveal a huge red welt. "I've got scabs from it."

"How do you keep from collapsing?" I ask.

"You just squeeze and go into a zone where you don't think about the pain," she says. "It's when you're done that you're like 'God, that hurts *so* bad.'"

Across campus, we arrive at the dorm where the spirit campers are staying. We crowd into an elevator and take it to the University of Memphis's floor. Lauren opens the door to the tiny cinderblock room she's sharing with Alicia Fletcher, another freshman on the squad. Lauren and Alicia are both "Mississippi Girls"—a group who earned their nickname because they live just over the Tennessee state line and come to the University of Memphis on a tuition waiver. Lauren and Alicia have cheered together for years, and both had their hearts set on the University of Memphis because of the All-Girl squad's reputation.

"I can't believe it—this is just so weird that *we're* cheering in *college,*" says Lauren, her blue-gray eyes intense. "We're going to be on TV!"

Alicia scrunches her nose. "When people ask, 'What's your major going to be?' I'm like, 'Cheerleading.' I'm going to college to cheer," she says.

A smile forms on Lauren's face. Today is a big day—her eighteenth birthday. Down the hall, some of the older teammates are getting ready to go out, but since clubs in the area have a twenty-one-and-up door policy, Lauren and Alicia will have a quieter celebration in their room. Casi walks by the door wearing a bright blue shirt, pearls, and a blue geometric-print scarf as a headband.

"I'm trying to disguise this," she says, pointing to a gash on her chest. "This is from one of the heavy top girls who doesn't know what she's doing. I'm pissed off—she broke my sorority necklace into three pieces. This scab will be here at least a few weeks." We assure Casi that she's covered her battle wound with the pearls.

As the older squad members leave, Lauren suggests hitting the convenience store down the road for a celebratory snack. We open the door to the bodega and it's yet another surreal moment. The store is packed with cheerleaders grabbing granola bars and chips, their chatter overwhelming the light rock streaming out of the radio. Lauren makes her selection and joins the end of the line, which snakes around the perimeter of the store. She waits patiently for forty-five minutes to buy a box of birthday Hot Pockets.

# CHAPTER 5

## "When a Coach Leaves, a Program Either Drops Off or Goes to a Whole New Level."

*The Stephen F. Austin Lumberjacks*

THE STEPHEN F. AUSTIN squad could pretty much sleep through stunt class. It's like NASA astronauts taking Introduction to Astronomy, yet the SFA squad claps as the staff talks them through every detail that bases and flyers must think about in the split second it takes to do a stunt.

It's SFA's second class at Southern Methodist University's Spirit Camp in Dallas. The gymnasium we're in looks similar to the one where SFA's tryouts were held—blue mats cover the basketball court, and the bleachers lining the room are being used as a backpack depository. The team drove here from Nacogdoches in separate cars, and since almost everyone arrived here late, this is the first time I'm seeing the squad together. There's only one problem: I can't find Coach Brad.

One of the SFA guys walks by me on his way back from the bathroom. "Where's Brad?" I ask him.

He looks at me like I'm speaking Russian. "You didn't hear?" he asks.

"Hear what?"

"Brad quit. He moved to Little Rock," he says. "Trisha's our new head coach."

I feel like an atom bomb has been dropped on me. Brad never even hinted that he was considering leaving his prestigious, full-time coaching position. Not to mention the fact that he had an impeccable track record—each and every of his three years as coach, SFA brought home a National Championship trophy. Trisha served as Brad's assistant coach last year, and while she's proven that she can be a great second-in-command, she's young—she graduated from SFA only two years ago. Many of the current squad members are her former teammates. Will they accept her as the law?

I run into the hall and frantically dial Brad's phone number. He answers, and I launch at him with a million questions. After apologizing for not letting me know sooner, he explains. "I'd always sworn that as soon as I finished my master's at SFA, I was going to go. I finished my degree over the summer, so I had to keep my own promise," he says.

Brad has a long list of reasons for moving to Arkansas. He and his wife just had a baby, and, in Little Rock, Brad's mom can babysit him during the day. Brad's parents also offered to sell them one of their newly renovated rental homes at the same price they bought it for years ago. Brad could pursue a doctorate in education at the University of Arkansas–Little Rock, and he happened to see the perfect job listing for a teaching position at a junior college in the area.

"For seven years of my life, pretty much everything I did revolved around SFA cheerleading," he says. "I love the team, I love SFA, I love Nacogdoches. But it quickly became a situation where I couldn't say no."

"So Trisha is the new coach?" I ask.

"Yes," he says. "Michael Preston and I batted around a few names, but the obvious choice was Trisha. If you can't find a coach from inside your program, you're not doing something right. There have only been five coaches in the history of SFA competitive cheer, and they were all in house. The only way to learn is to jump in feet first—that's what I did."

I hang up the phone and peek back in the arena. The cheerleaders are still rapt in the proceedings, but there's no sign of Trisha. I call Michael Preston, who oversees the spirit program, for some more insight.

"I thought cheerleading was always going to a be a part of Brad, but as the baby got closer and closer, it became a reality that it was time to move on," he explains. "I was surprised by the timing—I only had about a month to find a coach. Rumors were flying, and I had cheerleaders calling left and right, saying, 'Who's going to be coach? I'm quitting.' So far we haven't lost a single one."

I ask him how he decided to hire Trisha. "She's relatively inexperienced, but she's excited and that's going to rub off on the team," says Michael. "From an organizational standpoint, she's better. Brad was disorganized and a big-picture guy. Trisha looks at the details."

I walk back into the arena and take a seat in the bleachers, near a group of SFA alumni who've made the two-hour drive to cheer on the new squad. We sit quietly, watching the cheerleaders watch the staff. Nestled among several other teams, the thing that seems to separate SFA from the rest of the cheerleaders here is genetics. The SFA women are just a little more petite, the men just a little bulkier.

I look up and see Trisha walking toward me. Her hair is redder than I remembered, and she's wearing an SFA T-shirt with matching flip-flops. She has the same petite stature as the women on the team—her purple "Lumberjack" backpack is nearly as big as she is, and she leans forward slightly to balance the weight. She sits down near me and says hello. There's a shyness to her voice, one that makes me wonder whether she can rule this team with an iron fist. Will she be able to handle a herd of guys who are twice her size and, in some cases, older than her?

"Congratulations on becoming head coach," I say, and she blushes.

"It was kind of sudden. One day me and Brad are making plans for the year and the next, he just threw at me that he wanted me to apply for head coach," she says. "I've been coaching since I was fourteen. I remember that the SFA coach before Brad told me, 'You could be the first female to run this program.' It's something I've had in the back of my head for a while."

Besides Trisha, only one other person put in a resumé for the position—Doug, the insurance agent who came back to SFA because he missed cheerleading so much. Michael decided to make him the assistant coach, a move that made both Trisha and Doug happy. "Doug came straight over to my house and we ran around the neighborhood yelling like little kids," says Trisha. "We feed off each other wonderfully. He'll think of something and I'll add to it. In the end, it's very cool."

Before camp, the squad met in Nacogdoches for a week of pre-camp practice. Trisha watched as different flyers and bases worked together, trying to find couples who matched well in strength, style, and timing. She found the perfect partner for Samantha—Tyrone Lyons. "He's five feet tall and five feet wide," says Samantha. It's hyperbole, but at his side, she appears even longer and leaner.

Tyrone is half Puerto Rican and half Cuban, and his light brown skin probably fools many into thinking he's African American. A former college wrestler, he says, "I didn't mess with cheerleading in high school." I can see why Samantha was drawn to him—his demeanor is laid-back, a joke thrown in when needed.

On the mat, the NCA staff members ask the campers to try the stunts they've just demonstrated. As the SFA cheerleaders walk toward the back of the mat, the stunters pair off into their partner couples. Trisha points to Samantha and Tyrone as the couples form a circle, the women lining the center, their partners behind them. "They're one of those pairs you put together and the stuff they can do together is like 'Whoa!'" she says. "They're amazing."

Doug calls the circle to attention. "Full Up Libs," he shouts. The guys toss their partners in the air, the women spinning as they fly. They land in their partners' palms and pick their knees up for Liberties. The first one goes up, then the next, then the next—a cheerleading version of a wave. In the end, only one of the SFA women drops. "Yay," says Yvette as the women hop down. Samantha gives Tyrone five.

Sierra leads the next wave. Her new partner is James Brown, whose name evokes exactly the wrong image. James is white, a refrigerator of a guy with a Cro-Magnon brow. The only thing keeping him from looking intimidating is the dimple in his cheek. Sierra is thrilled to have him as a partner. "We were hitting stunts the first time we tried them that I'd *never* hit before," she says. "On other teams, I felt like I was being held back. Now I feel like I have an advantage cause I have one of the big guys."

Sierra's hands grip James Brown's wrists behind her. The two of them dip and he hoists her straight up, a flash of platinum hair. As she flies, Sierra kicks her left leg up and grabs her shoe, landing with her right foot in James Brown's hands. The rest of the wave goes up, the last couple botching it.

"Real nice," yells one of the SFA alumni. "We heckle our own."

Yvette and her partner, Jason Larkins, start off the next wave. Yvette is one of the few people who is still working with her partner from last year. They came in ninth in the Partner Stunt Competition at Nationals last year—not as high as they would have liked, but perfectly respectable for a first appearance. "Jason says being my partner was the best thing that ever happened to him. He never would have been able to compete in Partner Stunt with anyone else," she says. Unlike many of the guys on the team, Jason is tall and slim, his short afro and facial hair making him look like a smooth talker from a seventies blaxploitation film.

Jason tosses Yvette into a Heel Stretch. She scissor-kicks her legs, replacing her right foot with the left in a move called a Tick-Tock. But Jason isn't able to stabilize her as her second foot comes down. He grabs her waist as she falls, lowering her to the floor. "Sorry," she giggles, lightly hitting him on the chest. "I went slow."

Half an hour later, stunt class is over. While the squad has a few minutes before their next class, I ask some of the teammates how they feel about Trisha being their new coach. "I liked Brad a lot. Trisha is different, but things are going well so far," says Jason. "My big concern over the summer was that some of the rookies might have second thoughts. When a coach leaves, a program either drops off or goes to a whole new level. Some people don't want to take that chance."

As she chugs from a water bottle, Sierra explains that she is happy with the switch. "Brad's gonna have a new little baby and he wasn't going to be able to completely devote himself to us," she says. "I would have loved to have Brad as a coach, but this is what's best."

More than anything, Sierra is thrilled that her new coach is female. At her first college, where she learned the language of anorexia, she described her coach as a "twenty-four-year-old really hot guy." "He talked down to us and we'd get weighed in all the time. I wasn't eating and lost a lot of weight, and he seemed to like me so much more," she says. "He liked me for the wrong reasons—whatever I weighed, I still had the exact same skills."

At the junior college where Sierra transferred, her coach was a woman, and the difference was like night and day. "Honestly, I was kind of worried about coming to SFA and having a guy coach," she explains.

Kali Seitzer, a second-year senior at SFA with light brown hair that tickles her shoulders and the kind of cheeks that look muscular from smiling all the time, was all the way to angry when she heard Brad was leaving. Kali will be one of this year's female captains, so she speaks quietly as she voices her discontent.

"After tryouts, I pulled Brad aside, looked him in the eye, and asked, 'You're going to be here this year, right?' He said he was gonna be here *for sure*," she explains. "I know Brad. I understand his coaching style. I'm not good with change."

Neither am I. What had seemed like a sure-win year just a few months ago now seems like a gamble.

## "It's Like Letters for a Fraternity."

"We're going to have TEAM time—Together Everyone Accomplishes More," says an announcer on the stage. "We want to identify the strengths of your team and set your goals for the year."

NCA staff members hand out goal sheets and golf pencils to all of the teams sitting on the basketball floor. The SFA cheerleaders lay down on their stomachs, their heads toward the center of the circle. Their shoes face out, gaping holes where their toes have tried to escape. "It takes so long to break shoes in, you put off getting new ones as long as possible," says one of the women, explaining that they'll get nicer ones before competition.

Trisha sits down next to the circle, a purple binder in her hand. Across the front it reads HEAD COACH BRAD PATTERSON. She hasn't even had time to switch the names.

Team captain Kali picks up the paper and pencil, and acts as the stenographer. "What are our goals for the year?" she reads.

"To be patient and communicate with each other," says Yvette, sounding very Girl Scout-ish.

"To win Nationals," someone says. Kali writes it in uppercase letters.

"To pass classes." The team erupts in laughter.

"What are our strengths?" asks Kali.

"Cohesiveness."

"Um, talent?" says Trisha.

"What are our weaknesses?" asks Kali. She looks at some of the guys. "Goofing off," she writes without consulting the others.

"Inconsistency," says Yvette.

"How can we overcome our weaknesses?" asks Kali. Everyone goes silent.

"Practice," says Sierra.

"Don't settle," says someone else.

Kali moves on to the final question. "How do we want to be remembered ten years from now?" she asks.

"LCLM," shouts one of the guys. Kali writes it in huge letters across the bottom of the paper.

These four letters keep popping up. They're prominently placed on all of SFA's T-shirts, they're in their cheers, and I've even noticed a few LCLM tattoos. One girl has a dainty one on her shoulder, the letters framed by axes. Other guys have it starkly tattooed across their ankles.

I ask a group standing near me what LCLM stands for. "It's like letters for our fraternity," explains one of the guys. "It's the idea that we think of ourselves as a family, and that we always will be." But like what goes on in fraternity hazing, only the people in the group can know the precise meaning.

The NCA staff members hand out a second set of papers—it's time for their safety awareness test. The test was instituted two years ago by the NCA and the UCA. It consists of twenty multiple-choice questions designed to pound in the basic principles of safety.

Before the test, the camp director reminds the cheerleaders that two-and-a-half-high pyramids, basket tosses, one-arm stunts, and twisting tumbling are now outlawed at games. The SFA team collectively groans. "Man, we can't do anything anymore," says one of the tumblers.

The announcer on the stage acknowledges their grievances. "You can perform these things at halftime *if* they are done on a mat," he reminds them.

"Yeah, we're gonna roll out the mats," says Trisha sarcastically.

The staff hands out answer sheets for the test. "Please get these right, y'all," pleads Trisha.

The announcer calls the first question. "Who's responsible for safety in cheerleading? A) The student government; B) Every member of the team; C) The frat boys; D) None of the above." Most people laugh, while others instinctively call out "B."

"Don't cheat now," says the announcer. "Which surface has been approved for two-and-a-half-high pyramids and basket tosses? A) A mat or grass; B) Concrete; C) The basketball court." The squad writes down their answers.

"How does a coach determine a cheerleader's readiness to try a new skill?"

"When I say I want it," Trisha jokes as the squad listens to the answer options. Across the court, a cheerleader spells out the letter C with her arms. "Just pick the longest answers," notes one of the SFA guys. After three questions in a row where the dummy answers are one word, while the correct answer is a string of jargon, he is completely right.

While it's clear that the AACCA, the NCA, and the UCA are taking active steps and succeeding in lowering the number of cheerleading injuries, this test (along with the open-book, take-home test that coaches take for safety certification) has left a bad taste in my mouth. With just a few simple alterations—making the questions more sincere, having it administered individually and silently, and having the grades actually count for something—I wonder if the number of cheer injuries wouldn't drop even more.

### "Can We Go to Naptime Class?"

The coliseum is littered with bottles boasting names like Tab Energy, Red Bull, Full Throttle, Amp, and (my personal favorite) Diet Rockstar Energy. It's the third day of camp, and cheerleaders are relying on these drinks to carry them through their exhaustion. The camp is doing cheer-aerobics to warm up, and some of the SFA tumblers stand to the side doing goofy dances. "We have the most ADD guys on our team," says Trisha, sitting in the bleachers amid a clump of coaches.

"The guys can be so dumb," says another coach. "I said before camp, 'No drinking.' The guys were like, 'Well, can we get drunk?' *No*."

Trisha rolls her heavily mascaraed eyes. "My guys asked, 'Can we get beer and bring it back to our rooms?' I said no and someone asked, 'Can we drink in our car?' Um, no, stupid."

"We just did it—we didn't ask anyone," says a third coach, reminiscing about when the three of them were campers just a few years ago.

"I was so drunk that I threw up and punched my coach in the back of the head in the same night," says the second coach.

"You amazed people, not because you were good but because you were so drunk the night before," says the first. They all laugh.

The SFA squad moves to basket toss class at the other side of the gym. Trisha grabs her backpack and follows. "Can we go to naptime class? Where they show you the proper technique of how to place a pillow under your head," asks one of the SFA guys as he sits down to watch the staff demonstrate baskets.

Four bases stand in a semicircle, locking their hands together. The flyer uses their hands as a step and hops on, steadying herself between two of their shoulders. This is called "loading in." The bases quickly stand up, using the force from their legs and arms to launch the flyer high in the air like a cannon shooting straight up. She comes back down, her butt toward the floor so that she can throw her arms around two of the bases as they catch her in a cradle. On the ground again, the flyer describes how she squeezes her muscles so she can go as high as possible—this is called "riding the basket."

Sierra is the first SFAer to try it, kicking her legs to the side as she reaches the top of the toss. She lands with a thud in her bases' arms, a look of joy on her face.

Kali goes up next. "I've never ridden it that high," she says, back on the ground. "That made my stomach queasy."

Yvette spies a puddle of glitter on the mat. She crouches down, collects some of the silver flecks in her hands, and rubs it in her glossy black hair. She walks over to a group of guys, who link arms to toss her. She flies high toward the ceiling, pulling her body into a Tuck at the top. But on the way down, she stops spinning. Her head plummets toward the ground, her knees still tucked to her shoulders as she falls out of the air. Everyone in the gym gasps.

Her bases frantically step to the right as she falls like a baby bird out of the nest. They catch her, her head just a few feet away from the ground, and sit her down on the mat. "Are you okay?" they ask in unison.

Tears come to her eyes, as if the bubbliness has been knocked out of her. "I haven't done a Back Tuck basket in years and my muscles didn't remember what it felt like. I freaked out," she says, taking a deep breath and walking to take a seat in the bleachers.

"Yvette, that looked like *The Matrix* or something," says Trisha.

On the mat, Kali calls over the smallest guy on the squad, whose hair is spiked with gel. "Have you met my brother?" she says, putting her arm around him.

Kali and Michael Seitzer have their dad, a former gymnast, to thank for their tumbling ability. Growing up in North Carolina, their parents put them in gymnastics classes when Kali was seven and Michael was four. They both caught on quickly and earned scholarships at their gym. When she was thirteen, Kali switched over to cheerleading and soon fell in love.

When they were young, Kali and Michael had a lot in common—both quick, powerful tumblers who spent long hours perfecting gymnastic moves. But in high school, they grew apart. "My mom and dad were not good with drugs and alcohol," explains Kali. "My senior year, I moved out of my house and got two jobs to support myself." Kali lived in an apartment above her cheerleading coach's house while Michael stayed at home with their dad. When Kali graduated, she left for a junior college in Texas. "We just never talked," she says of her brother at the time. "I had no idea who he was or what to say to him."

A few years later, Michael followed an identical path, heading to a Texas junior college. Because he is stunning to watch as he crosses the mat, twisting and turning like a balloon with the air let out of it, SFA recruited him. When Kali heard that Michael was trying out, she suggested that they be roommates. In the past two weeks, they've talked more than they did in four years.

Michael and three other guys lock arms to propel Kali in the air for another basket toss. As she stands up, her hand is over her heart. "Phew," she says.

"I love basket tosses. They're so much fun," says Michael.

I'm surprised—even the big guys keep wincing as they catch their flyers. "All the tumblers love them," he explains. "We're naturally quick, so we can go from a deep squat to hands over our head quickly. Some of the big stunters are a lot slower."

As class ends, Trisha, in her cropped jeans and T-shirt, walks up to a group of guys. The other SFA cheerleaders gather around them, cheering. She loads in and sails up, up, up, flipping before coming back down. The team applauds as she stands up. Trisha throws her head back and laughs, her long hair falling loose from her bun.

## "Trick or Treat."

Blue fuzzballs blow across the mat like cheerleading tumbleweeds. For the first time in days, only two people are standing on the mat. The rest of the campers sit in the bleachers watching the Top Gun Partner Stunt Competition. Every now and then, the crowd pops out of their seats, clapping for particularly impressive moves.

For the SFA partner couples, this competition is the highlight of camp—it's their chance to show off and establish themselves as contenders for the Partner Stunt Competition at Nationals. About twenty couples stand in a line beside the mat waiting to perform, and over half of them don SFA T-shirts or sports bras.

Yvette and her partner performed a few minutes ago, but it did not go as well as they had hoped. Their opening move boggled, setting a bad tone for the rest of the 45-second routine. "It's not like when we do a team routine, where you do one tiring thing and then get a little rest while you walk to the next formation," says Yvette. "It's constant stunting, everyone looking at just you."

One of the guys near her pulls a bottle of Aleve from his backpack. Yvette sticks out her hands. "Trick or treat," she laughs as he pours pain relievers into her palms.

Sierra and James Brown are up next. Sierra has dolled herself up for the occasion, extra eyeliner around her eyes and trails of blush across her cheeks. James stomps his feet on the mat like a bull as he gets into position behind her. Sierra flips and he thrusts her in the air, catching her in his left hand like a torch. He brings her back to the ground and they do another Rewind, Sierra landing in his right hand this time.

"Wooo!" screams the audience as Sierra smiles wide. So far, the routine is flawless.

They go for yet another Rewind, but as James catches her this time, his arm drops. Sierra grunts, and James's Winnie the Pooh face wrinkles as he pushes her back up. She aggressively pulls herself into a Scorpion and bobs her head as if to say, "Mmm-hmm."

The audience roars. "That girl's badass," someone behind me says.

Sierra runs off the mat, excited. She throws her arms around me. "This is our fourth day stunting together!" she says. "I can only imagine what we'll look like in eight months at Nationals. I'm ecstatic."

Soon, Samantha and Tyrone have inched to the front of the line of competitors. Tyrone's wide, curving back reminds me of a stegosaurus, his neatly trimmed Mohawk adding to the effect. Samantha, red ribbon in her hair, waves excitedly as they step onto the mat.

Their routine begins well, with an explosive quality as they nail stunt after stunt. I almost wish Brad was here as the entire camp watches Samantha. "Whoever gets her as a partner will pout," he'd said in the deliberations after tryouts, explaining that her height would bar her from being a top stunter. But Tyrone is far from pouting.

He lowers Samantha to the floor by her waist and slides her between his legs, holding her parallel to the mat, just a foot above it. This is a move called a Superman—from here, Tyrone will swing Samantha straight above his head. But his palms are sweaty, and he loses his grip. Before Samantha has processed what's happening, she is face-planted on the mat.

"Ooh," gasps the audience.

Samantha and Tyrone both laugh. Samantha stands up, and they finish their final move to applause.

"Maybe we can create a new stunt where you start on your stomach?" says Tyrone, as they walk off the mat.

The Top Gun Competition comes to a close, and it's clear that an SFA couple has won. But I have no idea who will get the trophy. Tyrone and Samantha are out. Sierra and James Brown had the hardest routine and hit it with only one bobble. Yvette and Jason's routine had a less noticeable error, but it was less difficult as a whole.

I ask Jason and James Brown who they think won. "If Tyrone hit, it would have been him," says Jason. "They're flashy. On our team we have power stunters, technical stunters, and flashy stunters."

"My routine is about power," says James Brown, as if I hadn't noticed.

Jason pats him on his broad back. "It's between you and me," he says, forgetting to mention the women.

## "Can You Imagine If There Were Kegs?"

*Girls Gone Wild* would pay a lot of money to be where I am right now—at a cheerleader pool party. Some of the campers are still in practice clothes, while others have changed into swimsuits. They swarm the deck chairs beside a large wading pool. On the far wall, a waterfall cascades down.

The SFA cheerleaders have gone back to their dorm to change, so for the moment, I am on my own. A group of women walks by wearing garbage bags—it's initiation for their rookies. Other teams point and laugh.

"Are you ready for the Ms. SMU pageant?" yells a DJ set up by the wading pool. The Ms. SMU pageant is a dance competition that seems to be a tradition at camp. It starts off tame, the first contestant prancing and kicking up water from the wading pool as she dances.

But a few contestants later, it escalates. A group of women come out shaking their rumps and chests to Sisqo's "Thong Song." Two of the cheerleaders dance in the waterfall, reaching up and grabbing onto a pole, stripper-style. Another pair grinds against each other, and the guys around the pool cheer. Then the two women start making out.

"Okay, that's almost inappropriate," says the announcer as they separate a little. One of the women in the waterfall starts to take off her top. "Oookay," he says, cutting off the music.

"S! F! A! Go Jacks! S! F! A! Go Jacks!" I hear in the distance. It gets louder until the team bursts through a gate. The rookie guys march in front, each of them wearing a Speedo, an absurdly small piece of fabric for some of these large men.

"That was out of control," one of the guys says, catching the tail end of the dance contest.

"You should have seen it a few years ago," says Kali. "People acted crazy to win—it was the most distasteful thing."

"It's just college kids having fun," says Yvette. "Can you imagine if there were kegs?"

"We don't ever enter," adds one of the SFA women.

"We don't have anyone with boobs or a butt, so we wouldn't win anyway," laughs Yvette. "We just make our guys wear Speedos."

"Last year they had a belly-flop contest," says Kali. "That was much more fun."

## "Smile, Fucker."

Kali stares at herself in the bathroom mirror. She pokes at her stomach. While the others on the team have trim tummies that curve in from their hips, Kali's is straight up and down, muscular, like the star gymnast she trained for years to be. Her face registers only one emotion this morning: stress.

It's the final day of camp, and the Lumberjacks will be competing in an hour. When they ran through their spirit routine last night before the Top Gun Competition, they were fantastic, bringing a tear to the eyes of one of the SFA alumnae. "I want to be out there with them so bad," she said, clapping her ass off.

But this morning, the alumni's comments are critical. "That was sloppy." "You look like a wiggle worm." "If you have to bump around, what the fuck are you doing here?" After a late night of partying, none of the stunts in the spirit routine are hitting. One guy slams his foot into the bleachers, making a noise so loud that I jump.

"I'm stressing," says Kali quietly. "I'm supposed to be a leader, but I keep messing up. I don't want to be the one falling."

Back in the gymnasium, Trisha gathers the squad into a huddle. Doug puts his hand to his head like he's massaging away a headache. Others have bloodshot eyes. "Right now, this looks like shit. It doesn't look like you're having fun. It's all here," says Trisha, waving her hand over her face.

"I know you're tired, but pull it out of your ass," says Kali, trying to wipe the worry from her voice. "Be positive, be awesome, be excited about *everything.*"

"We're SFA. Don't drop a thing," says Yvette, uncharacteristically stern.

As they watch the first few squads perform, Yvette takes a vanilla body spray out of her backpack. "Can you spray me?" asks Kali, as Yvette mists her. Sierra sits down behind one of the guys. They both lean back and shut their eyes for a moment. Yvette sneaks over to snap a photo.

A guy near them stares blankly into space with an expression on his face like his puppy just died. "Smile, fucker," one of the alumni cheer-leaders snaps.

Their toughest competitors, Oklahoma State University, stand up and do a killer routine. "Oooo! Ssss! Uuuu! Cowboys!" they chant as they walk off the mat. Their mascot, a cowboy with an enormous plastic head, shoots his cap gun.

SFA is up next. Trisha motions for the team to stand up. "S! F! A!" they chant as they walk in a group to the side of the mat. "S! F! A!"

When they practiced this routine, the squad always started standing in their formation. But now, when their music comes on, they'll jog to their positions from the side. Michael and the rest of the tumblers lead the group throwing Fulls and Tucks, the others jumping, clapping, and cheering behind them. Kali does her best to pump up the audience as she moves to her spot. But before she knows it, the intro music is up. She misses the first beat of the routine—the rest of the flyers are already a flurry of bodies back-flipping into Rewinds. Kali's partner grabs her waist and sends her up a second or two late. On the other side of the mat, one of the Rewinds crumbles.

The women are touched back down to the mat. They keep their hands on their partners' wrists and go right back up for Full-Ups, their hair whipping in unison as they spin. Everyone lands, and they kick their legs up like Rockettes. They twist into Double Downs.

Tumblers crisscross in the front of the mat as Sierra, Kali, and Yvette shoot high in the air in basket tosses. The squad moves into their final formation—two 2-2-1 pyramids. I'm relieved when the women on each side land in place and throw their arms up in the air.

They hop down, clapping and smiling as they walk off the mat. Their routine looked good to me, but out of the spotlight, their faces shift to frowns.

"That was embarrassing," one of the guys says.

"I couldn't get up for the first stunt," says Kali, close to tears. "I let people down. It's a really big deal to miss a stunt."

Doug's nostrils flare. He turns his back to the squad and walks off alone. I head toward him to ask what happened, but his eyes narrow into slits and anger radiates off of him. I turn around in my steps.

The rest of the squad sits down in the bleachers near Trisha, Michael Preston, and the Lumberjack alumni. They look like a group of teenagers midway through a slasher movie.

"They weren't thinking," says Trisha. "Dropping a stunt happens. What I'm frustrated about is that a guy had to chase down a flyer to put her in the air—that's just not using your head. It's mental mistakes. Last night, I had to chase them out of the bar—even Doug. I was so mad."

"Every year it's the same issue," says Michael Preston. "Overconfidence. They spend all summer sitting on their butts and they think they can come in and hit the elite stunts."

Trisha glances at the squad, sitting silently. "When I'm mad at them, they don't talk to me," she says.

Michael Preston nods. "You have to say, 'If you don't listen to me, we will crash and burn.'"

## "And the Winner Is . . ."

In less than half an hour, SFA's spirit camp will be over. All they have left is the awards ceremony, only none of the SFA cheerleaders feel much like celebrating. They eye the blue holographic trophies that stand in neat lines on a table in front of the mat. There are far more trophies than there are teams here—in the spirit of "everyone is a winner," cheerleading organizations hand out trophies for nearly everything imaginable.

An NCA staff member picks up the first trophy. "The winner of the Top Gun Stunt Competition is . . ."

Sierra and James Brown exchange a hopeful look. Near them, Tyrone shrugs at Samantha. Yvette stares straight ahead.

"Lola and Jerrod from Stephen F. Austin University," says the announcer.

A woman with feline eyes jumps up and hugs her partner. The two of them are tall—at 5'5", Lola Medved is a cheerleading giant with legs so thin that I could wrap my thumb and forefinger around them. Even though Jerrod Vanover is a team captain cheering for his sixth year, the two were considered underdogs in the competition. The squad goes crazy. Many teammates stick up their hands for Lola and Jerrod to slap as they proceed through the crowd to claim their award.

"I knew that was gonna happen," says Trisha, clapping.

"Oh my God," yells Doug. "I'm happy for them. Jerrod has been a spotter in past years, so I'm glad he gets to step up."

But the rest of the ceremony doesn't go as SFA had wanted. The most spirited award goes to Oklahoma State University, and the first-place trophies for the three routines go to other schools.

"And now for the best all-around . . . ," says the announcer. Best all-around is the most prestigious award at camp, and it comes with a lot of bragging rights. Each team and staff member casts a vote for who should win, so as cheer legends, SFA has a good chance of taking it home despite their less-than-stellar performance earlier.

The Lumberjacks stare at the announcer, hoping to hear their name. "Oklahoma State University." The OSU cheerleaders jump up and hug each other. "Oooo! Sssss! Uuuu! Cowboys!" the whole auditorium chants with them.

SFA looks disappointed; many of the guys' mouths slope in severe frowns. Others hop up the second the ceremony is finished, as if they can't wait to get out of this place.

But Michael Preston isn't surprised at the outcome. "Every year in basketball, a top-ranked team loses early in the season to an unranked team," he says. "It's a wake-up call."

# CHAPTER 6

## "Coach Will Go Crazy If We Win That Award."

*The Southern University Jaguars*

THE SOUTHERN CHEERLEADERS HAVE been on the road for more than fifteen hours. They've played multiple rounds of Cheer Factor, a game they invented to pass the time on long road trips, and have attempted to sleep sitting up. They finally pull into Myrtle Beach, South Carolina, at 11 a.m.

Coach James has a job interview for a principal's position at the school where he works, so for the first time in thirteen years, he is not accompanying the squad to camp. In his place, he's sent Wallace Thomas, who cheered with Southern in the late '90s. "I'm a wreck because I want to be there," Coach James tells me over the phone. "It's like sending your kids off on a school trip."

Despite the absence of their coach, the Jaguars file off the bus all smiles and jokes. Jasmine has an easy, breezy grin across her face, and her mocha skin gleams. Tarianne saunters behind her. They head to a grass field between two buildings of the Springmaid Beach Resort, where their spirit camp will be held.

Coach James has managed to recruit a few new members—he worked with a girl from tryouts and two new guys all summer so they'd have the skills to join the team, even if he has to hide them in the back. Two flyers from last year's squad decided to come out of senior-year retirement. So did a captain from last year, Tremayne Baker, once he heard that the squad's numbers were so low. The squad is now up to eighteen members, but they're still two short of what they'll need for competition.

The sun is merciless as we walk across the field, the beach just over a sand dune. Two palm trees stand at the far end of the field, an NCA Spirit Camp banner strung between them. Several squads stand in front of a platform stage, listening to music that pours out of the speakers.

As Southern walks toward the stage, a favorite hip-hop song comes on. Without cueing each other, they begin a dance. They do a hip thrust and dip to the left with a snap and a leg shake. They repeat the movement to the right, dipping lower and pointing a finger in an arch in the sky as they slowly turn 180 degrees. "Ahh," they say, as they shake their knees out and pop their hips to the left.

Tarianne leads the group, throwing her head back as she goes. Up close, her features seem to compete—eyebrows that angle toward the center of her face, a prominent nose that slopes down between graceful cheekbones. Beside her, Jasmine does the same moves with a touch less attitude.

The other squads on the lawn watch them intently. "Southern, come up here," an announcer says. They step in front of the crowd and turn it up a notch. At Southern, these dances are called catch-ons, and it's not just the cheerleaders who do them—they're eight-count movements that one person starts and repeats as more people, well, catch on. They're a constant at Southern, but the other schools here, none of them historically black colleges, just observe.

The song ends, and the Southern Jaguars walk back beside the other squads. The opening ceremony begins, just like at the University of Memphis's camp. James Turner watches the staff do their routine through the screen of a video camera. "I tape everything—we can use it for inspiration," he says, his long eyelashes eclipsing his brown eyes. "We come to camp to see what other teams are doing. It makes us push to see what we can come up with."

Like the rest of the team, James is wearing a gray Southern University shirt. Other squads here have had specialty cheerleading shirts designed for each day of camp, but Southern's spirit budget doesn't allow for that. Instead, they coordinated buying shirts from the campus bookstore, and the women headed to Wal-Mart to pick out matching shorts and sports bras.

"I have a few announcements," says the camp director. "Don't let yourself get exhausted this week. Drink plenty of water—it's *very* hot out here. And I know you might feel like you've gained a few pounds over the summer, but this is not the time to go on a diet. Don't skip meals. We'll work it off of you."

He looks down at his notes. "We'll be giving out a few awards this year. You're going to select one team as the best all-around—that means not just talent, but the team that's spirited, that best portrays a collegiate image, that provides leadership. And there's a twist this year. The team that wins the best all-around award will get a trophy . . . *and an automatic paid bid to Nationals.*"

James's pupils dilate as he processes the words. He turns to Jasmine, and grins creep across both of their faces. Winning best all-around this week would be better than having a fairy godmother—this could be their chance to lead their team back to the castle.

Wallace and James Turner call the team into a huddle. "Coach will go *crazy* if we get that award," says James. "That would mean no raising money this year, no car washes, no bid videos. *Whew,* that would be nice."

Wallace cuts him off, his words clipped. "Listen. I know you didn't get a lot of sleep last night, but you have to bust your tails to get that award," he says. Tarianne and Chassity nod. "You gotta scream, cheer, mingle with the other teams—that's the only way you're gonna win. Think about it, they pay for *everything.* Hotel, food—everything."

"We walked away with a lot of awards last year," adds James.

"Hands down, every year Southern wins most spirited," says Tarianne.

"Be friendly," says Jasmine, ever the diplomat. "Everyone here will be voting."

Tarianne claps her hands. "I miss that adrenaline running through my body," she says. "I came to SU 'cause I thought we'd be going to Nationals every year and so far, no. This would mean so much to the team."

Jarel nods. "I'm not gonna lie, that's what I want to do—compete," he says.

The squad puts their hands in the center of the huddle. "Teamwork," they shout and break immediately into a cheer. They raise their left arms, pointing toward the stage. As they chant "Ssss! U!" they circle their right arm around, clapping their left hand every time they begin a letter. They speed it up, "S-S-S-S-S-S! U!" moving their arms faster. Then they slow it down, "Sssssss! U!"

People from other squads are mesmerized. Many of them throw their arms out and join in.

## "Give It Some Southern Style."

Jasmine looks lost. She stands with her left hand on her hip and her brow furrowed, as camp instructors teach the fight song all the squads will have to perform on the last day of camp. She uses her right hand to shield her eyes from the sun as she stops to study the movements.

High V, low V, arms circle around, punch right, hug yourself, drop a knee to the ground. These are simple motions—only a few women from the fifteen other teams on the lawn are having a problem picking it up. But many of the Southern women keep stopping in frustration.

"They look a mess," says Wallace, sitting with me under a palm tree, the only shady spot on the lawn. I'm confused—I've seen them master much more complicated dances in much shorter periods of time. A blonde NCA staff member comes to the rescue, and the Southern women crowd around her to watch the steps. "That's better," she says, watching Jasmine try it slowly.

"Everybody meet with your squad and work on your fight song," says the camp announcer. The teams gather in clumps around the lawn. For their performance on the final day, each team will repeat the dance they've just learned twice, putting in their own eight counts in the beginning and middle of the routine. Most teams are using these counts to do simple stunts or to break formation and walk into the crowd cheering.

But Southern has a different idea for how to choreograph their fight song. "We gotta twist it," explains James. "Give it some Southern style."

James wants to add in a dance the squad learned at tryouts. Chassity practices the steps—a Michael Jacksonesque turn, ending with her legs crossed. She pumps her arm twice from the elbow and rolls her hips into a squat. She leans forward, putting the back of each palm against a knee. She flutters her hands back and forth, one hand chasing the other.

The music comes on, and the Southern cheerleaders run through the fight song roughly, beginning with their eight counts and going straight into the dance the camp learned together. But the two dances don't mesh. The cheerleading moves have a balletlike uprightness—the arms are always perfectly straight or bent at exact angles, giving the motions a rigid crispness.

Southern's dance, however, comes from the hips, stomach, and butt. The moves flow from the center, the arms and legs following freely. The difference in style is even more pronounced with the guys; during the Southern eight count, they do the same motions as the women, but as soon as the camp dance begins, they stand still, moving only their arms for high Vs and claps. Now it makes sense that the Southern women were struggling to learn the fight song—for them, it's like learning another language.

"Y'all like it?" asks James as they finish running through the two dances welded together. Some of the squad members nod.

"Don't make it harder than it is," says Wallace, urging them to do something more traditional.

"When we punch, do we turn all the way around?" asks one of the women. " 'Cause some people are only doing partway."

"Can the girls when we finish do like this?" says Tarianne, holding her hands up in jaguar claws.

Japaul Winston, the sophomore who wore his sunglasses through tryouts, looks annoyed as he wipes sweat off his dark brown forehead. "If Coach was here, it'd be so much better," he says. "We're accomplishing nothing."

The announcer's voice comes over the loudspeakers. "We will only play the music one more time," he says. Southern runs through the dance again. It's still chaotic, and I can tell some of them aren't sold on it. But I have a feeling it's gonna be good.

## "Off the Chain!"

The sun has set over Myrtle Beach. Camp is done for the night, and many of the squads have headed back to their rooms. The Jaguars linger on the lawn determined to iron out the fight song. "Thank y'all for your input," says James Turner. "But we can't have fifteen people saying things at once. So tonight no, 'Why this?' or 'Let's try this.' Like Coach always says, 'Drink a sixty-four-ounce of shut up.' We just gotta figure out our formations and stunts."

James points each member of the squad into position, forming four lines (two women, two guys) and staggering them so everyone is visible. Jasmine and Tarianne are in the center of the front line. The team starts counting 1-2-3-and-4, going through the dance, but Jasmine gets lost again. "I'm a slow learner," she says as she tries to cover up a yawn. "I'm the type that has to go back to my room and practice while looking in the mirror."

"We're trying to do too much," says Japaul, playing with the sweatbands on his wrists. "Let's keep it simple. They just want it to be clean."

"We gotta give it our flavor if we want to win that bid," snaps James.

"I'm not feeling it," says Japaul, scowling. "Seriously, I want to quit."

James ignores the protests. He's plotting which stunts to throw into the mix. He tells the stunt couples in the back to do an Extension, a flyer's foot in each of her partner's hands. In the front he wants Shoulder Sits, where the women are placed on their base's shoulders like they're about to have a chicken fight. They'll do the stunts after the first repetition of the fight song and again at the very end of the routine.

James steps back to watch as the squad goes through the whole thing. "It's coming together," he says. "It's coming together." Wallace nods.

It's been an hour, and all the other squads have left the lawn. The sound of the ocean over the dunes has become more pronounced. But finally, James is happy. "It's gonna be off the chain!" he exclaims, dimples flashing.

"Bring it in," says Wallace, calling the squad into a huddle. "I'm really proud. When Coach picked this squad, he said that you guys were something special. I'm seeing that now."

James puts his arms around the two women next to him. "When we started, there were so many complaints," he says. "After we got quiet, everything fell into place." He looks at the ground and back up at the squad. "I'm not Coach. I don't have that fantastic eye. But if you be patient with me and simmer down, we can look better than all these squads."

And there, under the thinnest sliver of the moon and a bright smattering of stars, the Southern squad forms a circle, holding hands. They bow their heads, and Jasmine leads them in a prayer. "Thank you for protecting us and guiding us," she says. "I just pray that the other teams and staff see our specialness."

"Amen."

## "He'd Pass Out from All Those Steroids."

Cheerleaders swarm the buffet at the Springmaid Beach Resort's restaurant, piling their plates high with grease-laden food. I walk through the room of cafeteria-style tables and have a flashback to high school as I search for familiar faces.

Finally, I see the Southern Jaguars. And, score, they've saved me a seat. As we eat and talk, an enormous NCA staff guy walks past the table. "That guy did twenty-five Tick-Tocks with his partner yesterday—he said that was his record," says Tremayne. Short and compact with a stoic face, Tremayne is Chassity's stunt partner.

"He won the Partner Stunt Competition one year," someone adds.

"And his partner's not but seventy-five pounds," points out Tremayne.

"One Louisville guy last year was so huge," one of the guys describes. "He couldn't come out from under the shade. He'd pass out from all those steroids in his system."

"If they started drug testing . . . ," says Wallace, shaking his head, "hoo boy. All those guys—Louisville, Kentucky, SFA . . ."

At camp, it's hard not to notice guys who look like they might be "juicing up." Some of their muscles are just a little too defined, their hair slightly thinning, their faces a touch bloated—often telltale signs of steroid use. Without a drug test, it's impossible to know if it's natural or drug-induced, but either way, cheerleading culture seems either unaware of the problem or willing to turn a blind eye. The NCA and the UCA do not condone steroid use, but they also don't have explicit rules against it. As the president of the NCA tells me, it's not a problem they have had to confront in the same way as injuries. For now, it's almost a don't-ask-don't-tell policy.

I wonder if performance enhancer use could be a side effect of having so many coaches right out of college rather than the absolute "adults" who coach other sports. Earlier, I'd noticed a guy with leathery skin whom I'd interviewed at Nationals in 2005. At the time, he'd openly admitted that he used steroids to improve his physique—"It helps to be a big guy," he'd said. Two years later, he's a coach for a top cheer school.

"Does it frustrate you that guys take steroids?" I ask the Southern men.

Tremayne nods. "This is cheerleading—you don't need to be all that," he says. "You see little guys who can do all them stunts." Tremayne himself is a perfect example. For a cheerleader he is downright petite, yet he is the best stunter on Southern's team.

I move to the other end of the table, where James Turner sits surrounded by six women. "I did three hundred fifty this week," one of the women says.

"Just three hundred fifty crunches?" asks another, skeptically.

"No, three hundred fifty push-ups," she says. "Thousands of crunches."

James Turner picks up his tray and swivels his hips as he stands up. "Is that a stripper move?" one of the women asks, as everyone cracks up. James looks indignant, his eyelashes fluttering as he stares straight at her. "Yeah," he says, smiling.

"Wait, you're a stripper?" I ask.

James lets out a bellow of a laugh. "I'm an exotic dancer," he says. "I've been dancing a little over a year now. I had a few companies ask me if I was interested in dancing. At first I was like, 'I'm not doing *that*.' But then I thought, 'Maybe I could use it to my advantage.'"

I'm fascinated. At least to my knowledge, I have never met a male stripper before. "Where do you work?" I ask.

"Sometimes I'm at a club, but I've done mostly bachelorette parties," he says. "It's been good to me—I've gotten to travel a lot of places. I've been to Miami, Atlanta, the Bahamas. I usually get one hundred fifty dollars an hour, not including tip. If I have to travel, everything is paid for."

"Do you have a police costume or anything?" I ask.

He laughs again and rubs the peach fuzz on his head. "Nah, but I do have a costume that's kind of like *The Matrix*—there's a cape that comes all the way up to my neck," he says.

James glances at his cell phone and sees that there are only a few minutes left until the squad has to be at their next class. He is saved from this conversation by the bell.

## "The Whole Camp Wants to Watch *Us.*"

It's nighttime again, and the Southern University squad is back on the lawn practicing their fight song. In twenty-four hours, it has become smooth and confident. One of the women came up with an ending that is sure to get them points for creativity. The guys grab the women's sides as the women swing their legs back and lock them around their guys' waists. They lean forward, arching so their faces are toward the crowd, both hands out in dramatic jaguar claws.

The female staffer who helped them yesterday walks up, a guy staff member strolling behind her. "I came to show him your fight song," she says. "I've been bragging about you all day."

"I heard it's awesome," says the guy.

They go through the dance, and as they finish, the staffers call them into a huddle. "I want to give you props," says the guy. "You're some of the best cheerleaders here."

As the two head back to their rooms, Wallace turns to the squad.

"Coaches keep coming up to me—I had four just today—saying, 'Y'all are amazing.' They are the ones who'll be voting for best all-around tomorrow," he says.

James looks triumphant. "The whole camp wants to watch *us*," he says. "No one else in camp has this dance."

Wallace watches as they practice one last time. He shakes his head. "These kids give up *all* their time to the school, and the school acts like they can't send them to competition," he says. "We gotta get that award tomorrow. Otherwise, we'll be calling Oprah. There's a nine out of ten chance we're not going to Nationals."

The squad finishes and forms a circle, the lights from the hotel making their shadows look ten feet tall. They clasp hands, and Tarianne begins a prayer, bowing her head. "Lord, thank you for keeping us safe," she says. "Keep our attitudes in check, keep our families safe. And *please* help us get to Nationals."

As she says these words, I realize that I am no longer just observing. I am a part of the circle holding hands with the team, my head bowed, too. I'm a white Jewish girl who lives in New York and rarely prays, among a group of black Christian folks from Louisiana who do it almost every day. And yet here, under the stars, I'm saying "Amen" with them. All I want in this moment is for them to win tomorrow.

## "It's in the Bag."

The Southern cheerleaders wake up for the final morning of camp with that specific combination of excitement and nervousness you only feel when you know something big is about to happen. The men pull on their uniforms—light blue Southern jerseys and pants. The women make sure the straps on their cornflower tops cross perfectly in the back. They zip the zippers on their flat-front skirts and painstakingly straighten their hair with a flat iron, even though it'll frizz by the end of the hour from the humidity outside.

The squad feels confident as they walk to the beachfront lawn to practice. "Y'all are awesome," says a Louisville cheerleader as she walks by. It's a good omen—in just a few hours, the camp will vote on the best all-around squad.

While the squad members can't shake that feeling in their stomachs, I know something they don't. *It's in the bag.* At Stephen F. Austin's camp, I had a feeling that SFA wasn't going to win best all-around. I knew it was going to go to Oklahoma State—the squad that everyone complimented, the squad always on their feet cheering. I remember at the awards ceremony that when OSU began their chant, nearly everyone in the coliseum joined in.

At this camp, Southern is that team. It's almost irrelevant how they do in the competition today—their practice run of the fight song yesterday afternoon brought the entire camp to its feet. The staff member judging their routine was compelled to stand up in the middle of their dance and pumped his fist Arsenio-style. That moment—and their chanting and dancing all week long—is what each squad, coach, and staff member will remember as they cast their votes.

The Southern cheerleaders put out their left arms and begin circling their right. "Ssss! U! S-S-S-S-S-S! U!" they chant. As they go through the chant a second time, many people stick out their arms and circle along with them. Yes, it's in the bag.

James gathers the team for a last-minute pep talk. "Coach always tells us that the extra flair we have makes up for what we mess up on," he says. "Go out there and have fun, don't go out there and try to be like any other team. This is the time to do what we do best—be Southern University cheerleaders."

They sit down to watch the University of Louisville, Jasmine's movie star makeup sparkling in the sun. She claps as they give a flawless performance. "We're pumped up. When we performed yesterday, we got such a response," she says, bringing her hand softly to her cheek.

The Southern Jaguars stand up, jumping up and down. It's their turn to perform. They run to their positions on the grass shouting "South-ern Jags! South-ern Jags!" The music begins, and they launch into the Michael Jackson turn-and-knee-slap sequence. The moves look great—like one person reflected in facing mirrors to infinity.

But as they begin the required dance, their faces don't light up quite the way they did yesterday. In the second row, a guy gets lost for a second. He quickly corrects himself and starts counting out loud to make sure he's on the right beat. In front of him, the women sway and twist with precision.

The partner sets get into place for their first stunts. A guy in the front row lifts his partner for the Shoulder Sit, but she gets caught awkwardly on his head. He brings her down to the floor—the simple stunt has failed.

The other women pop down and begin the fight song sequence again. Tarianne puts extra oomph in the movements to try to make up for the mistake, and her eye contact with the audience is intense. The partners rush to their places for the final stunt. The women jump and lock their legs behind their partner's backs. "Jags, Grrr," they yell, as they make claws with their hands. The other squads clap and whistle.

"That was good, but it wasn't the same as yesterday," says Jasmine, sitting down again. "Yesterday when we walked off, it was like, 'Yeah! We did good!' You can tell the difference today." The team sits quietly and watches the last few performances. When the competition is done, Southern does a chant that's an ode to the valley girl: "A-W-E! S-O-M-E! Awe-some! Awe-some! To-tal-ly!"

They sit silently in a circle waiting for a staff member to bring them their evaluation. "Crowd appeal overtakes little mistakes," says James, trying to reassure them all. "Crowd appeal overtakes little mistakes."

An NCA staffer walks over, a sheet of paper dangling from his hand. He kneels down on the ground in front of the squad and brings the paper up to eye level. He reads the judges' comments. "Great energy." "Sharp movements." But the judges noticed the mistakes—the guy losing his place in the dance, the botched Shoulder Sit. Still, James's theory is right—they get a score of 46 out of 50. They jump up and yell.

As they settle back down, the staffer asks for their votes for best all-around. They talk it over and, around the lawn, I can see that other squads are doing the same. I hope that they are all saying "Southern University."

Jasmine isn't so sure anymore. "I felt a whole rush of confidence before," she says, her voice quivering. "But now that it's the last second, I don't know if we're going to get it."

The camp announcer calls everyone to the stage for the awards ceremony. "Bang! It's an S-U thang!" chants Southern as they walk, throwing finger guns in the air as they chant. "Bang! Bang! It's an S-U thang!"

While most of their nervous energy is directed at best all-around, there's a lot riding on the first award as well—most spirited. It comes with a special trophy, a silver megaphone attached to a plaque, and Southern has won it for the past thirteen years in a row. They know Coach James will be disappointed if they don't bring it home.

"The most spirited at camp is . . . Southern University," says the announcer. James Turner jumps up to take the trophy, and the squad goes crazy.

In the next few minutes, he collects several more trophies—they get the teamwork award and second place on the spirit routine. They hold in their hands more trophies than the other teams here. The stars are aligning.

"And now, your best all-around . . . ," says the announcer.

For the first time all week, the chatter of hundreds of cheerleaders dies down. The camp is silent, and I notice the excited yelps of children playing on the beach over the sand dune. Overhead, a cloud passes under the bright sun, and a shadow travels across the lawn. I look up at the hotels towering over the lawn—dozens of spectators are sitting on their balconies watching the proceedings. I wonder if they realize how much is riding on the announcer's next words.

Jasmine's head is bowed. Chassity leans forward slightly. "We really, really need this," mutters James, almost silently, like a last-minute prayer under his breath.

"The University of Louisville All-Girl."

The Louisville women let out a collective scream. They stand up in their red shirts and matching lipstick and bounce up and down, a frenetic mass of energy.

I'm shocked. Louisville doesn't need a paid bid to Nationals—their athletic department is booming and sends three squads to competition every year. My face is flushing. I feel angry, like a kid discovering for the first time that the world is unfair.

I turn to see how the Southern cheerleaders are taking the news.

I'm hoping there are no tears. But James, Jasmine, Tarianne, Jarel, Chassity—even Japaul—are all applauding sincerely for Louisville. I drop my notebook and join them.

Camp is dismissed, and the teams stand up, trophies in hand. The Southern Jaguars walk back to their hotel rooms, their spirits much higher than mine.

"It was almost too good to be true," says Jasmine as she walks. "It wouldn't have been a giveaway, but if they had given it to us, other teams would have been like, 'Oh, Southern's good, but there's other squads here who are better.'"

"We're not going to be disappointed," says James, shaking his head. "We can still get to NCA. We've shown Coach that we have the work ethic, but it's really going to take us captains forcing it—Coach is not big on fund-raising at all."

"If it's for us, we'll go," says Jasmine, happy to leave the decision to fate.

## "That Bid Would Have Been Nice."

Over the next half hour, Coach James gets phone calls from Wallace, James Turner, Jasmine, and several others recounting the day's events. "All week, they called me for the smallest things. Someone even sent me a camera-phone picture of one of the girls eating pie because they're not supposed to eat stuff like that," he says. "After the awards, everyone told me a slightly different version of how they were looking at it. It was like the Bible with the Gospels and the Book of John— what they said was different, but the story was the same."

Coach James can't help but be frustrated. "Don't get me wrong," he says. "Louisville All-Girl is phenomenally talented. But I disagreed with the selection process. I thought the paid bid should go to a team who was talented enough to go to Nationals but not financially able. If you see a team who would bring something different and who doesn't have the means to go, wouldn't that be a better choice?"

He sighs. "The team thought I was going to be upset with them for not winning, but I don't expect them to be perfect. The only award that I wanted was most spirited. That, they *can't* lose."

"Did you get the principal job you were interviewing for?" I ask.

"No, I didn't," he says, and I sense a hint of self-blame in his voice. "I wish I had known that they were giving out a paid bid before camp. If I had been there, it probably would have made an impact. The coaches and staff there are good friends of mine."

He pauses. "Every year, I spend ten thousand dollars on camp before the season even starts, and I always ask myself, 'Do I forfeit this training and have money left to go to competition?' It's something I struggle with every year," he says. "That bid would have been nice. It would have been *nice*."

# PART THREE

FOOTBALL SEASON

SEPTEMBER–NOVEMBER

# CHAPTER 7

## "Hey, Mom, I'm on ESPN."

*The University of Memphis All-Girl Tigers*

AT LEAST FOR TODAY, Memphis, Tennessee, is crazier about football than it is about Elvis. It's the day of the University of Memphis's biggest football game of the year, against their foes, the University of Tennessee. Everywhere I go, from hotels to restaurants, banners proclaim EAT 'EM UP TIGERS in royal blue or LET'S GO VOLUNTEERS in traffic-cone orange. On nearly every car, a small flag, either blue or orange, flaps from the antenna, proclaiming the driver's allegiance.

The University of Memphis cheerleaders are meeting at 8 a.m. in a parking lot on campus. It's only a five-minute drive to the Liberty Bowl Memorial Stadium, but the cheerleaders expect it to take an hour, and since parking will be tight, they want as few cars as possible. I get to the meeting point ten minutes early, and almost all of the All-Girl cheerleaders are already here, decked out in blue and making last-minute adjustments to their hair and makeup. I rolled out of bed a few minutes ago, but some of the cheerleaders have been up for hours getting game-ready.

Casi stayed up past 3 a.m. straightening her hair so that it hangs straight, curving in under her chin. But you wouldn't know by looking at her that she only got a few hours' sleep. She sits in the driver's seat of her silver PT Cruiser, the door open and her legs swung around so that her feet rest on the ground. She holds her cell phone in her hands and her fingers move diligently, typing a text message at world-record pace. She presses the Send button and looks up.

Casi's life has changed a lot in the past six months. When I first met her, she was happily engaged to a soldier stationed in Iraq. They were going to get married and move in together when he arrived back, but all that changed with a ring of her phone. "I got a call right before camp from a girl my fiancé was friends with in Iraq," says Casi. "She told me that they'd been sleeping together. I was just like, 'Well, I guess it's over.'" She relays the story as if it's had no effect on her whatsoever.

"I'm sorry," I say, a reflex when someone tells you bad news.

"Don't be," she says. "It's better that I find out now. I wouldn't have wanted to spend five years with him and *then* find out. I checked his profile on Facebook and saw that he's already in a new relationship. I think he was cheating on me for a while."

"How did people on the team react when you told them?" I ask.

"Oh, I didn't tell people. If someone asks, 'Where's your ring?' I just say that we broke up."

Casi is already over the drama. "I found the guy of my dreams," she says with a sigh. "He's a tattoo artist. I'm trying to get him to open a tattoo shop with me. I'm a business major, so we'd get filthy rich." The tattoo artist and the cheerleader—it's not a combination most people would expect. "He's gonna give me another tattoo this weekend."

"What are you going to get?"

"A picture of Casiopea," she says, referring to the mythological queen whom Poseidon turned into an upside-down constellation. "I'm named after her."

Casi puts her cell phone in her car's cup holder and taps her fingers on the steering wheel. On her long acrylic nails are three letters: I-A-N. It's her new boyfriend's name. "I haven't seen him in twenty-four hours," she says, pounding on the steering wheel.

A few parking spots away, Courtney and Ashley sit in a red sports car. Courtney is in the front seat holding an eye shadow palette and, putting on a layer of makeup in the vanity mirror. "I woke up late," she says, the whites of her eyes slightly red.

Ashley examines her hair in the rearview mirror. "You look pooty today," she says.

"Yeah, real pooty," says Courtney sarcastically.

I pile into a car with Casi and a few others, and we begin the drive to the stadium, singing along to Kelly Clarkson's "Since U Been Gone." Three blocks later, we're stuck in a traffic jam. On the four-lane road, only one of the lanes is moving. A squad member in the front seat rolls down her window and leans out to speak to the car in the next lane. "We're the cheerleaders," she says, pointing to her uniform. The car lets us merge in front of them. We're moving now, but barely.

As we inch closer to the Liberty Bowl, I have a lot of time to check out the scene in the distance. The 62,000-capacity stadium is shaped like a gigantic pair of concrete lips plopped in the middle of miles' worth of parking lots. To the left of the stadium, a lot hosts the Mid-South Fair, which always coincides with Memphis's biggest football game of the year. It has everything I loved about state fairs growing up—livestock races, rickety rides, bright carnival lights, and funnel cakes.

Across the street lies a neighborhood of one-story houses. In hopes of making a few bucks off today's game, many of the residents have turned their front lawns into extra parking. Hand-painted signs on poster board proclaim PARKING $5. A middle-aged man on one lawn directs an SUV into a narrow spot by some shrubs.

We inch past five blue cars to our left. "I want a Memphis blue car," says Casi, pausing to laugh at herself. "I call it Memphis blue, like that's a real color. Royal blue."

We reach the entrance to the Liberty Bowl and drive up to a police barrier. The officer waves us in the other direction. Casi rolls down her window to show him her uniform. He lifts a cone and lets us through.

The parking lot is even more amazing than it had looked from afar. Hundreds of RVs are parked in orderly lines, like a miniature city. Many of them have awnings, and people sit underneath in lawn chairs—one family even has a TV built into the side of the RV. They watch as if they were at home in their living room. "People started tailgating *yesterday* morning," says a brunette in the backseat. "There are tailgate breakfasts, tailgate lunches, tailgate dinners."

It's 10 a.m. and there are three hours until kickoff. People everywhere are in bright blue shirts—this section of the lot is for Memphis fans. Casi edges her car into a space between a fence and a truck whose bed is filled with five Memphis fans drinking cans of beer. "Go Memphis," they yell as the cheerleaders step out of the car.

The smell of barbecue wafts through the air. A man standing near a grill, holding a spatula, yells, "You go, girls."

The feeling is elated, but as we get closer to the gates, I remember there's one problem. After a comedy of errors between me and Frankie, I don't have a ticket to the game. "Don't worry," says Casi. "Stay close with us—they won't be able to tell the difference." She offers me her Memphis sweatshirt to make me look more legit.

We walk toward a security guard. The women wave, but I avoid eye contact. Is he going to kick me out? Will he really believe that I'm a cheerleader, even though I'm six years older and thirty pounds heavier than any of these women? And what about the fact that I'm wearing long shorts while everyone else is in a short skirt? The guard glances at me and nods. We pass through the gate without a problem.

We enter a dimly lit concrete hallway. At the end of the tunnel, I can see the bright sun and the green of the football field. But six more security guards stand in my way, looming by the entrance. In front of us, a man with a professional camera walks toward the guards, and they shine a flashlight on a badge he shows them.

I'm toast—I can't believe I've come all the way to Memphis for a football game only to get turned away at the doors. My heart starts racing. I glance at Casi, but she looks calm and collected, a faint smile across her face. She waves at the security guards. *Pretend like you belong. Pretend like you belong,* I tell myself. I swallow my nervousness and turn on my highest-wattage smile.

Before I know it, I'm standing on the field, the green grass under my feet. Even though it's AstroTurf, I swear it smells freshly cut. The white lines seem to jump off it.

No one has been let into the stadium besides the cheerleaders, band, food vendors, staff, and a few random VIPs. Standing on the grass, looking up at all the empty seats, it's strikingly quiet. Casi points into the stands, where cushioned seats have been clamped to the bleachers. "We had to install those VIP seats," she says. "We sell them as a fund-raiser."

A few squad members stand to the side of the field, pristine in their sapphire skirts. Their halter tops are the same blue, with a white upside-down triangle that comes to a point at their belly buttons. The word *Tigers* is embroidered in delicate cursive letters. White bows dangle from their half-ponytails. One woman holds a can of hair spray in her hands. "I go nuts with the spray," she says, a cloud forming around her.

Another looks close to tears. Her roommate, a freshman on the squad, had way too much to drink last night. "I tried to get her up this morning and help her put her uniform on. She was like, 'I'm not going,'" the girl explains. "She's going to get in so much trouble. She's lucky Carol's not here yet."

"Do you think she'll get kicked off the squad?" someone asks.

"I hope not," the girl says, choking up.

Kristen walks toward us. Her skin looks especially creamy today, her hair extra blonde against her blue uniform. "We're going to the front gates to pass out thunder sticks and game faces," she says to the squad. The women follow her in a single-file line up the stadium stairs.

"What and whats?" I ask Casi.

"A game face," she says, pointing to a temporary tattoo on her cheek of the letter M with a tiger jumping over it.

"And thunder sticks?" I ask.

"They're those sticks you blow up and bang together to make noise," she says.

We walk through a concrete arch and into a large hallway filled with concession stands. As the cheerleaders walk by, the employees at the booths stop to clap. "Yay," they yell. "Go Tigers!" The cheerleaders laugh, soaking up the attention with Miss America–style waves.

We reach the front gates. A line has formed outside, thousands of fans wrapping around the side of the building. "We're opening the gates in ten minutes," a security guard tells us.

Monica runs up, panting. Beads of sweat look out of place on her perfectly made-up face. "I had to walk like a mile," she says. "I drove with my family so they could get good parking, but traffic wasn't moving. I was afraid I was going to be late." She puts her hands up to feel her pearl earrings.

As Monica walks to the bathroom to put on her game face, she hands me a Memphis decal on a slip of paper. She wets a paper towel, sticks the decal to her cheek and rubs. I follow suit. The game face makes my cheek feel tight, like a clay mask. "Is that right?" I ask. "It's perfect," she says. "Some of these girls have been on the squad for years and don't do it that good. Sometimes you lose a paw."

In front of the main gates, the women position themselves behind tables. They rip open boxes and make stacks of thunder sticks, game faces, and posters. The front gates open, and the fans pour in. "Go Memphis!" yells Courtney, handing a teenage boy a set of thunder sticks. He blows them up and clangs them together. The booms mix with the sound of chatter.

Because I can't stay on the field without a pass, I'll be sitting in the Memphis student section, where the seats are given on a first-come, first-served basis. I rush to beat the crowd. Within five minutes, the section is packed, students squishing in the bleachers to try to accommodate more people. Almost everyone wears a Memphis football T-shirt—a few women have dressed up in royal blue halter tops and lightweight sweaters.

The University of Tennessee football team walks onto the field to warm up, and the Memphis student section jumps to their feet. "Boo!" people yell. "Boo!" Many of them have had a few drinks before the game. A guy spills a cup of Coca-Cola near me, and it reeks of whiskey. Beside me, a group of women draw on a piece of poster board laying across their laps. HEY MOM I'M ON ESPN, it says. Another goes for a play on the University of Tennessee mascot: VOLUNTEER THIS.

A group of guys behind me whip off their shirts, revealing a rainbow of flesh tones from white to whiter. One of them takes a tube of blue face paint out of his bag. Each guy finger-paints a big blue letter on his stomach. Together they read *Tigers*.

I sit quietly, sipping on an iced tea and hoping not to get beaten up. I've neglected to wear blue today.

## "You Might Have Paid Off the Ref, but We Have Better-Looking Cheerleaders."

"Bullshit! That's bullshit!" yells a Memphis fan behind me.

"Get it together, guys!" screams someone else.

"I can play better than you!" taunts a woman a few rows back.

When the University of Memphis football team ran onto the field in a burst of fireworks (yes, fireworks) an hour ago, no one expected that at halftime they'd be down twenty to nothing. It was a terrible first half. As a Tiger player ran toward the end zone with the football firmly in his grip, the entire audience jumped to its feet, the clapping of thunder sticks around the stadium sounding like a herd of noisy seals. But as the player spiked the ball with a self-congratulatory flourish, a flag went up on the play. Offside. The six points on the scoreboard dissolved back to zero. Meanwhile, the Volunteers scored touchdown after touchdown.

Before halftime, the band played an upbeat song, and the entire crowd sang along, school pride beaming across their faces. "I'm so glaaad, I go to the U of M. I'm so glaaad, I go to the U of M," they sang. "Glo–ry, glo–ry hall–elu–jah. I'm so glaaad." But now, as the band plays the song again a few minutes into the second half, the Memphis audience sings much less enthusiastically. People file out of the student section mid-play, as if watching their team get creamed is just too painful. Soon, the section becomes a graveyard of thunder sticks. I take advantage of the exodus and move to an open seat on the sideline.

The University of Memphis All-Girl cheerleaders are doing their best to keep spirits up. "Gooo!" they yell as they bend from their waist, their pom-poms in their hands, rolling their fists like they're in a conga line. "T! I! G! E! R! S! Tiii–gers!" they yell, spelling each letter out quickly with their bodies. Their halter-top uniforms reveal their buff shoulder blades.

Courtney runs past me to get water. "Is it hard to cheer when they're down by this much?" I ask.

She uses her pom-pom to shield her eyes from the sun as she looks up at me. "I just try to keep smiling," she says. "I usually don't know what's going on anyway." She laughs heartily and runs back to the squad.

The cheerleaders gather in six groups of four, and they send up a wave of basket tosses, an ESPN camera following them as they go. The baskets land and the women walk in a big clump toward the camera. I've seen this shot so many times before while watching college sports—a gaggle of pretty faces, decals on their cheeks, pointing and mouthing words into a camera. Across the field, the University of Tennessee cheerleaders seem to be having a blast. The cheer they do on repeat is spelling genius. "T! E! Dou-ble N! E! Dou-ble S! Dou-ble E! Tennessee!"

I notice a giant cage in the corner of the field. I'm not sure how I didn't see it before, because a real Bengal tiger naps inside, barely noticing the noise of the game. "They give him a shot so he goes to sleep or walks in a circle," says Casi, talking to me as she takes a swig from a bottle of water.

As if on cue, the band starts playing "Eye of the Tiger," the theme from *Rocky III*. The women spring into action. They punch their arms toward the ground and swing them around in a full circle. They walk forward, swinging their hips, and crouch down. In a wave, they spring up straight. They step-touch in a circle, weaving through each other and back to their original spots.

"One more time," says a creepy thirty-something Memphis fan behind me, gnawing on a grilled turkey leg.

The women move on to a cheer. "What do we want? TD! What's that? Touchdown!" the cheerleaders yell, swinging their arms behind them. The University of Memphis has the ball. The crowd is on their feet, willing something to happen. A pass snaps up into the air and soars toward a player. Kristen jumps up and down and screams.

But the cheerleaders don't get their TD. Instead, they get an interception. A few minutes later, Tennessee reaches their end zone—the score is now thirty-four to zero. One of the cheerleaders traces a fake tear down her cheek, then smiles as she blows an air kiss to a friend.

"You might have the ref paid off," says the turkey leg guy to a friend in a University of Tennessee shirt. "But we have better-looking cheerleaders." He shakes his head as if he can't believe what's happening. "Except maybe that one," he says.

I try turning around subtly, like I'm looking for someone just beyond him in the stands. His finger is pointed at Casi, who's stretching on the field.

"Why's she even in a uniform?" the guy continues.

I turn around again and look him squarely in the eye, trying to use my glance as a protest. But he keeps on going. "She's got thunder thighs," he says.

This man is pushing 300 pounds and has turkey juice dribbling down his chin. His words hit me like punches to the stomach. I turn back to Casi. Her black eyes sparkle as she cheers, and her smile, complete with its gap, looks so natural. Her arms look solid, like she can open jars and lift heavy objects. Her legs are muscular and wider than the others, but nowhere near "thunder," wherever that demarcation may be.

Still, he won't shut up. "She does *not* need to be a cheerleader," he says. Casi smiles as she tosses a cheerleader onto her shoulders and holds her there. Doesn't he see how strong she is? Doesn't he understand that it's not exactly easy to lift another human being in the air? But like so many times in my life when I wanted to find that perfect retort that would make my opponent sink low in their seat, I wimp out. I don't defend Casi. I let the conversation happen in my head.

Excited shouts from the stands bring me back to the game. Everyone in blue is on their feet. Memphis has scored a touchdown.

"We finally got points," yells Courtney, pointer finger to the sky. "We're number one!"

A man brings his daughter down to the sideline as the band begins to play Memphis's fight song. This girl has curly hair and wears a kid-sized version of a Memphis cheerleading uniform. She wraps her little hands around the bar, her tiny nails dipped in red nail polish. She sways and bobs her head, staring adoringly at the All-Girl cheerleaders as they shimmy. The score is forty-one to seven with three minutes. There's no way Memphis is going to win, but they might as well go down putting on a good show.

## "I'm a Daddy's Girl."

"I'd like a crawfish étouffée," says Monica to a food vendor wearing several strings of Mardi Gras beads around his neck.

He looks carefully at her in her blue cheerleading uniform as he punches numbers into his cash register. "You worked so hard for nothing," he says, taking a string of beads from around his neck and handing it to her.

Her turquoise eyes look down at the beads and back up at him. "I love you for giving me these," she says.

Monica's family has a tradition after the University of Memphis/ University of Tennessee game—they head to the Mid-South Fair and stop for gumbo at Crawdaddy's Café, a kiosk restaurant with tables all around it. Monica has a full-scale entourage who came to see her cheer—her parents (who've driven two hours), her boyfriend (who's flown in from Florida), her godparents (who also made the trek from Florida), and her brother (who goes to the University of Memphis as well). "My parents didn't care about sports until I got to college, but now they're fanatics," she says, looking at her dad as she talks. "Dad just likes to take pictures of me. I'm a Daddy's Girl."

"They showed you doing a flip on TV," says her dad.

"I know," says Monica. "I saw myself on the screen as I was going up for a pyramid and I was like, 'Yay!'"

Her dad turns to me. "I used to be a cheerleader for a small-town school in sixth, seventh, and eighth grade," he says. "I loved it."

Monica pipes up. "Cheerleaders were elected then, so it was all the popular guys."

Today, Monica's parents are both cosmetologists. They own a hairdressing shop in Dyersburg, Tennessee. They're a remarkably pretty, blue-eyed family—the kind you'd expect to see in a soup commercial. They seem laidback around each other, cracking jokes with ease as they sit down to eat their étouffée and gumbo.

Monica's namesake is also at the table—her godmother. "My parents loved the name because they've been friends forever," she explains. "And also because of Monica on *General Hospital*." She pauses and looks across the table at her godmother. "So I'm Monica and she's Ms. Monica."

Off to the side, disconnected from the banter, sits Monica's boyfriend. He's cute and clean cut—the kind cast as the Southern charmer on *The Real World*. He graduated last year and moved to Florida. I'm not sure what he and Monica were like before he graduated, but now they are awkward together. It's as if in the few months they've been long distance, they've forgotten how to interact.

While her family finishes their food, Monica and I explore the fairgrounds. She seems like she's trying to avoid her boyfriend. "It's not the best of situations," she says diplomatically. "We both wear the pants in the relationship, and it creates some conflict."

We walk down pathways with flashing carnival lights and signs advertising everything from deep fried oreos to your name on a grain of sand. Monica spots a booth set up by the local sheriff's station. She runs over and picks up two plastic sheriff's badges. She pins one onto her halter-top uniform and hands the other to me.

An older woman taps Monica on the arm. "Y'all did a good job out there," she says, nodding sincerely.

"Thank you, ma'am," says Monica.

Monica's boyfriend walks toward us, holding a string of carnival tickets. "Let's go on a ride," he says.

Monica looks at the Zipper, a series of metal cages turning fairgoers in nauseating directions. She shakes her head. "I can flip all day, but not on a ride," she says.

"Come on," says her boyfriend, grabbing her hand and pulling her toward it. Monica gives in and steps into one of the metal cages with him. I watch as they fling up and around.

Back on the ground, Monica is ready to leave. "Let's go home," she says. We reach the edge of the fairgrounds, and she turns around to get one last glimpse of the fair and the Liberty Bowl in the distance. "Football and basketball—here it's what you live for," she says.

## "We Have to Play the Cheerleaders? You're Kidding, Right?"

The night air feels cold and staticky as Monica and Kristen hurry across campus to the intramural football field. They're bundled up in sweatshirts and warm-up pants, but the sneakers on their feet are not cheer-leading shoes—they're cleats. The two are on their way to play football.

For the second year in a row, the Memphis cheerleaders have put together a twelve-woman flag football team to compete in the university's intramural league. They compete against teams from the law school, the campus ministry, and an assortment of sororities. The cheer-leaders have appropriately dubbed their team "the Sideliners."

"Every time we play, people are like, 'We have to play the cheer-leaders? You're kidding, right?'" says Kristen, the team's quarterback and secret weapon. "They automatically think, 'We've got this in the bag.'"

But once the game starts, the cheerleaders beat the pants off their opponents. The Sideliners have won every game this season. In fact, they haven't let another team score a single point on them all year. Even the teams that strolled on the field confident, their coaches hold-ing thick playbooks and the teammates wearing matching jerseys with their names on the backs, got creamed.

The Sideliners are coached by Kristen's older brother, James. But when Kristen first brought the idea up to him, he was skeptical. "Kris-ten told me she's good, but I thought, 'Yeah, right,'" he explains. "When I got to practice, I was impressed. They can really play football."

James stares at his sister, the quarterback. "She's an absolute cannon," he says. "They take this as seriously as possible. It's life or death. We played one game where we took out our best players at halftime be-cause we were winning forty-two to nothing."

In that blowout game, Monica got her first opportunity to play rather than sit on the bench. "I was the wide receiver to the left," she says. "The quarterback threw the ball to me, and I saw that no one was coming. I ran." She scored a touchdown, bringing the score to forty-eight to zero. The game was called before time was officially over.

Tonight is a big night for the Sideliners. It's the intramural champi-onship. Not only do they have a chance at a title—something that the competitor in them craves—but they can earn serious bragging rights if their defense can end the season with a perfect record. But across the field, their rivals—the track and field team—look fierce. James is worried. "They're very, very fast. I don't know if we can keep up with them," he says.

Even Kristen is nervous. "This game is going to be very hard to win," she says. "They're good athletes, and some of them are pretty big."

But midway through the second half, the score is still zero to zero. Nearly every call in the game seems to be going against the Sideliners. Kristen fumes. "They're calling us for things that are *not* a big deal," she says. "Meanwhile, they're literally tackling us and knocking our players over." A referee threatens to eject her from the game.

James feels the game slipping away. He calls a time-out to calm the team down. "Listen, we've got this game under control," he says. "They can't score on us. No one has scored on us all year. We have to be patient. We will score eventually."

The women take deep breaths and focus. They walk back on the field with five minutes left to play. The women line up and crouch down, gritting their pearly white teeth as they stare down the track stars. The ball is hiked to Kristen. She grasps it, her head turning right and left, right and left, surveying the field for her players. A Sideliner cuts toward her, and Kristen looks like she's going to hand off the ball. The track defense rushes toward them.

But it's a fake out. Kristen whips her arm back and lets the ball fly long, toward her teammate Christy, near the end zone. The ball arcs through the air. Christy jumps. Several track defenders do the same. They desperately grope for the ball, but somehow Christy jumps just a little higher and snatches it out of the air. She lands in the end zone, clutching the ball to her chest. Touchdown.

"Yeah!" yells Kristen.

"Nice throw!" yells one of her teammates. They high-five as the Sideliner fans give them a standing ovation.

The Sideliners hold off the track team for the next few minutes. As the referee calls time, they run toward the 50-yard line, hugging and screaming. They have won the intramural football championship.

"I'm thrilled," says Kristen. "I'm so competitive. If there's a pool table, I want to play. If there's a dartboard, let me at it. I'm in a bowling league with my family and I always want to be the girl with the highest average." She pauses. "This takes away every doubt people have that cheerleaders are athletes. We can beat every team in football."

Monica, who warmed the bench tonight, is ecstatic, too. "I just hope we do as well at Nationals as we did tonight," she says.

# CHAPTER 8

## "That Was the Most Fun I've Ever Had

## at a Game."

*The Stephen F. Austin University Lumberjacks*

SFA'S FOOTBALL STADIUM LOOKS more like a high school facility than the gigantic metal and concrete structure in Memphis. A track runs around the field, and the bleachers are built into identical hills that overlook the field like an amphitheater. On a grassy slope, the letters S-F-A have been shaped out of red flowering bushes, and an intrepid landscaper has also created two footballs out of shrubs to bookend the letters. A United States flag flaps in the breeze above the scoreboard, sandwiched between two massive Texas flags.

From my seat in the bleachers, I can see 360 degrees of sky—a rarity for someone who lives in New York City, where the most you get is a narrow sliver between buildings. Tonight the sky looks more painted than real—sweeping swirls of blue and pink mingling with gray clouds. The cheerleaders stand on the track, about ten feet below where I sit. Sierra pops up into an Awesome, her skin slightly orange from tanning. She winks at the audience.

A few feet from her, Doug rubs his shiny head. "If it starts raining, no stunting," he yells.

A mass of purple helmets runs onto the field, and the crowd hops to their feet. The SFA women fly into Extensions. "Give 'em the axe, Big Jacks! Give 'em the axe!" they chant, as they pump their arms like they're saluting. Sierra's voice sails over the others.

Tyrone, his Mohawk dyed blonde today, tosses Samantha up for an Awesome, both her feet in his right hand. "Yay," she yells as her kohl-lined eyes survey the stands. She puts her arms down by her side and begins to twist as Tyrone slowly moves his hand back and forth, keeping her in the air as she wiggles.

During the first quarter, the sky changes color, an inky blue creeping in from the east. The stadium lights turn on, and moths fly around like they're drunk. One hits me like it's on a kamikaze mission, and as I brush my back, the crowd starts screaming. I look up in time to see an SFA player running into the end zone. The cheerleaders go crazy.

From the far corner of the field, a group of ROTC soldiers in fatigues sets off a cannon. The noise startles me, and the smoke travels slowly across the field toward the cheerleaders as they jump and clap.

I notice a guy with a full beard, an axe in his head. He wears a red-and-purple plaid shirt with suspenders. He drops to the ground and does seven push-ups as the cheerleaders gather around him and count. This is the SFA Lumberjack. After the mascots at camp with elaborate fur costumes and plastic heads, there's something quaint about having a mascot who's an actual person.

James Brown snaps at a moth with a bandana. "Be nice to it," says Sierra. He snaps again. "Oh my God," yells Sierra. "Bug killer." James starts snapping her. "Stop," she screams and runs away.

"Behave," says Doug.

A raindrop plops on my nose. Another hits my shoulder. Umbrellas go up around the stadium, multicolored overlapping dots. The football players remain unfazed. The cheerleaders stay in place on the track, following Doug's order not to stunt. The raindrops drift slowly in front of the stadium lights, like snow blowing in the wind.

The first half is over, and the football players head back to their locker room. The guy cheerleaders kneel on the ground, putting out their right knees as the women sit down on their legs. They turn and watch the field.

A voice comes over the loudspeakers. "Our show begins with the styling of the Twirlajacks," says an announcer, like a '50s TV ad for Tide. "Fifty years ago, the term *Twirlajack* was coined. It's come to represent the smooth style that's influenced other lines around the country." A troop of baton twirlers in sparkly leotards struts on to the field, batons spinning like plane propellers.

"And now, the boldest sound of the oldest town—your Stephen F. Austin marching band," says the announcer. The SFA marching band high-steps on the field in bright purple uniforms topped by tall, fuzzy hats. They move into formation as they play "Love Train." "People all over the world, Join hands," the cheerleaders sing along.

The rain falls more aggressively. As it quickens, the women go from being perfectly coiffed to looking like cats taking a bath. Their hair droops with water. Sierra's running mascara trails down her cheek. "I'm melting," yells one of the guys, mimicking the Wicked Witch of the West.

A streak of lightning rips across the sky. "Because of the lightning, we will take a fifteen-minute break," says the announcer. The few people left in the stands jump to their feet, some heading toward an overhang, others walking straight for the exit. The football team and marching band leave the field.

"Can we go?" one of the guys asks Doug.

"No. You have to stay and cheer," he replies.

Puddles form on the track, new raindrops creating bubbles as they fall. "Give 'em the axe, Big Jacks! Give 'em the axe!" Sierra yells at the top of her lungs as she jumps in a puddle. A woman snaps a wet pom-pom in one of the guys' faces, water flying off the plastic strips.

"This would be a good time to run laps," yells Doug. Two guys and two girls take off, making their way around the track, water splashing as their feet land.

If a cheerleader is late, drops a stunt, or messes up a tumbling pass at a game, he or she has to run laps. It's a new rule implemented by Trisha and Doug. Trisha, at a friend's wedding tonight, explained the rationale to me earlier: "We need to put off a professional vibe, and it looks really bad when you have stunts fall or a tumbler touches down," she said. "They should be able to do this stuff in their sleep."

Music comes on over the loudspeakers. I don't recognize the songs, but the cheerleaders certainly do. "It's five o'clock somewhere," one of the guys sings along with a country ballad.

"Who is this?" I ask.

"Alan Jackson," he says, looking at me like I must be some kind of robot imposter.

Behind the goalpost, a giant mat used for pole vaulting is covered with a tarp. Tyrone and Samantha spy it and run toward it at full speed. They dive head and arms first, sliding on their stomachs across the mat like an impromptu Slip 'n Slide.

"Whoa, look at that," says one of the guys near me, who takes off to try it out, too. Half the squad races toward the mat, competing to see who can slide the farthest.

Near where I stand on the track, observing the chaos, a brunette flyer pulls the rubber band from around her ponytail and shakes out her long, wavy hair. "You could be on *Baywatch*," says one of the guys. The woman's cheeks flush bright red.

Soon, the rain slows to a drizzle. "We'll start play again in ten minutes," says the announcer. The football players appear from the corner of the field, and the marching band files back into the stands in slickers. The fans make their way back to their seats—there's about half as many people as before. They use napkins to dry off their seats.

The cheerleaders get back into their two-line formation, but the formality of the first half has disappeared. As the band plays, Samantha and Tyrone start a conga line, weaving in and out of the other cheerleaders. Their image flashes across the movie-theater-sized screen on the scoreboard, even though play on the field has started. "Thank you, I'll be here all week," yells Tyrone, bowing.

Forty-five minutes later, when the ROTC cannon blasts, signaling the end of the game, the cheerleaders don't seem too disappointed that SFA has lost. "That was the most fun I've ever had at a game," says one of the guys.

## "We Heard We'd Have to Tumble in Our Underwear."

The sun is blistering as the members of the SFA squad gather at a lawn on campus, the grass under their sneakers dried to a brown crisp. Now that they've cheered as a team for about a month, it's time for the new cheerleaders to be initiated.

Most years, the veterans on the squad far outnumber the newbies. But this year, over half the team is new. Most of them, like Sierra and Samantha, have transferred from junior colleges. A small percent are true freshmen. Marly Campos—still only seventeen—moved all the way from California to join the squad. Her girl-next-door face ends in a pointed chin.

Since camp, Marly has become close friends with Shelley Egan, another freshman from Sunnyvale, Texas. The two of them are nervous about what today's initiation might entail. "We heard that we're going to have to tumble in our underwear," says Shelley, sighing. "I just don't want to have to do anything against my morals."

On the lawn, the veterans tell the newcomers to link hands, forming a human chain ranging in size from tiny girls to one guy whose nickname is Shrek because of his ogre-like stature. The men lead the line, jerking the women behind them as they jog. Together, they chant, "R-O-O-K-I-E-S. Rookies! Rookies! Are the best!" to the tune of, "I don't know but I've been told." The whole thing feels very boot camp.

As they cross a road, a veteran yells, "Drop and do twenty-five push-ups." The rookies obey, hoping that any cars will stop for them. They place their palms on the hot concrete, many of them wincing. They stand up and continue to jog until a veteran barks the next instruction.

"You have one minute to spell 'Lumberjacks' with your bodies on the ground. Ready, go." The rookies scramble to contort themselves into letters, Marly and Shelley forming an L at the beginning of the pack. But the group quickly runs out of time.

"No time limit this time. But you have to do it with no talking," says another veteran. Marly and Shelley look at each other and lie back down in their L. A rookie guy motions that he needs two people for the U, and two step forward and get into place. They go through all the letters, and finally accomplish the mission. A veteran steps forward with something behind her back. "Congratulations," she says, handing them a wooden letter L.

Another veteran hands the rookies a clue to the next location on campus where they must run. "The cafeteria!" someone shouts, as they link hands and start jogging. Some of the veterans run beside them, while others take a car—the cafeteria is clear across campus. "R-O-O-K-I-E-S. Rookies! Rookies! Are the best!" they yell on repeat.

In the cafeteria, the veterans give the newbies their next mission— they have three minutes to make up a cheer that rhymes. "At the end of the cheer, all the guys have to be in the air," explains a veteran. Someone comes up with a rhyme right off the bat. "S! F! A! The best we'll ever be! National champs since 2003!" The women brainstorm simple motions. But they pause; the women can easily lift the smaller tumblers, but some of the rookie stunters are enormous.

It takes a few minutes to come up with a plan. Two women will face each other and hold hands. The guys will sit down softly in the cradle and lift their legs off the floor. But there's one guy left without women to lift him. As they show the veterans the cheer, he jumps as high as he can. A veteran steps forward and hands the rookies the letter C along with another clue.

The rookies link hands and jog to the football field. The air feels heavy, and everyone is dripping sweat. "I can't run anymore," says one rookie girl. A guy slings her across his shoulder and carries her the whole way.

"Come on, everyone. Keep yelling," says Sierra. "R-O-O-K-I-E-S. Rookies! Rookies! Are the best!"

At the football field, the rookies have to roll down a big hill, the shriveled grass sticking to their skin. "It's like itching powder," says Marly, wiping herself off. Next, they do a series of races—suicide runs, crab-walks, a wheelbarrow race. The veterans line them up and have them do squats followed by Standing Back Tucks. Even Jane Fonda would never be so cruel.

"What does all this mean to you?" asks a veteran as the rookies take a minute to rest.

"Dedication," says one of them.

"Teamwork."

"Family."

A veteran hands them the letter L with one last clue, leading them to a statue of Stephen F. Austin that everyone on campus refers to as "Surfin' Steve." The rookies link arms and run. They reach the circular fountain and sit around the edge, their bottoms burning on the hot marble. In the center, Stephen F. Austin appears to rise from the water on a star, one hand touching his heart, the other stuffed in his pocket. A carved cape billows around him.

"Everyone has to kiss Surfin' Steve's boot," says a veteran.

One by one, each rookie wades through the fountain. Some of them can reach the boot easily, while others have to jump to plant their lips on the bronze shoe. "This feels nice," says Samantha as she wades.

As the last rookie kisses the statue, the veterans clap. One of them reveals the letter M from behind his back.

"What does that spell?" asks a veteran.

"L–C–L–M," yell the rookies.

"What does it mean?" asks Shelley, not meaning to say anything out loud.

One of the veterans turns his face toward her. "When you're ready, we'll tell you," he says.


## "I Was Little Miss Texas in 1990 and 1991."

Sierra Jenkins is two parts mesmerizingly perfect and one part total chaos. It's Sunday afternoon and we're standing in front of her apartment in a complex near Nacogdoches's main strip. But she can't find her keys.

She rummages through her bag, her brown roots threatening to overtake her blonde ponytail. Giving up, she lifts a plastic chair and rests it beside the five-foot wooden fence that surrounds her apartment's patio. She hops onto it and attempts to boost herself over the fence. But she gets stuck, her stomach balancing on the top of the fence, her arms grasping the edge to keep from falling forward. Her legs flail behind her, and she reaches one arm back to pull down her camouflage print miniskirt.

I run to help, but before I can get to her, she hits the floor.

"Are you okay?" I ask, as we both crack up.

"Yeah," she says, still laughing as she pulls on the porch door and window, only to find that both are securely locked. "Maybe my neighbor is home?" she says in her I-smoked-too-many-cigarettes-last-night voice.

For the first time this year, I'm beginning to see the chaos part of Sierra—the part that is often locked out; the part whose phone rarely works; the part with the wild twinkle in her eye; the part she tries hard to mask by being the best.

Sierra has been performing her entire life. She started dance practically out of the womb. At age five, she was a gymnast. At age ten, a champion horse rider. Through all these activities, Sierra's mom entered her in beauty pageants. "I had JonBenét Ramsey hair, and I remember her pulling down my eyelid to put on eyeliner," she recalls. "I'd win all the time—I was Little Miss Texas in 1990 and 1991."

"Seriously?" I say, as we sit down on her patio to wait for her roommate. "What was your talent?"

"I sang 'Babyface' and tap danced. I was a horrible singer," she says, laughing. "That's why I started gymnastics—I wanted to do back handsprings. When I was eight, I remember being in pageants with twelve-year-olds. I look at tapes now, and it's funny. It'll be tall girl, tall girl, short me, tall girl. I asked my mom why she put me in competitions with older girls and she said, 'I wanted to get you started performing early.' "

"Are you happy she did that?" I ask, realizing as the words come out of my mouth that I sound like a therapist.

She nods. "My mom was a single mom—her and my dad divorced when I was one year old," she says. "My life was my mom's life—I was her prodigy child. All I always heard was, 'You're amazing.' I still feel like I want to impress people."

Sierra pauses and takes a pair of brown-rimmed glasses out of her bag. She slides them on her face, a perfect match to her eyes. "In high school, all that mattered was that you were an amazing cheerleader. But in college, you have to be beautiful, you have to have a six pack," she says. "You're judged on how white your teeth are and what color your nail polish is. I'm hard on myself—when I have a zit, I don't even want to go to practice."

She shrugs her narrow shoulders. "Sometimes I just start crying thinking, 'James Brown doesn't like me.' He always says little things like, 'My last partner was only ninety-four pounds,'" she explains, the pace of her words quickening. "The other night I saw him at a party, and I had a few beers. The next day at practice, he said, 'I think you weigh more.' He was fuming and grunting about it, like 'roid raging on me."

She looks around, as if to make sure he's nowhere in the vicinity. "I mean, I love being around James, but I get nervous eating in front of him. I don't want him to ever be able to say, 'Well, if you hadn't eaten so much . . . ' I've never cared so much what my partner thought of me, but I've never had a chance of winning a Partner Stunt National Championship before," she says. "I just don't want it to be like he's busting his ass for us and I'm not."

She interrupts her own thought and leans back in her chair. "I'm self-conscious, I don't know," she continues. "It doesn't help that all the guys on the team are hot. It's like a buffet of good-looking guys."

"Have you made any friends outside of the team?" I ask.

Sierra nods. "But when I hang out with normal people, I can see their eyes glaze over," she says. "Ninety percent of what I talk about is cheerleading. I'm obsessed. It's boring to me to talk to normal people."

Sierra's phone rings and she flips it open. It's her roommate—he's on his way to unlock the door and save the day. Sierra jumps up from her seat and does a little dance.

## "Here I Was, Thinking I Was a Hard-Ass."

The next weekend, Sierra heads over to a teammate's house to hang out and enjoy a bright Texas afternoon. The grass is green and dewy in the backyard. Two guys gather around a punching bag, a tall, black vinyl column on a weighted base. They take turns pounding their fists into it, the bag snapping back ever so slightly with each punch.

"I wanna try," says Sierra, walking over.

She curls her right hand into a fist and hurls it toward the bag in front of her. Her knuckles make contact, and the impact ripples through her body. "Oww," she screams.

She falls to her knees, clutching her right hand. "Oh my God!" she howls. Tears overflow from her eyes.

The guys stare in disbelief. "Are you okay?" one of them asks.

"Let me see it," says another, reaching for her hand. It is red, swollen, and her right pinky looks deformed. The guy's eyes widen looking at it. "You broke your hand," he says. "That's a boxer's fracture."

"There's no way I broke it. There's no way," says Sierra, shaking her head, as if saying it enough times will change what just happened.

"We're taking you to the hospital. *Now,*" says one of the guys, reaching for his car keys.

"No," sniffs Sierra between sobs. "My health insurance doesn't cover me going to the emergency room. I don't have money to pay."

"You have to go," says one of the guys sternly. They help her up and bring her to the car, still crying and muttering the occasional curse word.

At the hospital, a doctor x-rays Sierra's hand. He pins the x-rays up in front of a light board and shows her the bones underneath her skin.

"My hand is broken all the way from my right pinky to my middle finger," she tells me, shaking her head violently. "I've done all these crazy cheerleading things—I've landed on my face, on my back—and I'm fine. And now I'm doing something stupid, thinking I was a hard-ass, and I *broke* my hand."

By the end of the day, Sierra has calmed down. The doctors have put her hand in a splint. They'll need to look at it in a few weeks to determine if she needs a hard cast or surgery. And just like that, Sierra's cheerleading season is put on hold.

### "She Got Burned."

I feel like I'm at a rave circa 1995. It's the night before SFA's homecoming game, and hundreds of students are gathered in front of a building with a broad staircase leading up to a columned façade. The sky is dark, and on the steps, green and red lights flash behind a band playing covers of everything from Led Zeppelin to Weezer. Hundreds of blue glow sticks dance in the air like possessed radioactive twigs.

The SFA cheerleaders jump around as they dance, singing along with the band. Tyrone sticks two blue glow sticks in his nostrils and two more in his ears. Near him, Doug looks giddy. "Trisha and I did a two-hour cover shoot for *Cheer Coach & Advisor* magazine today," he says. "I'm excited to see how it turns out."

Near us, one of the guys cracks open a glow stick and swirls it around in the air, sending neon liquid flying. The women gasp, running from the DayGlo shower. The guys stand their ground, marveling at how the liquid forms glow-in-the-dark spots on their warm-up suits.

The band plays their last song and the students grasp hands, creating a long, single-file line. The leaders hold torches to guide the way. The cheerleaders fall into the end of the line and walk slowly down the campus sidewalk. James jumps on one of the tumbler's backs, insisting on a piggyback ride. "Thanks James Clown," the guy says.

Sierra stays as far away from James Brown as possible. A splint covers her right hand, and over it she wears a soft cast that looks like a tan oven mitt. For the past week, she's had to sit out of practice. She's barely spoken to James and thinks he might be giving her the silent treatment. But her frustration isn't obvious tonight. "Give 'em the axe, Big Jacks! Give 'em the axe!" she chants along with the others.

The line of students snakes through a patch of trees to a wide-open field. Hundreds of students are gathered in clumps, talking and laughing, the red glow of alcohol on their faces. At the far end of the field, an orange plastic fence ropes off a mountain of wood, cardboard, and packing crates.

The leaders of the procession approach the pile and toss their torches onto it. Sparks fly, and orange flames jump from the wooden pile. Black smoke funnels into the sky. It's impressive—the closest my college got to a bonfire was someone pulling the dorm fire alarm in the middle of the night. I breathe in deeply. The field smells like a fireplace in winter. On the road at the far end of the field, several fire trucks are parked, just in case.

A space is cleared beside the fire, and the Twirlajacks prance into it. Each stops in front of a man holding a torch, dipping the capped ends of her baton into the flames. Holding their flaming batons, they walk calmly into a two-line formation. They spin their batons so quickly that they create circles of light. The cheerleaders clap.

The women catapult their batons into the dark sky, like fireworks minus the boom. They reach out their hands to catch them in unison. A woman in front flinches, and lets her baton drop to the ground. It rolls on the grass toward Tyrone.

Amazingly, the grass doesn't catch fire, and the rolling does not extinguish the flames. She picks up the baton and continues in the routine with the others. "She got burned," jokes Doug. Finished with their performance, the twirlers stop to have their batons extinguished with wet towels.

It's the cheerleaders' turn to perform. They tumble into the clearing, the fire looming behind them as they perform one of the routines that they cobbled together at camp. The audience claps and hollers as eight flyers corkscrew into Full-Ups. But I'm disappointed. At games, their most impressive stunts, pyramids, and tumbling passes are outlawed, since they stand on hard surfaces. But tonight, they're performing on grass. They could do anything they wanted to, and yet they chose a routine filled with simple moves. I wish they'd pulled out all the stops—tried their own version of twirling with fire.

After they perform, Trisha sees the perfect photo opportunity. She points the squad over to an open area on the far side of the bonfire. The stunt partners form a line, friends and alumni cheerleaders standing before them. Trisha calls the name of a stunt—Liberty, Awesome, Scorpion—and the women fly up. In front of the leaping flames, their bodies become black silhouettes without faces. Camera flashes go off all around.

The fire slowly gets shorter, and half an hour later, it's the size of a campfire, a huge mound of soot and smoldering embers.

## "I Think It's Perfect to Weigh Three Times as Much as My Partner."

I'm sitting on a U-shaped black leather couch with Tyrone and five other big guys from the SFA squad. One of them looks like the kind of guy who would usually have a hunting rifle in his hand. Another is tall and wide, with shaggy hair. Jason, Yvette's partner, has taken the middle seat. Beside him is team captain Jerrod, tall and compact, black stubble covering his chin and head, like a towel wrapped around his face.

SFA's homecoming game ended about an hour ago, and after a long day of marching in a parade through Nacogdoches and cheering on the sidelines under the hot sun, the cheerleaders are ready to party. One of the teammate's mothers has prepared an Italian feast for us at his house. Only the guys are here so far. The women are taking longer at their respective dorm rooms and apartments to shower and change into civilian clothing.

The living room is sparsely decorated in that way guy's houses usually are—besides the couch, there's a big-screen TV and framed *Godfather* and *Scarface* posters. Several pans of lasagna sit on the kitchen table, along with a salad and a sheet cake with the SFA logo in purple icing on top. The guys pile food on their plates to the point where the plastic bends. "Salad? That's healthy. I don't want that," someone says.

The group sits down to eat, and for one of the rare moments in my life, I become one of the guys, privy to their gossip and thoughts. "Remember last year, James Brown was droppin' stunts and people were ripping into him. He said, 'Instead of making each other feel worse why don't we support each other. I mean, I know that's gay, but we should,'" recalls the shaggy-haired guy.

The rest of the group cracks up. "'I mean, 'I know that's gay,'" someone echoes, his mouth full of lasagna.

It's interesting that they brought up the word *gay*. The idea has percolated in American culture for decades that guy cheerleaders are most likely gay. It's another perception of cheerleaders that doesn't line up to the reality. While I have definitely met one or two guy cheerleaders who are openly gay, and a few others who set off my gaydar, the grand majority of male cheerleaders are straight. In fact, it's a culture of manly men—the kind who lift weights, drink beer, and butt heads.

Still, even though teams are full of good-looking men and women, there isn't nearly as much hooking up as you would expect from people in the party phase of their lives. Male cheerleaders tend to view the female cheerleaders on their team like little sisters, and vice versa.

On SFA's team, there are currently three couples, but, interestingly, none of the pairs say that they stunt well together. "A lot of cheerleaders just date cheerleaders," one of the guys explains. "But it's hard to date someone on your team because you're around them *all* the time. If you do it, the main thing is that you have to leave everything off the mat. If you're fighting, you can't bring that into practice."

Back on the couch, the guys continue to make fun of James Brown, who isn't here to defend himself. "We set up a video camera before telling him that Sierra broke her hand," says the shaggy-haired guy. "He turned red, started yelling, and ran into the bathroom. I guarantee he cried that night."

Two of the guys hop up for seconds of lasagna, while the others lean back and sink into the couch's leather. "I want to weigh myself," one of them says, jumping up and running into the bathroom. The other men follow him, a procession of hulks, crowding around a bathroom scale. "I'm 218," says Jerrod, stepping off the scale with a satisfied grin. "I used to be 180. I was so embarrassed."

"You realize this is something no woman would ever do—get on a scale right after pigging out," I point out.

They laugh. "Yeah, we're just curious," someone says. It's the ideal weighing time for them—the exact moment when they are at their heaviest.

"There's sort of a 200-line," explains Tyrone, a labret piercing poking out under his lips. Since cheerleaders must remove all jewelry, he takes it out at practice and games.

"My partner's ninety pounds," says one of the guys. "I weigh three times as much as her. I think that's perfect. It means I don't move when I catch her."

"I think as long as you weigh two times your partner, you're good," says Tyrone.

Another group walks into the room, James Brown at the rear of the pack. As deep food comas set in, James picks up the remote control. He turns on the television and flips through the sports channels, pausing on boxing and football scores. The score of the homecoming game they just cheered at flashes across the screen. "SFA loses," someone says. *"Again."*

# CHAPTER 9

## "I Was Addicted to the Attention,

## Not the Cocaine."

MARY* COMBS HER DIRTY blonde hair with her fingers as she flirts with our tall, dark, and handsome waiter. He cracks a joke and she throws her head back, laughing the kind of full-bellied laugh that makes you want to join in even if the joke isn't very funny. Her face is soft and her gaze is wide-eyed.

This is a 180-degree-change from the Mary I met two years ago at NCA Nationals. That Mary was a freshman flyer at a Texas college whose most prominent feature was the sharp clavicle bone that protruded over her uniform top. She had a reticence in her voice and rolled her eyes a lot. I would never have guessed it, but back then, Mary was a cokehead.

After hearing that I was writing a book, Mary, who's since left college cheerleading behind, said that she wanted to tell me her full saga. "No one has the balls to talk about it, and I want to be that person," she explained, the word *balls* sounding out of place in her sweet-as-pie accent. Rather than talk over the phone, I decided to drive several hours

---

*At her request, her name and identifying details have been changed.

in the wrong direction on my way home from SFA's homecoming so we could meet in person. We're at a Tex-Mex restaurant in the town where she lives, and since the sky is gray, we're the only ones on the outdoor patio. She begins to tell me her story.

In high school, Mary never worried about her weight. "When I left for camp my first year of college, I weighed 113 pounds," she says. "My coach looked at me and said, 'You look disgusting.' " The harsh words inspired her to start a diet. She watched what she ate and worked out every day for three months. But at her next team weigh-in, she'd only lost three pounds. She was devastated and cried on her boyfriend's shoulder.

"My first month in college, I'd never tried drugs or even thought about it," she says. "But my boyfriend was tired of hearing me complain about my weight. One day he said, 'If you really want to lose weight, try cocaine.' He did it with me for the first time—we did an 8-ball over a week and I lost nine pounds. *In a week.* I thought, 'This is a miracle.' "

"What is it that makes you lose weight?" I interject. "That you have more energy and run around all the time? Or do you forget to eat?"

She picks up a taco and stares at it. "I would *try* to eat, but I couldn't even swallow—food just felt strange in my throat," she explains.

Mary's teammates quickly noticed that her physique was getting sleeker. "They were like, 'You look so good. You're so sexy.' My stunts were getting better, and I was so happy that people were noticing me," she says. "It built up my ego. It was like I was addicted to the attention, not the cocaine. Everyone seemed to love me."

Ditto for her coach. "He'd compliment me and criticize everyone else. He'd say I was the best on the team," she says. "I had a messed-up relationship with my boyfriend, and doing so well at cheerleading made me feel like not just the worthless puppy dog that I felt like."

But after a few months, Mary was no longer "the newly skinny girl" who everyone fawned over—she was just "the skinny girl." The exhilaration of the previous few months melted away. "No one told me how good I looked anymore," she says. "I got paranoid that people would think, 'She's skinny because she's a cokehead' and judge me. I felt lonely—cocaine was there for me when no one else was."

"Can I ask how much all of this cost?" I ask.

"An 8-ball would cost me $200 and last for a week," she says. "I'd earned a lot of scholarship money for academics, so my cheer scholarship check went directly in my pocket. I had lots of money for drugs."

The following school year, Mary and her boyfriend broke up, but her cocaine habit was still going strong. She got an apartment with a close friend on the squad. "We'd been best friends, but one night we got into a big fight and stopped talking for a month. I'd go to my room, shut the door, and do coke by myself. Then I'd make myself pass out with shots," she says. "I'd wake up in the morning and go to class."

At this point, Mary's personality had changed. She describes herself as outgoing and friendly before, but after, she found herself reclusive. Cheerleading practice was the highlight of her day. "But even at practice, I'd be anxious to go home and do a bump. All I could think when people on the squad talked to me was, 'You don't know my secret,'" she says. "I got so used to seeing myself as skin and bones, that all I wanted was to see one more rib pop out."

One night, after not talking for a month, her roommate opened the door to her room. "She said, 'I'm leaving school. Every time I eat, all I can think about is what it will taste like when I throw it up,'" Mary remembers.

Mary was shocked to find that her roommate was struggling, too. "I had been trying so hard to keep my problem under wraps that I didn't notice she was in her room throwing up in the trash can. We were both embarrassed because we knew what we were doing was wrong, but we were fighting, not realizing that we were going through the exact same thing," she says.

"Did you tell her?" I ask.

Mary nods. "I said, 'Do you know how I'm staying skinny? I do coke all the time. Why do you think I've been in here so much? I have some right now.' I basically introduced *her* to cocaine."

"Do you feel bad about that?" I ask.

"Oh yeah," says Mary, shaking her head. "I remember one night I was going out, and she grabbed my wrist and started screaming, 'Don't leave me. Don't leave me.' I tried to calm her down and she said to take her to the emergency room. I did. After that, she started seeing a doctor and got on antidepressants."

Mary pauses. "In retrospect, I should have gone to a doctor too, but I told myself that there was nothing wrong with me," she says.

"When did you start to think, 'Okay. This is a problem'?"

Our waiter swings open a screen door, interrupting the conversation. He plops down another round of sodas on our table. Mary smiles at him, silent. As he walks back inside, she picks back up exactly where she left off.

"About a month later, I went on a binge—I did an entire 8-ball in one day. I remember seeing a bug on my bed. I started feeling like there were bugs all over me. I pulled the covers and sheets off my bed, and tore off all my clothes. I looked in the mirror and my pupils were so big you couldn't even tell what color my eyes were," she says.

"I was freaking out—I started trembling. I went into the bathroom and turned on the shower, still feeling like there were bugs everywhere. My heart was beating out of my chest. I sat down in the shower and pulled my knees to my chest as the water poured over me. My body was twitching out of control. I actually thought I might die.

"I stayed in the shower for three hours, sitting there bawling. I started to analyze everything—I couldn't believe that I'd let this need to be skinny control me. I'd totally blown off school and fucked up my life. That was the first time I ever thought of myself as a drug addict."

Mary looked online to find a rehab center, but the high price tag per night was a big problem—she'd blown all her savings on coke. "I'd literally spent thousands of dollars in a year and had nothing to show for it but ribs popping out of my chest," she says. "But I didn't have a choice, I had to kick it. So I just stopped. The next few days were a blur."

"Was that it?" I ask.

She nods. "I only did it one more time. A friend offered me some at a party, and I don't know why, but I took a bump," she says. "As soon as it hit my head, I was back in the shower freaking out. It was actually good—it took away *all* the appeal."

Mary left school a few months later and moved back in with her parents. "I remember walking through the door of my room, and I just felt like myself again. I sat down at my desk and saw the journals I used to keep. I started reading through them, and they reminded me who I used to be—a good-hearted, straightforward girl, not someone with all these problems."

It's been over eight months and Mary is still clean. She quit cheerleading but recently joined a team at a local all-star gym. And she saw her former roommate recently. "She was at my birthday party and she seemed good—she said she hadn't thrown up in months," says Mary. "I just can't believe how much our personalities changed in that year. I'm glad we can be friends again."

"Do you think this is an experience you would have had if you were not a cheerleader?" I ask.

"I don't know," says Mary, bringing a manicured hand to her face. "But I'm not the only cheerleader who's had a problem. I know one girl who took Ecstasy every morning to suppress her appetite—she did so much of it that she didn't act at all like she was fucked up. Other people take Adderall, some smoke a lot. Others get obsessed with working out—I know one girl who would go out every night running, even if it was pouring rain."

"If you met someone who was going through what you went through, what would you say to them?" I ask.

She takes a bite of her taco. "I'd just tell them that it's really not worth it. You might look better and you might be a better cheerleader, but really, it's self-mutilation. It's killing yourself," she says. "As much as I love cheerleading, it's just a sport."

The waiter comes back with our check and Mary glances up at him, the girl-next-door with a little spice. She leaves with his number.

# CHAPTER 10

## "I Know We Cheered Our Hearts Out,

## 'Cause My Voice Is Hoarse."

### *The Southern University Jaguars*

*PEP RALLY.* **THE TWO** words seem redundant, yet they appear together so often that the phrase has its own entry in the dictionary. It's one of the most basic American scholastic sports traditions, but as the Southern University basketball arena buzzes with people, the concept feels foreign to me. I've never been to a pep rally. My high school had them and attendance was supposedly mandatory, but they were held during the last hour of the day, making it far too tempting to skip. I'm not sure if my college ever had them, but if they did, I never got the memo.

It's the day before Southern's Homecoming—the second-biggest game of the year, topped only by the Bayou Classic against archrival Grambling State University over Thanksgiving weekend. A stage has been set up on the basketball court floor for today's rally. An S and a U crafted out of blue and gold balloons bookend the stage, so much helium concentrated in one place that it could float away at any second. A curtain hangs behind the stage from the rafters, among the retired jerseys and banners proclaiming Southern the SWAC champions.

The Southern cheerleaders are nowhere in sight, but in the distance, I hear a familiar chant. "Southern fans! In the stands! We're number one!" they yell, the words mingling with the hip-hop music and chatter of students. I walk toward the curtain and find a break in the fabric. And there are the Southern cheerleaders in their electric yellow uniforms. They're practicing a short routine, paying no attention to the concrete floor beneath their feet.

James Turner spots me and taps Jasmine on the shoulder. "Hey," he says, his dimples cutting like slits down his face. Jasmine waves as if she's presiding over a float.

"How's everything going?" I ask them.

"Real good," says James. "Our stunting is coming on up, and we're dancing like we're one now—you can't tell the new people anymore."

"Yeah," says Jasmine, her golden eye makeup looking like she just spent hours in a makeup artist's chair. "It's going really good."

"But it's still too many chiefs, like at camp," says James.

Jasmine nods heartily. "When the captain has something to say, everybody should just listen."

Coach James is conspicuously absent today. Missing camp started a trend for him. Even though this is Southern's Homecoming weekend, he is on his way to his own alma mater's Homecoming, hours away. It's a move that inspired eye rolls from several of the cheerleaders.

James Turner and Jasmine have had to step up their leadership to make up for Coach's absence. As James commands the squad to practice their routine one last time, I part the curtain and walk back to the front of the arena. The auditorium is packed, many students dropping their shoulders with the bass beat of the music.

As I make my way to an empty seat in the bottom section, eyes settle on me. "Look, a white girl," someone says, like he's just seen an alien walking down the sidewalk holding a tennis racket. I'm not sure how to respond, so I smile and wave. He does the same.

The cheerleaders run through the curtain. "Let's go Jaguars!" they yell, though the audience stays firmly in their seats. Jasmine smiles bashfully as Jarel sends her up for a Scorpion. She lifts her right leg and brings it behind her, like a figure skater beginning a spin. She points into the audience as several people clap.

Tremayne tosses Chassity. She flicks her small, powerhouse leg up as she glides toward his hands, hitting her Heel Stretch position before she lands. In the air, she smiles like a kid in a candy shop, her right hand waving at the crowd.

Near them, another couple attempts a Double Down. But the flyer under-rotates, and her partner catches her awkwardly on her stomach. At other schools, a fall like this would garner a gasp. But here, a group of women bursts into laughter.

"She busted," says a guy beside me, bringing a fist to his mouth.

"Somebody gonna get hurt," replies his friend.

It reminds me of something one of the alumni cheerleaders told me earlier in the year. "Southern is the worst crowd to perform in front of," she said. "It's like being at the Apollo. If you drop, people boo. If your rhythm's off, it'll be in the school paper the next day." She was right.

The football team shuffles onto the stage wearing blue jerseys and jeans, many with their hands shoved in their pockets. "They need to be practicing while they're up there," a guy near me says. Their season, apparently, hasn't been going well.

In the distance, horns blast. The audience jumps to their feet. At Southern, the marching band, the Human Jukebox, is as big a deal as the football team. The trumpet players emerge from the hallway, swinging their instruments in unison as they toot. The band marches in neat lines, their movements highly coordinated. In the back of the formation, the drummers dance as if they're in a club and don't have a heavy piece of metal strapped to their chests.

The cheerleaders line up in four rows. Smack in the front, Tarianne begins to dance. She leads the squad in their catch-ons, assembling their repertoire of twenty-five dances into whatever pattern matches the music. The others study the way she pumps her fists, and they join in on the second repetition. As Tarianne makes quick figure eights with her hips, it's impossible not to watch her. She dances without a hint of self-consciousness. "Technically, it's an honor," she once told me about leading catch-ons. "But I don't think about it like that. I just go wherever my body flows."

Behind the women, Jarel leads the catch-ons for the men. They jump, picking up their knees like they're running over hot coals. They cross their arms over their chests and bounce from side to side.

The audience whips blue and gold pom-poms so fiercely that they make snapping noises. "We have the best cheerleaders," says a man on the stage. "They cheer for us each and every day, so give 'em some love." The audience lets out a round of screams as the cheerleaders jog to their positions for their routine.

The town gathers in a clump in the middle of the floor, two sets of two guys lunging so that their knees touch. James and Tremayne each step onto a pair of knees as if they were stairs. They reach down in front of them, where two flyers stand, and grip their waists. The women are flung overhead, topping twin 2-1-1 pyramids with the same tapering shape as the Eiffel Tower. "Ssss! Uuuu!" the squad yells. James and Tremayne power the women higher in the air, each shifting his partner's feet into one hand for two very tall Awesomes.

On the stage, a Southern football coach grabs the microphone. He introduces the football players one by one, each getting healthy applause. One of the last players called is the team's lone white player. He turns around, lifts up his jersey, and shakes his butt like he's dancing on a bar. "Ohhhh," screams the audience, loving it.

In a few minutes, the pep rally is over, and the arena has cleared out. I sit down with James Turner, Jasmine, and Jarel. "That was one of the best pep rallies I've been to," says James. "I know we cheered our hearts out 'cause my voice is hoarse."

Jasmine shakes out her wrists. "When I tumble on the concrete, it feels like my wrists are about to cave in," she says.

"You weak," snaps James. She reaches out and punches him lightly on the arm.

I tell the three of them about the student who said, "Look, a white girl." We all laugh. "Some people," says Jarel, shaking his head.

For these three, coming to Southern was culture shock. They all went to predominantly white high schools—Jasmine in Dallas, James outside New Orleans, and Jarel in Wichita, Kansas. "I didn't even know how to dress when I got here," says James. "I would go to class with a button-down shirt tucked into khakis. Then I thought I had to wear

Gucci every day." He's since settled into T-shirts, hoodies, and jeans—casual, but polished, perpetually ready for the pages of a catalogue.

"As soon as I open my mouth, people are like, 'Where are you from?' They can't place it," says Jarel, touching the soul patch on his light-brown chin.

James nods. "People always say to me, 'Why are you talking proper?' "

"The Louisiana accent sneaks in for me," says Jasmine. "I'll always be country." She blinks her gigantic, almond-shaped eyes. She is so pretty that it would be easy to hate her for her stunning genetics. But she happens to be down-to-earth and genuine, one of those women it's impossible not to like.

Every year, Southern holds a Miss Southern pageant, a hybrid of a beauty pageant and a student government election. The idea struck me as contradictory at first (do you really need to look good in a bathing suit to institute programs on campus?), but queen pageants are a long-standing tradition on many historically black college campuses, a leftover from when Miss America excluded black women. This year, Jasmine decided to run.

The competition was stiff. For months, James Turner and Jarel headed up Jasmine's campaign committee, passing out flyers, key chains, shirts, even CDs of her singing around campus. Jasmine walked through nearly every Southern dorm, knocking on doors and meeting people. Jarel came up with a campaign slogan Jasmine adored: "Your Southern University Dreamgirl. You're Gonna Love Me."

The night of the pageant, Jasmine stepped on the stage and belted out Donny Hathaway's classic, "A Song for You," followed by the song that captured Jennifer Hudson her Oscar for *Dreamgirls*. "She killed 'em, from beginning to end," says James Turner. "I was standing right behind her, my chin on her head when they announced she won. I started screaming, and when I turned around, she was crying."

Jasmine blushes. "I'm just excited to try something new," she says modestly. "I'll be able to reach out to people and be remembered for making changes."

James Turner stares at her, shaking his head. "I can't believe we're graduating this year," he says.

"Do you have any ideas for what you're going to do next?" I ask. As soon as I say it, I remember hearing this question over and over again in the months before I graduated college, and the amount of anxiety it produced each time.

But none of these three seems fazed. "I've always known deep down inside that I'm gonna end up doing music," says Jasmine, bringing her hand to her heart. "I'm planning on moving to Atlanta after I graduate. It's the place to be for music."

"By the grace of God really, I'd like to continue with modeling and acting. There's not too many black actors. We need someone to fill the void," says James, pointing to himself.

"I want to be a backup dancer. That's why I'm moving to Atlanta—there's so many auditions there," Jarel says. "Atlanta's the place to be for anything if you're a minority."

## "If They Get Mad, They'll Get Great."

"Don't break nothin', cause y'all are old," yells James Turner, dimples widening as he laughs. In the yellow school desk where he sits, he leans back and rests his arms behind his head.

On the mat in front of him, two former Southern cheerleading captains try an Extension. Melisha, the aluma cheerleader who gave the women a reality check after tryouts, is petite with short hair. Avery, also in his mid-twenties, is tall and light-skinned, with cornrows whose ends peek out from the nape of his neck. He grunts as he sends Melisha airborne. "On the *first* toss," she yells with we-still-got-it excitement as they hold the stunt in the air.

"I heard bones pop," laughs James.

At Southern's Homecoming game, cheerleaders from past squads, dubbed "oldheads," will join the current squad in pumping up the crowd. For the oldheads, this is one of the rare opportunities they get to stunt, and because the Southern audience is so critical, they want to make sure they do it well. They'll have the next few hours to prepare; though they're out of practice, they are determined.

The current cheerleaders are not required to be here, but if anyone is doing anything cheer-related on campus, James Turner will be there.

He walks behind Melisha and puts his hands on her waist. He tosses her into an Extension. "Are you scared?" he asks, looking up.

"Nah," she replies, but her scrunched-up face tells a different story.

"Well, try an Awesome," says James.

James dips and passes her feet into one hand, Melisha standing like a broom balanced in someone's palm. They hold it for a millisecond, then James loses his grip. "What shoe size do you wear?" he asks, passing the blame even though it looked like his mistake.

"A five," she says with an are-you-kidding-me? tone.

The room we're in has changed since tryouts. It's no longer a classroom—it's been converted into a fitness facility, with weight machines and treadmills lining one side. Multicolored desks still sit around the room, but the cheerleading mats are now a permanent fixture.

Two more oldheads walk in the gym. A girl with long, shiny hair in a Southern cheerleader jacket hugs Melisha. A bald guy with the build of a professional wrestler takes a seat in the desk next to me. I remember seeing him at tryouts as well. "It's exciting to come back and see what they're doing," he explains. "It's like watching a baby learn to walk. They stumble and fall, but by the end of the season they get it."

James talks quietly to Avery on the mat, but he hears this comment. He whips his head around. "You're the rough draft. I'm the final product," he says.

James tells Avery about the disappointment of not winning the paid bid to Nationals at camp. "The system is not designed to entice a struggling historically black college team," says Avery. He crosses his arms over his chest, bringing one hand up to his chin. He stares James in the eye and asks *the* question on all the oldheads' minds. "Are you planning on going to Nationals?" he says.

"We seriously in our hearts want to go, but we don't have the money," says James, the skin on his forehead morphing into three worry lines. James saw Avery struggle with this same situation just a few years ago, so he feels comfortable letting out his frustration. "Why have we gotta go around hustlin' for money? The school should fully support its teams."

Avery's tone has turned serious. He points to the other oldheads in the room. "Our years we went to Nationals, and we didn't have the money then either. The difference was that coach was head-over-heels in love with the idea of going, so he wrote sponsorship letters to everyone he could think of," says Avery. "Saying we don't have the money is a cop-out."

I sympathize with Coach James. It's no small task to make thousands of dollars materialize out of thin air, but Avery does have a point. There is a reason cheerleaders are famous for holding car washes and selling booster pins—cheerleading is expensive.

It goes back to cheerleading's split personality. From a college's perspective, cheerleaders exist to root for other teams. Schools are happy to provide costs related to that duty, but a relatively small number see the value in pumping in an additional $40,000 a year to fund their cheerleaders as competitors. Perhaps this will change as more people come to see cheerleading as a worthwhile sport in and of itself. But for now, most teams are left to fend for themselves.

On the mat, James Turner takes a minute to process what Avery has said. He diplomatically rushes to Coach's defense. "We wanna do a lot of fund-raising," he says. "In twenty-four hours the other week, we raised $2,000 for our friend whose family was killed."

"You know what I think," says Avery, cocking his eyebrow in my direction as if a little scared of saying this in front of me. "I think in 2002, Coach *arrived*. We came in *second* at Nationals, and we only lost because of one fall. He proved himself to the people in the NCA. Now the goal's become, 'We have to be the best in the Southwestern Atlantic Conference.' Best in the SWAC? That doesn't prove our worth."

Though it makes me uncomfortable, I agree that there might be something psychological in Coach's detachment from the squad, in addition to the fact that he is overextended. Even if Southern raises the funds to go to Nationals, there's no guarantee that they'll place as well as they did in 2002. Heck, only half of the teams at Nationals make it past preliminaries. Every year, great teams are eliminated simply because they had a bad day. It's a risk.

Avery's words seem to set off a lightbulb in James's head, too. His brown eyes focus on Avery. "It's like we're just coasting," says James softly, seeming to agree.

"I think the program is taking a step backwards," says Avery. "In

1997, we had to take guys and make them cheerleaders, and now we're having to do that again. The program should have momentum, where it's attracting talented people." He pauses for a second, looking up at the ceiling. "I'm worried about Coach's time. A few years ago, he was busy—he was a husband, a father, and working with the church. Now he does all that, plus he's an assistant principal *and* he has a JV squad. When you try to do too much, you can only do it at 80 percent."

James seems torn as he listens to Avery. On the one hand, he respects him and, at least to some degree, agrees with his diagnosis of the situation. But at the same time, he's compelled to defend his teammates and his coach. "Oh, Coach is dedicated," retorts James.

Melisha joins the conversation. "Personally, I see a lot of potential, but I think the work ethic has declined," she says. "Your girls are lazy."

James holds his hands up like a stop sign. "People are getting better," he says. He thinks for a minute, the pendulum in his mind swinging back to the oldheads' side. "Last year, we were off the chain. But this year, people seem resigned to not going to Nationals. *I* say we're going."

"The way you feel now," says Melisha, her hand touching her heart, "our *whole squad* felt that way."

"We *all* wanted to show that we were the best *cheerleaders,* not just the best *black* cheerleaders. Now the squad rests on, 'We're better than Grambling State,'" adds Avery, referring to another historically black college squad that has been a contender at Nationals.

The two other oldheads in the room walk over, drawn to the conversation like magnets. "Remember that one year when Coach called us into the gym and said, 'We're not going to Nationals'." Avery says. "We said, 'We will *make* something happen so we can go.' We piled into a fifteen person van with no air-conditioning and we drove."

"The van broke down on the way," adds one of the others. "We slid up under it and figured out how to fix it. We were determined. We didn't care—we were gonna make it to the castle."

"We can't say that we're second in the nation anymore—that was five years ago," says Avery. "I don't even know if we can say we're the best black squad anymore—Grambling State goes to Nationals every year." He pauses, collecting his thoughts. "As long as we compare ourselves to other black teams, we'll be happy. But we should be showing up the best white squads—Louisville, SFA."

James looks up, a new depth in his eyes. "I don't want to just look good for the students here," he says, trying to show his drive. "At camp we had the right mentality to show everyone just how good we are."

The oldheads nod. "It's about the heart of the cheerleaders. We had bold, aggressive leaders," says Avery. "*You* have to be that now."

"You have to work this squad hard. Who cares if they get mad," says Melisha.

"If they get mad, they'll get great," adds Avery.

Melisha chokes up. "In a way, I think this is our fault," she says. "We set the standard, but when we left, we didn't leave enough people to carry it on."

James looks her dead in the eye. "I've always had the mindset that I'm gonna leave a mark on this program," he says. "There's no way I'm gonna say, 'I was captain and all we did was go to SWAC.' I want to say, 'I was captain and we raised the money to go to NCA Nationals.'"

"I'll give you so much props if you do it," says Avery, resting his hand on one of James's muscular shoulders.

The four stand up and start to stunt again, the serious mood evaporating back into jokes. But James's demeanor seems different as he leaves the gym. His head is tucked down and his nostrils flare, like a general ready to lead his troops into battle.

## "The Bayou Classic Is Bigger than Thanksgiving."

It's Thanksgiving weekend, and as I drive toward the Superdome in New Orleans, I see hundreds of white RVs parked in neat, orderly lines. I've been in the world of college sports long enough that my first thought is, *Which team are they here for?* As I pull closer, I look for a banner or license plate that gives away a team allegiance. But these RVs are sterile white. They aren't the million-dollar motor homes that football enthusiasts buy to follow their teams during the fall season. These are FEMA trailers.

The trailers are one of the few visual reminders of Hurricane Katrina I've seen in New Orleans. Tourists can admire the French Quarter without thinking about how hard the city was hit a year ago. Even the New Orleans Wal-Mart, infamous for the footage of people looting it, desperate for food and water, reopened just a few weeks ago.

In accord with the city's return to normalcy, New Orleans is hosting the Bayou Classic this weekend. A football grudge match between Southern and Grambling State that started in 1974, the Bayou Classic was one of the first bowl games in the country. Every year for decades, fans traveled to New Orleans over Thanksgiving weekend for the game and the festivities that accompany it.

"For my family, the Bayou Classic is bigger than Thanksgiving," one of the women on the squad once told me. "It's a huge party—everyone comes over, we cook gumbo and watch the game. For years, I begged my dad to let me go. He finally took me. I remember I had my little Southern pom-poms. I saw the cheerleaders and thought, 'I want to be one of them.'"

Last year, with New Orleans in shambles, Southern and Grambling State faced a difficult decision—should they cancel the 2005 Bayou Classic? Rather than forgo it altogether, they held it in Houston, where a large percentage of New Orleans' black population had relocated. But today, with the Superdome reopened, the Bayou Classic is home.

Not everyone believes that this means all is well. A few weeks ago, someone told me, "It's unfortunate that you're not going to the Classic before Hurricane Katrina. It will be a shell of what it was before. The whole culture, the whole spirit of New Orleans, has changed." Before Katrina, the event regularly brought together 70,000 fans. No one knows how many will be here this weekend.

It's the night before the big game, and as I walk into the Superdome behind the Southern cheerleaders, the place is already hopping. In the three tiers of seats, you can almost draw a line down the middle separating the fans. On the left side, the fans wear blue and yellow to show their love for Southern. On the right, everyone dons gold and black for Grambling State. A banner hung from the ceiling says, THERE'S NO PLACE LIKE DOME.

The Bayou Classic is not just a clash between football teams. Though the game isn't until tomorrow afternoon, tonight will be the highlight of the weekend for many of the two schools' fans—the famous Battle of the Bands. Both Southern and Grambling State's marching bands are world class. Grambling State played at George W. Bush's inauguration, *USA Today* once named Southern the best marching band in the country.

The Southern cheerleaders are decked out in matching electric blue polo shirts with jeans or khakis underneath. As they walk toward Southern's VIP seating area, they dance to the music pumping through the arena. At the front of the group, Coach James smiles. He wears a Southern University shirt, where an S has been made to look like the Superman logo. But while he is Southern's coach and got his master's degree at the school, he is a Grambling State undergraduate alumnus.

"I'll have to run across the field tomorrow to sing my alma mater," he says, his smooth face interrupted by stubble. "I wear blue, but I'm a Grambling Tiger at heart. For the first few years I coached, I couldn't put on a Southern wind-suit, and I had trouble getting into games."

Coach James's face is even-keeled, but his schedule is out of control. In fact, this is the first time I've seen him face-to-face since tryouts. By day, he works at a Baton Rouge middle school. When he leaves, he heads straight to Southern for practice. "I feel like Clark Kent in the phone booth," says James. "I could write a book on the mechanics of scheduling a day."

"I'm excited to see them perform at the game tomorrow," I tell him.

He nods. "They started the year saying, 'Coach, this is too hard,' but they really caught on fast," he says like a proud father. "I have some very strong ones and some very weak ones—they're lopsided, which can make it hard to put together routines. I basically hide the weaker ones behind them."

"What do you think about their chances of making it to Nationals?" I ask. I know I don't need to remind Coach James that the clock is ticking—Nationals are only three months and a few spare weeks away.

"They have such desire to go," he says, sighing. "They're already writing sponsors. Talent is not the question, it's just the finances."

The squad's favorite song, DJ Unk's "Walk It Out," comes on over the arena's sound system, and the squad erupts into dance. Near us, James Turner moves his loafer-clad feet, dimples flashing. One of the women flaps her knees wildly and brings her arms in front of her and behind her, like a wicked Pee-Wee Herman.

"She tribal," one of the guys says. The woman sticks out her tongue and dances harder. Her image pops up on the LCD screens that line the arena.

"You on camera," someone says as she turns and smiles. Everyone in the huge auditorium is looking at her.

Down the row, Tarianne dances, the thick silver earrings by her face swaying as she moves. But her quiet demeanor shows that something is on her mind. For her, being back in New Orleans is both exciting and surreal. This is her hometown.

Around us the Superdome looks shiny and new. It's hard to believe that last year 20,000 New Orleans residents took emergency shelter here. As the hurricane pounded New Orleans, two giant holes were ripped through the roof and rain poured in, flooding the Dome. The news segments were gruesome—not enough food and water, few medical supplies, unsanitary conditions. Then came the reports—many of them still unconfirmed—of rape, gang violence, assaults, and vandalism. Three people died in the Dome before people were evacuated. It took $185 million to get the Dome back to the state it's in now. But psychological damage cannot be fixed as easily as a roof.

## "My Mom's the Type of Person Who Wouldn't Leave."

A month before Hurricane Katrina, Tarianne had a bad feeling. She didn't know exactly how to explain it, but she sensed that something was amiss.

"There was a small storm, and the next day I woke up and trees had fallen outside. The birds were flying, but it just didn't look normal," she remembers. "I felt like something wasn't right. I'm very in tune with nature, and you can tell a lot by how animals act," she says, her voice twirling upwards nonchalantly as she speaks.

"I started to freak out," says Tarianne, looking down her straight slope of a nose. "I put all my stuff in plastic bags. I wrapped it in duct tape and put everything on the top shelves. My mom knows I'm weird, so she didn't pay much attention to me."

On August 25, already back at school in Baton Rouge, Tarianne heard the news. A tropical storm that had formed over the Bahamas was about to hit Florida. Governor Bush had evacuated several areas of the state. By the next day, experts were predicting that the storm would pick up speed. It was headed straight for New Orleans, and broadcasters were calling it "the big one."

Tarianne was safe an hour inland, but her mom, sister, grandparents, and cousins were all sitting ducks in a city that is 80 percent below sea level. Her eyes stayed glued to the news all day, her fingers constantly dialing her mom. "I kept asking her, 'What are you gonna do?' " says Tarianne. "My mom's the type of person who wouldn't leave."

Over the next day, Tarianne watched the blob on the weatherman's map get bigger and bigger. On some channels, it churned in a green-and-yellow swirl; on others it looked like an animal's eye staring out of the television. The words the weatherman threw out scared her—"Category Three," "Category Four," "the strongest hurricane ever in the Gulf of Mexico." By the time President Bush declared a state of emergency, Tarianne, like many people, was in a full-out panic.

She heard that her grandparents were on their way to Baton Rouge to stay with relatives. But her mom and her sister were standing their ground—they were going to wait the storm out. "I was so scared," says Tarianne. "I just wanted them to get out of there."

On August 28, the news reports grew apocalyptic. Category Five hurricane. Wind speeds of 175 miles per hour. A National Weather Service bulletin that morning said, "Most of the area will be uninhabitable for weeks ... perhaps longer.... High-rise office and apartment buildings will sway dangerously, a few to the point of total collapse.... Power outages will last for weeks....Water shortages will make human suffering incredible."

Tarianne stayed glued to the TV as Mayor Nagin ordered the first mandatory evacuation in New Orleans history. Everyone was to leave the city, and the Superdome was to be a "refuge of last resort."

Finally, Tarianne got the phone call she'd been waiting for. Her mom and her sister were packing their car. They were leaving, expecting to head toward Houston. "I was like, 'Praise the Lord! Thank you,' " remembers Tarianne. " 'Now get out of there.' "

The next twenty-four hours were tense for Tarianne. Cell phone lines were jammed, and she couldn't get through to her mom. She heard radio reports that traffic out of New Orleans was moving at a snail's pace. She tried to distract herself with schoolwork and cheer-leading practice, but she was terrified that her family would not get far enough away in time. "I had no idea where they were," she says. Finally, she got a call from her mom—they were halfway to Houston and out of harm's way.

That night, Tarianne stayed in her room in Baton Rouge, glued to the TV as Hurricane Katrina pounded New Orleans just an hour and a half away. "I was waiting for any little news break. It was really weird seeing those clouds go over New Orleans," she says. "Classes were canceled, and some students were having a good old time, throwing Katrina parties. But I was just so scared."

The next morning, footage of New Orleans trickled onto the news. The storm had been downgraded to Category Three status just before landfall, and it had veered fifteen miles from plowing head-on through New Orleans. The damage from the wind had been less than predicted, but the city's levee system had been breached. A huge portion of New Orleans was completely submerged in water. The death toll was growing.

Tarianne watched the images of her hometown in shock. "We stayed on St. Claude Ave., right near the Circle Food Store," she says. "The whole thing was under water—all you could see was the top of the sign. I was just like, 'Are you serious? How could there be enough water to fill up the city?' It was devastating."

She had no way of getting in touch with her mom and sister, and she prayed that they were safe. She was also scared for her sister's boy-friend, who had taken shelter in the Superdome with his uncle in a wheelchair. No one had heard from them. Later that day, at her dorm's front desk, she got a message from him. "He was so happy to hear my voice," she recalls. "He was like, 'Have you talked to your sister?' I told him she was safe. So he gave me his number so that next time she called I could give it to her."

For Tarianne, it's still hard to talk about the days after the storm, when she watched, helpless like the rest of us, while the situation in

New Orleans got worse, the government seemingly turning its back on rescue efforts because the grand majority of the people remaining in the city were black. It took Tarianne a long time before she went to see the damage in person. "My house wasn't as bad as I thought it was gonna be," she says. "I guess there were drains nearby, because the water only got up to our steps."

But her grandparents lived in the devastated Lower Ninth Ward that borders the Mississippi River. "You couldn't even recognize their house—the piano was all the way in the kitchen," says Tarianne. "My grandparents lived there for forever—all the memories and all the pictures were ruined. They have seven kids and they had everyone's degree from Southern hung on one wall. They got all messed up."

Today, only a handful of Tarianne's relatives have been able to move back to New Orleans. Her mom and her sister are currently in Atlanta. Tarianne doesn't know if she could ever live in New Orleans again. She stares into the sky, her long, straightened hair blowing in the wind. "It'll always be home and I'll always come back, but . . . ," she says, trailing off.

## "We're Kind of a Risqué School."

Last night at the Battle of the Bands, the Superdome's industrial-strength lights were turned down. This morning, they are on full blast, turning the AstroTurf field a retina-burning green. The Southern cheerleaders stretch out on the sidelines. In the end zone, near where they stand, the word *Southern* is painted in big, blue block letters. On the opposite end, *Grambling* is emblazoned in red. People with television cameras on their shoulders wander across the field, but for now, the stands are empty.

The Southern women's uniforms reveal large swatches of brown skin. The light-blue fabric stops just under their chests, and a metallic ribbon wraps around their bare backs. The men wear baggy uniform tops the same color, and on their pants the same metallic ribbon slices down the side.

"We're a risqué school," says Coach James, who designs the team's uniforms. "It's never distasteful, but we push the button." Coach is also particular about how the women wear their hair—no bows or pony-tails. "They look more mature with their hair down. They can control the in-the-face thing because their hair doesn't move as much."

Across the field, the Grambling State cheerleaders practice a pyra-mid. Their team is huge—maybe forty people—and the aesthetic is the opposite of Southern's. The women's white tops look like nun-wear in comparison, with high necklines and no stomach showing whatsoever. As they build their pyramid, seven women are suspended in the air. Southern barely has seven women on their squad.

Fourteen years ago, Coach James was a cheerleader on Grambling's side of the field. His coach is still there—a tall man, with his arms crossed over his chest. "The biggest difference between our squads is that we have better stunters," says Coach James. "They have more ex-travagant pyramids."

The stands begin to fill with blue and red dots. Soon, the football teams walk onto the field, and balls fly through the air as they warm up. The Southern band enters in their full regalia—navy blue suits with a golden cape slung around their shoulders. On their heads, they wear furry hats that stand a foot tall.

A sophomore cheerleader, Lakeitha Harden, launches into a back handspring, but her foot buckles as she lands. She tries shaking it out, but she can't stand back up. James Turner scoops her up and walks her off the field. "I'll be back in a minute," she says to the squad as he plops her on the folding chair next to me.

"Aaaayy! Oohh!" the Southern fans chant as the band plays their fight song. Tarianne begins a catch-on. She steps seductively in a circle and crosses one hand over her stomach. With her butt to the crowd, she rolls her back slowly, like a belly dancer. To her right, Jasmine somehow makes the movements look modest, and on her left Chassity gives it a sugarcoated twist. Beside me, Lakeitha scoots to the edge of her chair and mimics each step as best she can while sitting down. "Go Jaguars!" she yells, as someone brings her a bag of ice.

There are just a few minutes until kickoff, and a pastor gives some introductory words. "Our Father, we thank you for the privilege of being back in New Orleans," he says. "Like Noah in the days after the flood, bless us. Bless these schools. Thank you for bringing us home."

The game begins. "Move it on down the field! Hey! Hey! Move it on down the field!" the cheerleaders chant as they do a funky step-touch. Lakeitha faithfully pumps her arms along with the squad, as if she's a student after a participation grade.

James, his wife, and several alumni cheerleaders sit in the folding chairs beside her. While Coach James discreetly cheers for Grambling, his wife is much more vocal. As Southern fumbles, she claps. One of the oldheads scowls at her.

Lacumba, Southern's mascot in a disheveled jaguar costume, walks toward us cradling a stuffed tiger in his arms. He pretends to be a doting father, tickling the tiger's forehead. But then he drops the tiger to the floor. He glances at it on the ground, lifts his elbow, and drops his body on it like a professional wrestler.

James's wife jumps up and picks up the doll. She holds it lovingly in her lap as she sits down, petting it like a real animal.

At halftime, Grambling State is up seven points. Southern's drum major, a slim guy with a fuzzy yellow hat towering over his head, marches the band onto the field, pumping a scepter in his hand like a nefarious nutcracker. He stops and places his hands on his knees. He rolls his body like a caterpillar, inching his back closer to the ground with each gyration. He tilts his head back so that the top of his hat rests on the AstroTurf. The audience screams.

Lakeitha, still unable to stand up, whistles. But I can tell she's been crying. "I've been waiting two years to cheer at the Bayou Classic," she says. "I didn't go last year because of Katrina. Now this year, my ankle."

While the band plays the halftime show, the cheerleaders run to the bathroom to change uniforms. They emerge in bright, look-at-me yellow uniforms. Since everything at the Bayou Classic is a grudge match, it doesn't surprise me that there's an informal battle of the cheerleaders at the start of the second half. Coach James motions for the squad to follow him, and they cross into Grambling territory. A few of the Grambling women give the Southern cheerleaders hugs—it's a battle, but a friendly one.

The Grambling cheerleaders sit down as the Jaguars walk to their marks for a short routine. Two women are lifted in the air facing each other, both holding their arms in an L to create a shape like a goalpost.

Behind them, a group sends a woman airborne for a basket toss called a Flyover. She sails through the air, arms out in front of her, going straight through the uprights like a perfectly kicked football. At the top of her arc, she tucks, and a second group of guys catches her in a cradle. The audience roars.

"Jaguar fans! In the stands! We're number one!" they chant together, ignoring the fact that they are facing Grambling's cheering section. As Southern finishes their routine, the Grambling cheerleaders clap like they've just seen a good tennis match. "That looked good," one of them says as they stand up for their turn.

They begin with simple motions and fewer acrobatics, but they end with the pyramid we saw them practice earlier—seven women zigzagging high in the air. Three more women are tossed through the empty spaces, creating another layer of intricacy. "We should be wiping the floor with them," says one of the Southern oldheads.

The stunt lines are next. Just as a high school band director picks a first chair for each instrument, each coach carefully watches his partner couples and lines them up from the weakest to the strongest. On the right side of the line, partners perform simple stunts. But as they progress left, the stunts become mini-routines—long strings of moves put together with creative flair.

The Grambling cheerleaders clap for the first four couples in Southern's line. Then Jasmine and Jarel step forward. Jasmine lies down on the grass and curls herself into fetal position. Jarel squats, cupping his hands over her feet as Jasmine locks her hands around his neck. Jarel swings her up overhead.

Jasmine faces the side of the arena. She curls into a Scorpion, her movements gentle in the air. Jarel gives her a slight boost, and she whips her body into a straight line. They high five as they step back into the line.

James Turner and Tarianne are next. James crouches down like a defensive lineman. Tarianne faces him, lifting a foot into his hands. They dip, and James tosses her five feet overhead. She swings her legs open into a split and drifts down. Her arms catch his shoulder, and his arms slide under her legs. "Wooo!" yells someone from the audience as

James bounces her in this spread-eagle position. The move is fitting for the sexy couple of the squad.

A second later, Tarianne shoots up like a rocket, James catching her feet overhead. Tarianne flexes both arms, her tiny biceps popping.

"She be doing like she's Hercules," someone says behind me.

Chassity and Tremayne, the top stunters in the line, step forward. It is no small accomplishment that the two of them are first. When Chassity tried out for the squad as a freshman, she had zero stunting experience. "Coach put me with Chassity because my old partner, we fought all the time," Tremayne once told me. "We didn't want to be the last, so we worked all summer. We shot for the number-one spot, and we got it."

Chassity stands in front of Tremayne, and he tosses her into an Awesome. He drops her into a cradle, her arms draping around his neck and her body forming a V. Their next move is called a Texas Tornado. Still cradling her back, Tremayne lets her legs go. Chassity straightens her body as her stomach rolls over Tremayne's back, like a bottle going round in a game of spin the bottle.

"That's crazy right there," someone says as Tremayne catches her legs again.

The Southern squad moves back to watch Grambling's stunt line. James Turner points to a man in the audience, a Joker grin on his face. It's his dad. "I wanted to make sure I did good 'cause my dad will say, 'You're dropping girls all over the place,'" says James. "Me and my dad always go back and forth in a fussing, joking kind of way."

It took a long time for James's dad to warm up to cheerleading. "My parents support me in everything I do, but I didn't tell my dad that I was trying out for the cheerleading squad," says James. "He saw me perform for the first time at a football game last year, but I didn't get too much reaction from him. He didn't say, 'Son, good job.' He's not that type of person."

Grambling State's stunt line is long, and many of their guys are bigger than the Southern men. But as the line begins, the stunts barely lift off the ground. Even at the top of their line, the couples show none of the ease of Southern's stunters. "We always show up the Grambling cheerleaders in stunts," says one of the Southern oldheads.

The Southern cheerleaders hug the Grambling State squad good-bye and jog back toward their side of the arena, visibly pumped up. "A-Let's Go Jag-uuaarrs!" yells James, bringing a blue megaphone to his mouth. "A-Let's go Big Blue!" Lakeitha chants along with them from her chair.

In the remainder of the game, Southern gets two more touchdowns. Chassity shakes her pom-poms over her head in celebration as her boy-friend, the quarterback, throws yet another completed pass. But Gram-bling will get one last possession. Their quarterback throws the ball for their final down, and it drifts dangerously close to the end zone for what would be a game-winning play. But as the ball drops to the AstroTurf just a few feet in front of the line, the Southern fans go crazy. They have shut Grambling State down. The band blasts their fight song.

A minute later the Bayou Classic is over. Southern has won. "Did you see the highlights!" yells Chassity, jumping up and down and tug-ging on her friend's arm. "My boyfriend got MVP. He's number 16, a quarterback. He didn't get to play much before Homecoming, but since then he's done so good."

Only one Southern fan looks sad—Lakeitha. Her foot is getting more swollen, and the football trainer who examined her foot during the second half said that she's going to need crutches. He used a phrase no cheerleader likes—"You should have a doctor look at that." Not only has Lakeitha missed out on cheering the most important game of the season, but she may not be able to cheer for the rest of the year.

# PART FOUR

BID VIDEOS
OCTOBER–DECEMBER

# CHAPTER 11

## "They Need a Little Cussing Out

## Sometimes, Bless Their Hearts."

### *The University of Memphis All-Girl Tigers*

THE HALLS OF THE Memphis Elite Cheer Station, Frankie's all-star gym, are like a mini cheerleading museum. Glass cases display championship jackets—silky black and white versions of the classic letterman—won by Memphis Elite teams nearly every year since 1992. Scattered around the jackets are dozens of medals, plus pictures of the teams who won them, beaming young faces in organized rows.

I peek into Frankie's office, but he's deeply engrossed in a phone conversation. I walk up a set of stairs, past a curly-haired thirteen-year-old sobbing uncontrollably, to a lounge with a wall of windows that overlooks the main gymnasium floor. In a row of wooden chairs facing the window, mothers sit like they're on the porch of a swank resort. Two of them discuss last year's Nationals. "I touched her face and she was burning up—she had a temperature of 103," one says. "I'm such a bad mom. I told her to just get over it."

The gym floor below reminds me of the orphanage in *Annie*—girls of all ages, heights, and hair colors are packed so densely you can almost smell the hyperactivity. A group of eight-year-olds practice their hand-springs, their tiny bodies folding over quickly. On the tumbling track, preteens bounce high on their lanky legs. Near them, a coach works with a girl who can't be more than four. In this gym, perfectionism is drilled in when they're young.

The walls of the lounge are plastered with team pictures and plaques, as well as several magazine and newspaper articles blown up four times larger than life. One is a piece Frankie wrote years ago. "Sound effects add much needed high points to your music. Use bings, boings, and bonks to spice up your routine," he writes. "People will look to their friends sitting next to them and say, 'Did you see *that?*' "

I head back downstairs to Frankie's office. The twisty black cord of his office phone is still held to his left ear, in addition to the cell phone now held up to his right ear. Even sitting down, Frankie hulks over his desk. His wire-rimmed glasses are perched on the top of his head, as usual. To his side, a window in the wall and another in the hall give him a view directly into the gym from his chair.

On a dry-erase board behind the desk, I LOVE YOU FRANKIE is written in bubbly letters. Near it, an ad that ran in the Memphis newspaper is pinned to a bulletin board. "Memphis Elite tryouts," the ad says. "We want *you*." Just like Uncle Sam.

Frankie's task for the day is getting the University of Memphis cheerleading calendars ready for printing. The calendars are filled with photos of the All-Girl, Coed, and Pom squads, with extra pages boasting ads for local businesses. "For our fund-raising, it's a big seller," says Frankie. "The printer prints them for free, and every team member has to sell $300 worth of ads."

Carol walks in, wearing a pink sweatshirt and a baseball cap, eyeliner rimming her eyes. She takes a seat on a couch, and Frankie tells her about a mother at the gym who got caught having an affair. "It's gossip central in here," he warns me.

For the past few weeks, Carol has worked with both the All-Girl and Coed squads on their "bid videos." In high school, cheerleading teams compete in regional competitions to qualify for Nationals. But because the college schedule is so crazy between classes and traveling with athletic teams, squads prove that they're good enough to go to

Nationals by sending in a video of their best cheering, tumbling, stunting, basket tossing, and pyramid building. The system is the same for both NCA and UCA, but teams submit a video to only one. Judges at each organization score the videos, rank the teams in all the divisions, and decide who should be invited to their Nationals.

By submitting a bid video, teams get a shot (or a second shot depending on their camp) at an all-expenses-paid bid. In each division, the crème de la crème will get this coveted prize. Partial bids are also given out to high ranking teams. With this carrot dangling in front of them, squads can spend months working on their bid videos.

The bid video system has its advantages. It's not a one-shot deal, so a team can shoot as many times as they need to get a component perfect. The catch is that the judges will be able to see it over and over, using slow motion and the pause button to catch tiny imperfections. Some squad members estimate that they'll do as many as thirty takes of a single move.

"How are the videos going?" Frankie asks Carol.

"Good," she says, taking a camcorder out of her backpack and hooking it up to a TV to show Frankie what each squad has taped so far.

"We have to do both of their cheers tonight," says Carol, as Frankie watches clips of the Coed squad.

"Coed seems like they're in a bubble," says Frankie. "They're not clueless, but—"

"Oh, they're clueless," says Carol. "They need a little cussing out sometimes, bless their hearts."

The first clip of the All-Girl squad is pretty amazing. Nine base/flyer pairs face each other in a horizontal line. Each flyer has a knee up, and her base grips her foot like she's going to boost her over a fence. The flyers push off, and the bases use all their might to stand up and lift, catching the flyer's second foot at shoulder-height. They hit these moves, called One-Man Walk-Ins, in a wave. The motion is smooth and easy, like a line of figure skaters lifting their partners above their heads.

"Wow," I say. "That's really cool."

"It's all technique and timing," says Carol. "The first night we tried them, six pairs hit. It took us three days for the others. We'll definitely do those for Nationals. It's a Coed stunt."

In the next clip, the squad stands in a triangle formation. They each do three Toe Touches, their legs flying out simultaneously to the sides. Once they land the final Toe Touch, they pull their knees up to their noses for a Back Tuck, all of the women landing on the same beat. Carol stops and rewinds the tape.

She points to a woman in the left corner. "Look," she says. As this girl flips, her hands brush the mat. The brunette beside her sees the mistake. She reaches out a hand and hits her on the side. Frankie and Carol laugh—both girls are still smiling on the tape like nothing happened.

"I didn't realize she fell. If you put your hands down, why not say something?" asks Carol. "We've already taped that ten times."

As we watch more of the video, Frankie seems pleased by some clips and disappointed by others. "That's sloppy city," he says, watching the squad's basket tosses.

"What are the chances of the All-Girl squad getting a paid bid this year?" I ask.

"It's higher than it's been in the past," says Frankie. His voice perpetually sounds like he's reading a bedtime story. "They barely missed it last year. The UCA is actually talking about splitting the bid up between teams—one team wins airfare, one team wins hotel. It's better to split it, because there's only one paid bid for All-Girl."

"Meanwhile, there's like a dozen paid bids for Coed teams," says Carol.

Frankie looks up at us. "Time flies," he says. "Seems like we were just at tryouts making fun of people."

## "Front-Row Girls Have to Be Cheesy."

It's 8:30 p.m. and the University of Memphis cheerleading practice will be starting momentarily in the Cheer Station gym. The last few minutes have been like listening to popcorn in the microwave. At first, there were rapid-fire bursts of noise as women ran through the door. Now the time between sounds has slowed to once every few minutes.

Near me, Monica stretches. "How has taping been going?" I ask her.

"Most years, I feel like we're going to win, but this year I don't know."

"What's different about this year?" I ask.

"We have so many new people," she says. "There's lots of talent, but we're really still rebuilding."

On the wall, Carol has taped up motivational signs. "Pain is temporary, pride is forever," reads one. "Somewhere, someone is working harder than you," taunts another. And my personal favorite: "If you don't think the grass is green here, you might be the one making it brown."

"Don't you love the quotes?" asks Callee Jackson, one of the squad's best flyers. Callee is the kind of woman cast as the pretty girl in '80s teen movies. She's a junior on the squad and often gets the honor of topping pyramids. Because of her position as a third layer flyer, she's one of the few women on the squad who constantly expresses body woes. At a Japanese restaurant the other night she stared at her fried rice. "My bases are gonna kill me," she said. "I'm the one who made Carol weigh in us top girls—it gives me a line I can watch. Carol was like, 'You can weigh in by yourself,' and I said, 'No, we all should.' I know I wouldn't want to pick up a big girl."

The Cheer Station's architecture is industrial, with vaulted white ceilings and visible piping. Blue mats cover 75 percent of the floor. On the far wall, a mural depicts women doing cheerleading moves, the word M ELITE in block letters under them. Shelves hung around the room display dozens of multicolored trophies. Through the window to Frankie's office, I see that he's still parked at his desk on the phone.

Carol stares at a clipboard, barely looking up at the women. Tonight, the All-Girl and Coed squads will practice together. Carol has put the camcorder away—the agenda is to choreograph both squads' cheers. It seems to be almost everyone's least favorite part of the bid video process.

"Work on your 2-2-1s for the cheer," Carol tells the All-Girl squad, as she walks across the gym to work with Coed.

The women quickly devolve into chatter. Kristen tries to keep them in order, but when Carol looks over a few minutes later, all she sees is one woman walking on her hands. "Guys, 2-2-1s. Three of them. Get in your groups and show me your Shoulder Stands," she yells.

Six bases line up across the mat, their flyers in back of them. The flyers climb onto their bases' shoulders, many of them gritting their teeth. Monica looks down at the muscular woman below her. "Do you like holding me?" she asks sweetly. Her base looks up and nods.

It takes twenty minutes for Carol to lay out the design of the cheer. As six Shoulder Stands go up, a group of women across the front of the mat do Back Tucks. They each pick up a sign and chant, "T! I! G! E! R! S! Tii-gers!" holding their letter in front of them as they walk backwards to meet the Shoulder Stands. They lift their signs up and the flyers grab them. They chant again. The top women throw the signs to the side, and the three sets of Shoulder Stands take a step toward each other to form three 2-2-1 pyramids. A top flyer is tossed straight through the middle of each pair, the women in the Shoulder Stands scooping their legs and holding them in place.

Or at least that's how it's supposed to go. But the squad barely gets through the first half. "Stop, stop," yells Carol. "I know this is stupid, but front-row girls have to be cheesy. Do not be boring."

I quietly ask Monica what Carol means by "boring." "It means we're just doing the motions," she explains, tightening her blonde ponytail. "You're supposed to get the crowd into it. We're supposed to do jumps and Back Tucks, wave our pom-poms, scream, and smile. We're supposed to fight for attention." At competition and on their videos, the team will get a mark for their facial expressions and enthusiasm. Winks, head bobs, and other exaggerated gestures are encouraged.

The women get back into their starting position. As they run through again, Carol turns to watch the Coed squad across the mat. "What are you doing?" she bellows. The Coed women hop down from their stunts, the floor shaking as they land at the same time.

Carol turns to me. "Now you see why I don't like to have the squads practice together. Coed needs someone to babysit them," she says. "Frankie's always saying, 'Why are you here so late? Have them practice together,' but I'd rather be here till one in the morning and be able to give each team my full attention."

Carol stuffs her hands in her pockets as she turns back to watch All-Girl, who are midway through their cheer. The women in the front row beam as they thrust their signs in front of them. Since it's a practice run, they've grabbed random signs. The letters on them spell: T-J-G-E-I-S.

Carol doesn't mind the bizarre spelling, but she does notice one flyer in the air. "Could you say the words?" she yells. "Your mouth isn't moving at all."

"At least our cheer is going to look better than theirs," someone whispers, motioning toward Coed.

Both squads begin again, Carol watching with a serious expression. She waves her hands in the air. "Stop," she says, her voice much louder than normal. "I don't think the word *sharp* is in anyone's vocabulary in this gym tonight. Your motions have to be clean. When you're holding a sign, punch it out in front of you."

Carol swings back to the Coed squad. "You guys look like you've never done a 2-2-1," she says in her speedy Southern accent. "If these girls on All-Girl can hold a Shoulder Stand better than you, something's wrong. You top girls need to lose weight. Push back the plate and get in here and work out."

Carol looks exasperated. She turns to me, as if to justify her outburst. "It's stupid to have all this cool stuff on their videos and then have the cheer look like crap," she says.

As the squad runs through the cheer again, it looks like a different group. If someone yelled at me the way coaches are famous for, I'd disobey out of spite. But maybe Carol is right, maybe teams do need to be cussed out sometimes. Because the cheer looks better—much better. Their motions sharpen. Their faces register thrilled instead of merely happy. Their stunts stick cleanly. Their pyramids look solid.

"I'm used to coaches jumping down my throat," says Casi as the squad finishes for the night. "When Carol yells, it motivates me. It means that stunt's gonna go 100 feet high."

## "Will You Marry Me?"

"I don't like old people," says one of the All-Girl cheerleaders sitting on the curb outside the Parkview Retirement Community, which looks more like a regal hotel than a nursing home. In addition to all their other duties, cheerleaders often devote time to community service. The squad has two hours until practice, and in the meantime, they'll be today's afternoon entertainment.

Ten cheerleaders, from both the All-Girl and Coed squads, wait on the curb in their blue-and-white uniforms. "They're old people, but there's not like anything wrong with them, right?" asks Ashley Chambers, as if we're about to walk into a leper colony.

Casi plays with the strings on her sweatshirt. "I hope we don't have practice later," she says. "I'm about to lose my job. They're always like, 'Can't you skip practice?' I'm like, 'If I could, then I'd be here all the time.'"

"No practice—yeah, right," someone says.

Casi shrugs. "What else do we have to tape?" she asks.

"The cheer," says Ashley. Everyone groans—they are still not over the annoyance of learning it the other night.

Kristen walks up to the curb with several other squad members in tow. "I love doing this," she says. "It's making someone else's grandparents happy the way I'd want someone to make my grandparents happy." The squad follows her up the stairs and through the door.

As we walk into a lobby filled with club chairs, an old woman with curly white hair stops in her tracks, her face lighting up at the sight of the cheerleaders. They wave and continue toward the ballroom, where a brass chandelier hangs over a parquet floor. About twenty elderly people sit in a semicircle of chairs. Smiles drift across their faces as the cheerleaders walk in.

A man in his forties, the home's entertainment director, stands up. "We're delighted to have the University of Memphis cheerleaders," he says. "They went to school all day, then they came here to see you." The crowd gives a wimpy round of applause.

The squads split into four lines, Kristen in the middle of the front row. "G! O!" she yells, her face telegraphing enthusiasm almost to the point of insincerity. The rest of the cheerleaders join her. "G! O! Go Tigers, Gooo!" they yell together, jogging in place. An old man bobs his head along with the staccato words.

The squads begin a medley of cheers. A Coed guy tosses a flyer into the air. The audience gasps, worrying that she may hit the ceiling. But she lands with about four inches' clearance. "That's scary," she says, tapping it with her hand.

The entertainment director laughs. "When we have social hour, our residents get that high," he jokes.

The cheerleaders disperse to converse with the nursing home residents. Kristen spots an old man and woman holding hands. "Hi. I'm Kristen," she says, with that high-pitched voice people adopt when talking to children.

"Thank you for coming today," says the old man sheepishly.

The woman shows Kristen a photograph. "You remind me of my granddaughter," says the woman. "She's a cheerleader, too."

While most of the cheerleaders don't quite know what to say to the senior citizens, Casi seems natural talking to them. She stands beside two men in chairs at the entrance to the ballroom. One of them is bald with beady eyes. The other has bright gray hair combed to the side. They banter like the eighty-year-old's answer to *Beavis and Butt-Head*.

Nearby Callee talks to a cute old woman. "Cheerleading's a lot of work, but I wish I could do it forever," says Callee.

The woman looks her in the eye. "These years go by fast, so you enjoy them. Before you know it, you're in a nursing home," she laughs.

Kristen walks toward the front of the room. A tall, noble-looking man reaches out and grabs her wrist. "Will you marry me?" he asks.

"My boyfriend probably won't like that very much," says Kristen.

The cheerleaders line up again, and the University of Memphis fight song plays on a boom box. The two squads spring into action, but they do not mesh well since they stand on opposite ends of the football field, they rarely perform together. They are horribly offbeat from each other, and their pom-poms don't move in unison. But the senior citizens don't seem to notice. They watch longingly, as if they're seeing themselves fifty years ago.

## "I Don't Regret Choosing Cheerleading, But You Know . . ."

A pink highlighter is parked at the top of Kristen's desk, resting on her light-purple Trapper Keeper. She hunches over the desk as she takes notes, blonde hair cascading over her gray Memphis sweatshirt. Every minute or so, she uncaps the highlighter and makes a steady pink line across the page.

We're a half hour into Kristen's American History 1865–Present class, and her professor is comparing Abraham Lincoln welcoming the South back into the Union to the story of the Prodigal Son. "It was treating the South like little kids," she says. "Like, 'That's okay. You got mad and broke your toy.'"

This professor is determined to be cool. Earlier, she said it was no problem if students got phone calls during class. And as she describes a research project, she says, "If everyone gets an A, we'll go get a keg or something."

Kristen laughs and fishes for her day planner in her backpack. She writes down the due dates for the project in swirly handwriting, highlighting them in pink. On the pages of her planner, team events seem to be highlighted in blue. Holidays are in green. It's easy to see why Carol selected Kristen as this year's All-Girl captain. She's organized and experienced—this is, after all, her fifth year of college cheerleading.

As a child, Kristen auditioned for *The Mickey Mouse Club.* "I wanted to show them that I could tumble, but a few days before, I'd been running around and fell on a nail. So at my audition, I tumbled on one arm." The casting directors were interested, but Kristen was eight, and the minimum age for the show was ten. "They kept my tape on file and called two years later. By then, I had already gotten really involved in cheerleading, so I said no. *Big* mistake," she says.

She quickly backtracks. "Well, not mistake. I don't *regret* choosing cheerleading. But you know . . ." I get it. Britney Spears, Christina Aguilera, Justin Timberlake, Keri Russell, and Ryan Gosling all got their start wearing Mickey ears.

History class is over, and Kristen goes to check her email and Facebook inbox. She belongs to a dozen Facebook groups, including ESPN Addicts, Former Catholic School Girl and Proud of It, and Cheerleading Gets Me Into Crazy Situations. Kristen points to a picture of herself in uniform beside a fair-haired guy on a football field. "That's my boyfriend," she says. "He plays football for Memphis."

She points to another friend on her page. "She's getting married, but I can't go because I have a game at the same time," she says. "Cheerleading comes first."

We drive to Kristen's house, a white one-story, complete with a porch and trellis. Inside, it's neat and orderly, with real furniture—no milk crates. Kristen's bed is made, and it's piled high with pillows and dolls. I spot a Memphis cheerleader doll with pigtails and pick it up. "Squeeze its hand," she says.

The doll comes to life, chanting, "Cookies! Cookies! Cookies and Cream! What's the matter with the other team?" Kristen laughs.

Lindsey, Kristen's roommate and a cheerleader on the Coed squad, walks in. "She dates a football player, too," says Kristen. "And our other roommate dates a baseball player."

"So the stereotype is true?" I kid them.

"Yeah, it's a cliché," says Kristen. "But we're not cleat chasers. We're good athletes and we love sports—we wouldn't have anything in common with someone who wasn't athletic. We're built muscular, so we want a guy who is, too."

For months, I've been hearing from All-Girl cheerleaders who resent the Coed squad because they're seen as the more important ones despite their less winning record. But as Kristen and Lindsey talk about bid videos, Kristen doesn't seem at all bitter. "Carol's tried very hard to split it up so that she gives us equal time," she says. "We're all old enough that if she tells us to do something, we can do it."

"How did you decide which team to try out for?" I ask them.

"Well, All-Girl does more tumbling and I can't tumble," says Lindsey. "I just stunt better with guys. I like *high* baskets."

"And I'm a little on the tall side for Coed—I'm probably taller than some of the guys," says Kristen.

"I saw you guys doing Shoulder Stands at practice," says Lindsey. "I can't believe you guys can do that. My boyfriend's always like, 'I couldn't do what cheerleaders do.'"

Kristen smiles. "Football may be harder, but we get hurt almost as much. Cheerleading's the number-one cause for injuries in women's sports," she says, sounding proud, like the statistic somehow legitimizes her hard work.

## "Is He Lying?"

The Memphis sky has turned slate gray. As I walk to a side door of the FedEx Forum, rain begins to pour down like water from a faucet. I've forgotten an umbrella, so I run, pounding into the metal bar of the double doors at full speed. The door gives way, and I walk into the arena's bright white hallway, dripping with each step.

The FedEx Forum, which opened two years ago, is home to Memphis's NBA team, the Grizzlies, as well as to the University of Memphis's basketball team. The Tigers will be starting their season in a few weeks, and today the All-Girl and Coed cheerleaders have been summoned for a kickoff party, where the athletic department will sell basketball season ticket subscriptions. The cheerleaders often make appearances at university and athletic department events to drum up enthusiasm—it's part of what makes them local celebrities.

As I round a corner, I see nine of the All-Girl cheerleaders standing in a circle in the forum's front foyer. Their top halves are dressed for the storm outside, bundled in heavy sweatshirts and warm-up jackets. But their bottom halves look disproportionately bare—thin, goose-fleshed legs exposed under short skirts. The group smells familiar, though it takes me a second to place the scent: Herbal Essences shampoo.

It's a bit ironic that the squad is here today for a basketball event. The squad doesn't actually cheer at University of Memphis men's basketball games—that honor goes to the Coed squad. "You know what we should do," says one of the women. "Why don't we just show up at a basketball game and say, 'We're cheering today.' "

Callee rolls her eyes. "There will be some excuse for us to cheer in the rafters," she says. Callee reminds me of a cartoon character when she speaks, her face registering outraged, sad, and annoyed expressions in rapid succession.

"For big games, we get to cheer, but only in the top sections," one of the women explains to me. "Last year, the security guards gave us a hard time. And the fans were like, 'Move. I can't see.' "

"We could get to the games really early and sit in the front row in our uniforms and just start cheering," says Monica matter-of-factly. Some of the others nod in agreement.

A woman in a skirt-suit interrupts the conversation, pointing to several boxes of Memphis shirts, bags, and beer cozies. The cheerleaders' mission today is to pass out free University of Memphis paraphernalia to the fans who are trickling into the forum. Near us, members of the athletic department sit at a table, ready to sell subscriptions. Thirty yards away, on a stage, an interviewer thrusts a microphone in the face of a Memphis basketball coach while a small crowd of fans hangs onto his every word.

The cheerleaders will pass out gifts in the center of the foyer. "I want one," says Callee, reaching into a box and pulling out one of the Memphis backpacks.

"They're for the *fans*," says Monica, giving her a disapproving look. Monica walks up to an elderly man and woman and hands them a T-shirt. She picks up a backpack and scurries over to another couple. "I'm gonna quiz you," she says, locking her turquoise eyes with a forty-something man in a Hawaiian shirt. "What color is Pouncer?"

"Orange," answers the man, sounding unsure of both his answer and why she's asking him this in the first place.

"Yay," says Monica, clapping. "The backpack's yours." She puts it in his hand and he examines it.

Across the room, Ashley Chambers hands out beer cozies to everyone who passes. Her acrylic nails are intense—striped with black and blue polish. This is one of the few times I've seen her without Courtney at her side.

The event has reached its apex—since it's pouring outside, only fifty people have shown up. Monica walks up to me, her hands behind her back. "Kate's a fan," she says, giving me a small brown velvet purse. "Thanks for coming out today," she says with a wink.

Half an hour later, the boxes are empty, and Callee is still clinging for dear life to the backpack she likes. "I swear to God," says Monica, sounding uncharacteristically stern. "Give it away. *Now.*"

I notice an All-Girl cheerleader with blue glitter all over her eyelids, standing across the room, talking to a mysterious woman at the athletic department table. The cheerleader's hands are crossed in front of her chest, and from far away I can see her nostrils flaring. But since I can't hear what the two are talking about, I watch as Callee sheepishly approaches a woman in her fifties and hands her the coveted backpack.

All of a sudden, the blue-glittered cheerleader runs over to us. "That woman just told me that we have a big-time sponsor. We're always hearing that we have no money," she says, sounding ready to pick a fight. Whoever this woman at the table is, she seems to think that the cheerleading program is a moneymaking operation rather than one that needs constant fund-raising.

The rest of the cheerleaders quickly gather around. "A sponsor?" says Monica, confused. "Who is it?"

This news, whether it's true or not, sends the cheerleaders into a tailspin. They get $500 scholarships each semester, which barely covers the cost of books; they give a huge chunk of their time to the squad; and they're often asked to fund-raise for the program by installing VIP seats at the Liberty Bowl or selling team calendars. They've been led to believe that the squad bank account is perpetually on empty, and the idea that there could be more money than they realized unleashes a floodgate of complaints.

Callee turns around to show me the back of her uniform, where two safety pins hold her skirt in place. She puts her finger through a big rip in the side of her top. "Look, we have holes in our uniforms," she says.

"When we get shirts, we have to pay for them ourselves," someone says.

"We don't even have the same shoes," says another. The comments are coming so rapid-fire that I can't keep track of who is speaking.

"Frankie tells us that he can't give us full scholarships," says one woman, sounding desperate.

"He always tells us that he's going to meetings trying to change that. Is he lying?" asks someone else, her voice trailing up an octave.

"We had a nice bus last year," someone chimes in. "But the band kicked us off and the school gave us an old bus. At the last away game, we stayed at the most ghetto hotel. We found out some girl had been killed there."

"Every other school has a trainer who comes to practice," says another cheerleader. "We don't. If our ankle's hurt, we have to tape it ourselves. And then we have to go to the football trainer the next day."

The women stand in a circle, a few of them on the brink of tears. Some of them seem to be imagining a scenario where someone is embezzling money that's rightfully theirs. Others seem more like jealous siblings worried that their parents are giving more love and attention to their brothers and sisters, a.k.a. the Coed and Pom squads.

It's a shame that the women don't feel like they're being taken care of to the highest degree, but I don't think anything shady is going on. It costs *a lot* of money to fund a top cheerleading team, and together the three Memphis teams (Coed, All-Girl, and Pom) are only allotted $36,000 a year. The University of Memphis program relies on a steady stream of sponsors and fund-raisers to keep them in the black—without them, they would be struggling financially, like Southern's team.

The one thing that I wish would change is the scholarship situation. Earlier in the year, Frankie explained to me why he can't give bigger scholarships to All-Girl. While the university covers twelve full scholarships for the Coed squad, Frankie pays for the All-Girl scholarships out of the program's budget. "All-Girl really should get full rides because they go to class and make 3.8 GPAs," he said. "But that would cost $20,000." In other words, if they got full scholarships, they wouldn't have money to compete. Surely none of them would want that.

The foyer is empty now. The TV crew has shut off their cameras, and all the fans have hoisted their umbrellas and run back into the rain. I suggest that we go get some food at a nearby diner. The women gather their belongings, and we walk in silence. They're clearly still upset.

"I'd be happy with new shoes," one of them says.

"I'll take a new coach," says someone else. "Carol's got too much on her plate."

"If I wasn't such a Tiger fan, there's no way I'd do this," says Ashley, shaking her head. "I'm in it for the love of the game."

Monica sweeps her hair into a ponytail. She doesn't seem convinced of a conspiracy, either. "We don't know the full story," she says. "So we can't complain."

"Unless we win a paid bid to Nationals," says the girl with the glittery eyes, in a eureka moment. "Then there's no excuse that we don't have money."

"But we never win it," responds Monica.

"Well, this year we better," she snaps.

### "Coed Squads Are Wussies Compared to Us."

Our table at the Big Foot Lodge, a diner in downtown Memphis, is smack in front of the window. The manager has calculated that eight beautiful women, most of them in short skirts, will draw a crowd. As people walk by the window, they crane their necks to see the cheerleaders in their full regalia. The restaurant walls are covered in kitschy wood paneling and taxidermied deer heads.

As we talk, the cheerleaders seem to have put aside the frustration of the last hour. They've gone through one favorite subject—*Grey's Anatomy*—and have moved on to talking about guys. "Did you kiss him?" one of the girls asks Alicia, a pretty freshman with light brown hair and almond-shaped eyes.

She nods, with a slight blush. "But I don't want a boyfriend," she says. "My last boyfriend was so sweet, but he was around all the time. I don't want someone stuck up my butt."

"Play him like a fool," says Monica. The leader of the group, she always seems to have inside information. "Trust me, he told me that he's not interested in a relationship."

One of the women launches into a story about a guy who's been calling her—only he's also sort-of seeing a girl on the Coed squad. "One minute, he'll call me like, 'What are you up to?' " she says, adjusting her headband. "Then I see him ten minutes later with her, and he acts like he doesn't even know who I am. I don't want someone who's gonna be like that."

"She has really bad motions," says Monica, talking about the other girl's cheering skills. " 'Cause that defines a person," she jokes as the rest of the girls crack up.

"Guys are so sneaky, I hate them," says Ashley, stabbing at her appetizer.

Monica lets it slip that she is dating someone new. The women at the table all turn to her and prod her for a clue as to who he is. "Nope, I won't say," she protests.

"I know," someone says, and Monica covers her face with her hands.

I actually know, too. After the disintegration of her relationship with the boyfriend I'd met at the Tennessee game, Monica met James,

Kristen's older brother, who coached the cheerleaders' flag football team. They instantly hit it off and started dating about a month ago. She hasn't told Kristen yet, but Monica knows that she'll need to soon. For now, it's a secret.

"I fall in love so easily," says Monica. "I'm just addicted to the kill, to getting them. Then I'm like, 'See you.'"

The women start discussing the trainer situation. "Erica, a girl on our squad, went into the football trainer because she hurt her arm. You could tell she was so hurt, but she didn't want to cry because she was in a room full of guys. They just gave her ice for it," says Alicia. "She's out this week because she's having surgery on her arm. I hope those trainers found out that it wasn't something you just put ice on."

It's a valid complaint. While some schools do have a trainer who works specifically with their cheerleaders, the majority don't. With the number of pulls, sprains, and concussions they experience, I still find it scandalous that cheerleaders don't automatically get trainers. It seems like such an easy solution.

"After a girl broke her neck, you'd think that we'd have them," says one of the women.

I nearly choke on a fried green tomato. "What happened?" I ask.

The women exchange glances. "Our friend on Coed broke her neck," explains Monica. "I was there. We were working on a pyramid for Nationals. She did a Front Flip off the top into a cradle. She made a mistake—she didn't flip, she just slid and no one caught her. She just lay there on the floor. We all freaked out. She wasn't moving, we didn't know if she was breathing. When the ambulance came, they didn't know if she was going to be okay. She's recovered now, but she can't cheer anymore. When she turns her head, she has to turn her whole body. It's really sad—she was a really good cheerleader. It was no one's fault—it just happened—but it irks me that we still don't get trainers."

It's interesting that even when severe injuries hit this close to home, they don't have a visible impact on the women. None of them wince as Monica tells this story—no one throws down her napkin and says, "I quit" or even, "That scares the mess out of me." They seem inured to it, and that might be adaptive—fear actually makes it more likely that they'll get hurt. Most of the injuries I've heard about happened when someone panicked in the air, letting her nerves take hold of her and preventing her from going forward in the way her bases expected.

Our waiter walks toward us from the kitchen, trays of food in hand. For a few minutes there's silence as we attack our meals. One of the women looks up from her plate. "I really want that paid bid," she says, wiping sauce from the side of her mouth.

I've been watching the team work on their bid videos for weeks, and while their material looks great to my untrained eye, it's hard to judge where they stand when there's not another team to compare them to. "What do you think your chances are?" I ask.

"Pretty good," says Monica, contradicting what she said a few days ago.

"For All-Girl, there's only one paid bid," one of the women points out. "*One*. It's frustrating because we're as good a competition as Coed."

"And people are saying this is the fiercest All-Girl field ever," says Monica.

"Who's your main competition?" I ask. In complete unison, the women say, "Morehead State."

The Morehead State University All-Girl squad is good. Though they didn't win at Nationals last year, they've dominated for years, winning five National Championships since the late '90s. They almost always get first place in bid videos.

"What have you filmed so far that you're proudest of?" I ask.

"Our 1-1-1s," one of the women says definitively. A 1-1-1 is a tough pyramid that few All-Girl teams can even attempt. A middle layer woman climbs on the shoulders of an extremely strong base. She lifts her knee to a 90-degree angle, and two bases brace her foot. Then a top flyer is launched up and lands standing on the middle layer's thigh. "It's the exact same thing the boys do on Coed squads, only we do it with smaller bases and bigger top girls."

Alicia pipes in. "If you think about it, the Coed squads are wussies compared to us. Give us those little Coed girls, and we can do anything."

"I gained three pounds this year and I got cussed out," says another freshman.

Monica takes the big-sister role again. "I got pills that take the fatty acids you eat and break them down. That's how some of those Coed girls got so small. If you saw them freshman year, you would have said, 'Dang, they're huge.'"

"Does that cost a lot of money?" asks Ashley.

"Like eighty dollars a month," says Monica. "When I'm on the beach, I'm confident that I have the best body out there. But when I get around y'all I get self-conscious."

One of the women nods. "You don't want to be the one at a game people point to and are like, 'Ugh,'" she says.

"I understand why you hear about actresses who compete to be skinny or who don't think they're beautiful," says Monica. "When you surround yourself with girls this pretty all the time, you can be really hard on yourself. Everyone in the cheer world is gorgeous, and you just want to be as cute as everybody else." Everyone at the table nods.

### "That's a *Joke*."

Carol dropped the University of Memphis All-Girl bid video in the mail a few days ago. The results won't be posted online until tomorrow morning, but after years of experience, Carol knows that the UCA office will be making calls today to tell the coaches where they stand. Like college hopefuls who pray for a thick envelope, Carol has noticed that teams who win paid bids get called early in the afternoon since there are so many arrangements to be made. The rest are called later.

It's now 7 p.m., and All-Girl practice will be starting in just a few minutes. Carol is getting nervous. Finally, her phone rings. She steps into the Cheer Station office and shuts the door.

She emerges about fifteen minutes later, her mouth in a straight line. "We got fourth," she sighs. "And this year, they decided to give out three paid bids in the All-Girl division. They told me it was between us and Indiana for that third paid bid, but they put us in fourth. It's a shock, but the girls are just going to have to man up, raise the money, and move along."

Inside the gym, the women are stretching. Courtney jumps up and down, a box of Nerds in her hand. "Can I get some?" asks one of the other cheerleaders. Courtney pours a handful into her palms. "Yay, energy fix," she says, placing the red dots on her tongue.

Monica sits nearby, her blonde hair in a low ponytail. As she takes off the sweats she wears over her cheer shorts, I notice a bandage on her leg. "I got a wart removed," she explains. "Kristen was always talking about it—she thought it was gross that when we do stunts she had to touch it all the time."

Carol half walks, half runs into the gym. The women turn and stare at her, knowing that she'll have news. "So guess what?" Carol yells as she approaches the team. "We got fourth."

"What?" asks Monica desperately.

"I was thinking at least second," says Kristen. "All the stuff on our tape was really, really good."

Callee's face scrunches up like she's smelled something foul. "That's disappointing," she says.

"You want to know something else?" says Carol. The women stare at her like she's about to tell them the secret of life. "They gave out *three* paid bids for All-Girl this year."

"What?!?" says Monica, shocked and upset.

"And we got *fourth*? That's a *joke*," says Casi.

Kristen looks confused. "We did One-Man Walk-Ins that only guys can usually do, and we did a lot of them," she says.

"At least it means All-Girl is moving on up," says Casi, looking for the silver lining.

Two of the freshmen women look crushed, and Carol attempts to reassure them. "Taping results don't mean diddly squat," she says. "It doesn't mean any other teams are better than you—all it means is that they get their way paid. Anyone can win."

The women try to brush the news aside for practice. But as she goes home later that night, Monica is still upset. She sits in her sea-foam blue room, which is decorated with a mermaid theme. She calls a friend who is high up in the UCA. What her friend tells her—whether it's true or not—does not cheer her up.

"I heard there were some fights in the UCA office about it," she explains. "Some of the judges thought that even though we did those

Sierra Jenkins and
James Brown

Coach Trisha O'Connor

Kali Rae Seitzer

Ashley Picard

Samantha Frazer and
Tyrone Lyons

Yvette Quiñones

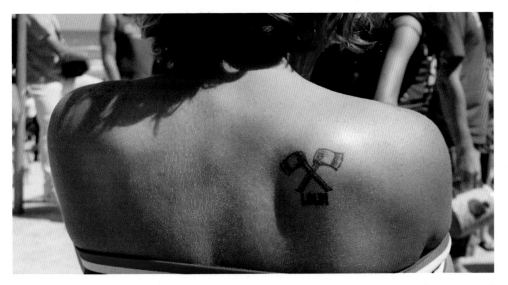

For the SFA cheerleaders, the letters LCLM are everywhere—on their shirts, backpacks, pillowcases, and jewelry. It's even tattooed on many of them.

The SFA cheerleaders practice before finals at the NCA Collegiate Cheer National Championship.

On stage at finals, giving the performance of their lives. That's Sierra in the front.

The SFA cheerleaders nail their pyramid. Ashley, Yvette, and Samantha scream their hearts out from the top.

Tarianne Green
and James Turner

Jasmine Smutherman

Japaul Winston

Jarel Small

Coach James Smith

Chassity Crittenden and
Tremayne Baker

After a prayer, the Southern cheerleaders say a quick chant before running on stage.

The Southern women sail up for the big pyramid. Tarianne stands in the center.

The pyramid morphs—that's Chassity on the top left and Jasmine on the top right.

Kristen Murdock

Coach Carol Lloyd

Courtney Powell and Ashley Chambers

Casi Davis

Monica Moody

Kristen Kern

The Memphis Tigers strike a pose before heading to compete in the UCA College Cheerleading Championship.

The Memphis women practice at Walt Disney World's All-Star Sports Resort the night before finals.

An audience gathered to watch them rehearse.

The Memphis Tigers send their flyers overhead to a round of applause.

Sandwiched between other teams at the awards ceremony, the women wait to see how they have placed.

One-Man Walk-Ins on tape, we'd never take a chance on doing them at Nationals. That's just stupid—we can obviously do it."

Monica isn't ready to throw out the idea of a conspiracy. "We've never gotten below second on taping, so I don't know what the deal is," she says. "Maybe it's because they know we have money, so they gave it to a squad that doesn't."

Even though she's frustrated, she is happy about one thing—that the UCA upped the number of paid bids they gave to All-Girl teams. "I'm thrilled that they're finally supporting us more," she says, sighing.

# CHAPTER 12

## "Pretend Like It's Nationals Every Time."

*The Stephen F. Austin Lumberjacks*

SIERRA'S CHEERLEADING SHOES LIE abandoned on the mat. Every square inch of the formerly white leather is covered in pink, blue, green, and purple swirls, hearts, and doodles. "Was she on shrooms when she made these?" asks one of the SFA guys, picking up a sneaker. Sierra sees him holding it out of the corner of her eye and darts across the gym. She wrestles the shoe free with her left hand—her right is still in the tan soft cast. She plops down on the mat and laces up her sneakers.

It's Friday afternoon, and the SFA cheerleaders are filing into the gym. Practice will be intense today; the team has started working on their bid video. After years of dominating Division 1 at NCA, it's almost expected that SFA will be the top qualifier. But—a big disadvantage of the bid video system—no team can see what any other team has up their sleeves. Come Nationals time, they'll have no idea what they're up against.

"Who've you been stunting with?" yells a guy across the gym as he hurls his partner in the air. He sounds like he's confronting his wife about having an affair.

"Everyone," says his partner with a sheepish grin.

"Don't *do* that," he snaps. "I can tell."

A guy standing near me explains the exchange. "So much of what makes good partners is having good timing. So you're territorial about other people stunting with your partner," he says.

Sierra and James Brown stand in the back corner of the mat. After two weeks of sitting out of practice, Sierra wanted to see if she could stunt without putting pressure on her right hand. "I asked James Brown if he wanted to try and he said, 'I don't want to get hit in the face with that thing.' So I started stunting with someone else. We were doing Rewinds, Full-Ups. Trisha said, 'Good job, Sierra,' and James Brown got all pissed off."

Once she realized that she could still cheer, there was no convincing Sierra to get the hard cast that her doctors recommended. "They have to rebreak my hand and put pins in to hold it," she says. "I can't do that now. I'll get that surgery *after* Nationals." Sierra is sure of this plan, but it's not the kind of thing a doctor likes to hear.

Even though Sierra has jumped right back into practice, the time she missed was vital. Stunt couples, just like teams, must shoot a bid video to earn a spot in the Partner Stunt Competition at Nationals. While Sierra sat on the sidelines, the other partner couples were working on their videos for UCA Nationals. SFA won't compete as a team until April at NCA Nationals, but to assert their total dominance in partner stunting, they send a select group of couples to the UCA competition as well. The program will pay for the four couples who place the highest out of the team. Couples who place lower can pay their own way and go, too.

While Sierra was sitting out of practice, James Brown—having no idea that she'd recover so quickly—asked another flyer to be his partner. "This is my last year cheering, and I'm not willing to pass up UCA Partner Stunt," he explained several weeks ago, his voice always meeker than I expect from such a daunting presence. "My goal has always been to win a Partner Stunt. I have to try to make that happen with somebody."

There's still two weeks until UCA bid videos are due. But even though Sierra is now able to cheer again, James Brown isn't backing out on his word to his new partner.

Sierra thinks at least an ounce of spite went into his decision. "I don't know if he did it because he was mad at me or if he did it because he's trying to get a piece of her, but it breaks my heart," says Sierra. "I want to go to UCA Partner Stunt so bad."

When it comes to the team video, Sierra and James Brown are still partners. But their relationship is strained. And today, none of their stunts are sticking. James Brown paces in a circle, shaking his large head. Sierra runs over to her bag and takes out her phone. "James Brown is crying about how he's blinded by the colors on my shoes," she says to a friend, her painted-on eyebrows lifted. "Can you bring me my white ones?" There's a pause. "Thank you, thank you, thank you," she says.

A few feet away, Samantha and Tyrone practice their bid video routine. Tyrone's arm begins to shake as he holds Samantha in an Awesome. "What's happening?" she asks as she quakes in the air. "Keep going," Tyrone yells, adjusting his grip.

"That feels better," she says.

The people in the center of the mat part like the Red Sea as a bare-chested tumbler runs through, flipping and kicking. "Did you lose your shirt?" Trisha asks sarcastically, scratching her head like she's confused.

Samantha follows him down the cleared path, twisting for a Full. I saw her do this at tryouts, sometimes landing on her knees, sometimes on her face. But as her legs strike the floor this time, she stands straight up. A slow clap begins, the same kind people give in movies. "Yeah," she yells, pumping her fist as the clapping speeds up.

Trisha gets in line to tumble, her hair in pigtails. She wears green socks, with frogs all over them, pulled up to her knees. "You still got it," someone yells as she does a tumbling pass.

She cups her hands to her mouth. "Y'all, 2-2-1s. We're gonna tape these tomorrow." The squad divides into three groups, and Trisha sits down in a plastic chair, resting her elbows on her knees. Doug sits near her, tapping his hand to the Blink-182 song playing on the stereo. His goatee is neatly trimmed, his skin peaches-and-cream.

"One, two, three, four," counts Trisha. On the left pyramid, Yvette is the top flyer. Sierra is doing the honors on the right. In the center is Ashley Picard, one of the team's smallest flyers.

As Trisha finishes her count, all three of the women should be suspended in the air. But none of them are. Yvette lands, but as she twists to face forward, her middle layer women drop her. Sierra's grab her toes instead of her ankles and she falls, momentum pushing her chest toward the floor. Her middle layer women clutch her feet as two guys reach up to catch her. Ashley's feet come nowhere near her middle layer women's hands, and she falls straight down.

"What the hell was that?" says Trisha, jumping out of her chair. "Pay attention. These are not difficult." She turns to Doug. "These girls don't fight for it on the bottom," she whispers.

The squad tries again. This time as the flyers are tossed straight through the middle of two Shoulder Stands, they land, but the top women have to swivel theirs hips to face the front. Doug claps his hands as he speaks. "You're not holding what you've got," he says. "Hold it and fight for it. Pretend like it's Nationals, *every* time."

"Thanks for catching me," Ashley says sarcastically to a base who let her drop just a little too far for comfort.

"No one needs to catch you if you stay up there," snaps Doug.

"You have to stay tight, baby darling," adds Trisha. But she's not convinced that Ashley is the problem. "I think it's the bases—James Brown's not throwing her up right," she says quietly to Doug.

"He knows how to fix it," says Doug, hesitant to correct someone so experienced.

"Watch. I'm telling you, it's the pitch, it's not the girls," says Trisha.

Doug walks over to the center pyramid and pulls James, Ashley, and the back base aside. He says a few words to both Ashley and James Brown. Everyone watches as the three practice the toss, Ashley popping straight in the air like a Japanese yo-yo. A few minutes later, Doug deems them ready to try again.

As they practice these pyramids ad nauseum, James Brown wipes his forehead. "I hate everyone," he says. "I hate life."

## "I'm a Ringchaser."

Samantha stands beside her white pickup truck in the parking lot outside her favorite pizzeria. A dainty woman beside an enormous truck, it's hard to see how any coach could have thought she was too big to be an amazing flyer. But five months ago at tryouts, she was on the chopping block for just this reason. Since camp, Samantha and Tyrone have established themselves as one of the fiercest stunting duos on the team. "They just keep getting better," Trisha said to me at practice.

Samantha's boyfriend, Hunter, now a tumbler on the Small Coed team, opens the door and holds it open for Samantha and me. Another cheerleading couple will be joining us for a post-practice dinner—Samantha's roommate, Ashley Picard, and her boyfriend, Kyle, both on the Large Coed squad.

As we sit down and order food, Ashley and Kyle congratulate Samantha on landing her Full at practice. Only Hunter remains quiet. He seems to withdraw from conversations about Samantha's achievements, perhaps because she made the Large Coed squad while he didn't. But Samantha doesn't notice the awkwardness, and basks in the praise. "My Full is better than I ever thought it could be," she says, her black-rimmed eyes resolute. "All the way through, I just pray not to land on my face. I'm a little mental about it."

Kyle interjects, flashing a boy-band smile. "Tumbling is 95 percent in your head. You have to make yourself stupid to be able to do it. The more you think about it, the harder it becomes. You're making your body do things it's not supposed to do."

Ashley smoothes back her chocolate brown hair to reveal her impossibly high cheekbones. "I've had my Standing Back Tuck since I was twelve," she says. "But when I came to SFA, I started to fall on my face. I haven't told anyone how hard I've been working to get it back because it's embarrassing. But I'll go out to the football field and do Back Tuck, Back Tuck, Back Tuck. There's no way that I'm not going to make the mat over a skill I've had for years and years."

As we get deeper into the fall semester, "make the mat" is a phrase I hear the SFA women use more frequently. While the Large Coed squad now has twenty-seven members, only twenty can compete at Nationals. It's pretty scientific who will get to perform—SFA usually brings seven or eight partner pairs and four to six tumblers. About twelve of the fifteen men on the squad will be picked. (Between the tumblers and stunters, more than half of the team is male.) At best, eight of the twelve SFA women will be on the mat. The rest will be alternates, and that's a position no cheerleader wants to be in—they will only get to compete if one of their teammates is hurt.

Kyle cracks a joke and Ashley giggles. She is unapologetically girly; she almost always wears pink, and she brings her Chihuahua, Bitsy, with her most places she goes. At 4'10" and eighty pounds, she is probably the smallest girl on the team. Her face is warm, with smile lines darting around her eyes and mouth.

"Have you ever heard the term *ringchaser*?" she asks. I shake my head no. "It's a person who bounces back and forth between schools trying to win a ring. It's a negative term—you're supposed to be with a team and stay there. But I'm a ringchaser."

SFA is Ashley's third college in as many years. She's traveled the farthest of anyone on the team to be here; she's from Boston, as the Red Sox sports bra she often wears to practice attests.

"How much of your college decision was based on cheerleading?" I ask her.

"One hundred percent," says Ashley. "I would not be in school if it weren't for cheerleading."

Kyle, a star tumbler on the Large Coed team, looks up from his plate of pizza. "I didn't even get a high school diploma," he says. "I got my GED so I could cheer in college."

"People don't realize how intense cheerleading is," says Ashley. "I'm basing four years of my life around it. I saw this squad when I was seventeen and said, 'I'm gonna go there someday.'"

The three of them discuss tryouts. Hunter gets up from the table without saying a word and heads outside to make a phone call. "I've never not made a squad, but this is the best squad I've ever tried out for," says Ashley. "I sent in a video, but on the day of tryouts, I didn't put my phone down."

Samantha smiles. "I thought at best I'd be a last resort," she says. "I'm pretty amazed at what I can do now."

Part of the reason for her improvement is, of course, Tyrone. "I just couldn't be happier with a partner," says Samantha, as Hunter comes back inside and sits down. "He's so strong, if we're a little off, he can hold his arm straight out and fight for it. Heck, he can lift the end of his car. No matter what, we don't blame each other. If something goes wrong, we always say it's *our* fault."

Hunter doesn't say a word as Samantha gushes about her partnership with Tyrone. He may just be a quiet person, but the tension feels palpable. With all the time stunt partners spend together, I imagine that it often becomes a sore spot between couples. I know I would be jealous if someone else got to be a "we" with my significant other.

Ashley is pleased with her partner, too, but because he relies more on technique than brute strength, she's had to make some adjustments. "I have what coaches call LGS—Little Girl Syndrome. It's where you get used to not doing much to make a stunt work. Like in a Rewind, I used to be able just to tuck my knees and my partner would do the rest. Now I have to work more on my technique."

Samantha smiles as she picks a piece of meat off a slice of pizza. "I'm peaking. Now I'm just scared to push myself too hard," she says. "To do something stupid and get hurt."

## "Ride That Bitch."

The light on Trisha's video camera glows like Rudolph's nose. For the past hour, the SFA squad has been filming their basket tosses. Trisha hopes to finish this section of their bid video in two days of practice or less. She watches the camera screen as four women reach the what-goes-up-must-come-down point, kicking their right legs out and spinning twice before landing in their bases' arms.

"Back Tuck," she says, looking pleased with what she just saw. "Sierra, get in the center." Sierra stands up and shakes out her injured hand. "It feels fine today," she says, looking at her oven-mitt cast. "It's extra motivation to come down right so I don't hit it on someone."

The five basket toss groups get into position. Sierra is in the middle, both James Brown and Tyrone in the group basing her. Samantha and Kali flank her on the sides. The women load in and spring high in the air.

"Good," says Trisha. "That might have been tape."

"We got it in one take," says Ashley in her girlish voice. "That *never* happens."

I've been hearing for weeks about how tedious bid video taping is. But this afternoon, everything is moving quickly. Trisha knows why. "We had a mat room talk last week," she explains. "Instead of letting things fester, we go into the mat room and everyone gets what they want to say off their chests. What is said in the mat room stays in the mat room—you don't pout about it. Last week, the veterans laid out exactly what was expected of the rookies, and I've seen a huge turnaround with the entire team since then. Before, it took us twenty-six takes to get a Liberty tape. Now their work ethic is better—they're trying as hard as they can."

"Kick Fulls," says Trisha, calling out the next basket toss. "You got this, babies."

The flyers step into their groups' hands. "Nope," says Ashley. "You can tell as soon as they dip if they're off." She's like a cheer psychic, sitting on the ground with her knees pulled to her chest.

Just as predicted, the five women reach the top of their baskets a few seconds apart from each other.

Half an hour later, the group tries this basket toss for the eight time. Ashley and another flyer are bored on the sidelines. They roll up their shirts and compare their abs. "I do leg lifts to the side," says Ashley, demonstrating a move copped from Tae Bo. "They rip you up." Her friend starts doing them instantly.

"You need to ride that bitch!" yells Yvette, smiling a big, bubbly smile. She turns to me. "When we're taping, I'm the one yelling profanities at everyone, trying to get them to do good," she says. "But once practice is over, it's 'Let's go get drunk!' "

The groups get into their positions again and the women fly high, finally coordinating their tosses perfectly. Trisha watches it on the camera screen. "That's a wrap," she says.

## "You're the Shit."

It's Sunday morning, and Kali is giving me the grand tour of her one-bedroom apartment. Her room is a white square with shag carpet and purple felt tacked in front of the windows to keep out the light. She leads me down a short hall, pushing a curtain to the side. This is Kali's kitchen, otherwise known as her brother Michael's room.

When Kali first told me her brother lived in the kitchen, I imagined a scenario straight from *After School Special*. But Kali and Michael have made their large kitchen into a cozy room with a bed in the corner piled high with flannel comforters. Michael sits on the end, a *Last Samurai* poster behind him. Her effervescent smile is almost identical to Kali's.

"We pay one hundred dollars each for rent," says Kali. "Most people couldn't live in a kitchen with a curtain as a door, but we don't need much." She glances at Michael and he nods.

As usual, Kali is feeling insecure this morning. I doubt other members of the squad would share this diagnosis, but she feels like she's having an off month. "I'm not too worried about making mat," she says, bringing her hands together in front of her chest in a prayer position. "But I can't gain any weight—I'm already the biggest girl on the squad."

Michael gives Kali an I'm-not-going-to-let-you-feel-sorry-for-yourself glare. "You forget that people think you're *the shit*," he says emphatically. "You can do everything—stunt, basket, tumble. Seriously, last night, everyone on the team was like, 'Your sister's something else.'"

Even though Kali was nervous over the summer about getting to know her brother again, their relationship has developed a special ease to it. It's amazing they can live in the same small apartment without one of them cracking. Not to mention the fact that Michael doesn't mind being in Kali's shadow. He even likes that the rest of the team calls him "Baby Seitz" rather than "Michael."

Kali picks up her car keys and throws a backpack over one shoulder. She's on her way to work—she gives private tumbling lessons at a cheerleading gym about half an hour from Nacogdoches. She wears a pair of athletic shorts that show her killer leg muscles and a long-sleeve T-shirt with a dragon on the front. Her dainty ankle is encased in an anklet she never takes off.

As we drive to work in her beat-up red sports car, Kali tells me that she got a letter from her mom, who's been semi-estranged because she struggled with drugs and alcohol while Kali and Michael were growing up. "She always collected cards, beautiful vintage cards. Lately, she's been sending them to us with long letters. Sometimes she'll tuck a ten-dollar bill in one," she says, laughing as she glances in the rearview mirror. "She's trying to help out—it's more symbolic than anything."

"Does she seem to be doing well?" I ask.

"Yeah, she's been sober and clean for a year now," says Kali. "But you'd be surprised—I've seen her bottom out after a year sober. But she seems like she's really trying to get her life together."

"What about your dad?" I ask. "How often do you talk to him?"

"Every now and then. He wants me to come home after I graduate. He's always talking about how he's fixing my room up. I keep trying to tell him I'm gonna stay in Texas," she says. "He came to Nationals last year, and I didn't even get to compete."

"What do you mean?" I ask.

"I didn't tell you this story?" she squeals. "Last year, a week before Nationals, we were performing our routine. I tumble faster when I'm in front of people, and the guy tumbling in front of me went very slowly. I somehow caught my feet on his shoulder and fell on my face. I was laid out in front of 300 people, bawling."

She turns her head to look at me. "Brad, our old coach, drove me to the hospital. He was freaking out, because I *don't* cry," she continues. "They got me in a room and gave me morphine for my arm. I remember very clearly that that was the first time Brad ever complimented me. It was small—he said, 'You're so on top of everything this year'—but it felt really good to hear."

"So you didn't get to go to Nationals?" I ask.

"I had this idea in my mind that maybe it could heal enough in a week," she says, shaking her head no. "A few days later, I tried to tumble, and my body just collapsed. Brad had to rechoreograph parts of the routine. I still went to Florida, and everyone on the squad wrote my name on their shoes so I could still be on the mat. But my eyes were tearing up watching them."

We pull into the parking lot of her cheerleading gym. Inside, on one wall, an old SFA jersey is framed and surrounded by SFA team photos. "This gym was founded by a Lumberjack," she says, clearly in awe.

Kali looks around the gigantic industrial space. "Me and Michael really want to open a cheerleading gym. It'd be so much fun. He does choreography and music, and I could teach tumbling," she says.

Many reasons have been given for the explosive growth of cheerleading over the past few years: cheer competitions airing on CBS Sports and ESPN2; USA replaying *Bring It On* every other weekend; the fact that while basketball generally stays the same every year, the skills in cheerleading are constantly evolving.

But I think this is a case of demand following supply. For top cheerleaders like Kali, the idea of leaving cheerleading behind after college is scary. They've been paid big bucks to choreograph routines and teach lessons, so they've seen that there's money to be made in solid coaching. Kali is not the first cheerleader I've talked to who's told me that she wants to open a cheerleading gym—on just these three squads, fifteen people have echoed this same desire. Let's say a fifth of them do it— that's three new cheerleading gyms. If they're successful in recruiting, that's potentially hundreds of new cheerleaders brought into the sport off the passion of these few. It's at least one reason cheerleading continues to be one of the fastest-growing sports in the country.

Kali's first student of the day walks through the door—a blonde, chubby-cheeked high-schooler who's taller than Kali. "She's been coming to me for two years," says Kali. "She's come a long way."

The student steps on the mat and Kali has her do handspring after handspring, drilling her on every minute component. "Keep your legs straight to get more power," she says. "Push through your toes." "Squeeze your legs together." "Bring your chest up quicker when you land."

Kali turns to me. "I'm picky, because in gymnastics, you can spend four years just working on getting one move perfect," she says. "I know that good technique helps you later on."

By the end of their hour-long session, Kali's student looks defeated. The critiques Kali's given are bite-sized, but this girl doesn't take the criticism well. She tries to keep a smile painted on her face as she bends over to rest, but tears well up in her eyes.

"You're so hard on yourself," says Kali, rubbing her back to comfort her. "You're doing so good. Don't be so hard on yourself."

I think back on all the conversations I've had with Kali this year about how she's not performing to the best of her ability, about her frustration with being bigger than other girls on the team, about her fear that people are disappointed with her. Sometimes I want to tell her the exact same thing.

## "It's Your Branch of the Family Tree."

I feel like I've stepped into an ancient spelling bee. Deltas, Gammas, Sigmas, and Pis stare at me, emblazoned on the sides of mugs, shot glasses, jewelry boxes, and sweatshirts. When Kali and Yvette, SFA's two female captains, told me we were stopping by the Greek store, part of me was expecting vases and togas. I didn't realize there were entire stores dedicated to sorority and fraternity paraphernalia.

We're here this morning because it's the cheerleaders' Lil/Big week—a tradition the squad has adopted from Greek life to form a group of unrelated people into something of a family. Yvette's deep brown eyes twinkle as she explains the tradition. "It's like your branch of the bigger family tree," she says. "You choose a Lil who fits in with your Big and your Grand Big."

Nearby, Kali bends down and looks at a set of glasses with the letters LCLM frosted on them. "Those are for us," she says. "We used to have to special-order LCLM stuff, but now they keep a lot in stock."

"Who is your Lil?" I ask. The veterans pick their faux-siblings by seniority, so Kali would have gotten her top choices.

"I'm in Trisha's family, so there was a lot of pressure on who to pick," she says. "I picked Sierra—I thought she would be the best family member."

The SFA cheerleaders truly think of themselves as a family. I've heard it from almost every member of the team. They live together, party together, and take classes together. In the past few years, there have been three LCLM marriages, with at least one more on the way.

Normally, Lil/Big week is followed by an induction of the rookie cheerleaders. But this year it's been postponed. "We just feel like the team isn't ready to be initiated," explains Yvette. "So instead, on Friday, we're going to go toilet paper and egg Trisha's house. It will be good bonding." She pauses for a second. "Just don't tell her about it."

I worry that "the team isn't ready yet" might be code for "we don't want to do our initiation while a journalist is here." But as I talk to Trisha later, she tells me another reason. "A very good friend of mine and a former SFA cheerleader broke his neck this week. He was doing a Double Full into a pit of foam at a gym, and he landed on his face, but his body kept falling over. Last I heard, he was sitting up and wiggling his fingers," she said. "A lot of old cheerleaders are flying in and I wanted them to go see him in the hospital in Dallas rather than feel like they had to come here for initiation. That's family."

Still, the squad is not letting their friend being in the hospital stop them from having a celebratory Lil/Big Week. The veterans have bought doodads galore and are giving their Lils presents every day this week. Kali is excited about the personalized stuff she's ordered. "I got an LCLM necklace and a flask," she says.

Yvette fiddles with her oversized sunglasses. "I wanna get an LCLM tattoo on the inside of my lip," she says. "I'm gonna do it by the end of the year."

She walks to a table in the center of an aisle where more SFA veterans are gathered. One of them has a wooden paddle laid out on the table with his Lil's name across the top, LCLM vertically down the middle, and his own name across the bottom. "It needs something here," he says, pointing to a blank spot on his paddle.

I search through the bins lining the aisle. They're full of letters (both English and Greek) and a remarkable assortment of baubles. I hand him a dolphin and a bumblebee, and he laughs. He looks through the bins himself and comes back with a Gothic cross. "My Lil Bro's religious," he says, placing the cross in the center of the paddle. He steps back to admire his work. "There, he'll like that."

## "I Want to Give Her a Lump of Coal."

Silly string, a jug of Captain Myers's Rum, feather boas, Crunch 'n Munch, cap guns, Blow Pops, ramen noodles, a *Pulp Fiction* DVD, and a pack of Marlboro Lights—all things that have made the Lil's gift baskets.

The SFA veterans gather around a picnic table on a lawn near the football field, laughing as they finish their gift bags and baskets. The rookies, meanwhile, are down at the football field, their view of the picnic table obscured by a hill. They still have no idea who their Bigs are.

A veteran woman walks by with six impeccably wrapped pink presents cradled in her arms. She walks toward a patch of trees and stacks them behind a tree trunk. A veteran guy crams Axe Body Wash and a bottle of ranch dressing into a basket—he gets the award for the weirdest present so far.

"Look what I got James Brown," says another veteran, holding up a pen shaped like a syringe. It's an interesting choice.

"Ohhh . . . ," the other veterans respond in the same tone my third-grade class used when someone told a good Yo Mama joke.

Kali puts the finishing touches on her bag for Sierra—a bunch of candy and some tubes of massage oil. She places it behind a tree with a note on top. "You can give your Lils gifts or you can make them do stuff for their gifts," she tells me. "I make mine do stuff. Sierra has to give one of the guys a foot rub for a full minute."

"Is everybody ready?" asks Trisha. They nod, and she takes out her cell phone to call one of the rookies.

Kali is giddy as the rookies materialize over the hill. "I'm so glad I'm missing class for this," she says, standing with the rest of the veterans, staring straight ahead so she doesn't give anything away.

Sierra trails the rest of the rookies as they head to the patch of trees. She says hello to me as she walks by. Her face looks long—not like someone on a hunt for gifts. I ask her if she's okay. "I've just had a bad day," she says.

The rookies swarm the trees and return to the table with their loot. "If your card tells you to do something, it's all in fun, but you have to do it," yells Yvette.

Michael, Kali's little brother, steps on the picnic table bench. He puts one hand on his hip, the other arm arched to the side of his body. He sings, "I'm a little teapot," to a loud round of applause.

A circle forms around another rookie guy. He holds the bottle of ranch dressing in his hand. He unscrews the cap. "My card says I have to chug this," he says, a little scared.

"Ew," gasps the crowd. I can't help but cringe.

He tilts his head back and brings the bottle of ranch dressing to his lips. His Adam's apple moves up and down as he gulps. A round of "Eww," "Nasty," and "That's foul," erupts throughout the squad. Finally he puts the bottle down and brings his head back up. "I feel dizzy," he says, wiping a lump of dressing from the corner of his lip.

Sierra holds her gift bag limply in her hand. Even though her card has told her that she has to give a guy on the team a foot massage, she stays quiet, hoping no one will call her out.

"Is that everyone?" asks Trisha. No one responds. She begins to give some group announcements. Sierra looks down at the grass, still flying under the radar.

Kali stands near Yvette. "Can you enforce this?" she whispers, pointing her chin toward Sierra.

Yvette cups her hands to her mouth. "Listen up," she says. "If your Big told you to do something, you have to do it. It's LCLM."

Sierra's eyes tear up. She dramatically takes off her hand brace and throws it. "Sit down and take off your shoes," she says to one of the biggest guys on the squad.

She kneels on the grass in front of him. "Who's got an f-ing timer?" she asks, a nearly hysterical combination of upset and angry. A few of the veterans shoot her a disapproving look as she scowls and opens a tube of massage oil. She holds it over the guy's feet and squeezes, the cream streaming out in a torrent over his ankles. She winces as she plants her hands, including the injured one, on his big sweaty feet. She swirls the lotion around. "Gross," she says, tears rolling down her cheeks.

"Get in between his toes," someone yells. She obeys, massage cream gooping out everywhere. "This is so wrong," she says.

"It's all in fun," one of the women assures her.

"Time's up," someone calls. Sierra stands up and scoots back as if she's just realized there's a bomb in front of her. She runs to a nearby water fountain to wash her hands, the tears still flowing.

Everyone claps to show support. "Good job," yells Yvette.

"You're a brave girl," shouts someone else.

The group disperses, and Kali and Yvette walk to their cars. They're not pleased with Sierra's performance. "Oh my God, someone had to chug ranch dressing and she doesn't want to give someone a one-minute foot rub?" says Kali. "I want to give her a lump of coal tomorrow."

Yvette nods. "Suck it up," she says. "We've all had to do our share of embarrassing things for LCLM."

## "Nothing's Ever Perfectly Safe."

Ashley Picard sits on a bench in a dimly lit cheerleading gym, braiding her brown hair into pigtails. She slides off her pink platform sandals and laces up her cheerleading sneakers. Near her, Samantha stretches out her long back. She takes off her sweat suit and puts on her purple-and-red uniform over her sports bra.

Trisha plugs her video camera into the wall. "All right," she says. "Let's get going."

Official practice for the SFA Lumberjacks ended hours ago, but because Trisha doesn't like to use regular practice time for partner stunt taping, she's been opening up the gym almost every night for the past two weeks. "Partner stunting is a privilege—you have to work on it on your own time," she explains. "It shows me who's willing to put in the time to get a perfect tape. Some of them are here every night. Jason and Yvette—they already have their tape ready to go."

The rest of the SFA partner stunters have a week before their video must be in the hands of a postal worker, on its way to UCA headquarters. Partner stunt videos will be judged just like team videos; judges will watch them over and over, looking for bobbles. Once the tapes are scored, the UCA will invite the top twenty couples to compete in January at Walt Disney World. For NCA Nationals in April, only ten couples will get a chance to take the stage. Of all the people competing in both partner stunt expos, almost half of them will be from SFA.

Tonight, Ashley and her partner, Jeremy, volunteer to go first. Trisha points them to the middle of the blue mat, centering them on her screen. Behind them, on a ledge about six feet high, is a long row of trophies grouped by color—some gold, some blue, some an American flag print. The trophies cut across the screen horizontally, subtle symbols that this is a team of winners. Through the three-inch screen, the gym looks sterile, like a hospital lobby.

"Come on, Ashley," yells Trisha as the pair begins their routine. The further they get in their routine, the more the tension builds, like a Jenga stack teetering after too many logs have been removed. About two-thirds of the way through, Ashley finally drops. Trisha presses the stop button.

James Brown walks into the gym, but Sierra is not at his side. Even though her hand is feeling better every day, he's sticking to his guns and is stunting with Cassie Valentin, a girl with hourglass curves and a face that resembles Alyssa Milano's, for the UCA Partner Stunt Competition. They will not be recording tonight, so they practice quietly in the corner, some things hitting, some things falling. They're hoping to be ready to tape in a few days, sneaking in just before the deadline.

Samantha and Tyrone give each other a high five and step on the mat for their turn. Trisha frames them in the viewfinder. As they begin with a One-Arm Rewind, Tyrone looks powerful, like a strongman in a competition pushing the sagging barbell over his head.

"Chest up," yells Trisha, and Samantha instantly obeys. They'll edit in music on the video so the judges won't hear any comments. Samantha drops into Tyrone's arms for a cradle, and he swings her back up as she spins into a Full-Up. "Too much, too much," someone yells. But Tyrone grabs her foot and stops her rotation just fine.

They go for another Rewind. But as Samantha's feet strike Tyrone's palms, she teeters and drops. Tyrone catches her by the waist and lowers her to the ground. She dramatically collapses to her knees and falls flat to the ground, like she's just been shot in a spaghetti western.

"You get so far and you just run out of steam," says Tyrone, panting.

They try their routine a few more times, but by the end of the night, they still don't have their tape. Tyrone faces the wall, the skin on his neck folding into three lines, like Mr. T's. Sweat rolls down his back. I expect him to be angry and frustrated, but when he turns around, he's smiling. "I'm happy," he says. "The little things are starting to click."

## "I Was Not Expecting That High."

Tyrone taps his pencil against his desk. His eyes drift into space—Hospitality 101 is boring today. His phone buzzes in his bag, and he stealthily reaches down to check his new text message.

It says only three words: RESULTS ARE UP.

Tyrone shoves his notebook in his bag and makes a break for the back door. Even though his professor is mid-lecture, no one seems to notice. He whips open his phone and dials Samantha. "The results are up," he says. "I'm on my way to the library to check them."

"Oh my God," squeals Samantha on the other line. "I just got a text message from Trisha saying congratulations. I didn't think we'd be getting results back for another few days, so I was like, 'Did someone enter me in something I didn't know about?'"

Tyrone hangs up the phone and walks quickly toward the computer lab. He opens the door and sits down in front of an empty terminal. He goes to *Varsityspirit.com* and looks for the UCA Partner Stunt listings.

He finds the page just as Samantha runs up behind him. He clicks on the link, and up comes the list of the twenty partner-stunting couples who have qualified for the UCA Partner Stunt Competition. They scan the list for their names.

And there they are. In seventh place. They will be going to Orlando, Florida, this January to compete.

Samantha puts her hand to her face. "I'm shocked," she says. "I expected that we'd do well, but I didn't think we'd do *that* well. I can't believe we're going!"

"Alright, cool," says Tyrone, a little hesitation, even a note of disappointment, in his voice. "If we pulled out one more stunt we could have placed a little higher. But anything can happen—anyone can win." The two stand up and wrap their arms around each other.

Yvette is at work at a Mexican restaurant when she gets a text message from her partner, Jason. "He's a cheer-holic," says Yvette as she opens it. "He's been checking the website all morning."

Yvette's eyes widen as she reads the words. She instantly begins jumping up and down—the rest of the waitresses look at her like she's crazy.

Yvette and Jason placed higher than they'd ever imagined, too—

they are fourth. And not only that, they've placed the highest out of all the SFA couples. "I'm just so excited," says Yvette. "I was expecting to be in the top ten, but I wasn't expecting this high. We really have a very good chance at winning. We have exactly what the judges like to see—cleanliness and confidence. If we can't hit it ten times out of ten, we don't put it in our routine."

Across town in her apartment, Sierra maneuvers the mouse of her computer using her right hand, still wrapped in a soft cast. Because James Brown submitted a video with another partner, there's no way her name will be on the screen. She's checking, hoping not to see James Brown on the list of couples who qualified for the competition.

The results flash up. James Brown and Cassie are in ninth place, and Sierra just stares at the screen. "I just want to give him the finger like, 'Dude. You're so full of yourself.' His new partner can't even do a Back Tuck on the ground." She shakes her head, her big eyes watery. "This just breaks my heart."

## "I Have to Go Take Care of My Mom."

There are only two weeks left in the fall semester. It's been a week and a half since the squad found out which partner couples would be heading to UCA competition. Their Friday practice has just ended, and the SFA cheerleaders file into a mat room talk. They form a circle inside the cinderblock cavern where their mats are rolled, standing on their ends like tree trunks. Behind them stands a pile of hockey goals and a folded Ping-Pong table.

Trisha has called tonight's meeting for a serious announcement. No one is quite sure what it's about. Even captains Jerrod, Kali, and Yvette seem baffled as they sit down on the concrete floor. Tyrone looks down at his neon sneakers—his favorite of his fifty pairs.

"Everyone, I need to tell you something," Tyrone begins, his voice shaky. "Last year, my mom had a brain aneurism. At the time, there was a pretty slim chance she would survive, but now her speech is a lot better, she's walking on her own, she can make her own decisions. But she still needs someone to take care of her.

"My sister brought my mom up to live with her in Connecticut," he continues, all eyes on him. "But now, my sister has made it into the police academy. She can't take care of my mom anymore because she's going to basic training in a few weeks. On Tuesday, I'm leaving for Connecticut to take care of my mom for a couple of months. I have to leave SFA."

Tears flow down Samantha's cheeks as she stares at the wall straight in front of her. Tyrone told her a month ago that his sister was applying to be a police officer, but neither of them braced themselves for what would happen if she got in. Tyrone only found out that it was definite last night. He considered telling her before the meeting, but he didn't want to distract her before practice.

"Oh man," someone says. Ashley Picard leans over and hugs Samantha. Samantha tries to keep it together.

"I didn't realize it started so soon," says Tyrone, choking up. "I thought if she made it into the academy, it would start next year or something. It sucks right now, but there's nothing I can do. I just hope to be back as soon as possible."

"Wow," someone says.

"I'm still going to UCA Partner Stunt," he says. "And I'll definitely be back next year."

One of the women stands up to hug Tyrone. Others follow suit. As the team files out of the mat room, Tyrone and Samantha throw their arms around each other. They don't need to say anything.

As she walks to her car, Samantha is doing her best to look on the bright side. "Thankfully we'll get to do UCA Partner Stunt together," she says. "Our relationship will still be really strong."

Though she tries not to show it, Trisha is upset, too. "Not only is Tyrone a phenomenal stunter, but he's also a very good tumbler," she says. "We'll just miss having him around—he always has such a great attitude."

There's just a month until the UCA Partner Stunt Championship. After nearly eight months of bonding and working their way up from underdogs to the seventh-best stunt couple in the nation, it will be Samantha and Tyrone's last chance to compete together. After that, Samantha will have to start from scratch.

# CHAPTER 13

## "Agendas Are Pulling Them in Different Directions."

*The Southern University Jaguars*

"THIS IS GONNA BE hard work—it's a true commitment," says Coach James, intensity streaming out of his eyes as he surveys the cheerleaders in the desks in front of him. He's dressed in a black button-down shirt with pinstriped pants, and he paces back and forth as he speaks. Southern's football season is over, and today Coach James has called the squad together for a team meeting.

The winter months are usually intense for the squad. Last year, Southern's basketball team qualified for the NCAA Tournament, and the cheerleaders traveled with the team to Greensboro, North Carolina, for their first-round game against Duke University. Duke prevailed on the court, but James Turner remembers the game fondly. "Our basketball team represented well, but it was the cheerleaders who stole the show," he told me earlier in the year, still relishing the national exposure the game brought the squad.

While they cheer on the basketball team, the Southern cheerleaders will also have to get ready for competition season. They have a month before the deadline for NCA bid videos, and they want to put together a good one in hopes of receiving a full or partially paid bid to Nationals. They also need to begin choreographing their competition routine—a task that can take months.

"It's pushing yourself far beyond where you think you can go. It's a sacrifice of your time and energy," continues Coach James. He sounds like the no-bullshit teacher from a classroom drama like *Stand and Deliver* or *Dangerous Minds*. "Starting today, let's get your mind into the training," he says. "Your bodies will be tired. Your attitudes will flare. You'll have done a million things during the day and then you'll have to come to practice. But be strong and know that the end is so much more important than the present."

James Turner and Jasmine sit in front of the group, returning Coach's blistering eye contact. Behind them Jarel, Tarianne, Chassity, and Tremayne listen attentively. But five cheerleaders are missing. Coach James knew not to expect Lakeitha, the sophomore who hurt her foot at the Bayou Classic. After an X-ray, her doctor confirmed that she wouldn't be able to cheer for the rest of the year. But Coach has no idea why the other four aren't at the meeting.

Over the next forty-eight hours, it becomes clear. "Lo and behold," explains Coach James, "everybody called one by one with a story about why they couldn't cheer next semester."

First came Tiffany and Terrica, two senior flyers who joined the squad over the summer. "I didn't do good in school this semester—it's hard to be in nursing school and cheer. I need to focus more on school," explained Tiffany. "And I didn't have as much fun as I did in years past. I guess I finally got too old." Terrica also wanted to put more of her energy into school, in addition to taking a night class that would conflict with practice.

Next, Coach got a call from Rishawn, one of the squad's strongest tumblers. "I had to start working. I wanted to stay, but I talked to Coach about how I could balance my schedule between work and cheer, and he said it wasn't going to work," explained Rishawn, who hopes to be back on the squad next year.

The last straw was Tiffany Jones—fourth on the stunt line, a great basket tosser, and the team's only strong female tumbler. "I have a class at five o'clock that I have to take for my major," she tells Coach. "It's a hard decision, but what I came here for was to get an education."

Luckily, Coach James soon gets a good phone call. G, one of the captains of last year's squad, heard through the grapevine that people were dropping off the squad left and right. He asks if he can rejoin the team and be a part of the competition routine. Coach James gives him a resounding yes.

"I lost five, but I gained one very strong one," says Coach James after the call. He can also ask the student who dons the jaguar costume at games to join the team—he can at least serve as a spotter. But even with these additions, the squad is down to just sixteen members, only five of them women. They need twenty to compete at NCA Nationals.

I ask Coach James if he is surprised that so many people quit. He sighs. "I could tell there were too many distractions. Particularly with the seniors, they had agendas that were pulling them in different directions," he says. "Even though some of those agendas are legitimate, they're still converse to what we need for a great competition season."

James Turner is surprised that so many of his teammates have bailed. "I had a feeling that two people weren't going to stick around after football season, but they were just okay cheerleaders," he says. "I was surprised about Tiffany Jones and Rishawn—I think Coach was a little hurt about that. They're really good, but we can't work our schedule around them."

Jarel, on the other hand, thinks Coach could have tried to make arrangements with each of them. "Essentially, they were given an ultimatum," he says, his normally political voice angry. "It was like telling them that cheerleading is their life. We're *college* cheerleaders—college should be our priority. As long as it's a required class, I think he should excuse it."

But with the squad's situation as it is, Coach James has made a big decision. "My team is dwindling. Even though they're very talented, there are outside influences pulling on them," he explains. "So I've decided not to make a bid video this year."

He pauses and takes a deep breath, a touch of mourning in his voice. "I can pretty much judge from the start of the year where they're going to be. In 2002, I knew from day one that they had the heart for making this thing work. But this team isn't as dedicated as I need them to be," he says.

James Turner has been hoping all year that his squad would be able to travel to NCA Nationals against the odds. Coach James's decision confirms his worst fears. "Coach is my coach, but we also have a father/son relationship," James Turner explains. "I've known him long enough, and for a while, I've been getting the vibe from him that we're not going to do a bid video. I'm not surprised—he says we don't have the money to go to competition anyway. But I wish he'd implement some ways to raise the money rather than sit back and wait for someone to give it to us."

Without a bid video, Southern's chances of getting to NCA Nationals have gone from a long shot to close to nil.

# PART FIVE

NATIONALS
DECEMBER–APRIL

# CHAPTER 14

## "Practices Have Been Scary Lately."

*The University of Memphis All-Girl Tigers*

FROM BEHIND, KRISTEN KERN is so small that she could easily be mistaken for a preteen. But her face is purely adult—all angles, with eyes that tilt toward her nose. She stretches out on the Cheer Station mat for the squad's second practice of the day, slowly lifting her leg behind her. "My body is so tired, I'm telling my leg to kick and it's not doing it," she says.

Kristen Kern, or "Kern," as her teammates call her, officially joined the squad a month ago, swooping in like a superhero to save the day when one of the team's best flyers unexpectedly quit. At twenty-three years old, it's ironic that Kern is the newest member of the squad—she's actually the oldest cheerleader in the room. During her freshman year of college, she cheered for the Memphis Coed squad. "I begged my coach to put me on All-Girl," she says. "I just didn't feel safe in Coed stunting. Everything went a lot higher, and I was always nervous."

During Kern's sophomore year (the same year Monica and Casi came on as freshmen), Frankie and Carol took over the university's cheerleading program. As if by fate, the squad performed perfectly at

Nationals and brought home the first-place trophy. Memphis All-Girl had established themselves as a force to be reckoned with.

But last year did not end like a fairy tale. Kern's stunt group nailed their stunts every time in practice—they were the group Carol had the others watch when they were having trouble. "We couldn't have hit that stunt more times," says Kern, "but during finals, I fell. I have no idea why—I just went flying."

Some squad members think that a base's hands were sweaty and Kern's foot slipped out of her grip. But no one is exactly sure what happened.

Even though she was coming back to the University of Memphis for a fifth year of college, Kern decided to quit cheerleading after her fall at Nationals. It was time for her to buckle down and get an internship instead of spending all her free time in practice. So when the squad needed a new flyer ASAP, a lightbulb went off over squad captain Kristen's head. She sent Kern a casual text message to ease her into the idea. "You wanna come stunt around?" it said.

Sure enough, Kern met the squad the next day at Cheer Station, decked out in the practice clothes she thought she'd never wear again. "They put me in a stunt group and we just started trying stuff," says Kern. "I had an idea they'd want to use me for Nationals. My dad and boyfriend were like, 'You're going to end up going to Orlando.' But my mom was like, 'No. I think she's really done with competition.'"

When Carol asked Kern to officially join this year's All-Girl Nationals team, Kern had several reasons for saying yes. "First, I just miss it," says Kern. "I feel honored that they asked me. And I want to prove to myself that I can do this. I don't care what the outcome is—I want to show myself that I can hit."

*Hit.* As Nationals draw closer, the cheerleaders say this word constantly. It's their term for performing a routine flawlessly—no falls or bobbles—with so much energy that they bring the audience to their feet. The squad is hoping that Kern can help them achieve this cheerleading dream.

But even with Kern's return, the last few weeks have been rough. While their classmates left for winter break, the cheerleaders stayed on campus for grueling two-a-day practices. People have been getting hurt left and right. "Monica tore some ligaments and hyperextended a tendon in her ankle," says Carol, twisting her tiny nose ring as she watches the women stretch. "Casi pulled ligaments in her thumb. Kristen, too. We are *struggling* right now."

On the mat, Kern eases herself into a split. Kristen sits on a bench in back of her, staring blankly in the distance. Beside her, Casi mummifies her hand with athletic tape. "I bent my thumb all the way back. I cried and said every curse word in the Bible," says Casi. "The doctor told me I needed surgery in two weeks, but he knew I would compete even if he told me not to. So he made my next appointment for after Nationals."

Ashley Chambers has also been an injury magnet—she has bruises all over her coffee-colored limbs to prove it. "My flyer's elbow slammed into my eye," she says, describing a beating she took during a Double Down. "It was swollen shut, like I had gotten into a fight."

"Someone went to the doctor a few days ago and the doctor asked point blank, 'Are you being abused?'" says Courtney, throwing a joke into the conversation.

It is exactly one week before the squad leaves for Nationals, and they have yet to complete a clean run-through of their routine as a whole. "Last time we did the routine full out, Carol stopped us halfway through because it was an abomination," Courtney says. "There were bodies all over the floor—we were in actual danger."

But Carol maintains that the squad is at the same place they are every year a week before Nationals. "We always have to change things last minute to make it work," she says. "I've changed things up until the day before they compete."

Carol motions to the women to gather around her. Courtney stands up and walks in her direction, revealing a T-shirt that reads OTHER ATHLETES LIFT WEIGHTS ... CHEERLEADERS LIFT ATHLETES. "There's just finals this year," says Carol, her voice hoarse from the past few weeks of yelling.

"What?" someone asks.

Carol strains to raise her voice a few decibels. "They're not doing semifinals for All-Girl this year," she says. "We just do finals."

"That's awesome!" exclaims Ashley. "We usually do semis in the morning, and then finals in the afternoon. Now we don't have to go through that stress of, 'Are we gonna make finals?'"

Kristen smiles. "Since I've been here, knock on wood, we've done better in semis than we have in finals. The first time has always been our best," she says.

But Casi isn't convinced. "Semis is like a dress rehearsal, where you get used to the mat and all the lights. Some of the freshmen could get out there and get stage fright," she whispers.

Practice begins. The women break off into five groups to work on the first set of stunts they'll do in the routine, called their "elite stunt sequence." Monica is the first up in the air.

"Good," yells Carol.

Callee goes up beside her. But halfway through the sequence, her butt pokes backwards. For the bases to hold their flyer in the air, her weight has to be in a perfect line down the center of her body through her heels. Callee folds like elbow macaroni and falls, one of her bases reaching out to catch her.

"Do not bend your knees," yells Carol. "And do I need to tie your shoelaces to get your feet to stay together?"

Callee's eyebrows are lifted so high that they make her seem in perpetual shock. "We just switched bases the other day and we're not clicking," she explains to me. "We're all doing our part, but we're working against each other. It's frustrating, because Carol expects so much of us so quickly."

Michelle, the squad's alternate, watches attentively as Callee tries again. She's brought her six-year-old cousin Hannah, pigtails in her hair, to practice today. "No boys?" her cousin asks.

"No," replies Michelle. "We don't need boys."

Carol hits Play on a CD player. Like many college cheerleading squads, she has worked with a music editor to create a high-energy sound track for the team's routine. Cheerleading music, while just 2 minutes and 15 seconds long—like the routine itself—can contain six, seven, even eight songs, along with a slew of random sound effects. "Memphis All-Girl," chants a voice that sounds like a pumped-up voice-mail operator. The music quickly cuts to "Eye of the Tiger," the theme song from *Rocky III*. All five flyers spin while their bases hoist them overhead for Heel Stretches. The music switches to Run-DMC.

The flyers spin again, this time swinging their right legs behind them and leaning their chests forward for Arabesques.

From here, each flyer is supposed to throw her chest forward and flip as if she's on the edge of a pool. Her bases are supposed to release her and form a cradle to catch her as she comes back down. But it's easier said than done. Monica, in the back center, stops herself before flipping, looking too freaked out to go forward. In front of her, Kern knocks Courtney over as she lands.

"That Front Flip scares the mess out of me," says Courtney, standing back up. "If she hesitates at all, she will kick us. I've gotten hit 500 times in the same place."

Still, alternate Michelle seems impressed. "That's the best they've done it," she says. "Usually they don't get all the way through the sequence. Our practices have been scary lately."

Carol yells to the group. "Talk to each other all the way through it," she says. "Remind each other of what's coming. Tell each other what's going on."

The squad moves on to practice the cheer—the portion of the routine where the music shuts off and the team pretends they're on the sideline of a football game. Even though not all the women love waving pom-poms at games, this is almost everyone's favorite part of the routine. Watching them practice, I understand why. They've loaded the cheer with one-base stunts—the kind Coed teams do with no problem but very few All-Girl teams even attempt. "It's straight-up Coed style," says Casi, describing the cheer. "I guarantee you a million dollars that if we hit it, we will win Nationals. That's not me being cocky—it's true."

The cheer begins with six One-Man Walk-Ins, the move that impressed me on the squad's bid video. Each flyer places her foot in her base's hands. Both women bounce and—boom—the flyer goes up, twisting her body to come to standing in the air, facing the audience. There's no one behind the bases to help absorb the flyer's weight—it's the equivalent of bench-pressing about 130 pounds—and both women's timing must be precise to the nanosecond. The squad does the One-Mans in a wave, Kern hitting first, Monica and Casi smack in the middle, and Callee last. They all look solid. It's all I can do to keep myself from shouting, "You go girl!"

"Looks better!" yells Carol.

"I never in my life thought that I would be able to do a One-Man," says Kern as they take a quick break. "But six of us throwing them? It's impressive."

"I'm so excited," agrees Casi. "Those are what the UCA said we couldn't do in competition. We're gonna be like, 'Shove that.' "

After the One-Mans, the squad builds two 1-1-1s, a three-person totem pole pyramid that's difficult even for Coed teams, who can put their biggest, strongest guys on the bottom. On the right side of the mat, Monica climbs onto Casi's shoulders. Monica pulls up one knee, and two other bases brace her foot below. She leans into them to take some weight off Casi. Behind her, a group tosses Callee. She flies like an exclamation point in the air, her feet coming down on Monica's thigh. Monica loops her arms around Callee's legs to hold her in place as the group chants "Let's! Go! Ti-gers!"

Across the mat, Kern tops the second 1-1-1. But she misses, pulling the people below her into a heap on the floor. Everyone in the room gasps.

Carol jumps up. For a second she looks like a parent whose kid has had a collision on the playground slide, eager to make sure everything is okay. But, seeing all the women stand up, she pauses. "There is no reason these are not hitting," she screams. "You have to be aggressive. Again!"

Both sides go up and crumble. "Again," says Carol. "Maybe I should have you do twenty-five push-ups first."

"No," mutter some of the women.

"Let's get these," yells Casi. "I have two people on top of me, and it weighs a million-billion pounds. Come on."

They try again, and both 1-1-1s stand triumphantly. "Good, y'all," says Carol. "It has to be like that *every* time." Monica and Casi high-five as they hop down.

"Are you ready to learn the dance?" asks Carol. I assumed that with just a week until competition, the routine would be completely cho-reographed and the squad would know it inside and out. But that's not the case.

"The dance is always the last priority," explains Michelle. "Everyone can learn it quickly."

Carol points each person into a spot in a triangle formation. Kristen, the squad's best dancer—not to mention the one with the longest legs—is front and center. "You start with two head swings," says Carol, crouching down and swinging her elbows to each side, following the momentum to face right. "Now try it to the music."

The music speeds the dance up considerably. Only Kristen can keep up. But within a few tries, almost everyone has it. Carol shakes her head at the others. "Talk about some slow learners," she says. "You better go home and practice."

Carol moves on to the next four count. Facing the side of the room, she swings her arms to a point over her head, and then down to her sides with her hands out at ninety-degree angles. "Now, you're gonna shuffle your right leg to the back and shake your hands to your side." The women try it—it looks like something out of "Thriller."

"It's so fun," says Kristen, practicing it over and over.

Monica takes her hair out of her ponytail to try again. Long blonde hair swishes in front of her face as she dances.

"Anyone have a tampon?" someone yells across the mat, grabbing her side. "I really need one." Another girl walks to her bag and hands her one.

"Listen up," says Carol. "We're going to do the whole routine from the beginning, full out."

Monica looks at her like she's crazy. "I'm getting you tired," explains Carol. "If you can do this now, you can always do it."

The women get into their starting positions. Carol presses Play, and the routine begins. It starts well, but most of the flyers come crashing down in the elite stunt sequence.

"What happened in the stunts?" yells Carol over the music. "Keep going."

They move into the cheer. The One-Mans look good, but a 1-1-1 goes haywire. "That's just stupid, someone's gonna get hurt," yells Carol.

They begin the dance, their faces lighting up for Carol's choreography. All they have left now is their final pyramid—Callee and Kern atop 1-1-1s, each placing a foot in a center girl's hands, connecting the sides like Tinkertoys. "Tigers!" the squad yells to finish it off.

The team gathers around Carol. She gives the usual comments, but, overall, she's pleased. "You guys got better tonight," she says. "Being tired is no longer an excuse. You don't have practice tomorrow, so use the day to rest. You're dead dog tired tonight, and you hit."

Monica pipes in. "Do not go out drinking tonight," she warns. "No more alcohol until after Nationals. It has an effect on your body."

The squad gets in a circle and grabs pinkies. Kern bows her head and closes her eyes deeply. "Our Father, who art in heaven, hallowed be thy name . . . ," they recite together.

The squad's mood is lifted, but, as they walk out to the parking lot, Callee shakes her head. "We should be more prepared than this," she says. "At this point, we should be able to do our routine blindfolded."

## "I Need to Knock on Wood—Now."

"Boring, right?" says Monica as she makes a fart noise and points her thumb toward the ground. She glances out on the basketball court, where the women's team is losing by more than twenty points with just a few minutes left to play. The cheerleaders are in the throes of perfecting their Nationals routine, and today is their only day off from practice all week. It seems cruel that they should have to be here, cheering for a lost cause. "The only ones who come to women's basketball games anyway are old people," says Monica.

She's right—there aren't very many people in the stands. But the fans who are here are hard-core. In front of me, a woman sports a pair of tiger ears. A few rows away, a man has dyed his beard blue. As the team falls irredeemably behind, he gets riled up. "What's the matter, Ref?" he yells. "Is your whistle broke?"

Memphis calls a time-out, and the cheerleaders head to the center of the floor. The band plays "I'm So Glad I Go to the U of M" with no nod to the fact that they're getting killed on the court. The cheerleaders step-touch mechanically to the music, shaking their pom-poms with less enthusiasm than normal.

The All-Girl squad was supposed to perform their Nationals routine yesterday at a University of Memphis men's basketball game during halftime, watering down the moves that aren't allowed on hardwood floors, but Carol canceled the performance last minute. "It's too scary and there are too many injuries for us to think about doing anything at the game," she explained. Coed, of course, got to cheer during halftime, like usual.

The clock announces that only two minutes are left in today's game. In vain, the squad begins a cheer. "We! Want! A bas-ket, Ti-gers."

Memphis calls another time-out. The basketball players huddle around their coach, and I wonder exactly what she thinks the team can do at this point to gain any traction in this game. The women throw their long arms around each other—almost every one of the players is tall and lanky. Behind them, in the distance, the cheerleaders look even shorter.

"Tigers! Shoot it! For two!" the cheerleaders yell as play resumes. As if out of spite, a Memphis player jumps up for a three-pointer. But the cheerleaders can't complain—it's something.

The buzzer goes off, and Memphis has lost by thirty-three points. The cheerleaders jog to pick up their bags, like they can't get out of the gymnasium soon enough. As Casi, Monica, Courtney, and Ashley walk through the parking lot in a clump, their conversation has already turned back to Nationals, just six days away. "We've been through so much crap this year. If we hit, it's going to feel so good," says Ashley.

"The judges don't care about your story," says Courtney. "They don't care who quit or who got injured. Two minutes and 15 seconds is all you get."

The four women approach a pole. Monica and Casi stay on one side, while Courtney and Ashley peel off to walk around it. "You split the pole! You split the pole!" yells Casi, freaking out about an old-fashioned superstition. "Now we're gonna lose Nationals!"

"Calm down," says Ashley.

But Casi is practically hyperventilating. "I need to knock on wood. Now!"

## "I Hope the Unexpected Elements Give Us the Edge."

The University of Memphis women sit in chairs crowded around a television, staring at the screen like zombies. Over the last two days, they've made steady progress—their stunts and pyramids are sticking in place with much more consistency. The squad has the feel of the routine, and today they're working on "cleaning it up," nitpicking every detail to make sure that all the steps, gestures, and movements are crisp.

"A lot of times people don't realize the mistakes they're making," says Carol, explaining why she's videotaped the squad for the last few nights. "They'll watch the video and be like, 'Sorry. I thought it was sharp.'"

On the screen, the team opens the routine with tumbling passes. The pattern at first looks random—the cheerleaders tumble toward each other, like they're bound for a pile-up at the center of the mat. But, at the last moment, everyone passes by each other. "The tumbling looks better than I thought," someone comments.

"Woo hoo," says someone else, her enthusiasm dulled by how tired she sounds.

Mapping out a routine like this is an intricate process, almost like a game of chess. Carol plots it out on paper, deciding who should go where and then working backwards to the start. "We don't have good tumbling, so we have to be creative to make up for that," she says, explaining the opening.

She turns back to the television and shakes her head as several women stumble landing their Triple Toe Touch Backs. "We're gonna perform this in one week," she says. "Some of you rookies, I don't know where you're from, but you cannot bust on that. Stepping forward is just as bad as putting your hands down. Do whatever you have to do to get around."

All five flyers go up for the elite stunt sequence, the wall-length mirror behind them making it look like ten. But by the Arabesque, two flyers are down. Carol whips her head toward one of the girls who fell. "It used to look like you were just stepping into air. What's going wrong?" she asks. "Stop toeing it."

Alternate Michelle has become my interpreter when Carol throws out a cheerleading term I don't know. "When you stunt, your foot needs to be flat," she explains. "If you point your toe, your weight goes to the front of your foot and it's unsteady."

Across the room, Kristen claps, watching the stunts. "This is getting better and better, y'all," she says.

The flyers throw their bodies forward for the Front Flip, and while it's better than the last time I saw it, it's still out of sync. Carol shakes her head. "You guys can't make these flips look good without killing yourselves," she says. "We're probably going to have to do something else there."

"Nooo," someone protests.

"I don't want to change it, but they're so far off," replies Carol.

She turns to me and whispers, "I'm gonna give them another day to work on it, and then I'll change it to something easier."

We turn back to the television, where the squad hits their first pyramid. It looks like two dining tables with legs that are two-people tall, Callee and Kern forming the tabletops. They change their body positions, and the pyramid morphs like a hologram. "That's cool," I say to Carol.

"The judges really look at transitions—how you get from one thing to the next. You have to create a visual effect," she says. "There's actually not a lot of All-Girl pyramids, but there's different ways to get to them. I watch Coed teams and figure out how to make their pyramids All-Girl."

Carol looks down at the pages of notes she's scrawled. "Everyone, when you walk, keep your hands straight at your sides with your hands in a fist," she says. "Some of you are doing different things."

Carol watches the One-Mans go up on screen, but she isn't pleased with the women whose job it is to rile up the crowd across the front of the mat. "You girls in front gotta hit the crowd—be in their faces," she says. "I'm gonna be pissed if you're not."

"How did you guys decide to put in the One-Mans and the 1-1-1s?" I ask Carol as the totem poles are built on-screen.

"Normally, you don't put crazy stunts in the cheer that will take away from leading the crowd," she explains. "If you can't make it look easy, it shouldn't be in the cheer. But some of these bases make it look like a guy's holding it. So we had to do it."

"Dang," says someone else, watching four Rewinds that come three-quarters of the way through the routine. "Those look good." As they land the Rewinds, the flyers go straight up into a basket toss. It's a creative transition, and I compliment Carol yet again.

"Cheerleading routines all have the same sections—tumbling, stunts, pyramids, the cheer," says Carol. "So I try to make it surprising, like you don't know what's coming next. I hope all the unexpected elements will give us an edge."

Carol turns back toward the screen and sees the squad beginning their dance. "Look at us go," someone says.

"I look really tan on camera," notes Ashley.

"Yeah, Courtney," someone yells, watching her ham it up in the front line.

Carol is quiet as the squad begins their final pyramid. She pauses the video as Callee and Kern get into place to climb to the top. "Look how badly the timing for the two sides is off. I watched it in slow motion so we could get it right." She has the team visualize this part of the routine and gives them new counts—flyers flip on two, kick their leg back on three, everyone dip on five, bases lift flyers into position on seven—to make sure both sides of the pyramid are mirror images of the other.

What's been going on for the last half hour seems trivial, but as she packs her bag, Callee tells me it's the key to winning. "Memphis is known for being sharp," she says. "If we aren't, we will be penalized, because that's what the judges expect from us. Honestly, I'd rather be sharp than do badass stuff and be sloppy."

As the women file out the door, Carol stays for a second, putting away her video camera. "From what you've seen this week, do you think they have a chance?" I ask.

She looks up at the ceiling and pauses. "It's anybody's game."

## "Somebody Ate Their Wheaties."

Just three days remain until the University of Memphis cheerleaders leave for Nationals. Carol sits on the Cheer Station floor, sketching a T-shirt on a piece of paper. In the center, she scrawls the words *Dream Team* in bubble letters. Above them, she draws a set of angel wings. She holds up the paper to examine the logo; these are the shirts the squad will wear at Nationals when they're not in uniform. She'll drop the design off at the printer today.

The squad adopted Dream Team as their moniker a few weeks ago, but it's not meant in the same spirit as the Michael Jordan–led Olympic basketball team. "We call ourselves that because when Carol told us about the routine, we were like, 'She must be dreamin'—there's no way we're gonna hit it,'" explains Casi.

Today, the squad is dressed in blue short shorts and black T-shirts. The Coed squad stands across the gym, also in matching practice clothes. Some of them tell me that this helps build team unity before Nationals. In the Cheer Station office, Carol has stored the squad's brand-new uniforms, which will replace the ones with holes in the sides that the women detest.

Having the All-Girl and Coed squads practice together is no longer a stress-inducing prospect for Carol. A second coach has stepped in to help Coed so that Carol doesn't have to juggle her time between the squads. The All-Girl squad is thrilled to have Carol to themselves. "We get her full attention now," says Monica. "We're her babies more than Coed ever was because, with us, she can win."

Coed's new coach, Chad, a muscular guy in his thirties, is one of the most popular Memphis Elite coaches. To kick off practice, he wants Coed to do a full rehearsal of their routine. He claps and yells, giving his team a pep talk. "*Nothing* comes down," he yells, jogging in place like a boxer entering a ring. He is the intense yang to Carol's yin.

Carol has the All-Girl squad sit down on the mat to cheer Coed on. "Let's go Coed!" yells Monica. Kristen reaches into her bag and pulls out a white spray bottle that looks like suntan lotion. "What's that?" I ask.

"It's Biofreeze," she says. "It's like Icy Hot, only better."

"We cover our whole bodies in it," says Ashley. The room fills with a menthol smell as the women mist themselves with the spray.

Coed's music comes on, and as they get to the halfway point in their routine, they are performing it perfectly. Their one-man/one-woman stunts look sleek and uncluttered. Their pyramids reach a few feet higher than All-Girls'. Their basket tosses glide toward the high ceiling. Chad yells like crazy. "Woo hoo!" one of the All-Girl women screams.

Casi watches as Coed does three 1-1-1s, the exact same pyramid she stands on the bottom of in her routine. The guys make sour faces as they hold the women stacked on top of them. Casi rolls her eyes. "It's the same thing we do," she says. "Only our girls weigh more."

A base sitting next to her nods. "One of the guys came up to me and was like, 'My top's so heavy. She needs to lose weight,'" she says. "I was like, 'Huh? Your top is one hundred pounds. Mine is taller than me and I still lift her in a One-Man.'"

Coed finishes their routine flawlessly. "That's the first time we've done it clean!" someone yells.

"That's what I'm talking about!" screams Chad, running to hug them.

The All-Girl team jumps up. "Let's do the same thing," says Courtney, leading her team to the mat.

"Show us what you got, All-Girl!" bellows one of the Coed guys.

The women gather in a circle at the center of the mat, and each reaches a hand toward the middle. "Dream Team All-Girl!" they yell, swinging their arms overhead. The Coed squad sits down and claps.

The music begins. "Pretty, girls, pretty," one of the Coed guys shouts, watching their opening tumbling passes.

All-Girl's stunt sequences look solid today—only one flyer in the back doesn't make it through the whole thing. "Those look really good and controlled," one of the Coed guys tells Carol. She shrugs her shoulders. As if on cue, one of the women in the front pauses and misses the Front Flip.

"That's rickety," says Carol softly as the squad builds their first pyramid. But the bases on the ground are able to push it up into place. Carol smiles.

The One-Mans pop up effortlessly in a perfect wave. "Someone ate their Wheaties!" screams one of the Coed guys.

The comment visibly excites the team. Their smiles get bigger and their voices get louder. They go for the 1-1-1s and—bam—both Callee and Kern proudly stand on their middle layer's thighs.

"That's so good," yells one of the Coed women.

"Them girls is strong up underneath there," bellows one of the guys. Casi's face lights up.

"Get down, hit da flo,'" sings Twista along to a ubiquitous ncha-ncha techno beat as the squad gets in place for their final pyramid, a latticework with Callee and Kern on the top, twelve feet off the ground. The pyramid goes up. But Callee comes right back down, taking her side of the pyramid with her. The rest of the women hop down. They instantly forget the success of 90 percent of the routine and walk off the mat like jetfighters who've failed their mission.

Monica holds her chest, panting. Ashley shakes out her hand. "My acrylic nail popped off," she says. Another girl spots it lying on the mat. She reaches down and hands it back to her.

"You better change that music," one of the guys says to Carol. "Because when it says, 'Hit da flo,' they hit the floor." Carol puts out her hand to smack him jokingly on the side.

Chad dismisses the Coed team, and they leave the gym still reeling from their perfect performance. All-Girl stays behind to practice more. "Opening pyramid," says Carol.

It's almost as if a light has been switched off. Just a few minutes ago the team was breezing through the elements of the routine, and all of a sudden, after one fall, they can do no right.

"Don't do this—this is not the day to mess up," yells Carol. "Y'all are making me nervous. There's too many stupid mistakes. You've only got one shot at this. You're not acting like a team who wants it."

The team stands there, stupefied. Some of the women anxiously retie their ponytails, as if fixing their hair will fix what's happening on the mat. The gym goes silent. "We're tired," says Casi.

Carol shakes her head. "You're in shape to do this. We've gone through every single thing and fixed it," she says. "I've done all I can do. It's up to you guys now."

The women leave the gym, a wrecking ball smashed through their confidence. Ashley and Courtney are uncharacteristically downbeat. "I *do not* want to go to Nationals on hope factors," says Courtney. "Some coaches rely on 'You'll have adrenaline.' I know for a fact that I'm gonna walk on the floor scared."

Callee is ready to nominate herself Most Likely to Fall in a Competition. Kristen tries to cheer her up. "We get down on ourselves, but when you compare this routine to routines in years past, it's much harder. If we can clean it up, we have a good chance," she says.

From what I've seen in the last few days, I'm not holding my breath. It seems unlikely that in the next seventy-two hours they can turn it around. But Monica has faith. "When we're at practice, we just kind of go through the motions because we know we have to do it five times," she says. "Once we start performing it, we'll find that unfound energy."

The next evening, the squad proves Monica right. At the team's Show Night, where family and friends come to watch them rehearse, they nail their routine for the first time ever. "I wish that could have been Nationals, we did so good. Carol was freaking out," says Monica.

Kristen agrees. "In the huddle before we went on, I said, 'We call ourselves the Dream Team, but it isn't a dream anymore. We can do this,' " she recalls.

## "I Have a Good Feeling."

The University of Memphis All-Girl cheerleaders stand up in the aisles, itching to get off the bus that's brought them from the Orlando airport to the All-Star Music Resort at Walt Disney World. The Memphis fight song blasts out of the speakers next to a UCA welcome tent, as if cued by a music director. The doors open and Kristen steps out first, gripping the railing to help her balance in her high heels. She's wearing a fuchsia rhinestoned top, and her perfectly coiffed hair flaps in the breeze. Behind her, Callee steps out in aquamarine, playing with a string of silver beads that hangs around her neck. Even casual-girl Casi looks done up in a striped top and heels, her hair ironed and curled under her chin.

In all the times I've met them, I've rarely seen the squad wear anything but their uniforms, grimy practice clothes, and maybe a sweatshirt and jeans to class. "All the teams get dressed up to travel," Kristen says. "We represent the school, so we can't just roll out of bed."

The squad picks up their bags. They'll only be here at Nationals for three days, but many of them have brought two suitcases. They head toward their building. The resort is typical Disney—everything bright and oversized to the point where you feel like a kid plopped down in a cartoon. Each set of buildings has a different theme. We pass one with a three-story pair of cowboy boots in front. We turn a corner, and Carol points to a building with an enormous red neon sign that proclaims it BROADWAY. The sidewalks are marked with street signs—34th Street, 42nd Street, and 5th Avenue. It's bizarre to see Disney's version of my city.

"That's us," says Carol.

"Cool," responds Kristen.

Carol hands out the room keys. The women will sleep four to a room, two to a bed. Monica, Kristen, and two friends will share the first room. They walk in and turn on the lights; the inside looks like a standard motel room, lacking on the Disney magic.

"Carol told us we had to bring our uniforms and our shoes in our carry-on because they're the most important things," says Monica as she unpacks. "I also brought bread and peanut butter," she says, taking an entire loaf out of her suitcase. Next, she pulls out a tiny piece of yellow Lycra. "And we packed bikinis." She doesn't show me two huge bottles of vodka nestled among the luggage—either they plan on taking a lot of shots this weekend, or they got a little too excited at the airport duty-free shops.

I pick up a mix CD that Jessica McManus, one of the squad's strongest bases, made for the team to listen to on their way to Nationals. On the front cover is a photo of Memphis cheerleaders gripping a big, gold trophy. I open the liner notes. "Normally I just put a tiger head on this CD, but this year I came across a picture of when we won in 2003," it reads. "I just want you to imagine—tomorrow, that could be *you*."

I look closely at the photograph and recognize three faces—Monica,

Casi, and Kern. All three of them look ecstatic, happy tears in their eyes. I flip the case over to see what songs are on it. Kenny Rogers's "When You Put Your Heart In It." Nelly's "Heart of a Champion." Danity Kane's "Show Stopper."

The women change into the blue T-shirts that Carol designed last week. "We're going to go outside and warm up our stunts and pyramids," says Monica, who knows the drill, having done this same thing for the past three years. "It's for intimidation factor and so that when we run out on the mat tomorrow, people will want to come watch us."

Standing outside the squads' rooms, Carol looks nervous. "I saw Morehead practicing and they look good," she admits of the squad's biggest rival. "I had to change the stunts this week—I took out all the Full-Ups. I didn't want to, but it just wasn't consistent." Her voice sounds like it's on its deathbed.

The cheerleaders trickle out of their rooms. "Where do you want to practice?" Carol quietly asks Kristen.

"Just out front?" Kristen says, unsure. Because two-thirds of the cheerleaders are staying at Disney's All-Star Sports Resort across the parking lot, if the squad practices here, not too many people will see them. If they walk to the football-themed buildings at All-Star Sports, they'll be on public display.

Coed's coach, Chad, walks up to the group clapping, encouraging that I-know-we're-the-best vibe. "Guys, I watched Morehead practice and I wasn't impressed at all. They're sloppy and their cheer looks bad," he says. He completely contradicts what Carol just told me, but it's exactly what the squad wants to hear. Courtney and Ashley exchange an excited glance. "Our cheer's the bomb," someone says.

"You need to go out and practice at the football field," says Chad. "You need to *want* to be seen."

"We just need to worry about ourselves," says Carol. But instead of walking the team out front as planned, she leads them down the resort's sidewalk, through the parking lot, and over to the All-Star Sports Resort.

We pass a building where enormous baseball bats serve as columns. Another building is adorned with tennis rackets only a giant could use. But the football hotel is my favorite yet. Two identical buildings face each other, forming a courtyard that's been crafted to look like a football field. In front of each building is a brightly colored helmet as tall as the three-story building.

It's close to dusk, and a cheerleading team passes wearing matching red berets. Further down the faux football field, a Coed team practices, cheerleaders lining the outdoor hallways of the hotel to watch them.

The Memphis women stretch on a blacktop that's been painted green to mimic grass. From what I saw last week, they have no business practicing on a surface this hard, but none of them seem concerned. Carol searches for an outlet to plug in the team's boom box but can't find one. They proceed without music.

"Stunts," says Carol as the women gather in their groups. It's the part of the routine Carol changed since I last saw the team practice.

In each group, three bases face their flyer, palms out, like they're trying to boost her over a tall fence. The flyer steps in and is hoisted overhead. Heel Stretch. Three sixty spin. Arabesque. I'm expecting the Front Flip that freaked everyone out, but they've changed this part, too. Now, the flyers lean forward and roll down as the bases lock hands and form a bridge to cradle their backs. This move, called a Miami Walk-Out, is similar, but it doesn't take your breath away the way the Front Flip did. But each stunt group looks ten times more confident than they did last week.

Carol is too much of a perfectionist to be pleased. "Sharper," she says, in her just-gargled-rocks voice. "These should be crisp."

A small crowd begins to gather. Another All-Girl team, wearing matching shirts, sits down on the edge of the blacktop. A group of parents leans on the second-floor railing, "oh"ing and "ah"ing as Monica, Callee, and Kern fly high in basket tosses.

Michelle talks to the flyers. "When you look up before the basket toss, smile," she says. "Right now you do it like, 'Oh shit. I'm really gonna do this.'" Since she can't be on the mat, Michelle has taken on the role of an assistant coach.

"You gotta smile," echoes Carol.

The squad moves on to the dance. They've added in some vocals to get their energy and enthusiasm up before moving on to the final pyramid. When they throw their arms up, they yell, "Oh!" As they point their toe and whip their heads toward the audience, they now yell, "Shut up!"

"Ha," says a cheerleader watching the practice near me. "That's so cute."

But the ending pyramid is presenting more of a challenge. Neither Callee nor Kern pops into position on the first try. Both of them fall, arms out, pulling the others down like a barrel of monkeys.

Carol jumps up from where she's sitting cross-legged on the ground. "Why did neither side go up?" she yells.

"I know it's like putting someone on top of a building and asking them to fall gently," says Courtney, who's at the base on Callee's side of the pyramid. "But don't come down grabbing people."

The women try their ending pyramid again, this time with much more ease. "That was perfect," yells Carol. "When you control it, it looks really good. Why can't you do that *every time*?"

Carol has saved the best for last in tonight's practice. The squad snaps into show-off mode as the One-Mans go up, 1-2-3-4-5-6. Each one hits.

"They make that look easy," comments a woman behind me.

Almost as if responding to the positive feedback, the two 1-1-1s go up and stay up, like matching totem poles. The crowd hoots and hollers.

Practice is over, and the women head to the cafeteria. "If we hit, no one can touch us," says Ashley, an irrepressible smile on her face.

Courtney nods. "But if we don't, we'll be at the bottom of the barrel."

Kristen is hesitant to make predictions. "A lot depends on our warm-up tomorrow . . . ," she says, her voice trailing off.

"I have a good feeling," says Ashley.

Monica nods, her turquoise eyes sleepy. "Especially after Show Night, I have that same feeling I had freshman year," she says. "That we're gonna win."

# CHAPTER 15

## "He Can Do Rewinds with a Horse."

### *The Stephen F. Austin Lumberjacks*

BY DAY, THIS STAGE at Disney-MGM Studios is home to the Indiana Jones Epic Stunt Spectacular, where Hollywood stuntmen and women dodge fire and gigantic boulders. Some of the set is still in view, a re-creation of the Cairo marketplace where Indiana Jones outsmarts his pursuers in *Raiders of the Lost Ark*. But tonight, this stage will feature the twenty couples competing in the UCA Partner Stunt National Championship. The blue cheerleading mat is sprawled in front of the scalloped arches of the market, a rack of costumes standing haphazardly behind it, as if someone forgot to take it backstage.

Seven SFA partner couples have made the trek to UCA Nationals to compete, along with Trisha and Doug, to show SFA's complete dominance in the realm of partner stunting. On the mats backstage where the competitors are warming up, Lumberjack purple and red seems omnipresent. Only one of SFA's best partner stunters is conspicuously absent—Sierra. She is at home in Texas, where the rest of the team remains. James Brown, the dimple on his right cheek like a meteor crater, is here with his temporary partner, Cassie. She tightens the red ribbon in her hair.

"How did you pick Cassie from the other stunters on the team?" I ask him.

"I had to do what I had to do," says James Brown, shrugging. "Cassie's good, but she didn't have one of the better partners on the team. I thought we could stunt really well together." His mind drifts to Sierra, too. "Sierra and Cassie's styles are completely different. Cassie gets herself in the air very well, but her body positions aren't always great. Sierra lets the guy get her into the air, but she has *really* good body positions."

Near them on the mat, Yvette's eyes light up as she stretches, black curls falling over her shoulders. Near her, Jason has trimmed his afro and gotten rid of his sideburns. "A lot of my friends from high school and junior college cheer for UCA teams. I was only decent back then, so they're surprised to see me competing in Partner Stunt," he says. "I'm definitely one of the smallest guys here, but I know I can stunt like a big guy."

Samantha and Tyrone practice a few feet away. In their uniforms, the two of them look like polar opposites—everything about Samantha is long, from her swanlike neck to her narrow face. Tyrone stands only a few inches taller than her, and everything about him is wide. Even his Mohawk is an exaggerated strip.

Out of all the partner couples warming up, these two have had the least time to practice their routine since Tyrone left school a month ago to take care of his mom. "He met us in Nacogdoches two days before we left," says Samantha. "He came right over to my apartment and we were so eager, we went out in the front yard and started stunting. We were like, 'Yep, we still got it.' We talked while he was home about what we wanted to do, but we only got to practice for two days, maybe six hours total."

"It's just a blessing that we got here," says Tyrone.

Samantha and Tyrone are distracted from the conversation by a partner couple from Morehead State, who step onto the mat. The flyer tumbles toward her partner, flipping into a perfect Rewind. "They're flawless," says Samantha, clearly in awe. "We really can't be disappointed if we don't do well because of the circumstances."

The first few teams on the performance roster line up near the entrance to the stage. Samantha and Tyrone watch from the wings as a University of Delaware flyer begins their routine laying on the floor, her face propped up in her hands. Her partner straddles her and takes hold of her waist. He pops her straight into the air as she flips, landing for a stunning Rewind. The audience roars.

"Man, we had that idea at camp!" says Samantha. "We told Trisha we wanted to do a Superman Rewind, but she said, 'No, that's illegal.' Maybe they sent in a video and asked if they could do it? That's a bummer."

From where Samantha and Tyrone stand backstage, they can see that every inch of metal bleacher in the auditorium is packed. By the time the tenth couple in the competition takes the mat, it's standing room only. Samantha begins to feel butterflies in her stomach. She bows her head and says a quick prayer. "Please God, I ask you to bless us. This is our last and only time to do this, so just let us be proud," she says.

There are only two more couples before Samantha and Tyrone are on, and a UCA staffer has them line up in the wings. They're directly behind the couple from Morehead State who had looked so incredible in the warm-up room. But as this couple steps to the mat, their routine is a disaster—a long string of drops.

Samantha makes eye contact with Tyrone. "A lot of people haven't hit tonight," says Samantha, grabbing his hand. "If we just hit our routine, we will automatically be ahead."

"Don't worry about nothing," assures Tyrone. "It's just me and you."

"And now, from Stephen F. Austin University . . . Samantha Frazer and Tyrone Lyons," says the event's announcer.

Samantha gulps. She jogs toward the mat, waving at the audience, her half-moon smile in full force. Tyrone follows behind her, his usually unexcitable face animated. Bright lights pound on them, obscuring the audience and dilating their pupils. Samantha faces the crowd with her fists out to her sides. Tyrone opens his legs wide and squats behind her.

"Go Tyrone!" shouts someone from SFA's cheering section.

Their music begins. Samantha swings her arms in a circle and lifts off, Tyrone hoisting her and catching her two feet in his right hand. Her toes point toward the floor, and she quickly flexes her feet. She swings her right foot up into a Heel Stretch.

Tyrone brings her down, holding onto her waist as he brings her through his legs and straight back up, where she twists for several more effortless stunts. They go for a second Superman, this time with Samantha flicking her body straight and pulling her leg up as she sails through the air. She lands in Tyrone's hand with both legs slightly bent, one directly under her, the other held up to her ear. Her eyes squint as she presses with all her might. Like an inchworm flattening against a tree branch, she manages to fully straighten her body. Her bottom jaw drops as if to say, "I can't believe I just did that."

"Go Sam!" yells one of her teammates in the cheering section.

Samantha Doubles Down and steps right back in front of Tyrone for their final stunt. Tyrone boosts her for a picture-perfect Rewind. As he touches her down to the mat, he pulls his fist to his side, like a basketball player celebrating a slam dunk. Samantha jumps, blonde hair soaring in slow motion behind her.

The SFA cheering section jumps to their feet and the auditorium echoes with applause.

Tyrone faces Samantha. He throws his arms around her with such force that I'm afraid he might crush her. Her thin arms wrap around him and she jumps up, curling her knees around his waist. Her legs stay wrapped around him as he walks off the mat. They stand hugging to the side of the mat. "Y'all won, y'all won," someone says, passing by them in the wings.

Samantha's eyes are full of tears. "I couldn't have asked for anything better," she says. "For it to be our first time and to know that other people in this competition are doing it for their third, fourth, fifth time ... Any doubt I ever had in myself, it's gone."

The pair walks down the stage steps to where the SFA cheerleaders who've already performed sit. Several of their teammates rush toward them. "That was the best so far," someone says.

"But James Brown is on next," adds someone else. "And he can do Rewinds with a horse."

As the announcer calls his name, James Brown hulks onstage, cute Cassie at his side. He pushes her sky bound in a solid Rewind. Cassie comes down again, and he sends her back up, this time spinning like a screw twice before landing in his hands. He pops her high in the air as she dives into a flip, uncurling in time for him to catch her in a cradle. "Ohhh," gasps the audience. So far their routine is fierce.

"Hit it, Brownie, come on!" someone yells.

Cassie curls her body into a ball, in a transition stunt where James Brown holds her at chest level, then boosts her back to standing. But as he grips her back, she boggles, like a basketball slipping out of his hands. She reaches out in a panic toward his shoulder, and James Brown recovers his grip just in time. But messing up on such an easy stunt after nailing all the hard stuff doesn't look good to a judge.

James and Cassie finish their routine, and Cassie tries her best to smile. But her head hangs as she descends the staircase toward the SFA cheering section. Someone whips open a camcorder to show James Brown the routine. He shakes his head, angry with himself. "It was going well until that bobble," he says. "It didn't feel bad, but watching it, it looked a lot worse than it felt. It's usually the opposite. That stunt is normally really easy for us."

Yvette and Jason are the last couple from SFA to take the stage, Yvette blowing kisses to the audience as she walks. She stands a few feet in front of Jason.

"Go Evie!" people shout, as the drumbeat of their music begins and she back handsprings toward Jason. He reaches out and grabs her waist, flicking her up and around. She spins like a teetering top over his shoulder and comes perfectly to a stand, facing the audience. Everyone claps. She comes down and swings into a Rewind, Jason taking several steps as he catches her.

"I'ma get, get, get, get you drunk." A line from the Black Eyed Peas "My Humps" is oddly cut into the music.

Yvette pulls the hem of her short skirt down before handspringing toward Jason again. As she goes up, she dips like a car driving over a pothole. Jason struggles for a split second to get her back in place. Yvette does her best to curl herself into a Scorpion and Doubles Down.

As they walk back toward the stage's wings, the pair looks unsure. "It felt good," says Jason. "I've done worse."

Yvette nods, tiny jewels by her eyes. "We didn't drop, but we could have done better," she says. "All I care about is that one of the SFA couples gets first. I think Sam and Tyrone might have done it."

In the audience, Trisha and Doug stand identically, hands crossed over stomachs, backs against a stone wall, as the UCA staff calls all the couples to the stage for the awards ceremony. The women stand in a semicircle, their partners directly behind them. Tyrone places his hand on Samantha's shoulder.

The announcer begins with nineteenth place, but as he gets to number eleven, he has yet to call a couple from SFA.

Trisha jumps up and down. "We have seven couples in the top ten! That's amazing," she says.

"In tenth place," says the announcer, "We have a tie. Lola Medved and Jerrod Vanover from Stephen F. Austin University and Kristen Wilkerson and David Bowden from Stephen F. Austin State University." Trisha and Doug hoot and holler as the two of them step forward to claim their golden trophies.

"In eighth place, Chelsea Craiker and Tim Wegner from Stephen F. Austin University."

Samantha reaches back and touches Tyrone's hand, still on her shoulder.

"In seventh place, we also have a tie," says the announcer. "Ashley Picard and Jeremy Plemel from Stephen F. Austin University and Tony Crump and Brittany Kaczetow from Morehead State University."

James Brown visibly exhales.

Sixth and fifth places whiz by, and Trisha begins jumping again. "Three in the top four!" she says. "Amazing." The odds are in her favor—there's a three-in-four chance that one of her pairs has captured first.

"In fourth place," says the announcer, all the remaining competitors bracing themselves, "Cassie Valentin and James Brown." James Brown raises a thick eyebrow as they walk forward to claim their trophies. I wonder if he's thinking about what place he could have gotten performing with Sierra.

Yvette turns to Jason. Samantha tightens her grip on Tyrone's hand. "In third place . . . Yvette Quiñones and Jason Larkins," says the announcer. The two of them hop up, Yvette winking at someone in the audience. As they take their trophy, Yvette beams.

Samantha swings around and hugs Tyrone, his thick arms pressing her toward his hefty body. It is down to them and the couple from the University of Delaware. Whoever doesn't hear their name next has won the Partner Stunt National Championship.

"In second place," says the announcer, pausing just long enough for

Samantha to squeeze her eyes shut and say a quick prayer. Trisha taps her foot in anticipation.

"From Stephen F. Austin University, Samantha Frazer and Tyrone Lyons."

Samantha squeals. Tyrone nods his large head as Samantha starts jumping. But their celebration is eclipsed as University of Delaware cheerleaders and fans swarm the mat. They calm down just long enough for the announcer to call the winners' names and hand them the biggest trophy of the pack.

Samantha and Tyrone hug. Eight months ago at tryouts, Brad Patterson had said that Samantha would never be an elite stunter. Now she's one half of the second-best partner couple in the nation.

Still, for a brief second, she thought she might be first. "Second is a tease," she says. "It's bittersweet—I'm disappointed that we didn't defend SFA's title from last year, but at the same time, it feels like first. It's hard enough to make finals, and we traveled all the way up to second. It's awesome."

"How does that happen?" says Tyrone. "After they called third, I was just thinking, 'I can't believe we did this good.' "

James Brown steps away from the celebration. It looks like someone has ironed wrinkles into his forehead. "I'm a little disappointed," he says. "We should have been higher." He takes a deep breath and walks back to the group.

In her hands, Samantha grips her trophy—three golden columns with a gold cup placed on top. She leans her elbows on its top as she relays her victory to her family on her cell phone, her eyes filling with tears of happiness as she speaks.

Tyrone looks at the trophy and shakes his head. "This is just crazy," he says. "I can't believe we did this."

Trisha gathers the group to take a team photo. They line up all fourteen of their trophies in a semicircle, the guys lifting their partners to a seat on their shoulders. Samantha and Tyrone sit down in the middle, their larger trophies in front of them. They throw their arms around each other and flash victory smiles as Trisha snaps a picture. Trisha looks at the photo and smiles. "There's not room in the van for all these trophies," she says.

# CHAPTER 16

## "I'm Shit-My-Pants Nervous."

*The University of Memphis All-Girl Tigers*

IN THE CORNER OF her hotel room, Casi pulls on her bloomers under her royal-blue cheerleading skirt. "These are my lucky panties," she says. "I've worn the same panties and sports bra for Nationals since middle school." She pulls on a pair of warm-up pants and yanks her skirt down over them.

Around the room, four women tear through open suitcases, running into each other as they rush to get into their full cheerleading regalia. Finals is only four hours away, and they're supposed to meet Carol in forty minutes to take the bus as a team to Disney's Wide World of Sports Complex, where the competition will be held.

Casi looks down. "I forgot lotion," she says, taking the pants back off and rubbing white moisturizer into her mocha skin.

"Are you nervous?" I ask.

"Oh, I'm shit-my-pants nervous," she responds. "I couldn't sleep last night."

She looks at her computer's iTunes list. "I need some inspiration," she says, stopping the Dave Matthews song that's currently playing. She turns on her favorite hip-hop song and starts to dance.

Two doors over, Monica sits in bed with the covers pulled over her as she puts on blush and eyeliner. "Woo hoo," she whistles as she checks herself out in the mirror. All the tables in the room are covered in McDonald's cups and bags—Kristen's brother went on a fry run for them late last night. They're listening to Common and Will.i.am's "A Dream," the song based on Martin Luther King's famous speech, on the team's mix CD.

"I didn't shave my armpits, since we don't need to," says one of the roommates, staring at the uniform that's laid out on her bed. Each uniform has three pieces. The first is a blue spandex turtleneck with silver and white bands that snake around the elbows. Over that, they pull on a slim-fitting V-neck that's blue, with white triangles nipping in at the waist. Across the center, the word *Memphis* is written in block letters. The squad's skirts are simple—bright blue with a triangle-shaped slit cut into the right side. A white ribbon runs around the edge of the skirt, following the shape of the triangular slit, like an arrow pointing upwards.

One of the roommates sits on the edge of her bed as Kristen brushes bronze shimmer powder up and down her legs. "Do they look longer?" the girl asks.

"So much longer," jokes Kristen.

Across the room, Monica is way ahead of the rest of the group—her uniform is on and her hair and makeup are done. She laces her cheerleading sneakers, sits up straight with her back against her headboard, and wiggles her feet. "We're gonna be done in four hours," she says.

Next door, in Courtney and Ashleys' room, things are more chaotic. Belts, high heels, and other articles of clothing are flung everywhere. The TV blares a Daffy Duck cartoon. "We were supposed to wake up at 7 a.m.," says Ashley, "but we didn't actually get up until 7:39 a.m. Oops."

Ashley and Courtney jockey for position in front of the room's only mirror as they comb their hair into tight ponytails. One of their roommates is still in bed. "Get up," their fourth roommate yells. "We have to leave in fifteen minutes."

"I don't feel good," says Brittany, a freshman flyer on the squad, gripping her stomach. "Does anyone have any Tylenol?"

"I have Tylenol PM," says Ashley.

"Do *not* give her that," snaps Courtney. "Drink some water."

"The water from the tap makes me want to puke," says Brittany. Everyone seems to be ignoring her—maybe she's one of those people who always mysteriously feels sick before a performance.

"I feel like a robot in this," says Courtney, putting on her uniform over her sports bra. "The elbows are stiff."

"I'm hurtin' bad," says Brittany, pulling herself out of bed.

"Try telling Carol that and see if she cares," snaps Courtney.

"Can we just do it already?" says Ashley. "My stomach is going crazy just thinking about it."

Outside, Callee and Kern, who are sharing a room, are ready to go when Carol pops out of her door. "We had a system in our room," Callee tells me. "The girl with the thickest hair woke up first and got in the shower since it takes her longer to dry her hair. Then she got the rest of us breakfast."

Carol looks panicked that only a few members of the squad are outside and ready to go. She starts knocking on doors. "It's 8:30 a.m. you guys, come on," she says, her voice pretty much nonexistent. More women start to file out. Some of them hold flags over their shoulders the way a soldier holds a rifle, others grip signs with the letters that spell out Tigers. "Who has lipstick?" Carol asks. Kristen and Monica both raise their hands.

"Why don't people have their gamefaces on?" asks Carol. "That's part of getting ready." "Everyone have their poms?" "Why's your hair not up?" she barks to different people.

Ten minutes later, the team begins the walk toward the bus, Brittany and her friend trailing behind. "I don't feel good," says Brittany, hunched over with her hands across her belly. "My stomach."

Her friend does her best to raise her spirits. "I feel like Marcia, Marcia, Marcia with this ponytail," she says, swinging it *Brady Bunch* style.

Brittany's eyes tear up, and trails of salt water fall down her cheeks. "Seriously, I'm hurtin'."

## "It's Like Torture."

The squad looks like a flock of exotic blue birds as they jog up the stairs to Disney's Wide World of Sports Complex. They stand on line with other squads and a mass of soccer players also here today for a tournament. The women show the guards at the gates their Disney passes and walk quickly toward the Milk House, the building where the competition will take place. (It was built by the National Dairy Association, of course.) Carol opens the door. "I want to take a look at the stage," she says. The squad follows her into the hall and through a cinder-block arch that overlooks the indoor arena.

Two stories of stadium seating below, the mat has already been assembled and velcroed in place on the floor. Behind the mat, a Greek temple has been created out of white cloth and faux stone columns. Red and blue lights shine on it.

Rows of plastic chairs have been set out for spectators, and Kristen's mom has already saved a section for the Memphis fans, a blue and silver pom-pom on each seat.

Behind the chairs, a long table is on a platform that is so tall it requires stairs. This is where the twelve judges will sit. Six of them will score the cheer section of each routine, worth thirty-five points (plus fifteen for a tape of the squad leading a crowd at a football game). Six of them will judge the rest of the routine, performed to music, on a scale of fifty points. For each group, the highest and lowest scores will be thrown out, and the rest will be added together for a maximum of 400 points. With their bird's-eye view, the judges will be able to see every little mistake.

"It makes me so nervous seeing the stage," says one of the freshmen. "When the music comes on, I hope this feeling goes away."

"I just want to hit," Carol says, eyes glued to the stage. "Shit, I don't care if nine people hold something up . . . I just want to hit."

The squad walks outside to begin warming up, but Kristen lingers in the arena, holding onto a railing, staring at the stage. "I'm scoping it out for the last time," she says. "It's sad. This is all I've ever known."

"Are you nervous?" I ask.

"I don't get nervous—I'm the calm one. I calm everybody else down," she says. "Now, before the awards ceremony, I'm a nervous wreck. I think that's because it's completely out of my control then."

Kristen turns around and jogs to catch up with the squad. Together, they walk to a grass field, where the sunshine is almost blinding. Carol bends down to feel the grass. "It's wet," she says. "We can't practice on it." Instead, she has the squad spread out on the sidewalk to stretch. The girls laugh at Callee's shoelaces, which she's taped into a ball so there's no way they can come untied. "I'm sorry if I'm *pre-pared*," she responds to their mocking.

As they practice the stunt sequence, the women look excited, flashing uncontainable smiles at each other. But even I'm starting to feel that sensation in the pit of my stomach that tells you you're either very nervous, very hungry, or you've had way too much caffeine.

"Tighten your ponytails," says Carol as they finish the stunt sequence. It has to be a good sign that she has no major comments besides grooming tips.

"Is there any way to hold the S the other way?" asks Michelle, watching as the team practices the One-Mans. Callee holds an S sign that looks upside down—it's a printer mistake Carol didn't have time to fix.

Carol shakes her head. "I don't care if it says P on the end. We don't change a thing."

Coed's coach, Chad, walks over. "You have the prettiest stunts," he says as the girls gather around him in a semicircle. "The way to win today is to sell it. Whip your heads up with big, huge smiles. Put that Memphis magic on it. Make your claps sharp, keep your faces excited. Turn it on, on, on. Morehead can't make that magic happen."

He watches as the girls run through their final pyramid. "This was money last night," Carol tells him. Perhaps the concrete below is giving them extra motivation to not let anything fall, because again the pyramid goes up strong. Brittany, who is in the center, puts her hands out as Callee and Kern both pick up a knee to place their inner feet in her palms. She moves her hands like someone trying to find something in the dark—their feet are just out of her peripheral vision.

"Good," says Carol. "Good."

"I can never get their feet," says Brittany, gripping her stomach as they pop down.

"Just pretend," says Callee, whipping her hands out like a waiter holding two trays. "We'll find you."

Brittany nods and paces in a circle, near tears again. "My mom is bringing her medicine," someone says.

"Baskets," yells Carol. The women look at her like she's crazy—a fall on this concrete would send someone to the emergency room. "Everything we just did is illegal on concrete. We can warm up the baskets." The four basket tosses go up. Thankfully, everyone is caught perfectly.

The team is almost ready to go inside the Milk House. There's still an hour and a half before they perform, but their official warm-up backstage starts in half an hour. A few of the women take out mirrors to give themselves one last look over. "Spray all this crap back," says Carol, pointing to the hairs falling around her face. "I want to see all your pretty faces. Everyone put on lipstick."

Monica and Kristen pass around lipstick and gloss, everyone sharing tubes. Kristen puts on another layer of blush over her gameface, her cheeks vibrantly pink. Behind her, women point bottles of hairspray at each other's heads.

"Remember, it's not enough to hit," says Chad, turning to walk toward the Milk House. "You have to *sell* it."

"Everyone take out your earrings," says Carol. "And spit out your gum."

Casi looks down at her uniform. "Our uniform tops come up, so we should all take out our belly button rings, too," she says. Almost half the squad lifts up their tops slightly. They begin to unhook jewelry from their navels.

"My mouth is already dry," says Courtney.

The women pick up their bags, flags, poms, and signs and walk toward the Milk House. They open the glass doors and squeeze past five other squads into the hallway that now smells of Victoria's Secret perfume. The chatter feels syncopated—the nervous energy in here could power a small country for days.

The Memphis women sit down in a circle, and Carol plugs in her boom box. Their music comes on, and they close their eyes, visualizing the routine. They move their arms in mini-circles for the Triple Toe Touch Back Tuck. They put their arms up when they'll be lifting people and out when they'll be flying. They do a miniature, seated version of the dance. All the other teams stare.

Kern takes a stone out of her bag. On one side it says STRENGTH.

"My mom gave it to me one year when I couldn't compete because I tore my ACL," she says. "Ever since, I've had everyone kiss it before we go on." She holds the stone in front of each squad member's face. Each of them puckers up and plants her lips on it, lipstick outlines forming in layers all over its surface.

Through the plate-glass window in the hall, we can see Morehead State warming up on the sidewalk outside. They look like cheerleaders straight out of Toni Basil's "Hey Mickey" video. Their uniforms are solid white, the only embellishment a big blue M on the stomachs. Their hair is half up and half down, and it flops around as they practice. They all wear matching white athletic socks scrunched around their ankles. As someone later points out, this is the "Kentucky cheerleading look." But retro styling aside, they look impressive—their stunt sequence is loaded with difficult Full-Up spins, while Memphis took almost all of theirs out.

"Don't look at them," says Courtney, physically turning one of her teammate's heads.

The Memphis women head to the official backstage warm-up area, which is the size of several basketball courts. Three cheerleading mats have been laid out on the ground. On the first mat, each team gets three minutes to warm up their tumbling. Then they are called to one of the two remaining mats. Here, they get four minutes to run through their full routine and fix any trouble spots. To the left of the mats, Herbal Essences has set up a booth with row upon row of hair products and stage mirrors. MAY YOUR STYLE HAVE AS MUCH BOUNCE AS YOUR MOVES, reads a banner.

The Memphis women gather beside the booth, but they're too nervous to primp. Even though none of the teams warming up before them look top-notch, the squad members make a concerted effort not to watch them. Instead, Monica does a grand plié to stretch out her thighs. Ashley puts her arms up over her head and kicks her legs.

Casi makes fun of a cheerleader on another squad. "Please, Lord, forgive me," she says.

"He's gonna make you pay," says Courtney, shaking her head.

Casi looks toward the ceiling. "Just make me pay *after* today."

"University of Memphis. Three-minute tumbling warm-up," says a

UCA staff member. The women line up. Side by side, a pair of women runs and does the tumbling pass that they'll throw in the routine.

"Looking pretty, y'all," says Carol, as Monica and Callee whip their bodies into Fulls, landing as nonchalantly as cats.

The group gathers around Carol in a circle. "It starts right now," she says, trying to squeeze the words out as loud as she can. "Get pumped up."

"University of Memphis, four-minute warm-up," directs the UCA staff. The team runs onto the larger practice mat.

Their music comes on and the women snap into action. Everything looks solid—the tumbling, the stunts, the opening pyramid, the One-Mans. The excitement builds in the team's eyes with each thing they hit. They get to the 1-1-1s in the cheer. On opposite sides of the mat, Callee and Kern are launched up to stand on their middle layer's leg. Callee's feet slip out from under her, but Monica holds on tight, keeping her up in the pyramid at a slight slant. The rest of the routine is mistake free.

"Callee's 1-1-1, go again," says Carol, hoping to get them to hit it once solidly to build their confidence. But this time Callee misses completely, pulling Monica down.

"Again," says Carol.

"Hurry, time's almost up," says alternate Michelle.

They try again, and this time they hit. "Looks good," yells Carol as the team gathers their belongings.

"Was that the warm-up you were hoping for?" I ask her.

She nods yes. "I just want them to feel the excitement of hitting this," she says. She walks toward a metal door. She swings it open and holds it with her back as the squad runs through. "Y'all, that was awesome," she says.

We descend down two flights of a dark stairway. "We're gonna hit it!" yells Carol, finding a few extra decibels in her voice.

"This is ours!" someone says.

"We got it!"

"Go Memphis!"

At the bottom of the stairs, we walk through an open doorway into a hallway with a checkerboard linoleum floor. The women book it down the hall. It almost feels like that scene in *This Is Spinal Tap,* where the band is trying to find the mysterious stage door, but everyone around me seems to know exactly where they're going. Nearly all of them have been here before.

The hallway feeds directly into the Milk House's main arena. We can hear the roar of the crowd's chatter, but we can't see a thing—we are separated from the stage and the stands by a series of black curtains that hang from the arena's rafters to the floor. We turn right into a narrow corridor between two curtains. For the past few months, the women have described being in "the tunnel" before running onto the Nationals mat. I thought they were being metaphorical, but we are literally in a tunnel, curtains billowing on both sides of us. Four teams are lined up in front of us like a stack of blocks—black, red, forest green, and navy blue.

The women gather around Carol one last time. "Listen up," she croaks. "You are the first of the best teams to go out there. *You* get to set the pace. Make yourselves the team to beat. Sell it, but don't overdo it. Control it."

She holds a Coke in her right hand, and Monica leans forward to take a sip through the straw. "Where will you be sitting?" she asks.

"I'll be to the left of the stage," replies Carol. Many people have told me that they watch Carol during the routine as a gauge of how they're doing. If she's jumping up and down, they're kicking butt. If she's in her seat, something is wrong.

Carol gives each cheerleader a tight hug. She turns around and exits the tunnel. No break a leg. No good luck. The squad is on their own.

In the arena, the national anthem plays. Sandwiched between the curtains, the Memphis cheerleaders put their hands to the hearts and sing along. All-Girl Cheerleading Finals is about to begin—the first team is called to the mat. They rush out of the tunnel, and the line steps forward.

One of the girls rubs her hands on her skirt. "My palms are getting sweaty," she says.

Callee looks at Casi. "The only thing I'm nervous about is our stunt sequence," she says. "If we get that . . ."

Casi nods. "I'm always scared for our side of the opening pyramid."

Behind the curtain, the thumping of the bass is strong as the first team's music changes frenetically between songs. High up on the wall, two projection screens hang so that the cheerleaders can watch what's going on out front. The women strain their necks to see. "I hate this part, standing back here," someone says. "It's like torture."

Brittany's face is blank. She stands silently, her arms crossed over her stomach.

Courtney starts singing Ace of Base's "The Sign." Ashley follows her in silly-song-singing with a "Wake me up before you go, go, Whoever doesn't is a ho ho."

Kern calls over all the flyers. "If you go in the air at any point in the routine, come over here," she says, her voice cracking. The flyers all grasp pinkies in a circle. "Lord, may you be with us today and keep us safe. Let the angels hold us up," she says. "Some of us might not be coming back next year. So this is it. It's in God's hands now." Tears well up in her eyes, and she smiles softly.

Callee walks out of the circle, her animated face unusually still. "I can't be my yippity self now. I just need to be calm," she says.

"Let's own this!" someone says, as another squad heads out to the floor. Memphis is only one team away from the front of the line. It feels like the bottom is dropping out of my stomach, and my pulse is starting to race. Yet Monica stands silently watching the screen. Kristen looks serene beside her. "Look, they did that Front Flip we were gonna do," says Courtney as dance music blasts through the auditorium.

"Was it good?" someone asks.

"Nope," says Courtney.

The navy blue team in front of us jogs onto the mat. The Memphis women look at each other and step forward. Just three minutes until showtime.

Kern drops to her knees and says a prayer to herself, her eyes closed and her bottom lip quivering. She stands up. "I'd never fallen in a competition until last year. Having that possibility again . . . ," she says, shaking her head. "I'm so jittery. I just have to lock my legs and my body out."

Courtney turns around and looks at the rest of the squad. "Can we just go on already?"

### "Show Them That Memphis Magic."

In front of the curtains, the Memphis parents are getting nervous. "This isn't like other sports where you have four quarters and if you mess up in one, you can fix it," says Kristen's mother. "You only have one shot."

Monica's parents sit nearby. "I'm real emotional," says Monica's mom.

Her dad nods. "I don't think there's a parent with a senior girl who's not sad," he says. "We complain, but when it comes down to it, us parents get hooked in as much as the girls do."

The competition announcer leans into his microphone. "Up next, the University of Memphis Tigers," he says as the Memphis fight song plays. The parents wave their blue pom-poms in the air. The Memphis Coed squad, seated on the floor in the front of the rows of chairs, jumps up and screams.

The Memphis women run through an opening in the columns. Ashley and Courtney look pumped, clapping as they jog. Monica waves to the audience—although the women tell me they can see nothing but bright lights when they're on the mat, she knows exactly where her family and boyfriend are sitting. The squad members carrying flags line them up at the back edge of the mat, while the women with signs and poms place their props at the front.

I rush to the coach's observation area and sit down beside Carol, who is perched on the edge of her seat. "The music's on! The music's on!" someone yells.

"Come on," screams Carol, straining to get the words out.

The women wait for the first beat of their music. Several shrug their shoulders harshly, either trying to release the tension or to get in a deep breath. Brittany, who was in tears earlier, reaches down to adjust her shoe. It seems like minutes elapse before the music starts. But then the metallic voice shouts from the speakers, "Memphis All-Girl." The women spring into action. "It's the eye of the tiger, It's the thrill of the fight," sings Survivor, as if cheering on Rocky as he climbs the stadium stairs.

The women hurtle up, throwing their hands overhead to gain momentum, and launch into their tumbling passes. Heading in six different directions, the women tumble toward each other, each person looking like they're about to hit someone else. They weave past each other like lines in an Escher drawing. "Yeah!" yells Carol. "Yeah!"

At the back of the mat, six of the women move their flags in a rainbow motion, the word *Tigers* flickering by on the blue flags in perfect unison. The teams walk into their three-line, triangular formation for their Triple Toe Touch Backs. They jump up, their legs scissor-kicking straight out to the sides. One. Two. Three. The women land and spring back for their Back Tucks. Not a single hand touches the ground, not a single person lurches forward. Their upper bodies are folded down in front of their straight legs, and they whip their head and shoulders up on the same count with Cheshire cat smiles.

Carol cups her hands to her mouth. "Wooo!" she yells along with the rest of the crowd.

The women walk backward, ponytails swishing, into their five stunt groups. The bases turn to place a hand in the center of their group. The flyers step in and are hoisted up.

All the flyers are in the air. They kick their left legs up into Heel Stretches. Kern is in the front, right side of the mat, her body line unwavering. Beside her, Brittany smiles like she's never felt better in her life.

"Come on!" screams Carol.

All five flyers bring their left leg down and bend their knees slightly as their bases spin them 360 degrees, like five planets making a year's worth of rotation in a split second. They straighten again as their bases bring them back fully overhead, this time facing right. On the same count, their front legs kick straight behind them and their upper bodies come down, creating a long straight line in an Arabesque. They turn their heads in unison to face the crowd. Callee nods as if to say, "We're the bomb."

The flyers fold their upper bodies down, interlocking their arms with their bases, and they roll forward for the Miami Walk-Out. "Ohh!" responds the audience.

"Yeah!" yells Carol next to me, jumping out of her seat. "Yeah!"

I turn around to see the parents. Many of them are up, waving their pom-poms. Others are busy snapping pictures.

The women walk into the positions for their opening pyramid, shaking their heads for extra flair. Once in position, they throw their arms in the air, like *Fame* dancers reaching for the sky. "Can't touch this," sings MC Hammer as the squad begins to build the pyramid.

On the left side of the mat, Monica scrambles onto a base's shoulders as a woman on the other side of the mat mirrors her. They face the center, where two groups of bases have lifted Callee and Kern curled into balls, facing each other. The groups dip, and Callee and Kern kick their legs straight out behind them, toward the edges of the mat. Below them, the bases push two women into Shoulder Stands, still holding onto Callee and Kern's hands. Callee and Kern land in push-up position, their backs like tabletops, one middle layer woman holding their legs and another their hands.

The applause in the arena turns up to 11. Carol jumps up again. "Come on!" she shouts. She had been worried that, in a repeat of last year, someone would fall in the opening section of the routine, setting a bad tone for the rest of the performance. But so far, it's stunning.

The middle layer women lower Callee and Kern, turning them on their backs, and they bounce up in the middle in an Arabesque position. The whole group dips and transitions to a new pyramid. Monica and her mirror each grab their top flyer's leg. As the group dips again, they pull their top flyers to standing on their thighs for a 1-1-1. Callee and Kern lift their inner knees and place their inner feet in the hands of the Shoulder Stands in the center of the formation. It looks like two sets of facing staircases.

The audience yells. Carol is on the edge of her chair. Across the auditorium, the Memphis Coed squad is going crazy.

Callee and Kern bend at the waist, letting themselves fall backwards into a cradle. The music stops. It's time for the cheer. This is where the squad can pick up a lot of difficulty points.

"T! I! G! E! R! S! Ti-gers! Ti-gers!" the squad chants together, their Tennessee accents bending their "I"s into "Aye"s. Some women spell out the letters with their bodies. Others wave their poms in the air. Some pepper in their own words. "Let's hear it!" "Come on!" they scream.

Behind them, the six One-Man partners face each other. The bases squat down, putting their hands out in front of their hips. The flyers put their hands on their bases' shoulders and step their front foot into their palms. "T!" The first group dips and then Kern sails up, swinging forward so that her second foot rests in her base's free hand. She hoists up her T sign. "I!" The second One-Man goes, her I sign held high in the air. The G goes up, and then the E. Casi swings Monica up for the R, a look on her face that seems to say, "What? You can't do this?" Callee follows with her S. All the One-Mans are in the air. The squad has proved the UCA staff wrong—an All-Girl team can do this kind of stunt in competition. "Let's! Go! Ti-gers!" the squad shrieks. Their faces glow—they can tell from the booming audience that they have hit it.

"Good! Come on, girls!" Carol jumps up and circles her fist in the air.

"Breathe!" shouts Michelle.

"Memphis fans, let's hear you yell!" the squad chants, as three women run forward with signs. Behind them, the rest of the squad gathers into three groups. On the left side of the mat, a shoulder stand goes up. Behind it, Courtney and another base throw Kern straight up to land on the middle layer's knee, which is bent and being supported by Kristen underneath. Kern gets there, holding up a sign that reads LET's. They've completed one of the hardest things in All-Girl cheerleading—a 1-1-1 where the third layer girl is tossed into the stunt.

Beside them, in another wave, an Extension goes up in the middle, with Brittany hoisting a GO sign. Callee follows in a split second, landing on Monica's knee for the second 1-1-1. She raises her TIGERS sign. Both 1-1-1s are up. I feel a wave of pride surge over me.

"Oh, shit," says Carol softly, bringing her hands to her mouth. I survey the mat. Nothing seems worthy of a curse word.

And then I see it. Kern's knees are bent and she's sliding off her middle layer's leg. As Kern's 1-1-1 collapses, it falls softly, like a house of cards. The audience gasps as Kern flutters down, her body in a straight line. She knocks down her middle layer, their bases having the wherewithal to reach up and bring them safely down to the mat.

The women in the fallen pyramid stand there, stunned. I can't tell if the others have seen what has just happened, because they continue to chant "Let's! Go! Tigers!" Brittany and Callee raise their signs proudly. The women dismount and throw their signs toward the back of the mat.

"T-I-G! E-R-S! Let's Go Tigers!" they chant as they walk into four groups, some women out front.

"Come on!" yells Carol again, as if to reassure them that all hope is not lost. Their Rewinds go up. Callee, Monica, Kern, and Brittany all flip backwards as their bases grunt to hoist them up, and they all land with their feet in their bases' hands at shoulder height. Their arms go up in a V-shape. Callee gives some spirit fingers.

"Wooo!" yells the audience.

The music pumps back on. "Get down, hit the flo'." The flyers squish down into a ball and look up at the crowd on the same beat. They smile like kids digging their tongues into ice cream cones. And, bam, they're launched in the air like batons, their bodies in straight lines.

The bases interlock their arms, and the flyers come down. All four land with their arms crossed over their chests. "Get down, hit the flo'," the music repeats as the women hustle to their places in the triangular dance formation.

Kristen swings her head side to side excitedly with all eyes on her, front and center. She throws her right elbow up, and then her left, following the pendulum movement back to her right side, where she squats. She dances like there was no fall twenty seconds ago, like there's no way her team could lose, like this isn't her last time on a cheerleading mat.

She jumps to standing, her arms swinging wildly over her head and then to her side, palms perpendicular to her body. I catch her eye as she shuffles her feet "Thriller" style, her hands shaking out to her side with attitude. She points her toe and pops her leg out, whipping her head to the audience with a "Shut up."

The audience screams, loving it. Carol is back on the edge of her seat. "Come on! Go!" she yells.

The team lines up for the last thing in their routine—their ending pyramid. "Come on y'all," screams Michelle. If they do this cleanly, even with Kern's fall earlier, they could still have a chance of winning.

Two tumblers crisscross on the front of the floor, drawing enough attention to give the squad time to start building. On the right side of the mat, Monica climbs on Casi's shoulders as their mirror on the left does the same. Farther out, Callee faces the right side of the auditorium and does a Rewind, Kern doing the same on the left. Their bases catch them at waist height.

The groups bounce, and Callee and Kern each kick a leg toward the center of the mat as they put their hands on their base's shoulders. The group bounces again. Monica grabs Callee's leg and places it on her thigh. The bases below hoist Callee up, and Monica scoops up both of her legs, bringing Callee to standing on her leg.

On the other side, Kern does the exact same motions, kicking her leg back, her middle layer grabbing hold of her foot, too. Her bases bounce and hoist her. But it's not smooth and controlled like Callee's side. Kern doesn't stand up on her middle layer's thigh. Her momentum keeps her moving, and she falls toward the center of the pyramid.

In the middle of the mat, Brittany goes up in an Extension and put her hands out in anticipation of Kern and Callee's feet. She desperately gropes back and finds Callee's foot. But Kern's sails straight past her, kicking her on the way down. Three bases rush toward Kern with their arms up, catching her as she falls out of the air.

"Memphis!" the squad yells as their music stops. They're used to ending the routine in glory, the pyramid triumphantly in the air. But instead, their pyramid looks like a Roman ruin, only half of it intact, the rest of the cheerleaders standing in a clump like a pile of ancient rubble. Kern looks stunned—her feet are back on the mat, but her arms are around the shoulders of two of the bases who caught her. The audience cheers, and Courtney throws her hands up in a congratulatory High V. But Memphis has committed the cardinal sin of cheerleading—they've missed their final stunt and left a bad taste in the audience's mouth.

Carol looks like she's just been slapped across the jaw. She gets up from her chair quietly and follows the cheerleaders off the floor in silence. I turn back to see how the Memphis parents are taking it. Everyone is firmly planted in their chairs with concerned looks on their faces.

Courtney's words echo in my head: "If we don't hit, we're the bottom of the barrel."

## "Why Did It Come Down?"

The Memphis squad walks through an opening in the black curtains to the right of the Nationals mat, the bounce in their step flatlined. They walk through the checkerboard hall into a small room where two flat-panel monitors have been set up. Since it's impossible for the cheer-leaders to know what their routine looked like as a whole, the UCA has set up this area so the teams can see exactly what the judges saw.

The women look devastated, like they're on the way to a funeral. Kern darts past the group, already crying, booking it to the nearest bathroom. No one even seems to notice her. Kristen and Carol trail behind. "It was good," Carol says, trying to reassure Kristen. "It was fine."

Tears roll like tiny rivers down Kristen's cheeks. If the sage of the team is crying, the situation must be bad. Christy, the middle layer flyer who holds Kern's legs in both 1-1-1s, gasps for breath. "I'm sorry, y'all," she whimpers. "I tried as hard as I could. She just didn't stand up."

The flat-panel screens flash on, and the squad crowds around them. They're non-reactive as the opening section of the cheer looks solid. Most of them know what is coming. Even if they were looking in the opposite direction during Kern's falls, they heard the crowd's gasps.

The playback hits the mid-point of the routine. On the screen, the 1-1-1 pyramids go up. I squint my eyes, willing the pyramid to stay up this time. But still, Kern falls, taking the others down with her.

"It was up there," says Carol, shaking her head. "Why did it come down? It looks like she just bent her knees."

Monica's eyes brim with tears, but she's not outwardly crying like the other girls. Callee, standing beside her, sobs quietly. Monica pulls Callee toward her, and the two hug, swaying slightly, each one like a mother trying to comfort her baby.

Casi sits down, sliding her back against the far wall. She is not cry-ing. I see something different in her—anger. It oozes out as she stares at the checkerboard floor a few feet in front of her, like she's trying to burn a hole in the floor.

Carol groans as the final pyramid falls. She surveys the room. "The rest . . . the rest is so badass," she says, her voice still begging for a cough drop and bed rest.

Courtney and Ashley stand near each other, tears pouring out of their eyes. "That was the *best* routine I've *ever* had in my *life*, and . . . ," says Courtney. She stops, not wanting to pin the blame on one person. "Ugh, I just hate messing up."

Michelle, the team's alternate, shakes her head. "She just buckles under pressure. If she hit the first 1-1-1, she probably would have hit the second," she says. "That could have been the winning routine. It was perfect."

The "she" everyone keeps referring to is, of course, Kern. She swooped in to save the day, and ironically it was her mistake that cost the squad a perfect routine. She is not ready to face her teammates yet. She sits inside a bathroom stall, sobbing. "I just want to be alone—I don't want to see anybody," she says. "If they're mad at me or if they're like, 'It's okay'—anything they say is still going to upset me." I remember what she'd said a week ago—that she just wanted to prove to herself that she could come through when it really counted.

Back in the viewing room, the UCA ushers shoo the Memphis squad from the area. "The next team's on their way in," a man in a polo shirt says. The women file out, theirs heads lowered. Half the team heads inside the arena to watch the rest of the competition. The second half wanders through the halls of the Milk House, trying to calm themselves down. Their rivals, Morehead, won't be going on for another forty-five minutes.

Jessica, the base at the bottom of Kern's 1-1-1s, shakes her head. "I felt it bobble for a second," she says. "But I thought they could stand up on it."

"You did what you could," someone reassures her.

I've vowed to keep silent and let them mourn—I'm worried about saying the wrong thing. But an unsportsmanly thought slips out of my mouth. "Isn't there a good chance some of the other teams will drop, too?" I ask.

Michelle shakes her head, her ponytail waving behind her. "The likelihood of another good team having two drops is not good," says Michelle. "It sucks that one person messes it up for everyone else. For the *second* year."

"It's hard not to blame her," says Ashley. "It looks like she was just like, 'Okay, I'm gonna fall now.' Like she didn't want to be up there."

"She could have stayed up," someone says.

Behind them, I see Kern's head pop out of the bathroom, her once-perfect eyeliner transformed into raccoon-like shadows. She's contemplating coming out of exile, but once she hears "She could have stayed up," she turns right back around and heads back to her stall.

"Let's sit and sulk," someone says as the women head toward a concession stand for comfort food.

Inside the arena, Kristen and Monica have joined their families. "Good job," says Kristen's brother. Her eyes are bright red. She sits down in front of her mom's chair, and her mom rubs her back. Tears begin to roll again.

Monica's legs are thrown across her boyfriend's lap; his arm is wrapped around her, and her head is on his shoulder. In her hands she holds a stuffed fish—Flounder from *The Little Mermaid*. "I'm proud of myself because I went through four years of college competition never falling," she says. "That's incredible." Her turquoise eyes look past me. "But it just stinks. I felt like this was our year."

Near her, the rest of the squad squeezes into a tiny area on the carpet. They sit like cross-legged sardines, barely talking and moving. They stay like this for routine after routine, each one blending together. The music coming from the loudspeakers sounds like a late-night commercial for Now That's What I Call Music! Volume 16—choppily edited snippets of the year's biggest dance songs, from "La La La" to "Fergalicious" with a lot of Justin Timberlake thrown in. These are songs the women love to dance to, yet they sit there, eyes puffy and makeup askew, barely reacting at all.

I sit down next to Callee. "Part of me is happy because I hit my stuff," she says. "It's just heartbreaking. Now we have to watch all these squads who are not even close to us but will rank higher."

Her face crumples like a pug, and she begins to cry again. "I'm sorry. But just look at this team, this cheer is ugly. It's just slop," she says. "These girls are my best friends and now I'm not going to get to see them every day anymore. I love Kern, but come on, it's your fifth year. You know what to do."

I see Kern walk into the auditorium with her boyfriend. They take seats far away from the squad. "Have you talked to her?" I ask Callee.

"What's there to say? 'It's okay?' It's not."

"Why couldn't we have had prelims?" asks Casi. "It's like 'All-Girl—get them out of the way fast so everyone else can go.'"

A few minutes later, Morehead takes the mat. As they get in their positions and wait for the music to start, Courtney whispers to her teammates, "Someone told me the Morehead girls were like, 'Memphis fell—good.'"

In their white socks, the Morehead flyers soar up for their stunt sequence, spinning like dreidels that just won't fall over. They hit a pyramid and begin their cheer. "M! S! U!" they yell. "Go! Big! Blue!"

"It's good, but nothing's sharp," says Callee, as Morehead tumblers crisscross the floor for a second round. "But I have to give it to them on tumbling. There's no way we could do those passes at the end of the routine."

On the stage, the Morehead flyers shoot up into the air, and their white uniforms become a blur as they do a Front Flip stunt similar to the one Carol cut. Behind me, Courtney and a few others make "Pfff" noises. "They're trying to blow the stunt over," says Callee. But nothing falls. Morehead's routine is solid. The squad walks off the mat high-fiving.

Casi tugs on her hair. "If I could hate someone, it would be Kern," she says. "She's done this shit two years in a row. We could have won easy and now I don't think we'll even place. We're sixth."

"There's no way we're higher than seventh," one of the squad's juniors chimes in.

A woman hands out flyers for an audition tomorrow for roles in *Bring It On 4*. They're hoping to cast real cheerleaders. Normally, the women would be excited, but they pay the flyers little attention. The sheets of paper float to the floor.

"Let's just burn down the Milk House," says Callee.

## "Sometimes Cheerleading Is All Luck."

The judges' scores have been tabulated, and the UCA staff sets up for the All-Girl cheer awards ceremony. It's been a few hours since the University of Memphis women stepped off the mat, but Kern can't stop replaying the routine in her head. "I remember going up and thinking I was up," she says, eyeliner still smudged. "I remember wanting to stand back up really bad. I don't know what happened—if it crumbled underneath me. I hope I'm not the kind of top girl who just crumbles. Maybe I did—I don't know. That's where it shuts off for me. The rest of the routine was straight adrenaline."

Kern sits down on the carpet with a video camera someone has snuck into the Milk House. She watches herself fall in the cheer and rewinds, watching it over and over again.

Across the arena, the squad stands in a clump. Kern gets up to join them, staying on the outskirts of the circle. This is her first time seeing her teammates; she's spent the past few hours with her boyfriend, who's done his best to cheer her up. "We went outside and I was still just bawling," says Kern. "These two kids came up and were like, 'Can we take a picture with you?' I didn't want to say no, so I did it, but I was just like, 'Really? I have to smile right now?'"

While a small handful of her teammates have made a point of telling her "It's not your fault" or "Don't blame yourself," many are giving her the cold shoulder. "There's nothing to say," says Ashley Chambers, usually one of the team's most forgiving members. "Every time I think about her, I'll know what happened."

Kern is doing her best not to take it personally. "Some people want to blame me, but that just comes with the territory of being where I am in the third layer," she says. "Sometimes cheerleading is all luck—it's your day or it's not. That's what makes people argue about whether it's a sport."

On the mat, the UCA staff places the trophies on two tables covered in black tablecloths. This isn't like the Olympics where only the top three competitors will hear their national anthem—in cheerleading every team gets a trophy. Thirteen of them are small, standing about two feet tall. But the last three—for the third-, second-, and first-place teams—rise like a staircase. The Memphis women stare at the large trophies wistfully. The consensus seems to be that they placed somewhere between tenth and fifth.

"Would all All-Girl Division 1 teams report to the stage for the awards ceremony," calls the announcer.

Kristen leads the sapphire precession to the mat, Carol following behind them. The UCA staff directs the teams into a semicircle that looks like a twisted rainbow, color stripes slicing vertically instead of horizontally. Nearly every woman wears a hair ribbon—some are polka-dotted, others striped, others metallic. Memphis's ribbons stand out because they're pure white.

Monica, Casi, and Kristen squat down in the front row, their knees folded under them. Behind them, the squad stands in neat rows. They all try to smile as their parents and friends reclaim their seats and the auditorium settles down.

An announcer walks in front of the trophy tables, holding a microphone. "I hope when you look back on this competition, you will remember your friends and coaches," he says. "I hope you won't let these two minutes determine the rest of the year." It's very true for Memphis, but a strange note to begin an awards ceremony on.

"In sixteenth place . . . Syracuse University," the announcer says. A member of the Syracuse squad pops up excitedly to claim their trophy. Even though they've technically placed last, the glory for them was in making it to Nationals.

As the announcer calls fifteenth through eleventh place, the Memphis women look calm. But as soon as the announcer gets to tenth place, the tension creeps back onto their faces.

"In tenth place," calls the announcer, "Texas State University." Two women hop up in maroon crop tops and approach the table. The team does not celebrate—their lips remain in straight lines.

"That's a fluke," says Kristen. "They looked really good."

The Memphis women look nervous. One girl in the middle of their clump anxiously chews on her lip. Several of the others begin to adjust their hair. But as the announcers call ninth and eighth places, there's no mention of Memphis at all.

"In seventh place," says the announcer. Casi looks up, ready to accept her fate. "Ball State University." The team hops up and hugs, their fans cheering from the stands.

The first table of trophies is empty, and the UCA starts picking up trophies from table number two. "Sixth place goes to . . ." The announcer pauses and looks over his notes. "The University of Miami."

The team stands up in their green uniforms lined in orange. I remember seeing them in the warm-up area. "Whoosh! Whoosh! We got some Canes over here," they'd chanted. The hurricanes? In Florida? That's kind of like a New York City sports team calling themselves "the Terrorists."

"In fifth place." The auditorium once again goes silent. The Memphis women grasp hands. Casi brings a knee up, as if she knows she'll be standing up this time. "San Diego State University."

The Memphis women exhale in unison. "I thought San Diego would win," says Casi, eyes widening. "They hit and they did like twenty baskets."

The truth is that until the scores are announced, it's hard to tell exactly how a team has placed. The judges watch the routines in a different way than spectators do, giving scores on the skills as well as in categories like "sportsmanship" and "use of motions and placement." The scoring is as standardized as possible. However, as with any artistic sport, the judging is largely subjective.

The Memphis women turn to look at each other. One blonde in the back starts jumping. "There's no way we got this good," someone whispers.

"Coming in fourth place," the announcer says. He seems to pause forever. One of the women wipes fake sweat off her forehead, another clasps her hands in front of her in prayer position. The Memphis parents strain their necks to see their daughters. "Indiana University."

For the first time in hours, smiles come back to the faces of the Memphis women. Monica looks out in the audience. Courtney's eyes widen the same way they do when she tells a joke. The women squeeze each other's hands. They were prepared for the worst, but now they know they've placed in the top three. They will be going home with a big trophy. But which one? Several women in the back of the clump jump up and down with excitement.

"Third place goes to . . ."

Carol faces the audience. "You might win," another coach mouths to her.

While I watched the women cry for the past few hours, I felt an overwhelming need to fix this for them. I kept hoping that it wasn't as bad as they thought. If the announcer just calls another name or two before them, perhaps Kern won't be traumatized and the squad won't feel like their entire year was a disappointment. Maybe Kristen, Monica, Casi, Courtney, Callee, and Ashley will feel happy with their final year as cheerleaders. *Not Memphis,* I plead silently. *Anyone but Memphis.*

The auditorium is silent.

"The University of Memphis," the announcer calls.

Some of the squad members squeal, others let out full-scale screams. They jump up and down, hugging each other. It's not the unbridled thrill that made Brandi Chastain whip off her soccer uniform. It's controlled, the equivalent of a heartfelt "Phew." I watch Kern, in the back of the group. Tears of relief roll down her face.

Kristen walks toward the trophy table. A UCA staff member hands her the trophy, a set of golden columns with a big, shiny cup on top. She holds it overhead, like Atlas, the rest of the team rushing toward her. Monica reaches out to grab one side of the trophy. I feel like a surgeon whose patient has just made it through surgery.

The Memphis women go back to their places in the semicircle, Kristen cradling the trophy like a baby. As the announcer calls out that the University of Cincinnati has placed second, the Morehead fans in the audience begin yelling in triumph. Like when the first runner-up is called in a Miss America pageant, they know that their team has clinched first place.

"Your All-Girl Division 1 National Champion is Morehead State University," says the announcer as the whole arena applauds. The women in white step forward, socks and all. They are ecstatic—screaming, hugging, and jumping at the same time. They've won six National Championships since 1998, but the Memphis squad doesn't let it distract from their own celebration.

Ashley and Courtney bear hug. "When they passed sixth I was just like, 'What? *What?!* We're in the top five?'" says Ashley.

"We can fall twice and still get third place! Are you kidding?" yells Monica to no one in particular. Their creativity and the cleanliness of their routine are no doubt what saved them. A UCA official explains it to me. "We ask our judges to start at zero and build points—you don't start at the maximum and deduct," he says. "With deductions, it's more difficult to win if you have a fall. If you put pressure on teams to worry about mistakes, the routines won't be as creative and entertaining." He guessed that Memphis's clean lines, the difficulty of what they were doing, their synchronization, and showmanship helped them build enough points to squeak by teams that didn't have falls.

Audience members rush the mat, weaving past each other to get to the team they're here to see. The Memphis parents instantly start snapping photos of the squad with their third-place trophy. "Will the top three teams report backstage for your medals," the announcer says.

The women bend down and roll their arms. "T! I! G! E! R! S! Ti-gers," they chant as they spell out the letters with their bodies. Carol walks backstage with a punch in her step and emerges from behind the curtain with twenty bronze medals slung around her arm. In her right hand, she holds several pieces of paper, which she is carefully studying.

She walks excitedly back to the team. "We got 322 points!" she says, her voice practically gone. "And Morehead 339 got points. We're only thirteen points away from first."

"I cannot believe that," says Kristen.

"Only thirteen points away from first?" one of the seniors asks, her voice trailing up. "We're pretty badass." They're so excited that I don't have the heart to point out their math is wrong. That's a seventeen-point difference.

"The judges are saying if we hit one more thing, we would have won," says one of the squad's freshmen, who either has an inside source or is totally BSing.

Even Casi looks excited. "But I'm still never gonna talk to Kern," she says. The two were never the closest of friends, but they were certainly cordial to each other before. "She could pass me at the mall and say hi and I'd just be like, 'Is someone talking?' "

Monica hugs her boyfriend. "We beat teams that hit their routines—that just shows how well we performed," she says.

The squad walks out of Disney's Wide World of Sports Complex quiet, but no longer depressed. They go back to their rooms to shower. Then they're off to Club Paris, Paris Hilton's uber-pink club in Orlando, where the owner has set aside the VIP room just for them.

### "Ask Me If I'm a Cheerleader?"

The following night, after watching the University of Memphis Coed team place a disappointing sixth place after hitting their routine, the Tiger women hang out in their hotel rooms. They drift from door to door, popping in and staying a while with whoever they find inside. No one says it out loud, but this is their last official night as a team.

In Monica and Kristen's room, four women are piled on each bed. They eat pizza out of a Papa John's box as Kristen flips television channels, trying to find something to watch. She stops on ESPN2—the U.S. National Jump Rope Championship is on.

On the television screen, a jump roper performs a complicated routine of handstands, flips, and twists as his rope spins so quickly it looks like a blur. "How do people realize that they're really good at this?" someone asks.

It's a great question—exactly what was going through my mind. But it's interesting—not only is ESPN2 the same channel UCA Cheerleading Nationals will air on, but no doubt many viewers will ask themselves the exact same thing as they watch the women build pyramids and stunts.

The screen cuts from a routine to a clip of a sportscaster interviewing the jump roper, using the word *athlete* to describe him. "Oh, so they're athletes but not us?" asks one of the women.

"People have no idea what we do," says Kristen.

"I know," someone says. "I was telling my boyfriend that my wrists hurt, and he was like, 'Did you clap too hard?'"

Kristen nods. "I went by a store one day after practice and I had my wrist wrapped. The guy at the counter asked what happened and I said, 'Cheerleading.' He looked at me blankly. I said, 'Let's just say that there are people on my team who could lift you.'"

"Does it feel strange to be done with cheerleading?" I ask.

"So weird," she says. "I've never had a football season go by that I'm not cheerleading. Next year, I'll still be at all the games but in the stands. It'll be like, 'I'm supposed to be down there.' But I'm ready. My body's ready."

Monica nods. "Part of me feels like I'm at my prime and there's no way I should be leaving now," she says. "But it's time. I have an internship with a hedge fund that starts right after we get back."

"Will cheerleading still be a part of your life?" I ask.

"Oh, yeah," says Monica. "I can always work for the UCA, or coach a squad. Cheerleading has made me such a strong person. Sometimes I hear people complaining and I just want to say, 'Shhh, I've been dropped on my head a million times.' I hope I have daughters who'll be cheerleaders."

A few rooms over, Brittany lies in bed in her pajamas. She's gotten steadily sicker over the course of the last twenty-four hours. Several women are gathered in her room, and her friend Lauren puts a cold washcloth on her forehead.

I remember talking to Lauren and Brittany at the beginning of the year, when they were both thrilled to have made the team and ecstatic about the idea of being college cheerleaders. But when I mention next year's team, they're quick to tell me that neither of them plans to try out again. Even though they'll only be sophomores, they're ready to hang up their skirts.

"I had all these hopes and dreams about what it would be like to be a college cheerleader," says Brittany. "But after this year, I was counting off days until the end of Nationals. I'm way too disappointed to do it again."

Lauren nods, her eyebrows rising. "It's just too hard balancing schoolwork with two jobs and cheerleading," she says.

Kern pops her head in the door. Many members of the squad are still ignoring her, but the freshmen women are making an effort. Brittany happily lends her a dress and red belt to wear for the night. Kern slips the dress over her tiny frame. "Does this look all right?" she asks. The others nod.

Kern seems to glow. For the first time since yesterday, her teammates are talking to her in a normal way. "No one has size five heels, do they?" she asks, as if she wants to prolong the moment.

Next door, however, Casi is still fuming. Rather than have to walk into the same room as Kern, she calls a friend one door over. "I don't want to talk to *someone*," she says.

Casi seems to be giving up cheerleading as if it's a bad habit. When we walked by a thirteen-year-old girl tumbling in the grass earlier, she said, "I wanna tell her to stop cheering while she can—before she gets addicted." There's little nostalgia in her voice as she thinks about not cheering anymore. "Now I'll get a promotion at work," she says.

Two doors away, about eight members of the squad are crowded into Ashley and Courtney's room. One of the women is toasted after drinking all day. Ashley and Courtney sit on a bed with her, trying to keep her from getting herself into trouble.

"Tuck check," says Courtney.

"What?" says the drunk girl.

"You should never be so drunk that you can't do a Back Tuck," says Ashley. "Why? Because you're a cheerleader."

The girl stands up to try one. "No. I can't," she says, collapsing back down.

Ashley shrugs and turns to Courtney with a big smile on her face. "Ask me if I'm a cheerleader."

"Are you a cheerleader?" Courtney says, indulging her.

"No!" yells Ashley. They will only be juniors next year, but both Courtney and Ashley are ready to retire.

"Do you realize this was our last Saturday cheerleading?" asks Courtney.

"Ever," says Ashley. "We're done."

I'm shocked that only a handful of the women on the team are planning on cheering next year. They all seem so excited, driven, and obsessed with cheerleading—it seems inconceivable that they would just pack it up with so little fanfare. As I say good-bye and head to the airport, I take their joy about retiring with a grain of salt. After all, when I first met Casi, she was dead set on not cheering for her senior year. Ditto for Monica and Kern—neither of them thought they'd be donning the uniform this year.

I think back to Memphis's spirit camp, when the camp director introduced a girl who was quitting UCA staff after thirteen years. "At some point all of you will move out of this profession and into another life—into the real world," he'd said. For people who've been cheering for years, leaving it behind symbolizes a giant leap toward adulthood. They feel the same way about quitting cheerleading as I felt in the weeks leading up to graduating college—it's a point of no return filled with both possibility and fear. I wonder which of these women is really ready for that. And I wonder whose tune will change when tryouts come and go, and the reality sets in that they've left their passion behind.

# CHAPTER 17

## "It's Like Race Car Driving—There's Always a Chance Something Could Go Wrong."

*The Stephen F. Austin Lumberjacks*

THE STEPHEN F. AUSTIN Lumberjacks started running through their Nationals routine two weeks ago, and so far it looks badass. They have the next two months to perfect it, peppering it with new flashy bits, before they head to NCA Nationals in Daytona Beach. They're the student you despised in elementary school for finishing his science fair project a month ahead of schedule while you were slapping together a papier-mâché volcano.

"Let's do it," yells Trisha as the team gets into their positions for the opening of the routine—a gaggle of tumbling backed by Sierra's patented Double Full basket toss. Trisha presses Play on the CD player.

"We call this the drive for five!" says a computerized voice. The team leans forward slightly, holding up five fingers with smirks. The women launch into Toe Touch Backs, the men whip into Toe Touch Fulls. At the back of the mat, James Brown and three other guys grip wrists. Sierra loads in, steadying herself between their shoulders. They bend from their knees and power her up, up, up, her bleached blonde hair swirling as she twists twice.

Sierra easily soars twenty-five feet in the air. I wonder what it's like up there. Does she open her eyes and see the gym spinning around her, or does she close them tightly like you might on a roller coaster when the car begins rolling down the big hill? She sails back down toward her bases, her body position perfect. But at the last second, she folds oddly, her foot kicking over James Brown as another base scrambles to keep her from hitting the ground.

From the front of the mat, everything looks normal, the basket toss blending into the dozens of moves going on simultaneously. But a few seconds later, Sierra is not in place for her tumbling pass. She lies at the back of the mat, motionless on the floor. The music keeps playing, Beyoncé singing her heart out, but the cheerleaders stop and stare.

Kali throws her hands up. "Why are we stopping?" she yells. "What if this was Nationals? We can't just stop. If you're hurt, roll off the mat so we can finish."

In cheerleading, people go down on occasion. They wince, grab a body part, lie on the mat, and stand up again—it's a part of putting their bodies in extreme situations. The pain usually subsides within a minute.

But Sierra is still on the floor. It's been well over a minute. "What happened?" Trisha asks her spotters from across the room. "Did she hit the ground?" Someone shakes his head no.

Sierra's eyes open and she slowly sits up. "Help her move to the side," Trisha tells two of the guys, assuming that Sierra got the wind knocked out of her when she landed.

Normally the most outspoken person in the room, Sierra doesn't make a peep. The guys hoist her up and walk her to the side of the mat, where they place her to rest. Practice resumes without her.

Trisha, not too worried, begins to work with two tumblers who keep stumbling as they land their Toe Touch Fulls. The partner stunters use the back of the mat to work on their elite stunt sequence, an impossibly long set of moves.

A member of the Small Coed team sits down beside Sierra and grabs her hand. "What happened to me?" she asks him groggily.

"You fell," he says. "I think you might have hit your head."

Sierra sits silently for a few minutes and then turns to him again. "What happened?" she asks, on repeat.

Something seems off. "We need to take Sierra to the trainer," he yells, scooping up her body in his arms and running with her down the hall. Trisha follows him, leaving practice behind.

They rush her to the trainer, about two minutes away on campus. As the trainer examines her, Sierra begins to speak. "I can't see," she says woozily. "I can't see." The trainer says to get her to the emergency room. Immediately.

Trisha drives Sierra to the hospital as quickly as she can. The emergency room staff puts Sierra in a wheelchair as she waits to be checked out. She speaks only occasionally. "What happened?" she says. "I can't see." It seems like her words are being looped.

Yvette walks through the hospital doors, several other cheerleaders behind her. They see Sierra in the wheelchair. Yvette says hello. Nothing. She waves her hand in front of Sierra's face, but no one is home.

"I didn't see it, I didn't hear it, I didn't feel anything hit the floor," says Kali, mad at herself for worrying about the routine rather than her friend. "Sierra's known for her basket tosses, and the people beneath her are massive—I think we all just thought, 'What could go wrong?'"

In the wheelchair, Sierra's body begins to shake. The hospital staff rushes her through the swinging doors. They keep her in the intensive care unit overnight. Her mom gets the call no parent likes to hear and begins the three-hour drive to Nacogdoches.

It isn't until the next morning that anyone on the team hears the report: major concussion, skull fractured in two places, multiple seizures. Sierra has been moved out of the ICU, a sign that her life is not in danger, but the fractured skull and seizures signal that she's likely sustained a brain injury. The hospital will have to run more tests, but it's possible that she will need neurosurgery. Recovery could be a long, hard road—it's almost certain Sierra will be out for the rest of the year. In fact, one bad basket toss may have ended her cheerleading career.

Sierra lies in the hospital bed, her practice clothes replaced with a patterned gown. She's hooked up to IVs and catheters and is heavily medicated. Her mom, Sharon Jenkins, is worried and irate. "Let's just say that it wasn't handled properly. Someone called me in the afternoon and told me that Sierra had a minor concussion. Then at 9:15 p.m., I get a call from the emergency room saying that she had a seizure and a fracture in her skull," she says. "I heard that the coach didn't even go over to see if she was okay. Sierra is tough—if she's lying on the ground saying that she can't see, something is really wrong."

With her mom and grandma at the side of her bed, Sierra sleeps through the next day, barely conscious of what is going on around her. When she wakes up momentarily, she tries to rip out her IVs. She mutters curse words to the nurses who try to restrain her.

A steady stream of visitors comes by. Trisha is one of the first. "This is my sixth year here and nothing like this has *ever* happened. I was a basket tosser and I had my fair share of falls to the ground. I thought she just got the breath knocked out of her," says Trisha, staring at one of her cheerleaders—a cheerleader in her LCLM family line—lying in the hospital bed.

Though Trisha talks to Sierra's mom many times over the phone, the two never meet face-to-face. "She's been very understanding and has kept me updated on how Sierra's feeling," says Trisha. "With this sport, there's always that small chance that something can go wrong. It's like with football or race car driving—there's always the chance."

James Brown stops by later in the day, squeezing into a chair by Sierra's bed. "I'm just hoping for the best," he says. "She's going to be okay, but they don't know if she'll be able to come back to the team."

The next morning, Kali comes to visit, begging the nursing staff to let her in even though visiting hours haven't started yet. "I feel psycho that my first reaction was to get mad and say 'Get off the floor—let's go,'" she says, wringing her hands. "I feel so bad about the way I acted. I'm just so sorry she's hurt."

And Yvette also visits multiple times. "I'm scared," she says at Sierra's bedside. "I just hope she's okay and that she'll be able to come back. We need Sierra. She's the one girl you can't take your eyes off—she's our eye candy. That's one of the reasons I started talking to her about coming here. I was like, 'What are you doing next year? You need to come to SFA.'"

Yvette chokes back tears. "You hear about people getting hurt, but it's never been someone I know and love so much," she says.

Sierra wakes up three days later in the sterile hospital room with no recollection of the past few days or any idea what happened. All she knows is that her hands are bound to the bed and she has tubes sticking in her in odd places. She opens her big brown eyes and turns to her mom. "Mom, am I in the loony bin?"

## "We Have an A Routine and a B Routine."

It's been two weeks since a run-of-the-mill practice turned into a nightmare for Sierra. After several days in the hospital, she was finally released. But because the doctors were worried about her having another seizure, they required her to have 24-hour supervision. She went home to Arlington, Texas, where her mom could take care of her around the clock. Until the doctors are confident that she is out of danger, she can't come back to SFA.

"It sucks waking up every morning to the reality that I'm stuck at home and not in Nac practicing with everyone," says Sierra. She sounds different—the excitement that usually pushes words loudly and quickly from her mouth is dulled. "I'm not even allowed to drive for fear of me having another seizure. I have anti-seizure medication that I have to take until August when I get another CAT scan. My medical bill came to $17,000 and my insurance is only covering $8,000. But Michael Preston said the school is going to pay the other half, because obviously it's not my fault—it's not like I was out drinking and hit my head."

"It just blows," she sighs. "It tears me apart that I can't be there."

Three and a half hours across Texas, the squad is struggling without her, too. Because she was such a central player, it's been hard to figure how the routine should flow without her. Ashley Picard has taken over the Double Full basket toss, but she looks so scared as she sails through the air that the effect is compromised. Cassie, who stunted with James Brown at UCA Nationals, has been upgraded from alternate status to fill in for Sierra as a stunter. But since she and James Brown aren't hitting the elite stunt sequence consistently, Trisha moved them from front and center of the geese-like formation. Sierra also held key positions in both of the difficult pyramids strung together in the final section of the routine. Other women have stepped in to take her place, but each time they try it, the pyramid rocks like a tree caught in a storm. The routine that was so solid two weeks ago is now a mess.

As she watches the team practice, Trisha stares blankly. "We have a routine A with Sierra, and we have a routine B," she explains. "We have to have the contingency plan because we don't know if Sierra's coming back. But the original is always going to be easier on the team." It sounds like wishful thinking; from everything I've heard, it's pretty definite that Sierra will not be cheerleading again for a while.

Upstairs in his office, Director of Student Life Michael Preston sits in his desk chair, hands clasped together on his desk. His hair is parted on the side, a modern homage to *Leave it to Beaver*. Lining the wall behind him are dozens of trophies, huge gold cups suspended in the air by pillars. The largest ones are the Grand National Champion trophies, topped by giant silver megaphones.

Michael Preston wasn't at practice the day Sierra fell. He heard about it when Sierra was en route to the hospital. "It was scary, but I felt like safety measures were in place. Trisha did as good a job as she could in the situation. Sierra got the medical attention that she needed," he says. "But it did show us that we need to change our procedure. Now if we even *suspect* a head injury, the paramedics will be called. Someone can hit their head and seem fine, but a few hours later something nasty turns up."

"When it happened, no one knew it was as bad as it was," he continues. "It's like the wreck that killed Dale Earnhardt. It didn't look bad compared to some of the crashes you see in Nascar, but the effect was catastrophic."

When Sierra was released from the hospital and it was certain she would be okay, the team's concern shifted. One of their biggest fears now is that the president of the university could say, "That's it. No more cheerleading." They worry that this could send ripples through the cheer world, like Kristi Yamaoka's fall at the NCAA tournament. SFA is a top-tier team, and Sierra is one of the best cheerleaders in the nation. If this could happen to her, it could happen to anybody. The NCA and the UCA could outlaw basket tosses as a result.

So far, none of these things has happened. But Michael Preston did sit the team down for a talk. "I told them that one is an accident, but two is a pattern," he says. "If there is another incident in the next year, there will be repercussions. I won't hesitate to ground them until we can figure out how to make it safer. It doesn't matter how competitive they are."

"Have you seen them run through their routine?" I ask. He nods. "How do you think it's going?"

"The day is coming when we will get on the Nationals stage and we will crash and burn," he says. "We've won four years in a row, and every year I get so nervous that something's out of our hands—even if it's the sun shining too bright or a bird pooping on someone's head. One of these years, we're gonna throw it up in the air and it's not gonna come down like we want."

## "It's Almost Like an Escape for Me."

Ashley Picard sips her coffee, her Chihuahua, Bitsy, curled up in her lap. Her eyes, normally bright, have a dark tinge to them, a sign that she has not been sleeping well. Her top is pink, and she plays with her dark hair over her shoulder. All of the members of the squad have coped with Sierra's injury in their own way, but Ashley seems to be taking it a touch harder.

"I have to do the Double Full Basket now," says Ashley. "I hate baskets more than anything. Especially since it's like, 'Sierra just cracked her skull doing this—now you have to do it.' I've been crying myself to sleep at night."

"Is that the part of the routine you're most nervous about?" I ask her.

"That and the pyramid," she says in her girly voice. "Pyramids are all muscle memory and consistency—the same people doing the same thing over and over again. It's hard to get used to new people. Sierra is very aggressive. If I didn't land right, she grabbed me. The new person in her spot—if I don't land right, it's good-bye."

"I know you had been worried last semester about making the mat," I say. "When did you find out that you were definitely in the routine?"

"In January," she says. "I got a text message from Samantha and I was just like 'Yay!' I'm not a 100 percent confident person, and at the level of cheerleading that we're at, we're a dime a dozen. I think every rookie had their doubts. I was really excited, especially since first semester was a tough time for me."

"What was going on?" I ask.

"Around Thanksgiving, I just missed my family so much. I second-guessed moving to Texas from Boston," she says. "When I get stressed out, it directly correlates with my eating disorder. My mom wanted me to come home and do an in-patient thing."

In all the conversations we've had, often over meals, it never occurred to me that Ashley was battling an eating disorder. She is tiny, her weight in the mid-80s, but I assumed she was naturally a miniature version of the average woman. It's just another reminder that in our culture, no woman is immune. It doesn't matter what size jeans you wear naturally or what your IQ is—eating disorders are equal opportunity.

"I'm bulimic, real bad," she explains. "It's been six years that I've had it, on and off. It did stem originally from having to be the smallest for cheerleading, but now it's so much psychological stuff beyond that. It's almost like an escape for me."

"When did it start?" I ask.

"I was sixteen, and the all-star team I was on combined with a junior team. All these teeny-tiny junior-high girls were now on my squad—they were like these sixty-five-pound little peanuts coming up and taking my spot. I'm small, but I was a junior in high school—I already had boobs. I thought, 'I'm gonna do what I have to do.' "

"It was me and a few friends—it was a group mentality," she continues. "Once I realized that I could do it, I did it a lot. My friends all got better, but I never did. I guess you either have an addictive personality or you don't."

"Have you done a treatment program before?" I ask.

"I've done two in-patient things and they helped a lot," she says. "You have to eat as a group. When you have bulimia, you don't know how to eat because you see food and think, 'I'll have this and this—it doesn't matter because I'm going to throw up in five minutes.' So it's a relearning process. If you go to the bathroom, someone has to come with you and check before you flush. They even supervise you brushing your teeth. You get no privacy, whatsoever."

"Has bulimia been a problem since you got to SFA?"

She nods. "First semester my weight dropped really low, so I started seeing a nutritionist twice a week. It really drives you nuts, it consumes you," she says. "I've been good, though—I haven't done it for a couple of weeks. I've put on some weight, and I feel more energized. With Nationals coming up, I want to be healthy."

"Is it something you've talked about with anyone on the squad?" I ask.

"I've talked to Samantha—I live with her, so she's noticed patterns. She tries not to buy junk foods, which can be trigger foods for me," says Ashley. "My weight drops a lot, so people know when I'm sick. When I'm sick, I get really edgy and use the people closest to me as punching bags."

"Do you think this is something that will be with you for life, or do you think it will end when you're done with cheerleading?" I ask.

"I've always wondered that," she says. "I don't know. I hope it will change. I could definitely see myself doing one more in-patient thing. I'm the type of person who knows I need help. That's the first step, right?"

# CHAPTER 18

## "That Dream Slowly Melted Away."

### *The Southern University Jaguars*

TREMAYNE BAKER IS THE only member of the Southern cheer-leading squad who has felt the Daytona Beach sun on his face as he nailed a routine at the castle. He was a freshman in 2002 when the squad made their legendary appearance at NCA College Nationals, coming in second. "It was one of the best experiences of my life," he remembers. "Back then, people saw a historically black college and automatically assumed that we were gonna be crappy. The minute we left the stage it was like, 'Where did you guys come from?' We were instant celebrities."

But this year, the castle has never seemed farther away. After not completing a bid video and losing five members of an already-too-small squad, the Southern Jaguars limped into February with some squad members still clinging to the idea of NCA Nationals. "We're still gonna try," James Turner said, sounding a touch delusional.

Others on the squad were hopeful, too. "Coach was still talking about doing fund-raising. So we thought, 'Oh yeah, we're going to Florida,' because he is not big on fund-raising," explained Chassity. "I really, really want to go before my time here is up."

But this isn't *Bring It On*. Seventeen thousand dollars doesn't just appear out of nowhere. No one swoops in at the last minute with an oversized check to save the day. "That dream slowly melted away," explains Tarianne.

Coach James had hoped that when he asked the school for money to go to Nationals, the answer would be different than what he'd been hearing his entire coaching career. "They told me the money just isn't there," he said. "Every year, I get excuses. I see it coming at this point and that's disheartening. When are you not gonna give me excuses? When are you going to say, 'We'll do it this time?' " He didn't acknowledge that by not making a bid video, the team couldn't get into the competition even if they had the funds.

It's now late February, and the squad has dealt with the fact that they will not be making the castle. "I'm upset, because I've never gone," says Jasmine. "But there's a reason for everything—it's just not our time."

Others cannot be so zen about it. Like some of the oldheads, Jarel worries that Coach isn't pushing hard enough. "I don't feel like his heart is in it anymore," says Jarel. "Practice isn't as concrete as it was my freshman year. I know I've gotten lax."

And while Tremayne is disappointed that the squad didn't make a bid video or fund-raise, he understands. "If Coach felt we were an NCA-caliber squad, he would break his neck to raise the money. Why waste other people's money? I would never ask people to sponsor me if I'm not comfortable I could go down there and do well," he says.

"Do you think the school will ever send you to NCA?" I ask him.

He staunchly shakes his head. "Unless someone is gonna replace who we have over at student programs, I don't see us going back to NCA for a long time," he says.

The truth is that the years Southern University went to NCA Nationals, they didn't go on the school's dollar. In 1998, 1999, 2000, and 2001, Southern took home the first-place trophy at the Black College National Championships, and part of the prize package was a free bid to NCA Nationals.

The next year, Coach James hatched a new plan to get his squad to Daytona Beach. He met two Baton Rouge rappers during a basketball game and asked if they would sponsor the team. They gave donations so that Southern could make the expensive trek to competition. But soon, they moved away, and James could no longer contact them. Southern went back to Black Nationals in 2004 and won. However, the competition no longer offered the paid bid.

The next year, Black Nationals disbanded altogether. "Every year, the organizer was going in the hole, so she sold the company," explains Coach James. "Another company took it over, but they made the competition February 1st to kick off Black History Month. But most colleges don't get back to school until January 15th. There's no way we can be ready for competition by February 1st. The company didn't make any money, so they canceled it." Southern's run at NCA Nationals was over.

"The best in the SWAC." I've heard the Southern cheerleaders repeat this line hundreds of times in their cheers. In past years, even if NCA was a long shot, the squad could always count on the cheerleading competition at the Southwestern Athletic Conference. A showdown between ten squads from historically black colleges in the region, the real contest is almost always between Southern and Grambling State.

But a few days ago, Coach James got a call with bad news—the SWAC cheerleading competition, like Black Nationals before it, is canceled. "They said it's because of finances," explains Coach James. Even the squad's backup has been pulled out from under them.

Coach James is worried. "A year of not competing can destroy a program. These are competitive people, and if you're not competing, they'll look elsewhere," he says. Wanting to give the team a consolation prize, Coach James has started looking into smaller competitions within a few hours' radius.

Local and regional competitions are the bread-and-butter of high school and all-star cheerleading, but because college cheerleaders have such intense schedules, the system has developed so that Nationals is the only competition most teams will attend. Still, some all-star competitions have divisions open to college-level teams. "I want something nearby," says Coach James. "But we need something large enough so that it's not some kiddie thing."

Though he hasn't made a definite decision yet, the best solution looks like the Worldwide Spirit Association's (WSA) Grand National Championship, which will be held in March in New Orleans. The squad actually performed at this competition last year in addition to SWAC. Because the WSA competition was moved to Baton Rouge from Katrina-ravaged New Orleans, Coach James made the last-minute decision to enter the squad. They didn't have to travel, and it didn't cost much to enter. "We had the highest score there and we were named the Grand National Champions," says Coach James. "We got jackets and everything, so it was a nice end to the season."

But even though they got a fancy title, some members of the squad don't remember WSA fondly. The competition included all-star teams, middle schools, and high schools, with cheerleaders ranging in age from six to a touch over eighteen. No other college teams showed up. "We didn't compete against anybody," exclaims Tarianne. "We just competed against the charts—like you had to get so many points to be first, so many to be second. That takes all the fun out of it."

Chassity nods. "We drive off the energy of competing against other people," she says.

James Turner wishes his teammates could get out of this mindset. "There may be other college teams this year," he says. "And I don't care if we don't compete against anyone, we have to set a standard for ourselves. We have to get respect, and we got that last year."

## "You Have the Talent and Drive to Pull This Off."

Jasmine, Chassity, and a third Southern woman hover three feet off the ground, their stomachs resting in the arms of a pair of bases. The women's bodies are in straight lines, arranged like the spokes of a peace sign without the outer circle. The three of them grasp hands, and they shoot high in the air, spinning like propeller blades, their bodies stiff. They each travel 120 degrees before they land, switching bases like musical chairs.

This is the opening sequence of Southern's competition routine, which they will be performing in four days at the WSA Grand National Championship in New Orleans. This stunt is aptly titled the

Helicopter. "It's a lot of fun," says Chassity, her feet safely on the ground again. "The women in it are looking at each other, so we make faces and sing along with the music."

Jasmine stands a few feet away. "You come down really, really hard, landing straight on your boobs," she says, smoothing her chin-length hair. A beauty pageant winner, I'd expect Jasmine to use the word *chest* rather than *boobs*.

Jasmine and James Turner are in charge of practice for the time being. Coach James has left them both messages saying that he'll be late—there's something he has to take care of before practice. G, who joined the squad to help out during competition season, is also missing. But James and Jasmine soldier on, having the squad run through what they can of the hardest sections of their routine—the Helicopter, the stunt sequence that comes right after it, and the shape-shifting pyramid in the middle of the routine.

Coach James walks into the practice room, his forehead crinkled. Stress seems to emanate from his body, but he does his best to disguise the concern in his voice. "James and Jasmine," he says. "Can I talk to you outside for a minute?"

Everyone stares at Coach. They can tell that something is wrong. James and Jasmine exchange a glance that seems to ask, "Do you know what this is about?" But both of them seem clueless as they follow Coach James down the hall and out the back of the building into the muggy air.

The three of them stand on a sidewalk that leads from the building to its parking lot. The sun shines down at a severe angle. Coach James turns to face James and Jasmine. He takes a deep breath. "I put the paperwork in to pay for registration for WSA this morning, and the person in student activities who had to sign the paperwork said, 'You're not going to the SWAC Championship to cheer for the basketball team?'" explains Coach James.

This weekend is not only the WSA Championship in New Orleans. Five hours away in Birmingham, Alabama, the Southern basketball team will be playing the SWAC basketball tournament. Coach James did not think the two would be a conflict, because after a stinker of a season, it seemed highly unlikely that the basketball team would even make it past the first round of the tournament.

Jasmine's face is frozen, her almond-shaped eyes pleading for there to be more to the story. James Turner doesn't wait to find out. "This is my senior year, there's no way in the world I'm not going to competition," he says. "We have to go. I have to go."

Jasmine nods. "It's like they don't care about *our* competition," she says.

Coach James puts up a palm. "I know," he says. "It became a huge conflict, a day-long ordeal. I ended up calling the chancellor, who has always been very supportive of us. He said, 'James, the team might not even make it to Saturday in the tournament. The band will be there to cover it. Take the kids to competition.'"

James and Jasmine let out sighs of relief. The look of shock on their faces showed that they thought another disappointment was about to be piled on the long string of letdowns they've endured this year.

In the parking lot nearby, a car drives up. G steps out of the passenger side door. He is average height and stocky, with a dark complexion. His face has an air of toughness to him, though as several people on the squad tell me, it's a façade. He sees the three talking and ambles toward them.

"I've got something to tell y'all," he says. Coach James and Jasmine turn around to meet his gaze. James Turner shoots him a *Not now* look.

"I didn't realize that we were performing at WSA on both Saturday *and* Sunday," he says. "I have prior obligations on Sunday I committed to before the squad."

It feels like a bomb has been dropped. Most squads have alternates in case something like this happens, but even with G, the Southern squad has only sixteen members. There's no one they can call to replace him. At this point, they'll have to put on the play with no understudy.

James Turner bites his tongue and his mouth closes tight to keep from yelling. "How could you not know about this before?" asks Coach James, his words carefully metered. He looks ready to scream, too.

"I didn't realize. I'm sorry," says G. "I want to go in and tell the team."

"No, there's no need. Thank you very much," snaps Coach James. He doesn't try to plead with G, and G doesn't offer any more detailed explanation. Without any further words, Coach James whips around and heads back into the gym. Jasmine and James follow a few feet behind him.

"It seems like he doesn't care," whispers Jasmine. "It seems like it really doesn't bother him."

James Turner is fuming. "I don't care what his conflict is about," he says, still trying to keep his composure. "If you came to the squad saying, 'I want to be in your competition routine,' that should be your sole commitment. You just find out a few days before the competition that something else is going on? That's crazy."

A few feet ahead of them, Coach James tries to calm himself down before going in to talk to the team. "We only have two more practice days before the competition," he says, his voice despondent. "We're gonna have to redo a lot."

Coach James left the gym with one problem and came back with an even bigger one. All eyes are on him as he walks toward the squad members where they stand on the mat. None of them knows exactly what is going on, but they know that something isn't right. They gather around Coach, James and Jasmine bolstering the outside of the huddle.

Coach James prefaces what he's about to tell them. "Everything works out the way it's supposed to, even if we don't like it," he says, a touch of preacher in his voice. "This is a test to see how strong we are."

He explains to the squad the conflict with student activities and tells them that G has just abandoned them four days before the WSA competition. "Do y'all want to go to competition?" Coach James asks, the question hanging in the air. The team's expression is blank—part shock, part detachment, part just not knowing what to do.

"That's messed up," says Chassity, as quietly as possible.

Tremayne, who cheered with G for years, is irate. "Not only is that a waste of his time but it's a waste of our time."

And silence again. As he surveys the dumbfounded cheerleaders gathered around him, Coach James makes his decision. "I know that you have the talent and drive to pull this off—you can do this," he says. "If you're leaning toward not going, think about the other people on the squad. Think about the team."

Around the room, people begin to nod. They've made up their minds, too—they are going to the WSA Grand National Championship. "If you want to do this, then let's do it," says Coach James. "Get up and let's walk through this routine so I can see where we need to make changes."

The squad gets into their first formation. Coach James looks carefully and sees the hole in the Helicopter where G used to stand. He moves another guy from a back spot position to the abandoned main base slot. The squad advances to the next formation, and Coach continues to shift people like living room furniture. G held many important roles in the routine, but half an hour later, Coach James has rearranged everything to work without him. The squad walks through the routine several times, Coach checking his handiwork.

"Let's run through it," yells Coach James, walking toward the stereo. He flicks on the squad's music—a remixed amalgam of Beyoncé, Yung Joc, and the Black Eyed Peas, with a line of RuPaul thrown in.

The squad begins with the Helicopter, and it lifts up just as it did an hour ago, before the bad news came raining down. Still, the squad seems skittish as they perform—a basket toss fails to go up, and half a pyramid crumbles. They hit their final beat, throwing triumphant fists toward the ceiling. In the back of the mat, Chassity tops an Eiffel Tower–shaped 2-1-1 pyramid. She hops down and the music stops. Everyone drops instantly to the ground to rest.

The squad looks up. It was one of the worst run-throughs they've done, and they're half expecting Coach James to yell. But his face is deadpan. "I'm not mad at y'all—this isn't your fault," he says. "The mistakes that are being made right now are happening because little things are new to you. But this is life. We'll get through this. We have one more practice before we leave, and we can do this."

## "To My Future Baby Daddy."

"I want a tuna fish sandwich," says Tarianne, as the teenage guy behind the Subway sandwich counter cuts her bread. "But will you hide some turkey in the bottom of it?"

The guy looks puzzled, as do I. Tarianne and I are both vegetarians who started eating seafood a few years ago. "So you want tuna fish with turkey?" the guy asks.

Tarianne shakes her head, long, glossy hair swinging. "I want the turkey, but I don't want to *see* you put it in there," she says as she turns her head toward the door.

"Okay," the guy says, shrugging. He rolls up pieces of turkey and scoops tuna fish on top.

Tarianne walks with her sandwich bag in hand to a booth near the restaurant's window. "He was looking at me like I was crazy," she says.

"Did you start eating meat again?" I ask, confused myself.

"Well," she says, inhaling, "I'm having a baby."

"Congratulations," I manage to say, though I'm caught off guard. Tarianne is twenty-one and has a long-term boyfriend, also a student at Southern, who seems smart and kind, sometimes even doting. But still, I'm six years older than her, and I feel far from ready to have children.

"I always said I needed to start having kids now because I want to have, like, five," she says, pausing. "But I didn't know it was really gonna happen. It was unexpected."

"When are you due?"

"In late August or early September. I'm almost three months now," she says, patting her stomach, which at practice yesterday looked just as toned as ever. "I always feel drained, so I decided to start eating chicken and turkey. But I still can't just eat a piece of chicken. I have to hide it in my food."

"When did you find out you were pregnant?" I ask her.

"About a month ago," she says. "I was late, and then when my cycle finally came, it only lasted a day. So I got a little pregnancy test and took it at home. Pink line, pregnant."

She pauses and takes a bite of her tuna/turkey sandwich. "I called my boyfriend at work and said, 'Baby, I have something to tell you. We're having a kid.' He was like, 'Are you serious?' He didn't say a word. Then he was like, 'I'm coming right over.' "

"Was that a hard call to make?"

"Not really, it's something we've talked about," says Tarianne. "Last Father's Day, I sent him a text message that said, 'To my future baby daddy.' We'd even picked out joke names. His name is Phillip Mason, so the first one—a boy—would be Mason Mason Mason. The second one is Uniquely Wonderful Mason. The third one is Curtain Rod Mason." She narrows her energy into her dark eyes, like a model preparing for the photographer's snap. "Maybe we joked about it too much."

"How did your boyfriend react when he came over?" I ask her.

"I showed him the test and he sat down and was like, 'We're gonna have a baby,' " she says. "I was freakin' out more than he was. I was like, 'Oh Lord, what am I gonna do? I'm still in school, I'm cheerleadin.' He really calmed me down like, 'It's okay, we can do it. I'll work and we can figure out a schedule to take care of the baby.' "

"Did you ever think about adoption or—"

Tarianne cuts me off before I have to say the word you're never sure how anyone will respond to. "I wasn't gonna get rid of it or anything like that," she says as she nonchalantly lifts a chip toward her mouth. "I made it, I keep it. No matter what."

"Was telling your parents hard?" I ask.

"No, that was easy. My mom, she's a very open-minded person. She lets people be," says Tarianne.

"What about Coach?"

"I told him a few weeks ago. I was like, 'Hey, Coach, I'm having a baby,' real casual. He was like, 'Congratulations, now get in line for the next stunt sequence.' He didn't think I was for real," says Tarianne. "After practice I told him again and he ignored me—he heard me, he just didn't *want* to hear me."

"Were you worried at all that you wouldn't be able to go to competition?"

"I talked to my doctor about it, and he said it's fine for now, but when you get to the third, fourth month, you want to take it easy," she says. "If I had gotten pregnant a month before, I wouldn't be able to do it. It was actually good timing."

"So, yesterday aside, how has everything been going with the squad in general?" I ask.

"Horrible," she says. "We just can't do the routine. I don't ever remember being so winded. I don't think it's choreographed right. It's like—we do a skill, we walk, we do a skill, we walk. There's no parts where we really get to show out. Routines in the past, they've always had a signature move where it's like, 'Oh, that's Southern.'"

"What about the Helicopter?" I ask. "That seems pretty unique."

"Yeah, but it's so high school. We don't have anything collegiate. We don't have any high, high pyramids."

Earlier in the semester, after she found out that SWAC was canceled, Tarianne told me that she didn't think the squad should go to competition at all. I ask her what she thinks after G quitting yesterday.

"Having to switch people around messes up the chemistry. I know in my basket toss, there was someone in my group just for extra support. Now it's a wide-open space, and it scares me," she says, sighing. "But now that we've spent all this time practicing, I really do want to go."

"Could everything be okay?" I ask.

"I hope so," she says. "There's a one in a million chance that everything goes right at competition. Everything can be a mess, but when you get on the floor, if you have that extra adrenaline and you really concentrate . . ."

She puts down her sandwich and touches her belly. "My baby's a cheerleader already," she says. "It feels like she's doing back flips."

## "I'm Looking for That Miracle."

Coach James rubs his brow like someone who's been battling a never-ending migraine. His eyes are bloodshot, the light red contrasting with his dark skin. He sits waiting for the squad to arrive. The WSA competition is now two days away, and this will be the team's final practice before heading to New Orleans. "I'm scared, I'm nervous, I'm optimistic, I'm excited, I'm panicking, I can't sleep at night, but at the same time, I'm encouraged," Coach James says, his long eyelashes punctuating each thought. "I just hope they do good."

At WSA last year, Southern had the highest score at the competition, earning them the title of Grand National Champions. But they are not guaranteed a repeat this year. With the changes they made to the routine two days ago, many people do not yet feel comfortable with their new positions. As of now, they are far from hitting the routine. If no other college teams show up—if Southern's competition is all-star kids and high school students—Southern would be the only team performing single-base stunts, which will boost their score. But other teams will have many more members, meaning that although their stunting may be less difficult, they will have a lot of it. Plus, all-star teams are known for top-notch tumbling—a weak point for Southern.

Coach James sits quietly, his elbow propped on his knees, his chin resting wearily in his hand, as the cheerleaders warm up. On the blue mat before him, a flyer goes up, shaking as she stands in her partner's hands. "You look like you had five piña coladas up there," Coach snaps. The girl hops down and laughs.

"Everyone, get up and in your spots," says Coach James a few minutes later. The squad scrambles to their positions, and Coach presses Play on the boom box. "It's on," he says to the squad, who are waiting with their heads bowed.

"G-g-g-g-guess who's back?" says a voice, repeating as if by a DJ's scratch. James Turner and Jarel, standing in the middle of the mat, fire imaginary guns at the audience as a woman back-handsprings toward them. They turn to each other and grip hands, the woman landing in the cradle of their arms. Jasmine and Chassity have done the same things from the sides of the mat, forming a triangle of women held in cradles. In the center of the mat, Tarianne soars toward the ceiling, kicking her legs out as she reaches the peak of the basket toss.

As "Ain't No Mountain High Enough" plays in the background, Jasmine, Chassity, and the third woman in the triangle flip in the air, unfolding to land on their stomachs rather than their backs.

The men walk the women toward each other, and the three link arms for the Helicopter. Normally, this is an easy part of the routine. But as the men bounce the women high in the air, all three come down awkwardly in the same place they started. It looks like a Helicopter losing power, about to plummet to the earth.

The music changes. "Some people think that I'm, Just sittin' on top of the world," croons Brandy over a dance beat as the team heads to their elite stunt sequence. Most of the stunt sequences I saw at the UCA competition are long, flashy combinations of moves performed by at least five flyers on a team. Not only is Southern's sequence relatively simple, but there are only three flyers able to do it. In a diagonal line across the mat, Chassity, Jasmine, and Tarianne glide into Liberties. In the back corner, Tarianne falls down just as smoothly as she went up.

Chassity and Jasmine smile sweetly as their partners turn them to the side. They kick their legs into an Arabesque. They wrap their arms across their chests and whip into Double Downs. Tarianne stays on the ground, James Turner not attempting to send her back up into position to catch up with the others.

The pyramid is next. Tarianne runs to the center of the mat, where two women lift her straight up in an Elevator. Jasmine and Chassity shoot up on either side of her, and they swing their inside legs, straight like tin soldiers, to meet her hands. The final two flyers on the squad are tossed into Shoulder Stands on the far ends. They connect their arms with Jasmine and Chassity.

The pyramid shifts. Jasmine and Chassity drop into splits, their bases bracing their legs and butts. The two women push back up to standing and kick their legs behind them, spinning like jewelry-box ballerinas. The two flyers on the far ends of the pyramid are supposed to catch their legs and stop their rotations. But on the left side, Jasmine loses her balance, and her spinning leg knocks over the second flyer. The two women stand on the ground and stare at Chassity as she hits the third and final position of the pyramid.

"Meet me in the club, It's goin' down," sings Yung Joc, twice as fast as he did on the original track. The squad rushes to the front of the mat and begins to booty shake for the dance section. Behind them, the squad's few tumblers pass back and forth, trying to make their acrobatics seem more abundant than they really are.

The squad poses for the final beat of the music. In the back of the mat, Chassity shakes atop the 2-1-1 and drops abruptly. I gasp as she comes down hard, taking out two bases underneath her. Coach James jumps up, beginning to rush toward her. She sits up and waves to him to let him know she's fine.

Around the mat, members of the squad collapse to the floor in exhaustion. Jarel and James both lay there with their knees up, panting. Tremayne squats down, his hands on his knees and sweat pouring down his back. "This routine is harder for those of us who are all-around than it has been in past years. I don't have a break in the routine *at all,*" he says. "It gets tiresome."

Coach James closes his eyes. Faces slowly turn to look at him, as if he has a magic wand in his pocket that he can wave to fix everything.

"Y'all, that was horrible, from beginning to end," he says, his voice softer and less commanding than usual. He turns to Tarianne and James. "If a stunt falls, there is no reason in the world not to get it back up there," he says. "You have plenty of time. Don't just stand there."

He looks at Jasmine. "Jasmine, if you can get tight at all in that pyramid, the guys can fix it," he says.

The cheerleaders hang their heads like puppies being punished for peeing on the kitchen floor. Jasmine and Chassity run to get a drink of water. "That pyramid makes me so nervous," says Chassity.

Jasmine sighs. "You'd think since there's more people under you, it'd be easier. But it's not. There's height differences, so one foot may be lower than the other," she says. "I'm on the left side—that side is harder for girls. When we fly, we usually fly on our right leg. So it's like trying to write with your left hand if you're right-handed."

Chassity nods. "It's rare that both sides of that pyramid hit at the same time."

They rush back into the practice room, and the squad runs through the routine again. While it looks better this time, it is still chaotic. Just getting through it seems to be a struggle.

"Is that the best you got? Because if you're proud of that . . . ," yells Coach James, his voice trailing off as he shakes his head. "I don't know what to say. If you perform like that, you will go from being Grand National Champions to being the last spot in Louisiana."

The auditorium is silent as the cheerleaders rest. "Stand still," says Coach James, his voice shifting to that of a patient yoga instructor's.

"Don't talk. Just breathe." The squad stands for a few minutes, silently, tension in the air.

They manage a great run-through next, but as Coach James has them do it yet again, it's a disaster. Coach James walks toward Tremayne, who's sitting on the edge of the mat. His skin looks liquid from sweat.

"Can you do it one more time?" whispers Coach James.

Tremayne shakes his head no. "I'm not trying to make an excuse, but I'm running from here to there," he says. "By the time the routine is over, I'm just fatigued."

The squad is sure that they will have to do the routine well at least one more time to satisfy Coach James. "Circle up," he says.

"Coach, we're gonna end like that?" asks one of the women.

"The ones who are doing everything, they ain't got nothing left," explains Coach. "I don't want to keep you here all night practicing— someone's gonna get hurt."

The squad gathers tightly around Coach James. "For Saturday, we are going to meet here at noon," he says. "I spent the last bit of money to enter you in the competition, so I had nothing left to get a bus. We're going to carpool."

And just like that, the squad has finished their last practice. They grasp hands in a circle, and Coach James leads them in a prayer.

Chassity looks frustrated as she gathers her things to go home. She's usually the most consistent flyer on the team, but today she struggled with every stunt. Her normally smiling cheeks blend straight into the rest of her caramel-colored face. "I usually have one or two off days a semester, and that was today," she says, shrugging.

Tarianne walks several feet behind her. "I'm looking for that mira-cle," she says quietly, not wanting anyone to hear. "I don't want to be the rotten egg of the team, but I feel like this just isn't going to happen for us. But I want it to, I really want it to."

Across the room, Coach James stands silently, watching his squad file out of the gym. "My spirit is a little low, but it will be fine," he says. "It's going to be okay." His voice trails up as if this is more of a question than a statement.

"I think if I didn't fuss, they would think something is wrong," he says. "They would think, 'Coach doesn't have any faith in us, because right about now he would be yellin'.'"

"Are you going to call them in tomorrow for a practice?" I ask.

He shakes his head slowly. "The day before competition is their time to get their minds together. I don't want them to stress—I know that when their adrenaline starts to flow, they can do this." He pauses. "I always forget the hell I go through getting ready for competition."

"Does it ever cross your mind that this should be your last year?" I ask him.

"Every year. As my career as an educator grows, I always think, 'This is it—I can't do these two jobs.' But then God says, 'This is not it.' I move by what He says," explains Coach James. "I've been doing this for thirteen years. After a time, everybody should be replaced—your ideas get old and your values shift. There's always someone behind you who's more creative and more excited. When I find that person, I'll know it's time."

I smile, not quite sure what to tell him as we step slowly out of the gym. Tarianne lingers in the hallway. "How do you think we're gonna do on Saturday?" she asks Coach James as he walks through the door. "Honestly?"

Coach James pushes a smile onto his face. "It's gonna be real good," he says, giving her a hug. "Real good."


## "We Didn't Pray Before We Left."

The atrium of the New Orleans Convention Center is overrun with cheerleaders. On the paisley carpet, teams sit in circles, stretching, while others practice parts of their routines. Some of the teams look like high school students. Others are kindergarteners, their cropped uniforms and poofy hair bordering on JonBenét territory. As many of the Southern squad members feared, they will be the only college team competing here this weekend. None of the other teams frozen out of SWAC have made the trek.

Tarianne, Jasmine, Jarel, and James Turner stand in royal blue polo shirts and jeans, surveying the scene. Not only does their skin color separate them from the majority of people in the room, but they're by far the oldest. "This is depressing," says Tarianne. She looks ethereal today, a dreamy quality in her heavy-hooded eyes. "Competition used to be like a cheer reunion, but I don't see any of the little girls I know. After the hurricane, a lot of people moved away. Or maybe I'm just old."

Jarel brings his hands into a prayer position. "Don't let anyone I know be here," he says.

A young voice breaks the conversation. "Miss Tweedy," yells a blonde in her midteens as she runs up to Tarianne. Her eyes have been extended like a cat's and doused in silver glitter.

"You just made my day," says Tarianne, giving this girl from her old gym a hug. "This is my last weekend cheering."

"Really?" asks the girl.

"I'm having a baby," says Tarianne.

"You're pregnant?" the girl asks in shock. Tarianne nods.

As the girl runs to join her team, James Turner pulls Tarianne in for a hug. "Do you realize that this is our last time as partners?" he says.

Tarianne nods. "I'm in a better mood now," she says. "Let's go in and watch."

It is dark inside the auditorium, where bulb-shaped lamps hang from the ceiling. In the center of the room, a stage has been erected to hold the mat. Above it, bright spotlights blast the performers in a fluorescent glow. Many rows of chairs are set up in front of the stage, but only a third of them are full. The audience seems sedate. Because all the teams will be performing today and tomorrow, their scores from both days will be added together, I have a feeling tomorrow will bring a bigger, more excited crowd.

On the stage, thirty preteens flip, turn, and twist in every direction imaginable. "If we had that many people, we wouldn't get so tired. We need to make clones of ourselves," says Jarel. "We're gonna be embarrassed. I don't want to look like a fool."

James Turner shakes his head. "We won't be embarrassed—we'll turn it on. Anyway, these kids have been cheering since they were infants." He turns around to face the others. "Remember last year when that lady came up to us and said, 'I didn't expect y'all to be so good.'

We were all scratching our heads like, 'Wow—was that a compliment, or was that derogatory?' "

Jasmine stands with her right foot at a 90-degree angle to the left. She is unusually quiet as she watches the performers on the stage. She has not put on her makeup yet, and it's the first time I've seen her looking anything besides perfect. "How are you feeling?" I ask.

"We didn't have a good last practice—there was tension," she says. "But somehow, it's going to come together. That spring floor will make it easier—it gives you a bounce."

Music plays between performances, and the Southern cheerleaders begin to dance. The mostly white faces in the audience turn to watch them. A little girl with bangs straight across her forehead gawks at Jarel as he swings his arms and flaps his knees. "We should walk on stage like this," he says, not noticing the girl. "Coach would have a fit."

"Come on," says James Turner, glancing at his watch. "Let's go get ready."

Jasmine and Tarianne head to the nearest women's bathroom. They disappear inside bathroom stalls and slip on their uniforms—white-and-blue one-piece jumpers with diamond-shaped cutouts that reveal their belly buttons. They step out and zip each other up. "I don't like this little jumpsuit—it's like a high school pep rally," says Tarianne. "Why did Coach put us in these?"

Jasmine shrugs and turns back to the mirror, where she has laid out several different shades of eye shadow. She leans forward and lines her eye, pulling back to judge each individual stroke. She sings a song from the team's sound track, Beyoncé's "Check On It." Her *American Idol*-worthy voice fills the bathroom, and younger girls stare.

Tarianne does her makeup beside Jasmine. "This is not coming out good. But at least my hair looks nice," says Tarianne, admiring how her long, dark brown hair moves as she twirls. She stops abruptly and leans into the mirror. "I swear you can see my nipples through this," she says.

Makeup completed and uniforms on, Tarianne and Jasmine join the rest of the squad where they've claimed a patch of carpet in the atrium. The guys' navy blue pants sit baggily on their hips. Across every chest, the word *Jaguars* is embroidered in cursive.

But three teammates are still missing. "They got lost on the highway," one of the guys tells me. "They got all the way to Mississippi before they realized it, but they're almost here now."

Coach James walks toward the squad and stares at Japaul Winston, a sophomore with the body of a refrigerator and the face of a politician. Over the year, Japaul has gained a reputation for being the team contrarian. While the rest of the squad is ready to go, his jersey is balled up in his hand, and he proudly wears a T-shirt for the all-star gym he cheered for in high school. "Put it on," snaps Coach James. "I don't know why you're so hardheaded."

Japaul stands there for a few seconds in a staring contest with Coach. Finally, he takes his uniform top and slides it over his head. "I'm causing controversy," he says.

Coach James motions for the squad to follow him. Like the pied piper, he leads them through the competition area to behind the stage, where several teams are warming up. All of a sudden, the lights in the convention center turn off and the music from the DJ booth abruptly halts. The auditorium goes pitch black. A wave of chatter arises. I'm just relieved that the outage happened when the stage was empty. I can only imagine how much it would scare someone in the air if the lights went out for no apparent reason.

"Maybe they blew a fuse?" someone near me asks. In front of us, a team continues to warm up. An iota of light creeps in from a hallway, but they don't seem fazed by the inky darkness.

Finally, the stage lights come back on. "And now I'm nervous," says Jarel.

Coach leads the team into the hallway. The squad crowds in shoulder to shoulder around him. Coach James's eyes open wide, like they're trying to escape from his head. "There are 150 reasons why you should not be here today—from money to your teammates driving all the way to Mississippi," he says, glancing at the three team members who've made it just in the nick of time. "But you're *here*. You got this far. This is your grand finale. Go out there and have a good time." Across the circle, a faint smile grows on Jasmine's face.

"I brought you back here because we didn't pray before we left. So we need to back up and start there," says Coach.

The teammates grab hands. I stand behind them until James Turner turns around. "You're not a reporter all the time," he says. "You better give me your hand." I drop my notebook and pen onto the floor and grasp his outstretched palm.

We bow our heads and the room goes silent, the sound of the thumping bass from the auditorium reminiscent of a heartbeat. "Lord, I ask right now that you lift them to the highest of their skill level," says Coach James. "We ask you right now, Lord, for no injuries, for nothing that falls. We thank you right now for giving them everything they've worked hard for."

Beside me, James lifts his hands to his shoulders. He squeezes with all his might, and I realize that his body is shaking. I look at him—his eyes are shut tight. I can't tell if it's nerves, excitement, frustration, or a combination of them all.

Coach James's voice crescendos. "Lord, we thank you right now that they will enjoy themselves, and that when it's all over that they'll leave everything right out there on the mat. We've been in this place before and always came out well because of you. We love you and thank you for everything. Amen," he says.

"Amen!" shouts Jasmine.

The team opens their eyes, and each member puts a hand in the center of the circle. "Fire it up! S! U! Fire it up!" someone yells. On the count of three, they lift their hands toward the ceiling.

"Y'all are the current Grand National Champions here," says Coach James as they walk through the door back to the competition area. "Take that on the floor with you."

Twenty minutes later, after the squad has rotated through all the warm-up stations, Coach James sits in the front row of the audience, clapping heartily. He glances up at the ceiling in a last-second prayer.

"G-g-g-guess who's back?" The squad's music begins, and a grin travels across Coach James's face as he watches the Helicopter spin quickly and precisely. The audience lets out a burst of applause.

The stunt sequence goes up, and Coach James leans forward in his chair, clapping sharply, like he's at the opera. On the stage, Chassity waivers in her stunt. She fights to push her leg into an Arabesque and loses her balance, falling into Tremayne's arms. Coach James sighs.

But as the pyramid goes up, the women forming peaks like a mountain chain, his smile returns. Laugh lines squiggle around his eyes as he watches them nail the dance, eliciting a roar from the crowd. His smile doesn't fade as the second stunt sequence goes up, even as Jasmine bails out of a Double Down, popping off from the stunt instead. Thirty seconds later, Chassity slides off the top of the final stunt, her 2-1-1. And still Coach James smiles.

As the music stops, the few Southern fans here today are on their feet. One woman puts her fingers to her mouth and whistles. The team's performance was by no means perfect, but it was miles ahead of where they were two days ago. Considering all they've been through, their performance was great, plus they'll get a second shot at perfecting it tomorrow.

I turn to my right to congratulate Coach James, but he has already disappeared. I walk around the stage to try to find him.

Backstage, sweat drips down Jarel's forehead. "We were so worried about that pyramid and that hit," he says. "But I'm upset that stunt fell." He turns to a female oldhead who's migrated backstage with the team. "How'd we look?" he asks.

"Good," she says.

"Stop lyin'," snaps Tarianne.

"That was weird—it felt like a dream," says Jasmine, her hair poofed up from all the movement. "It was in slow motion, but fast at the same time."

Several friends and oldheads have taped the routine, and with their chests still heaving, pairs of cheerleaders gather around the tiny screens to watch. "Right here," says Jasmine, pointing to where she dropped her stunt too early. "I was like, 'Oh Lord, I can't hold it anymore.' I didn't Double Down—my bad."

Chassity's smile dissolves as she watches her 2-1-1 go up, stay for a second, and come right back down. "I got so tired early from fighting for that first stunt," she says. "I never fought so hard for anything."

"Where's Coach?" someone asks. Everyone looks around, but he's still nowhere to be found.

James watches a camera screen over Tarianne's shoulder, a droplet of sweat from his forehead landing on the two-inch screen. "Damn, that pyramid looks good. I'm so happy," he says, glowing. He looks up at the squad members standing around him. "Y'all, I'm proud of you. Did you hear the crowd reaction for the Helicopter?"

Nearby, Jarel watches the routine for the first time. He notices something no one else has seen. "Japaul doubled," he says, watching Japaul's tumbling pass over and over. "He did a Double Full. That's illegal. He talked about it beforehand and we all told him not to do it because we could get disqualified. Man, Japaul is such a show-off."

"Are we disqualified?" someone asks, panicking.

"I bet that's where Coach is," says Jarel. "He's yelling at Japaul or trying to find out if we're disqualified." I don't see Japaul backstage either, so I'm guessing the answer is the former.

The congratulations quickly turn to anger. "If we get disqualified, I'm gonna punch Japaul in the face," says one of the women.

"I want to hear him get cussed out," says another.

A few minutes later, Coach James walks toward the squad. "Are we disqualified?" someone asks.

Coach James doesn't answer the question directly. "Scores will be posted on the web at 6 p.m.," he says. "We'll see how we did then."

The skin between his eyebrows is scrunched—the situation does not look promising. Over the loudspeakers, James Brown's classic "I Feel Good" fills the auditorium, but I feel exactly the opposite. I feel nervous, worried. I want to go ask some of the judges whether Southern will be disqualified, but on the off chance that they didn't notice the Double Full, I don't want to be the one to point it out. It doesn't seem fair that the squad has worked so hard and overcome so many hurdles to get here just to have their standing put in jeopardy because of one person's split-second decision. Not making it to NCA Nationals was one thing, SWAC being canceled another. I can't bear the thought of them now being disqualified at WSA.

The squad gathers around Coach James. "I'm not at all disappointed," he says, his voice soft. "It was 100 percent better than what it was, and you can only get better from here. Stay focused. It's not about individual effort, it's about the team. When you're out of breath, remember there are fifteen other people out there who are just as tired as you. It's about how good you look as a whole." He willfully ignores the obvious question lingering in the air.

The Southern cheerleaders walk to their cars, not knowing their fate. They don't get to spend the night in New Orleans. Tomorrow, they'll do the drive from Baton Rouge again. Hopefully, it won't be for nothing.

## "We Need to Be off the Chain."

Japaul sits in the hallway of the New Orleans Convention Center by himself. It's the second day of the WSA competition, and the rest of the team congregates about fifteen feet away in their golden uniforms, only talking to Japaul when they need to. His wide back is straight against the wall, and his knees are curled to his chest. "Coach was mad yesterday," he says, his teeth showing in a defiant smile. "I got cussed out. He said what I did was disrespectful. If we get a deduction for my Double Full, I'm off the team."

"Did you plan it, or did you throw it by accident?" I ask, aware that I sound like a lawyer trying to differentiate between murder and manslaughter.

"I had it in mind, but I didn't decide for sure until we were on the mat," he says.

"Why did you do it?" I ask.

"We're competing as an Open Squad Level 6, not as a college team. Doubles are only illegal in college rules," Japaul explains. "If they're judging by NCA rules, we'll get a deduction. But I don't think they are. So why not a Double?" His voice is calm and confident—there's no doubt in his mind that he's right.

He glances at his teammates. "I hope we don't get a deduction," he says. "But I don't think we will. I don't know why the NCA made Doubles illegal anyway. They said it was because people were hurting their ankles, but you're more likely to hurt your ankle on a one and a half."

Because of a computer problem at my hotel, I haven't seen Southern's score from yesterday. I was counting on the teammates to tell me how they did. But unlike at other schools, where squad members rush to a computer to see their results, no one on Southern's squad seems to know their exact score. One person tells me 410, another 415. And no one seems to know the answer to the looming question, did Japaul's Double Full disqualify them?

Finally, Coach James walks through the glass doors of the convention center. He holds a cardboard box in front of him as he strolls toward the team. Coach James looks for someone to hand the box to. His eyes wander to Japaul. "Japaul," yells Coach. "As mad as I am with you, you get to carry this all day." Japaul instantly obeys.

The squad looks at Coach James with expectant eyes. "You got a score of 418 yesterday," he says. The squad lets out a collective sigh of relief. "That's not bad at all. But you can do better today."

Because they are the only team competing in the Open Level 6 category, Southern is guaranteed to win their division. But winning the Grand National Champion title for a second year in a row is up in the air. Several teams are currently ahead of them—yesterday's high score was given to an All-Star Level 5 team. Southern is in striking distance, but they need to put in a flawless performance today to prevent themselves from being shown up by teenagers.

Coach James plops down on the floor near me. "When I saw that Double Full, I thought, 'Have you lost your mind?'" he says. "But when I saw the score sheets last night, I honestly don't think they caught it. At least it didn't reflect in the score."

"Will you let him do it again in the routine today?"

He looks me dead in the eye. "No, he will not," says Coach James, loud enough for Japaul to hear.

Coach James surveys the squad. "I think today is going to be good. Their nervousness is gone," he says. "This is the culminating day of the year for them—especially if it's their senior year, they're gonna give the best performance that they've got. I think they're gonna hit."

"What are their chances of winning the Grand National title again?"

"Really good," he says. "None of the other teams are doing single-base stunting. They look really powerful."

Powerful isn't the word I'd use to describe them at the moment—they look in need of a major caffeine fix. Jasmine curls up on the floor, using her backpack as a pillow. Within a minute, she is asleep, her eyes slits of eyeliner, her chest moving gently up and down as she breathes. Nearby, Tremayne lays down on his back and covers his face with a newspaper.

"He look like a bum," someone says as he naps.

James Turner throws a ball of tinfoil at Jasmine and hits her on the head. "I'm trying to enjoy my nap," she says, rolling over.

Sitting near her, Tarianne shakes her head. "All this waitin' is making me anxious," she says.

"We need to be off the chain today," agrees James.

Another squad member runs up to the group. "Guys, we're next for warm-ups," he says. "We're next."

The squad jumps up, hooking their backpacks around them, and rushes into the competition area. The auditorium is far more packed than it was yesterday and the audience is showing signs of life—they are on their feet, screaming for the squad on the stage. The Southern cheerleaders run by in a golden flash as they make their way to the empty warm-up mat behind the stage. At this competition, there is no tunnel—around the sides of the stage, the audience sits with its eyes glued on the performers.

The Southern cheerleaders proceed from a small mat, where they warm up their stunts, to a long, skinny one, where the tumblers practice their passes, to a full-size mat, where they rehearse bits and pieces of the whole routine. Time seems to be moving very quickly, a digital clock counting down from three minutes in big, red numbers. The squad sends up their pyramid, and it looks solid. They practice the Helicopter, and it spins perfectly. The partner stunters take the last minute to warm up the stunt sequences.

Jasmine has a relaxed smile on her face as she spins into a Double Down. But as her next stunt goes up, she falls. Jarel catches her by the waist, but she lands hard on her ankle. She winces and shakes her foot out. I can tell she's hurt as she takes a few tentative steps on it.

A cheer rises from the audience out front. Jasmine takes off her sneaker and Coach James quickly wraps her ankle in tape, spinning the gauzy material around and around. Neither of them says a word. The squad rushes toward a metal staircase that leads to the stage, Jasmine trailing behind. Coach James hugs each squad member and speed-walks away, disappearing around the corner.

"We got this!" shouts James Turner to the team as they line up behind him on the stairs. "Talk to each other through everything. Let's just go out there and make this happen!"

Jasmine squeezes past the others to stand beside him. She touches him lightly on the arm and looks up at him. "There's no way in the world this isn't going to be good," she says.

Applause roars. The squad before them has finished, and Southern will be called to the stage any minute. I dash around the front of the stage and take a seat beside Coach James in the front row. His wife and children sit behind him, already clapping. Music plays from the DJ booth, giving the judges another minute to score the last team.

Behind the mat onstage, a tall, vinyl backdrop boasts the letters WSA encased in a halo logo. There's a rectangular opening on the left side, where the back staircase meets the stage. Through the opening, I can see the Southern cheerleaders standing in a circle, their arms around each other. They sway to the music.

"Next up," says the event's announcer. "Southern University from Baton Rouge, Louisiana."

Southern's cheering section is three times as big as it was yesterday, filled with oldheads, friends, and the occasional significant other. "Wooo!" they scream as Japaul runs onstage, leading the group, pointing at people in the audience like a presidential hopeful accepting his party's nomination. James Turner makes an S and a U with his arms as he walks. Jasmine strolls near him, giving the beauty pageant wave she's been perfecting since the fall.

They find their places on the mat and bow their heads, bringing their arms tightly to their sides. Jasmine and Chassity are at the far corners of the stage, facing the auditorium's industrial walls. A third cheerleader forms the front point in the triangle, James and Jarel positioned a few feet behind her.

The first beat of their music erupts from the speakers. "G-g-g-guess who's back?" James and Jarel point imaginary guns at the audience.

Behind them, Tarianne loads in for her basket toss and sails up like a shooting star. She flies higher than the stage's backdrop and kicks her legs to the side, touching her toes. She drifts back down into her bases' arms.

The Southern cheering section lets out a burst of screams. A loud honking noise startles me, and I jump out of my seat. Beside me, a Southern fan presses the red button on a foghorn. The sound is so thunderous that I worry it might distract a cheerleader at exactly the wrong moment.

On the stage, Jasmine and Chassity hurtle backward for back handsprings. Instead of landing on their feet, two guys step in and scoop their arms under the women's backs lifting them into Elevators at shoulder height. "S! U!" the women scream, molding their arms into the letters and bobbing their heads with attitude. "Ain't No Mountain High Enough" plays on their sound track. The men send their women airborne, where they tuck into a ball for a miniature basket toss. But instead of being caught on their backs, the women unfold on their stomachs.

"Let's go y'all!" an oldhead yells. Coach James claps steadily to my right.

The pairs of men rush toward each other, holding Chassity and Jasmine with their arms extended in front of them, as if they're swimming through the air. They lock arms, each girl's hand wrapping around the next one's wrist. The Helicopter goes up, the women spinning like a roulette wheel.

The audience lets out a roar, and several Southern fans jump out of their seats. The woman beside me lets her foghorn boom again—I want to rip it out of her hands and throw it away. I turn to Coach James, who has an ear-to-ear smile as he hovers slightly above his chair in anticipation.

The squad walks into two orderly rows. They bound up in Toe Touches, the spring floor making their jumps impossibly high. The women bound backward for back handsprings, and the guys curl their knees to their chests for Standing Back Tucks. As they land, their right arms all shoot out to the side. "Jags!" they yell as, on their CD, Brandy chants, "Some people think that I'm, Just sittin' on top of the world."

It's time for the stunt sequence. The three partner couples stand in a diagonal line across the mat—Chassity and Tremayne in the front right, Jasmine and Jarel in the center, and Tarianne and James in the back left. The music shifts to a steady drum n' bass beat as all three women land in their partners' hands in unison. Three dings sound, a woman kicking into an Arabesque on each noise. The three of them pull into Double Downs, coordinated to the split second, like three missiles spiraling toward a target. They land in their partners' cradles and hop up, index fingers pointing toward the ceiling.

Coach James is on his feet clapping as the foghorn sounds yet again. "Yes!" he says quietly. The squad has nailed the Helicopter and the stunt sequence—I hope they can hit the pyramid as well.

Hands straight at their sides like a military brigade, the team walks to their positions for the pyramid. In the center of the floor, two women lift Tarianne into an Elevator. She smiles slyly and raises her arms in a V. On either side of her, Chassity and Jasmine are tossed into Extensions, each of them an arm's-length higher than Tarianne. Chassity and Jasmine lift their inner legs like excited aerobicizers, and Tarianne locks a hand around each of their ankles. Her brown hair cuts across her face like Jessica Rabbit's, obscuring one eye.

The team's two spare women go up in Shoulder Stands on the far ends of the formation. Chassity and Jasmine drop down with their legs wide open in a split, revealing their blue sequined bloomers. The bases below them grip their thighs and butts. The women on the far ends squat and grab their outer wrists, as Tarianne reaches down in the center and locks their inner wrists. The group bounces. And up Chassity and Jasmine go, spinning like the jewelry-box ballerinas until they face inwards, their front legs pointed straight behind them and held in place by the women on the far sides. So far, their pyramid is flawless.

The pyramid will morph a third time, like a billboard whose message changes every few seconds. Chassity and Jasmine snap their feet together and swivel their hips to face forward again as their bases slightly lower them. They shoot back up, bending their outer knees and stepping a foot into the palm of the women on the far sides. The five women stand there solidly, zigzagging like a line graph.

Balancing on the ankle she twisted not ten minutes ago, Jasmine looks shocked that she is standing in the air. Chassity gives the audience an exaggerated wink. They've hit the three hardest parts of their routine perfectly.

"Yeah!" shouts a squad mother behind me, her voice getting shrill. Coach James drops to his knees on the floor and pounds the concrete with his palm. He is ecstatic—the rest of the routine is smooth sailing.

The women run to the front of the mat, the men lining up behind them as a faster version of Beyoncé's "Check On It" plays. The women bring their elbows in front of their faces and open them, a cheerleading version of peek-a-boo. They throw their arms to the side and roll down to the carpet in a ball as Jarel and the men ham it up behind them. The women stand up, their backs to the audience. They lean forward slightly, shaking their butts, sequined bloomers showing under their short skirts. The women spin, moving their arms across their chests, around their heads, and back out to the side.

At the corner of the mat, Japaul runs for his tumbling pass, his arms swishing at his sides. Yesterday, he chose to do a Double Full. My muscles tense, and I try to send him a telepathic message not to do it again. Even though it didn't disqualify them, no one seems certain on the rules—it's possible that the judges just didn't notice it yesterday. It would be heartbreaking for the team to be disqualified today when they are putting on their best performance ever.

Japaul throws his hands to the mat, his bulky body turning two quick handsprings. He rebounds high in the air. His body twists slowly while he flips. After one rotation, his legs jut toward the ground. He's listened to Coach and has thrown a Single Full. I exhale, relieved. Behind him Tremayne and another tumbler whip and whirl their bodies across the mat. In the back, Chassity, Jasmine, and Tarianne sail up into Heel Stretches and twist into Double Downs.

"You don't want no drama," sings Fergie of the Black Eyed Peas on the sound track. "No, no, no, no drama."

James and Jarel walk front and center again, each with a woman beside them. Behind them, fanning out to the sides, are Jasmine and Tarianne, a guy positioned beside each of them. They begin a dance that reminds me of two ninjas sparring. The women kick a leg in front of the men and then duck as the men punch over their backs. The women turn their backs to the audience as the guys stick out an arm and rest it on their lower backs. The women turn back handsprings over their arms. The men duck this time, the women swinging a straight, pointed leg over their backs. The men stand up, jumping, their legs wide apart, pushing one hand triumphantly up toward the ceiling, like superheroes making lightning flash out of their fingertips.

In the back of the mat, Tremayne steps onto the thighs of two of his fellow guy cheerleaders. He reaches forward and grabs Chassity by the waist. She jumps as he catapults her high in the air. She lands with a foot in each of his hands, high atop a 2-1-1, the shape tapering in the middle. The audience screams.

Coach James is still on the ground, pounding the floor. Tears flood his eyes, and he claps so hard it shakes his whole body. The squad's friends and family are on their feet, throwing their fists in the air. An oldhead puts his fingers to his mouth and whistles.

On the stage, the Southern cheerleaders jump with joy. Tarianne bends from the waist and shakes her head with attitude. James Turner's dimples are visible from fifteen feet away. The spotlights turn off, and the squad rushes across the mat and down the staircase behind the stage.

"That was a miracle!" exclaims Tarianne, wrapping her arms around one of her teammates as they both jump up and down.

"That was the best we've ever done it!" squeals another woman.

"I'm ecstatic," says Jarel. "It felt so good! I heard the audience going crazy for the Helicopter, and I just went into the zone."

James Turner's eyes look watery as he blots sweat off his forehead. "I am so f-ing proud," he screams. "We really brought it. The Lord was on our side this time."

He locks eyes with Jasmine. "The last thing I saw was Coach pounding on the floor. I haven't seen him like that in a long time," she says. The two of them give each other a hug.

On cue, Coach James runs around the corner. "I'm almost in tears, I'm so proud," he says, his hand over his heart. "They get on my last nerve and then they come out and do something like that. They're in it for Grand National Champions," he says. He looks at the squad, whose family and friends have all made it backstage to congratulate them. "They know they did a good job. That's all I can really ask for."

## "This Year's Grand National Champion Is . . ."

The competition is over, and the fifty or so teams who've competed in Levels 4 through 6 scramble onto the stage. It's time for the awards ceremony, and they sit facing the stage's backdrop, the bright lights above forming a halo around each of their heads. The light glistens off the golden trophies lined up on tables in front of the mat.

"The Final Countdown," a synthesizer-heavy '80s classic, plays as the winners are called in dozens of categories. A narrow aisle forms in the mass of cheerleaders as WSA staff members present the division-winning teams with their trophies and a fist full of medals.

The Southern cheerleaders, in their DayGlo uniforms, sit toward the front of the mat. Chassity and Tarianne have relaxed smiles across their faces. "I'm just happy we did what we were supposed to do," says Tarianne. There's not much suspense about whether they'll win their division—they are, after all, the only ones competing in Open Level 6 category. But was their perfect performance today enough to win them the WSA Grand National Championship for a second year in a row?

Finally, the announcer gets to their division. "With a score of 836.9, first place goes to . . . Southern University," he says, pausing as if it is any surprise. One of the women hops up to claim their trophy. Chassity excitedly takes the medals, placing a red, white, and blue band around each teammate's neck.

"The Final Countdown" is now giving me a headache. But we are reaching the end of the ceremony. "Now, for our final award of the night," says the announcer.

James Turner kneels on the mat and looks up for the first time in minutes. Jasmine's eyebrows arch high above her lids. They both have their poker faces on. I can't tell if they are nervous or hopeful.

"This year's Grand National Champion, with a score of 926.4 is . . . Louisiana Cheer Force Level 5."

A group of young teenagers catapults up. They bounce up and

down, ponytails flopping, screams coming out of their mouths. They throw their arms around each other, and the tears start rolling.

The Southern cheerleaders watch them quietly. They clap, but I know what they are thinking: they've been beaten by a bunch of kids.

"I don't know how a Level 5 could beat a Level 6, honestly," says James Turner as he walks away from the stage. "I'll need to see the score sheet to know how that happened."

"Why are we not Grand Champions?" someone else asks.

"They're a more all-around team," says Tremayne, sounding level-headed. "They have more stunts, they can all tumble. But man . . ."

Jasmine sighs. "Oh well," she says. "Last year was our year, this year is their year."

Coach James calls the squad around him, sensing their disappointment. "You guys should feel good. I'm proud of you all tonight," he says. "Tomorrow at 5 p.m., we're gonna meet at the gym to turn all your stuff in. Bring all your uniforms—I'll have an inventory to make sure we get everything." For many people on the squad, tonight marks the end, but for Coach James the cycle is just beginning. In three weeks, he'll hold tryouts for next year's squad.

Still, he takes a minute and scans the cheerleaders with a Papa Bear grin on his face. "I'm proud of you. I really am," he says.

The team is headed to a celebration dinner at James Turner's house, but Coach James's family is itching to get back to Baton Rouge before dark. I walk him out of the convention center. "I'm going to try to forget that routine—I don't think it represented the caliber of routines I can do," he says. "All in all, this was a rough year. Once I lost so many cheerleaders, I think I just got very frustrated."

He stares into the distance, where the sun is beginning to set. "This is a great group of kids, but sometimes it's just not your year. The Chicago Bulls were such a force when Michael Jordan was on the team, and when he left, they had to rebuild. I think this year was a rebuilding year for us," he says. "I already have a much larger number coming to tryouts in a few weeks. Their skill level looks really, really strong. I'll have a good mix of my old cheerleaders, and I'll still have enough newness to really put together a force for competition."

Yes, for Coach James, the cycle is just beginning.

## "I Don't Think It's Gonna Hit Me until I Turn In My Uniform."

The hall of James Turner's house is like a museum of his life. There are pictures of him as a kid, playing with his older sisters. In the center of the hall, he stands with his arm around a prom date. A few feet away, he wears a maroon marching band uniform and holds a trombone. In some of the photos, James is a tad bit chubbier than he is now. But in all of them, his charismatic, dimpled smile shines through.

Since James's mom lives about twenty minutes from the New Orleans Convention Center, she has volunteered to cook dinner for the squad. In front of her modest brick house, she has set up a long folding table in the driveway. Several coolers filled with food and sodas are lined up on a porch lit by a single lightbulb. Everything is ready for when the squad arrives.

"Just leave the beers alone," says James's mom, Eliza Turner, as she opens the screen door and walks into the living room. James's stepfather is sprawled across the sofa watching a detective show, and she sits down beside him, placing her hand on his knee. On the wall above them hangs a Ten Commandments poster with gold lettering.

Outside, James speaks softly, so they can't hear. "My parents came to competition last year, and afterward I introduced them to everyone. They were like, 'You're not ashamed of us.' I'm the first in my family to graduate high school, I'm the first to go to college," he says. "But I'm not ashamed that my parents aren't lawyers or doctors. I told them, 'Anything you didn't get to do, you brought me into the world to do.'"

The cheerleaders arrive and load their plates with macaroni and cheese and red beans and rice. James lifts the lid on a cooler. It's filled with crawfish, their eyes and heads still in place. I don't recognize what's inside the next cooler. "It's turkey necks and pig's feet," one of the cheerleaders tells me.

"Are you gonna eat some crawfish?" asks CJay Jacobs, a sophomore on the squad with chin-length black hair and bright blush.

"If you show me how," I tell her. She walks to the cooler and piles a plate high with shrimp's uglier cousin. She demonstrates how to pull the tail free, rip open the shell, and get the tiny, buttery piece of meat inside. She sucks the heads, but I think that might be a little advanced for me.

Near me, Jasmine takes dainty bites of macaroni and cheese. "Does it feel weird to be done with your last performance?" I ask her.

She scrunches her nose. "I don't think that it's going to hit me until I turn in my uniforms tomorrow," she says. "I love cheerleading to death, but I'm excited to try something new. Being Miss Southern, I still get to be a representative of my school, but I'll be able to reach out to people and be remembered for making changes."

Jarel shakes his head. "I'm not gonna have my Jasmine next year," he says, shaking his head. "I've had her since my freshman year. If I don't cheer next year, I'd say I ended with a bang." Jasmine smiles.

"So you're not cheering next year either?" I ask him.

"I don't know," he says, swatting a mosquito from his forehead. "If my heart is not in it and I'm not giving 110 percent, I don't want to do it. But at the same time, I need the scholarship—I'm out-of-state and my parents can't really afford those fees." I can tell by the way he back-tracks that in three weeks he'll be back in the gym trying out for his senior year as a Southern cheerleader.

Across the table from us, Chassity takes a bite of red beans and rice. I've heard several people mention her as someone who might be a captain next year. I ask her if that's a position she'd like to take on. "I'm not going to say that I don't want it," she says. "But if I wasn't captain, it wouldn't bother me. Coach puts a lot on our captains. I would like it, but at the same time, I know it's gonna be a lot of work."

The cheerleaders finish their dinner, and James's mom urges them to take Styrofoam containers of food home. The table slowly gets emptier as people pile into their cars for the drive back to Baton Rouge. Soon, it's just me and James. We walk inside, where his parents are still enjoying their detective show.

He takes my camera and sits down next to his mom. He presses Play and shows her the routine from earlier in the day. "That's me," he says, pointing to himself as he dances. A smile grows across her pretty, but hardened, face.

It's obvious as his mom speaks that she's very proud of him. "He's always been outgoing—always a sports person. Look at him tumbling up in the air," she says, her accent gritty. "I hope he'll be a lawyer or some kind of famous person one day."

I call a cab to take me back to my hotel and say good-bye to James and his family. As I get in the car and close the door, the lightbulb on the porch flickers off.

# CHAPTER 19

## "That Pyramid Should Be Called the

## Wall of Death."

*The Stephen F. Austin Lumberjacks*

ON SFA CHEERLEADING'S MYSPACE page, a clock counts down the minutes until NCA College Nationals: 00 months: 04 days: 9 hours: 33 minutes: 04 seconds. In just a few days, the team will begin the eighteen-hour bus ride to Daytona Beach. Tonight will be their last, and most important, practice—a Show Off, where they'll perform their routine for several hundred friends, family members, and fellow students.

Under a bright purple JumboTron in the campus coliseum, the squad stretches on the mats that they've moved to the center of the basketball court. The Lumberjack women look more svelte than ever in their purple uniforms, their bodies like the anatomy models from a biology class, where every muscle striation is visible. Almost all of them have a matching, thumb-sized bruise above their right hip, where their partners push to spin them in stunts.

The guys look even more monstrous than the last time I saw them. "I put on thirty-five pounds since New Year's," one of them tells me with pride.

Kali ties a brace around her right wrist. Her newly highlighted hair is held back by a thin red headband, and she looks like a tanned Snow White. "I'm nervous about tonight," she says. "All my friends are here—even the kids from the gym where I work."

In the middle of the mat, Ashley Picard stands in her partner's right hand. He passes her to his left hand and back several times, as if he were bumping a volleyball. "Our routine looks *so* good now," says Ashley as he places her back on the ground.

Trisha stands to the side, dressed up in a shirt with a plunging neckline. Her eyeliner is darkened to the point where her eyes look like holes. The B-52s' "Love Shack" plays on the stereo. Samantha swings her golden hair as she dances and mouths the lyrics. If Tyrone hadn't had to leave SFA, he would no doubt be dancing at her side.

Out of the corner of my eye, I see a familiar hefty body and baby face walking toward me. Brad Patterson, the squad's coach for the previous three years, is here. It's his first trip back to Nacogdoches since he resigned and moved to Arkansas. Beside him, his wife holds in her arms the kind of baby custom-made for Gerber commercials.

Kali and Doug run to greet him. Kali rubs the baby's miniature back. The baby ignores her, staring straight at Doug. "Staring contest," someone says, as Doug kneels down, his eyes unwavering. The baby holds his own for nearly a minute, then squints and starts to cry. "I understand," I want to say to him. "Sometimes Doug scares me, too."

"Elites," yells Trisha, and the SFA partner sets line up across the mat to practice before the audience arrives. Just like at the University of Memphis and Southern University, the elite stunt sequence comes close to the beginning of the routine. But SFA's sequence is one of the most difficult on the books, chock full of Rewinds, Full-Ups, and Double Downs.

The partner couples stand in their formation, their eyes surveying the arena like they're waiting for someone. And then I see her.

Sierra rushes through the arena doors, a red bow flapping wildly in her curly hair. She is wearing her uniform top and a pair of boy-short bloomers, and she rushes to put on her skirt as she runs.

I'm so happy to see her. "On the first day of spring break her doctors released her to cheer again," explains Trisha, watching as Sierra hustles across the gym. "It was a huge relief, because she is so talented."

Sierra gets into her position in front of James Brown. Four partner couples stand behind them, forming an arrow pointing toward the audience. The women lean into their partners' hands and flip, their Rewinds uncurling within a split second of each other. They look like marionettes as the men drop them down. The women face their partners and lock their arms around their necks, straightening their bodies into lines. The men spin them so that they twist over their shoulders. The women reach toward the floor as the men lower them into handstands. The women kick their feet down to the floor and take deep breaths, facing their partners. They handspring toward the men, who flick them to vertical as they sail through the air. All five women land in their partners' hands and mold their bodies into Scorpions.

Sierra hops down and gives James Brown five. I wave, and she does a double take as she sees me out of the corner of her eye. "I'm back!" she says, walking to give me a hug. "The doctors told me that I wasn't going to be able to do any physical activity at all. I said, 'You don't know me. I have Nationals in a month and a half. I'm going to do it whether you release me or not. I will fake a doctor's note if I have to.' But they eventually said I was okay."

"It's kind of unheard of for someone to be back already," says James Brown. "I'm just glad she's okay." He doesn't say it outright, but I'm sure he's thrilled that he won't have to withdraw from NCA Partner Stunt Competition. Even if someone is injured, no partner substitutions are allowed.

"Have you guys had a chance to practice your partner stunt routine?" I ask Sierra.

She nods enthusiastically, her brown eyes bigger than ever. "It looks really *good,*" she says. "I'm thinking positive. Have you seen *The Secret*? Whatever energy you put out comes back to you, so you have to think about everything positively. We're gonna win. It's the law of attraction."

Trisha waves Sierra back to the mat—she wants the squad to practice the dance portion of the routine. They gather in a diamond formation and begin a series of squats, hair flips, and arm motions, like glitter falling through the end of a kaleidoscope. They shout words as they go, but I can't quite understand what they're saying.

"What do you chant there?" I ask Jerrod as he rests a few feet away.

"It's 'S! F! A! You catch our drift! National Champs! 1-2-3-4-Fif!' The 'fif' is from Dave Chappelle, when he says, 'I plead the 1-2-3-4-Fif!' " Jerrod explains, voice sailing up. "I came up with those words as a joke, but then Trisha wanted to keep them."

"Pyramid," yells Trisha as Jerrod runs back to the mat and lines up with the rest of the squad. From behind, three women are lifted above the group, arms straight out to the sides. A second later, they flash up again farther to the left. They zigzag to the front of the group, popping up again as their partners spin them. Behind them, three women—Kali in the middle, Sierra to her left, and another woman to her right—scramble into Shoulder Stands behind them. Kali crosses one forearm over the other as a guy tosses Yvette, who lands on her arms. At the same time, Ashley and Samantha are tossed from the side to top 1-1-1s on either side of her. The two of them swing their inner legs up to meet Yvette's hands. The formation looks like a five-year-old's crayon drawing of a two-story house with a pointed roof.

"One of the guys was watching cheer videos on YouTube," Yvette told me earlier. "Bangkok University did that thing where the women zigzagged forward like that. We thought it looked cool, so we adapted it."

Still standing on Kali's forearms, Yvette flips forward, Ashley and Samantha drifting backwards into their spotters' hands. A fourth woman joins the middle layer line in a Shoulder Stand. The two women in the center kick a leg out to the side, the outer women grabbing their calves and holding the legs horizontally. Samantha and Ashley sail up, landing on the outstretched thighs. They take a second to stabilize themselves, and then Yvette is tossed through the center of the whole thing—the topper on an elaborate wedding cake. The women in the center scoop their inner arms under her feet.

But Yvette doesn't quite get her footing, and she begins to cave in. She grabs onto Ashley, at the top right of the pyramid. The two women embrace each other tightly as they fall forward. Several spotters run to catch them, but the two brunettes fall with such intensity that it creates a five-person pileup on the floor.

"It makes us look like shit when that last pyramid falls," Jerrod yells.

"That pyramid has never fallen that badly," adds Kali. "And it never will again, right?"

Someone helps Ashley off the floor. "You gotta keep it up there, babe," Doug says to her.

She looks ready to protest, but then nods. "Okay, I'll stay up."

"What happened?" I ask her.

"Yvette came up and it kind of caved in," she says. "I had to make a choice whether to hold onto Yvette or let go and watch her fall. We made the same decision at the same time to cling to each other for dear life."

The purple seats of the arena begin to fill up. There are only a few minutes until showtime. "Thank you for coming out tonight," says an announcer, turning to face the audience. "This is the team's chance to perform in front of an audience before Nationals. The SFA Large Coed squad are eight-time National Champions. They are coached by first-year Coach Trisha O'Connor." As he calls the name and hometown of each individual squad member—it sounds like he's announcing the starting lineup for the New York Knicks.

The squad members run onto the mat, waving to their friends. "We call this the drive for five!" yells a computerized voice as four men at the front of the mat spring upwards into Toe Touch Fulls, the rest of the squad turning Toe Touch Backs. Behind everyone, Sierra flies toward the JumboTron, twisting for the same basket toss that sent her crashing to the ground just a month ago. Today, it looks perfect. She tumbles toward the front of the mat, pointing at the audience as she lands. James Brown steps in behind her.

The five women Rewind and begin the elite stunt sequence. They perform a complicated string of moves that is hard enough for one partner couple. In stereo, it looks powerful, all five pairs doing the exact same thing to the millisecond.

In the front point of the formation, Sierra makes a new excited face with each move, going from beauty-queen-who's-just-won-the-crown, to scared-woman-standing-on-a-chair-after-seeing-a-mouse, to flirty-woman-winking-at-a-guy-across-the-bar. She curls her leg into a Scorpion as the four women behind her do the same. "Yeah!" screams someone in the audience. Sierra pulls her foot even higher, flattening the O-shaped space between her back and leg. The audience goes crazy.

The middle section of the routine looks good, with only the occasional mistake. Jay-Z's iconic "Big Pimpin' " riff plays over the sound system, and the team begins to dance, the audience loving every moment of their flashy choreography.

It's time for the big finale—the pyramid. The women zigzag through the formation as the music does an about-face, cutting to Journey's classic power ballad. "Don't stop believin'!" sings Steve Perry, hitting the high note just as Ashley, Yvette, and Samantha land perfectly at the top of the first formation.

The audience jumps to their feet as Yvette bird flips forward and the middle layer women shoot out their legs to build the second, bigger and better portion of the pyramid. Ashley and Samantha sail up, landing in place on the thighs held like balance beams in front of them. Yvette blows a kiss to the audience as she flies through the center of it all, the middle layer women catching her sneakers and holding her twelve feet up in the air. Yvette links arms with Ashley and Samantha, just a step below her on either side. The women at the sides of the pyramid each step up a knee, creating a formation like a staircase that goes up and right back down.

"That pyramid should be named the wall of death," says someone near me.

"No, the wall of hot bitches," says one of the team's alternates.

The team pops down from the pyramid and claps. They soak in the audience's loud applause. Jerrod, so mad just twenty minutes ago, throws his arms up to the ceiling in celebration. "I spot Sierra in the elite," he says. "When she pulled up for that Scorpion and the audience went crazy, goose bumps popped up all down her legs."

Doug nods in his direction, a tough-guy's way of saying, "Good job." "They've been doing it to a blank wall every day," says Doug. "So it's good to see them actually perform it."

One the guys standing near us isn't so enthused. "It's still not near where it needs to be," he says. "It's about getting a huge guy and a not-so-big guy to stunt the exact same way, the tumblers to all tumble at the same speed. It has to look more uniform."

Kali agrees. "We still have some work to do," she says, as the team heads out the back door to their cars. "The odds are against us. We're going for five in a row and everybody wants another team to win. And underdogs want it so bad."

## "My Biggest Fear Is That We'll Be the Team That Lost It."

Yvette leans back in the hairstylist's chair. Her hair cascades into the basin and her hands rest over her stomach as a hairstylist washes bleach out of the last few inches of her glossy black hair. "I'm getting my tips dyed purple," she says, smiling.

She looks up at the twenty-something stylist and motions to her bag. "I brought my uniform in so you could match the color." The stylist picks up Yvette's SFA top, the same color as grape soda, and walks to the back of the shop. She comes back a minute later, swirling a purply goop with a comb in a plastic bowl.

Yvette's cheeks puff out as she smiles. "I wanted to do red, but Trisha said nothing too drastic—she doesn't want people's eyes to automatically go to me. If it looks crazy, we could get a deduction," she says.

The stylist stretches a shower cap over Yvette's head and places her under a dryer. "Wind Beneath My Wings" plays on the easy-listening channel the salon has tuned into. I sit down in the chair beside her.

"A lot of girls on the team have gone blonder this week," says Yvette, crinkling her nose. "Not me."

"What else do you guys do to get ready for Nationals?" I ask.

"Tan, tan, tan," she says, holding out a darkened arm. "Everyone will get their nails done and whiten their teeth. I like that Trisha is our coach. Brad always wanted us to look plain, but Trisha wants glitter, red lipstick, ribbons with sequins."

"When did you guys find out who made the mat?" I ask.

"In January, Trisha posted it online," says Yvette. "One girl took it really hard—she's phenomenal, but she doesn't have a Back Tuck. She was in a bad mood for a month straight. It got to the point where we had to have a mat room talk because her negative energy at practice was affecting us."

It must be frustrating to have picked a college primarily to cheer, then not be able to be a part of the competition squad. Alternates still have to attend practice, even though they mainly sit with their backs against the wall. They will, however, get to travel to Daytona with the rest of the team.

"What do you think of the routine?" I ask Yvette.

She claps her hands in excitement. "Trisha gave us a skeleton, and then we said, 'We want to try this,' " she explains. "She really wanted it to feel like it was ours."

"So you like her as a coach?"

"Oh yeah," nods Yvette. "It's the first time a woman is coach, and it's a business where most of the coaches are men. I always try to remind Trisha that she's doing an amazing job because coaching college boys is tough. I think she's really worried because it's her first year that we're not gonna win."

"Is there anything you're worried about?"

"The pyramid," she replies. "Right before the pyramid, I feel like I'm about to have an asthma attack. I sometimes feel like I'm gonna puke by the time we finish."

Yvette adjusts the shower cap over her head. "My biggest fear is to be the team that lost it—to be the one who broke the streak," she says. "At my junior college, they won for two years in a row. Then when I was captain, we lost. I really felt like it was my fault."

"Who are the teams you'll be watching out for?" I ask.

"Wichita State," she says. "They usually do well, but they don't have the difficulty that we're known for. This year, we really want Grands. That's the best team at Nationals—the team with the highest score. Louisville has won for as long as I've been here. But this year, I feel like if we hit perfect, we can win."

"How long do you have to wait until you know how you did?" I ask.

"Just a few minutes," she says. "We're usually the last team to compete in the division. There will be a team in the winner's circle before us, and we'll know their score and what we need to win. They announce our score a few minutes later. If we beat them, we'll start jumping up and down."

She sits up, the excitement already getting to her. "Competing on the stage at Nationals is just the most amazing feeling—I can't even describe it," she says. "Half of the team, if we win, is going to go get a tattoo or something pierced. We're all gonna go crazy if we win." She pauses. "That's what makes us so close—we party as a team. The town is so small that we really come together. Our team is like *The Real World* meets cheerleading."

A buzzer dings, and the stylist leads Yvette back to the sink. She rinses out the color and begins to blow-dry her hair. The ends of Yvette's hair are now a deep purple color. She swings her hair, admiring it in the mirror.

## "If You're Not Bleeding, Then They Think You're Okay."

On most nights of the week, the SFA cheerleading squad can be found together. Bullfrog's, a bar on Nacogdoches's main strip, is one of their favorite hangouts. Behind a patch of pool tables and through a wooden door is a feature that I've never seen at a bar before—a swimming pool. Outside, a group of college students plays volleyball in the water, their drinks perched precariously on the concrete ledge.

Sierra walks across the wooden pool deck in a striped bikini and matching flip-flops. In her belly button, a silver ring with a bird pendant hangs down, a falcon soaring across her muscular stomach. She holds a plastic margarita glass in each hand as she sits down at a wooden picnic table across from me.

A big toothy grin forms on her face as a tall, thin man in his twenties walks up to our table. He's the classic Southern gentleman. "This is my boyfriend, Adam," says Sierra. "He's a cheerleader, too. He's always wanted to marry a girl he could stunt with—that's why he fell in love with me." She kisses him on the cheek.

"Let's go jump in the pool," she says, grabbing his hand and pulling him across the wooden deck before he's had a chance to say anything.

She runs to the edge of the pool and back flips into the water. She swings her hair over her head like a mermaid and rests her forearms on the edge of the pool. Her boyfriend does a Full over her head, landing with a huge splash. "This is how I learned to do basket tosses—at the beach," she says to me. "In the water, when you land, it doesn't hurt as much."

"Does it normally hurt when you do a basket toss?" I ask.

She nods her head sharply. "Half of our team is big guys who just put out their arms and stand there to catch you—they're supposed to bend and absorb your weight. I'll land and feel James Brown's knee in my side. He's like, 'It's only my knee.' But his knee is like a tree trunk."

"What happened the day you hit your head?" I ask her.

"We were doing the beginning of the routine and I went to do a Double Full basket toss. When I opened up, my body started turning a little bit . . . ," she says, trailing off. "The next thing I remember, I woke up in the hospital, freaking out."

She pauses. "It's almost like a dream replaying in my head. When I woke up, I just thought, 'Did that really happen?'"

"What do you think went wrong?" I ask.

"I think it was just people getting too comfortable and thinking, 'We've done this basket toss a million times.' They're huge, and so they thought they could automatically catch me. But if something goes wrong, you have to be ready to make adjustments," she says. "They weren't ready. That's what pisses me off the most."

"Do you think Trisha and Doug handled the situation well?"

"They didn't even do anything!" she yells. "If you're not bleeding, they think you're okay."

"If someone lands on their head, you're not supposed to move them," says her boyfriend.

Sierra gazes at him adoringly. "If an ambulance came and picked me up, then I probably wouldn't have had that seizure—I would have been with a doctor sooner," she says. "Thank goodness I wasn't doing that basket toss on a basketball floor."

"You could have died," says her boyfriend. "It would have been game over."

A group of college students jumps in the pool nearby and begins a chicken fight. "We could take them," whispers Adam, with a wink.

"How are you feeling about leaving for Daytona tomorrow?" I ask Sierra.

"We're going to win!" she yells. "I am so confident."

"Is there any part of the routine that makes you a little nervous?" I ask.

She thinks for a moment. "The pyramid only hits about 70 percent of the time," she says. "Like at the Show Off, Ashley flew on top, all loose, leaning on Kali like a limp noodle. It looked like she was scared up there."

Sierra slurps the last few drops of margarita out of her cup. "I noticed you're in the middle for a large part of the routine. Why do you think you and James Brown got that spot?" I ask.

"We're not in the middle because of James Brown. Let's just say that the day I hit my head, they moved him. I'm in the middle because I'm the most flexible, I have the best facial expressions, and I'm the best performer," she laughs. "Sorry, my head is a little big right now."

"Right now?" says her boyfriend, cocking an eyebrow.

She throws her tan arms around him. "Daytona's gonna be so fun, especially since you're gonna be there," she says, kissing him on the cheek again.

A month and a half ago, I wasn't sure that Sierra was ever going to be able to cheerlead again. It seems unreal that in less than twenty-four hours, she'll be on a bus barreling down the highway toward Daytona Beach, Florida.

## "Make It Look Like You Can Just Wake Up and Do That."

The clock on SFA's MySpace page reads, "00 months: 00 days: 22 hours: 25 minutes: 37 seconds." Finals is less than a day away, but to qualify for the main competition, teams must first make it through preliminaries. About a dozen squads mill about outside the Ocean Center, a building that looks like a UFO that's landed in a patch of palm trees, in their last-minute preparations. They are so close to the goal of their entire season—to take the castle tomorrow, to dazzle the crowd as the Fox Sports Net cameras roll, and to have a shot at being National Champions. But only half the teams will make it to finals.

Across the street, I see the SFA cheerleaders marching toward the Ocean Center. From here, their purple uniforms look almost black, the letters SFA popping off the dark background. The women's hair looks big and curly, their uniforms sleek to their bodies. A white diamond cuts across each man's shoulders, making them look bigger and broader than the others guys here. Their stride oozes confidence, and a posse of alumni cheerleaders follows behind the team. One of the men swaggers in the lead, holding a Bose boom box on his shoulder. The music is soft at first but gets louder as they creep closer—riff-heavy rock music that doesn't belong in this world of pop.

"S! F! A! S! F! A!" they chant in an almost warlike tone.

The teams behind the Ocean Center reluctantly turn their heads, a touch intimidated. SFA is a cheer legend, on an unthinkable winning streak. If they win tomorrow, it will be their fifth National Championship in a row.

The SFA cheerleaders place their bags under a row of palm trees. All eyes are on them as the women sink into splits on the grass. The men tie bandanas around their wrists—red on the right, purple on the left—using their teeth to pull the knots tight. "Gives the girls something to grip onto," Doug explains.

Nearby, the SFA Lumberjack—a thin, muscular guy in plaid shirt and suspenders—grips a real axe. He puts it down on the ground and does one-arm push-ups, preparing for a cameo role in the routine.

Trisha emerges from the pack wearing a red T-shirt and a pair of jeans. Her small frame is weighed down by a huge necklace—a cord holding all the National Championship rings that the current team members have won during their college careers. The silver and gold rings glint in the sun, a ruby here, a sapphire there. In her right hand, she rolls a purple stress ball between her fingers.

In front of her on the grass, Ashley Picard is the first woman on the team to defy gravity, beaming as her partner tosses her. Beside her, Samantha goes up, looking long and lean.

James Brown's right eye is swollen, purple, and shiny. "How'd you get that black eye?" one of the alumni cheerleaders on the grass asks him, reading my mind.

"Someone elbowed me," he says, raising a Neanderthal eyebrow.

Sierra calls him over to warm up her basket toss. He gathers with two others as she steps onto their hands and flies up. As she comes back down, her body folds, like she's scared herself in midair. Her spotters take a few steps back and catch her.

"Slow down, baby," says Trisha. Sierra stands up, frustrated with herself, and Kali walks over to give her a few tips. Sierra stands silently, staring at the ground with her hands on her hips.

The other teams turn their heads and watch as SFA practices a pyramid. "You're amazing," Kali says to Ashley, as Ashley lands on her outstretched thigh perfectly.

"You make that look easy as hell," yells one of the alumni women as they pop down.

"Circle up," shouts Jerrod as the team and several alumni huddle around him. "We are doing this routine *two* more times and that's it."

"Don't overthink," says Yvette. "If you get ahead of yourself in your mind, you will mess up. Ladies, in that pyramid, squeeze your stomachs. If we squeeze hard, it won't waver."

One of the alumni adds in his words of wisdom. "Go through everything with fearless confidence. Make it look like you can just wake up and do that," he says, adjusting his baseball cap. "I want so bad for SFA to get the highest score we've ever gotten."

The team members pick up their bags and walk to the doors of the Ocean Center, still feeling their competitors' gazes on their backs. They walk into a gray room with dim lights, where they will have thirteen minutes to warm up on a tumbling track and another thirteen minutes to warm up on a full-sized mat. The superstitious part of me wishes the NCA had chosen twelve or fourteen minutes for warm-ups instead.

The Lumberjacks line up at the sides of the narrow tumbling track. Sierra goes first, stumbling as she lands her Full. Kali runs behind her, curling her body into a tight ball, punching her legs out, and spinning them back together before landing. It's a tumbling pass called a Ball X Full, and Kali doesn't know of any other women who can pull it off. "Hell yeah," someone says, the whole group clapping as she lands. "That's the best I've ever seen you do it."

Sierra's lips pout. She walks back to the top of the tumbling track to try her Full again. And for the second time, she stumbles. "It's gross," she says, her big eyes glossing over.

I've never seen Sierra this off—perhaps the pressure is getting to her. Her teammates seem to notice, too, and they do their best to reassure her. "It looks badass," says Yvette, rubbing her shoulder.

"Head to the next mat," an NCA staff member tells the squad. They step over to the big mat to practice all of the elements of the routine—the elite stunt sequence, the basket tosses, the dance, and the pyramid. Almost everyone looks confident; the only move that falls is Sierra and James Brown's Rewind. For Sierra, each botched move is becoming a self-fulfilling prophecy. She stands with her hands on her thighs, her back curled over. A worry wrinkle appears across her forehead.

The clock is ticking—the squad has less than a minute left in their warm-up. Sierra steps forward to try to nail the elite stunt sequence one time before heading to the competition floor. "Go, Sierra, go!" yells one of the alternates, trying to pep her up as she fidgets nervously with the bow on top of her head.

Sierra stands in front of James Brown. He sends her up for the first half of the sequence perfectly. She handsprings up for the second half, pulling her Scorpion high and twisting for a beautiful Double Down. "Perfect!" someone squeals. Sierra's face instantly brightens.

The team heads through an open door and follows arrows to the on deck area. It is similar to the tunnel at UCA Nationals, a curtain dividing the competition area from backstage. But rather than a tiny hallway, this is wide-open space. NCA staff members corral the six teams waiting to perform. In the corner, behind velvet ropes, the trophies stand—some modest, some close to seven feet tall.

Kali fans her face. "I got myself a little tired out in warm-up. I'm already dripping sweat," she says. One of the alternates swoops in and gives her a handful of Pixy Stix, as if they are some kind of cure-all.

Samantha stands near them. "I'm so nervous," she says. She grasps hands with her new partner, a husky six-foot man with tiny dreadlocks, and they swing their arms back and forth.

The team circles around Trisha. Her stress ball has been put away and her right hand now fiddles with the rings on the necklace. "Y'all, that practice was amazing. There's not one team here that can touch you. No one will have your level of tumbling. No one's stunts will be as clean. That pyramid is going to be one of the hardest thrown today," says Trisha. "You're the best in the nation. Now you just have to show it."

A fluorescent light shines directly on Doug's bald head. "Get Daddy a ring!" he yells. Several team members grunt as they line up in back of the next performers.

Trisha peeks through a break in the curtains. Doug and I follow her as she steps through and makes her way to the coaches' area, a raised platform at the back of the auditorium. We pass the blue competition mat lying on the concrete ground. Huge stars crafted out of metal piping stand on either side of the mat. Between them, a banner reads NCA COLLEGIATE CHEER CHAMPIONSHIP.

"And now, from Nacogdoches, Texas—Stephen F. Austin State University," says a *Wizard of Oz* voice.

"S! F! A! S! F! A!" the team chants as they calmly stroll to their positions. Blue and red strobe lights flash around them, and smoke billows from a machine at the back of the stage. The team members ignore the hoopla, and stare down at their feet.

For a minute, there's silence. Then their music comes on. The squad bursts into action. All of their opening tumbling looks solid. Sierra is launched above it all for a perfect Double Full basket toss, spinning like an Olympic ice skater in a double toe loop. Her bases catch her and place her on the mat. She tumbles forward, landing her Full cleanly in the clutch. She now stands at the head of the V formation. James Brown powers her up for the elite stunt sequence in perfect time with the four women behind her. The women drop, spin, and pop back up again, pulling their legs over their heads for Scorpions.

A round of screams rises from the audience. Fans clap their hands above their heads as the team moves on to their next formation.

In the back, Sierra and another flyer hurl toward the ceiling for more Double Full baskets. Sierra's looks good, but the flyer to her right stops short of her peak and moves far to the right. Her bases catch her safely, but it looks sloppy. Beside me, Doug flinches. A second later, Kali and Samantha go up in the front, their bodies flipping in perfect lines.

Three tumblers run from the back of the mat, throwing a pass that ends in a Full. On the right side, one of them falls to her knees. Kali prepares for her tumbling pass in the corner but pauses as she sees her teammate on the ground in her path. The girl jumps to her feet and scurries out of the way just in time. As another tumbler crosses the floor, he accidentally steps off the blue mat on his landing. Trisha groans—it's the third deduction in a matter of seconds.

Unlike at UCA, NCA judging is done by calculating a maximum score and deducting. Panel judges look at five categories—tumbling (up to eleven points); partner stunts (eleven points); pyramids (eleven points); basket tosses/jumps (eleven points); and motions/dance (five points). The panel judges' scores are averaged to determine a raw score, the highest possible a 9.80. A legality judge makes any deductions for safety, time, or boundary violations. Finally, a point deduction judge subtracts 0.05 for each bobble, 0.1 for each major mistake, and 0.2 for big falls to get the final score.

On the mat, SFA begins to dance, going for the full five points. I can see every wink, sexy glance, and goofy smile all the way across the auditorium. They are in the home stretch as they move to their positions for the pyramid. The first section hits with no problem, three tall lines with legs swinging out to create the roof. They dismount and go for the final pyramid. Kali, standing in the center on a guy's shoulders, kicks her leg to the left, the woman next to her kicking hers to the right. Sierra and a second middle layer woman on the right side of the pyramid hold the legs parallel to the ground. Samantha and Ashley fly straight up and land on their outstretched thighs.

Suddenly, Ashley's knees bend and she slides down Kali's thigh, her weight now pushing on Kali's upper body. The pyramid is about to cave in, like a soufflé collapsing under its own weight in the oven.

Out of the corner of her eye, Sierra sees Ashley and Kali falling. She grabs a tight hold of Kali's leg and pulls it sharply toward her. Kali's face grits as she tightens every muscle in her body, and she uses her free hand to force Ashley back in place. Their side is straightened just in time, as Yvette is tossed through the center of it all. She comes to a triumphant stand, the star topping the Christmas tree.

Trisha jumps up and down, her little body shaking the coach's podium. If the pyramid had fallen, her team would have received a 0.2 deduction for a major fall. By saving it, they'll walk away with a much less severe 0.05 bobble deduction. Their score would still have carried them to finals, but their confidence would have been shaken.

"I can't believe that save!" yells Doug as he and Trisha jog toward the team.

The audience roars along with them—it's almost as if they appreciate the impossible save more than they would a flawless pyramid. SFA has shown that they are the ones to beat both in their division tomorrow and for the Grands trophy.

But, as the team steps off the mat, their smiles disappear. Kali stands with her hands on her hips, stunned. "We did *not* do well," she says, hard on herself, as always. Ashley walks by, sobbing. Even Sierra, who turned around the energy of a terrible warm-up to give a fantastic performance, is upset. She takes an empty seat in the audience, her face flushed and a look in her eyes like she's ready to stab someone.

Doug looks straight at them. "Don't," he says. "You did *amazing.*"

The team walks in a loose clump back through the curtain, the darkness enveloping them as another team runs onto the mat in a burst of strobe lights and smoke.

The group gathers tightly around Trisha. "There were very few mistakes in that," she says. "They were stupid mistakes, but nothing that can't be fixed. Tomorrow is the day to be perfect. But y'all, that was phenomenal—the energy was fantastic. If you do that tomorrow and clean it up ... I'm telling you ..."

Jerrod stares at the concrete. "We can win our division with little mistakes," he says. "But there's no way they'll give us Grands. Tomorrow, all that needs to be perfect."

"Let's go back out there and wait for our score," says Trisha. "We know we made finals, so as soon as we get our score, let's leave."

Sierra stomps as she follows the group through the curtain and to three open rows of seats, where teams are encouraged to wait for their scores. "I'm still stressed out because I have to do Partner Stunt later," she says. "I need a huge cigarette."

As SFA takes their seats, Wichita State runs onto the floor. "They're our main competition," says Sierra, clapping as they hit a pyramid. "But

I still want them to do good." They end the routine with several stunts and return to their seats with excitement.

"We now have the score for Stephen F. Austin University," says the announcer. The team turns around in their seats and faces a large screen where their university name is displayed in block letters. Some of the SFA women grip hands.

*9.50.* The numbers flash in red on the screen.

Sierra throws a fist in the air. "Whoa!" she yells, hugging the person next to her.

"That's awesome!" screams Trisha.

Kali jumps up and down, her hair lifting above her head. "Oh my goodness, are you kidding me?" she yells. "That's a Grands score."

"It's definitely the highest score we've gotten in prelims," says one of the veterans. "It might be higher than what we got at finals last year."

"And that's *with* deductions," someone adds.

Once a team has qualified for finals, they are given a five-minute practice session on the outdoor stage where finals will be held tomorrow. The SFA squad has dubbed this time "Meet the Mat." To get there on time, Trisha motions for the team to stand up and follow her before Wichita's score is announced. She leads them down the steps of the Ocean Center, past the palm trees on the lawn, across the street, and through a hotel's lobby toward the beach. "We get to get a feel for the floor, the sun, for where the crowd will be," explains Trisha as she leads the parade, the necklace of rings around her neck clanging as she walks. "It's important for tumblers, especially because the floor feels different than in preliminaries."

We walk through a pair of stonework gates with an iron-wrought light fixture atop each post. In front of us is a stage shaped like a medieval castle, complete with stonework and a gothic tower on each side. This is "the castle" I've heard so much about. Built in 1937, it has housed concerts at Daytona Beach for decades, but in recent years it has become synonymous with the finals of NCA Nationals.

But the castle will serve mainly as a backdrop. Because the existing stage is not quite large enough to house a regulation-sized mat, the NCA has raised a platform in front of the stage. In front of that is a sprawling concrete space where spectators will sit on beach towels tomorrow. Around the perimeter of the arena are empty bleachers, which will soon be packed.

The SFA cheerleaders walk up a metal set of stairs to the stage. The wooden platform gives slightly under their weight, adding a spring to each step. "Tumblers, throw some passes to get the feel of it," says Trisha. "Then we'll do the routine." The floor creaks as they tumble much higher than they could on the preliminaries mat.

As the team waits to practice the routine that earned them a score of 9.50, one of the team members gets a phone call on his cell. "Wichita State got a 9.27," he yells so everyone can hear.

He puts his ear back to the phone, and a big toothy smile grows across his face. "And Louisville got a 9.48."

"Oh my God!" yells Kali, jumping up and down again.

"Wait, who's in first place?" one of the women asks.

"Us," everyone responds in echoing unison.

## "That Was Pimp."

Samantha sits in a clump of SFA cheerleaders on the floor of the Ocean Center, a wistful look in her Cleopatra eyes. Her hair has held its curl from this afternoon, adding some roundness to her normally thin face. She claps loudly as she watches the first couple in the NCA Partner Stunt Competition power their way through a clean routine. Her trophy for second place at the UCA Partner Stunt Championship is on her bedside table at home. Still, it feels unnatural for her to be here in the audience rather than backstage with the four SFA couples who are performing tonight.

"We would be competing now, but . . . ," she says. "It just sucks that Tyrone had to leave SFA." She hasn't seen him since they parted ways at UCA Nationals in January, but she talks to him on occasion and knows he is doing well in Connecticut taking care of his mom. While Samantha loves her new partner, the two of them aren't quite the caliber needed to enter a partner stunt competition. Samantha misses being a contender.

Yvette sits near her, her stage makeup from the afternoon out of place with her simple T-shirt. Earlier in the year, Yvette also expected to be in tonight's competition. She and Jason qualified in fourth place for the UCA Partner Stunt Championship based on their bid video, and on the Indiana Jones stage, they placed third overall. But even though they put together a video they thought was harder and cleaner for the NCA competition, they placed eighteenth. Only the top ten couples compete.

When the results were announced, the SFA team, Trisha included, was surprised that Yvette and Jason had placed poorly. It's an example of how cheerleading judging is subjective—one set of judges loved them while another panel didn't. Yvette wanted to let it go, but after watching other bid videos on YouTube, Jason wanted to take action. "I had people telling me, 'There's no way that I should've scored higher than you,'" Jason explains, a hand on his short afro. "I didn't think the videos were judged correctly."

Jason wrote an email to the NCA inquiring about his placement. The next day, he received a cordial reply explaining that while he and Yvette scored well on creativity and cleanliness, they received low marks on difficulty. Jason still wasn't convinced. "It seemed like other people scored higher for no apparent reason," he said.

He wrote a second email, and a full-out scandal erupted. An NCA official told Trisha about the emails, and she immediately called Jason into her office for a meeting. "It sounded like a fifth grader throwing a hissy fit," Trisha said. "One of the reasons SFA is a respected program is that our cheerleaders handle themselves with tact."

She ordered Jason to write an apology to every person he mentioned in the emails. The longest apology went to Yvette, who was fuming after she heard about the second letter. But now, sitting in the audience, she says that she's fine not competing. "It's a bit of a weight lifted off my shoulders," she says. "Now I can focus on the team."

Samantha and Yvette watch intently as the second SFA couple of the night performs. They clap and scream, and as the couple nails their finale, Samantha jumps up to clap. Her peripheral vision catches someone running toward her. When she turns her head, she sees Tyrone. The two run toward each other and hug tightly, a movie scene unfolding in real life.

"I decided to drive here yesterday," says Tyrone quietly as they sit down to watch the next couple perform. "I drove for twenty-two hours. It was a last-minute thing." Samantha hugs him again. I wonder if she's thinking what I am—that even though they haven't have been able to practice for months, if they'd submitted an NCA bid video, they might have been able to compete tonight.

Last year at this competition, SFA took first, second, and third place. It would be unlikely for SFA couples to sweep the first three spots again, but Trisha, Doug, and the rest of the team are hoping that an SFA couple can shore up first. With Samantha and Tyrone and Yvette and Jason out of the running, Sierra and James Brown are SFA's best chance. They're up next.

"This is Sierra and James from Stephen F. Austin University," says the event's announcer.

Samantha screams. "Go James Brown!" yells Tyrone beside her.

"Show 'em how it's done, Sierra!" someone bellows behind me.

On the mat, Sierra runs out as the smoke and strobe lights go off. Her pale blonde hair is piled on top of her head, and her skirt looks too long on her short body. James Brown lumbers slowly behind her, walking with his feet first, his arms hung dead at his sides. "S! F! A! S! F! A!" people in the audience chant.

James Brown pulls up the fabric on the legs of his pants and squats, his left hand on Sierra's back as their dance music comes on. She flips backwards, and he hulks her up to his outstretched right hand for an impressive Rewind. In the air, Sierra smiles like a sixteen-year-old who's gotten a car for her birthday.

"That was *amazing*," a woman near me says as James Brown taps Sierra back to the mat and hoists her up again to spin twice before she lands. She brings her foot back for a patented Sierra Scorpion. Her mouth opens, unhinging at the jaw. The audience roars.

"She's like Play-Doh," says someone in the audience.

Sierra Doubles Down and stands up, before James Brown sends her right back in the air for another Rewind. He gets his hands to her feet a little low and presses her back in the air, like a miner hoisting a heavy boulder to save his team from being trapped in a tunnel. Sierra pulls a foot up for a Heel Stretch. She Tick Tocks, scissor-kicking her legs as James Brown grabs hold of her other heel.

"Go James Brown!" yells Tyrone.

"Yeah Sierra!" says Samantha, as the audience behind them raises the decibel level.

Sierra drops into a cradle, and James Brown spins her over his shoulder before she handstands out. She pauses for a second, mouthing the word *breathe* to him. So far they have put in a clean, difficult performance—exactly what the judges look for in handing out the trophy.

Sierra's blonde curls bounce as she thrusts herself into a handspring. James Brown grabs hold of her waist and he pushes up with his left hand, down with his right, tossing her like a juggling pin. He reaches to catch her feet in his right hand, but as they make contact, his elbow dips. His hand is dropping out from under Sierra.

He quickly reaches up with his left hand to bolster her, turning a certain disaster into a bobble. Sierra raises her eyebrows and makes an O shape with her mouth. She pushes her right leg straight behind her and leans forward slightly.

The music suddenly stops. People in the audience glance at each other, confusion filling in the sound of silence. Sierra's smile evaporates. Their time is up. They won't be able to finish their routine as planned, and they'll get an automatic 0.1 time limit deduction in addition to the 0.1 deduction for two bobbles. Sierra's extended leg bends awkwardly, like a flamingo losing its balance. She looks down at James Brown in a panic. He pops her up, reaching out his arms to catch her in a cradle as she falls, ungracefully, like someone who's slipped on a wet marble staircase.

James Brown places her back on the ground and she claps softly as the audience applauds. She seems disoriented, walking in a circle until she spots the section of seats where the other SFA partners are watching the remainder of the competition. James Brown follows her. As she takes the first steps up the bleacher stairs, Sierra breaks into a run, sprinting out of the arena. The forty-five seconds she'd been working toward all year are over, and she cannot deal with the fact that she and James Brown messed up. She disappears through a set of doors.

James Brown takes a seat behind Ashley Picard and Jeremy, his legs spread wide and his elbows resting on his gigantic knees. His back heaves up and down as he breathes.

Outside the Ocean Center, Sierra is livid. She slams her foot into the wall, and tears begin to flow. Her boyfriend, Adam, and Kali try to comfort her. "It's okay," they say. "You did really good."

"I looked like an idiot," yells Sierra, her voice deep as she cries.

"What happened with the music?" I ask.

She shakes her head. "I told James Brown we should start ready, but he said, 'I'm going to wait until the music starts and then I'll get set.' Ugh, there's no arguing with him," she says. "The music came on and he took a few big breaths, then put his hand on my back. We just ran out of time."

She pauses, her tears stopping a little. "He was thinking on the spot—he told me to do that Arabesque. I would have Doubled Down, but I didn't know if he was ready and I didn't want to fall straight to the mat in front of a thousand people. So I popped off." She shakes her head. "It just looked like we were both confused."

In a few minutes, she's composed herself. She reenters the auditorium and walks toward the section where James Brown's large body is squeezed into a blue seat. "I thought you were going to catch me," she says, facing him. Her face crumples into tears again. "It made me look so stupid. I didn't know what to do." She sits down next to him and he swings a thick arm around her, an unspoken apology. They watch the competition silently.

Ashley leans forward. "Sierra, it really wasn't that bad," she whispers. She plays with Sierra's blonde curls, trying to comfort her. Sierra turns toward James Brown and hugs him, her salty tears mushing into his sweaty face.

A couple from Morehead State—a tall, wide black man and an itty-bitty mousy blonde—walks on stage. The girl stands at the edge of the mat, her back toward the crowd. She handsprings toward her partner and pulls directly into a Back Tuck, his hands boosting her high in the air for a Rewind. It looks superhuman—none of the SFA couples even attempted anything that flashy. The rest of their routine is equally effortless. The audience is on their feet, clapping and yelling.

"That was pimp!" screams Tyrone. "They *brought* it."

Samantha turns to him. "Yeah, but we beat them at UCA."

As the Morehead couple leaves the mat, the announcer says, "We have the score for Sierra and James from Stephen F. Austin University."

James pats Sierra on the leg, both of them silent. Ashley leans forward and rubs Sierra's shoulders.

"An 8.78." Sierra and James barely react to the number. They were hoping to get above a 9.0. With that score, they won't place above the two other SFA couples who have already performed.

"Let's go find the others," says Sierra, standing up.

Sierra and Ashley walk down the bleacher steps, the rest of the SFA partners following them. James Brown stays in his seat. He sits there, staring straight in front of him—a giant in a sea of empty seats.

Back on the floor, Trisha and Kali watch intently as a couple from Wichita State performs an amazing routine. "We're getting our ass handed to us right now," says Kali. Even if the SFA routines had been perfect, if the drops and bobbles obvious to the crowd had somehow been invisible to the judges, there's no way they'd have won over Morehead or Wichita State's creative, powerful routines. "Everyone stood up halfway through Morehead's routine," says Kali. "*I* felt compelled to stand up. It was amazing."

At the awards ceremony half an hour later, the couple from Morehead State walks away with the first-place trophy. Wichita State gets second. A partner set from Louisville steals third. Even though SFA had four couples in the competition, half of the playing field, they didn't manage to place. After a drop, Kristen Wilkerson and David Bowden earned seventh. Ashley and her partner Jeremy Plemel got sixth. Sierra and James Brown, who were so gunning for first, landed in fifth place. And Chelsea Craiker and Tim Wegner scored the highest of the SFA pairs, but still placed only fourth.

Sierra walks out of the Ocean Center, her face tear-stained. "I did the best I could, but Morehead did amazing. I've always told myself, 'Let the best person win' and they did. But it still hurts," she says, her eyes heartbroken. "I'm not a fifth-place kind of girl."

## "We Need to Give Them Greatness, Not Just Awesomeness."

The Stephen F. Austin cheerleaders pile into Trisha's hotel room, where empty Papa John's pizza boxes lay piled on the floor along with dozens of unopened Pop-Tarts. The women have all showered—several heads of hair are still wet—and many of them have changed into pajamas. The guys opt for shorts, and the most muscular members of the group go shirtless.

The seats on the bed are taken first. Samantha, Kali, and Doug pile onto one bed, as Sierra, team captain Jerrod, and a few others hop on the second. Jerrod now wears the necklace of championship rings around his thick neck. "Feel how heavy this is," he says, taking it off and offering it to me. I pull it over my head, and as I let it go, the cord pulls on the back of my neck. I look down at the mass of gold, silver, and huge jewel faces. LCLM, JACKS, DESIRE, THREE-PEAT are engraved into their thick bands.

"How many rings are on that thing?" someone asks.

"Fifty-eight," says one of the guys. "I counted."

On the turquoise carpet near me, a pretty brunette lightly tickles the two guys lying on either side of her. The vibe in here is slightly charged—a Coed slumber party. The door swings open, and in walks Ashley Picard wearing a Red Sox T-shirt, striped pajama pants, and big white fuzzy slippers. "Make like the Red Sea," someone says as the sprawled bodies part to let her through.

Across the room, Trisha is curled into a ball in a desk chair. "Listen up, y'all," she yells over the chatter. Most of the faces in the room turn to her, and one of the guys lets out a fart. Trisha ignores him. "I want you to see your video from today," she says, hooking up her video camera to the flat-panel television on the desk. The tape of the squad's performance this afternoon begins to roll.

"Sweet," someone says as the elite stunt sequences sail up smoothly.

As they finish the sequence, Jerrod loses a shoe, a big white blip on the perfectly blue mat. I hadn't noticed this during the performance, but watching on the screen it looks like an ominous banana peel, ready to trip someone. He keeps performing like nothing has happened.

The tumbling passes crisscross the floor, Kali's Ball X Full high and beautiful. "I can see Kali's penis," one of the guys says as everyone claps for her.

On the screen, the final pyramid goes up. It leans inwards as Sierra and Kali miraculously fight to keep the whole thing from collapsing.

"Look at Sierra," someone says. "She's like, 'Get back over here.'"

"Kali, I love you," exclaims someone else.

The routine ends, and we watch as Jerrod walks across the mat to collect his lost shoe. "I felt like such an idiot putting my shoe back on," he says.

Trisha stops the video. She holds several sheets of paper in her lap, the team's score sheets from earlier today. "I want to read you some of this," she says. "'Neat stunt sequence.' 'Creative, clean.' 'Great incorporation of tumbling skills.' 'Great save on that pyramid.'"

As she looks up from the paper, I realize that it's the first time I've seen her without eye makeup. She looks younger, more fresh-faced than usual as she claps her small hands together. "You can't even believe how happy I am that you've learned to save that pyramid instead of giving up," she says. "Your recovery is part of what makes you great. When that pyramid faltered, it could have left the judges with a bad impression. But because you saved it, you impressed them."

She continues to read comments from the score sheets. "'Straighten your legs on the baskets.' 'Watch the timing on the pyramid.' 'Keep the energy up.'"

She looks up again. "Your scores for motions, expressions, projection, and energy can easily go up," she says. "Act like you're having fun. Put in a little extra in those places where you know that it's dead. Boys, I need your flames on." She puts the score sheets down on the desk. "You've done this routine a thousand times. You know you can hit it perfectly."

The door to the room opens, and in walks Michael Preston. "Anything you want to say to them?" Trisha asks her boss.

"It was like fireworks today—just stunning," he says. "But what's so amazing is that it could still be better. I want Grands *so* bad. I want to beat the hell out of Louisville."

Michael Preston's assistant steps into the room behind him. "Guys, you have the chance to be *the best* in the nation in what you do," he says. "That's just amazing to me. How often do you get that chance? I'm getting chills just thinking about it, and all I do is bring you pizza." The room erupts in laughter.

Doug sits on the bed, his hands clasped between his knees. His bald head has gotten a little red from the sun. "Our score showed us that we have what it takes," he says. "But Wichita State looks awesome, and tomorrow they'll be out for blood."

Samantha nods. "Wichita State is really clean, and they're not far behind us," she says. "They could give us a run for our money."

Kali holds a hand over her stomach. "It's going to be such a different feeling tomorrow," she says. "There's nothing but sky and a mass of people. You'll feel like you can fly, like you can do anything in the world."

Trisha's eyes begin to water up. She pounds her fist into her other hand. "I can't even explain to you how awesome it feels to hug your teammates after you've all put on the best routine of your life," she says. Near her on the floor, Yvette fans her face. "It is the most amazing feeling in the entire world. I want you all to feel that tomorrow."

Tears spill out of Yvette's eyes as Trisha continues. "This is why you came to a school in the middle of nowhere," she says. "This is why you're here."

On the bed, Samantha pulls her shirt over her head and squeals. "I just want to thank you all for letting me be a part of this," she says. "I just don't want today to be the day we peaked."

"In finals, the judges expect you to be better than in preliminaries," someone adds. "We need to give them greatness, not just awesomeness."

Trisha nods. "Today, you came off the mat *mad,*" she says. "And that's what will make you the best, the fact that you're pissed off when you're not perfect because you know that you can be *perfect.*"

The team members stand up, reaching to the person next to them for a hug. Yvette's high voice sails above the babble. "Let's go out there tomorrow and live the dream," she yells.

## "Arrogance Will Be Their Downfall."

The Stephen F. Austin cheerleaders gather behind the castle. Finals have been going on for hours and, in twenty minutes, it will be the Lumberjacks' turn to take the stage. As I watch them stretch and look at themselves in their pocket mirrors, the words from last night's team meeting echo in my head: "You have the chance to be the best in the country." It is truly amazing that the cheerleaders in front of me are the best of the best—the gold-medal contenders, the ones to beat.

The Lumberjacks stand twenty feet from the castle's stage entrance, a rugged wood door with metalwork hinges, in their purple uniforms with pie slices of red on their torsos. The women's hair has been curled into the "big curls" Trisha requested, each strand of hair sprayed and wrapped around the barrel of a curling iron. On top of each girl's head sits a thick bow with sequin stripes of purple and red, which glitter in the sun. The men are situated in a quiet clump, each trying not to sweat in his thick polyester uniform. "Starting now, sunglasses off," someone says. "Let's get used to the sun."

Their warm-up was all Trisha could have hoped for, almost every stunt, tumbling pass, pyramid, and basket toss hitting with military precision. Trisha's light brown hair blows in the ocean breeze. The necklace of rings is still tied around her neck. She cups her hand over her eyes to block the sun and surveys the other teams standing in the area. She looks at Hawaii Pacific University in grayish-blue uniforms that cut away to reveal the women's shoulders. Near them stands Southern Arkansas University in cobalt blue. Across the sidewalk stands Wichita State, SFA's main competition in the Division 1 category. Their uniforms are white with splashes of yellow, the word *Shockers* in large letters across their chests.

Yvette looks at them with disgust on her childlike face. "Last night, one of our girls got off the elevator on the wrong floor. It was Wichita State's floor, and over their coach's door was a big poster that said, 'Dynasties end in 2007. Arrogance will be their downfall,'" she says. "Now I want to beat them so bad so we can be like, 'Arrogance, huh?'" Smile lines form around her purple-rimmed eyes. "Half our team doesn't even know what 'arrogance' means."

Kali sprays herself with vanilla body spray. "Ooh," she says, lifting her arm. "I forgot to shave my armpits."

On the back of Samantha's white, high-top sneakers she has written Tyrone's name. Others have names scrawled on their shoes, too—alternates, people who had to leave the team during the year, alumni, and others who cannot be on the mat with them. Tyrone is not backstage, but I saw him as we walked past the arena. He's parked his large body in the front row, ready to cheer loud for SFA.

Standing near me, Doug has a faint smile on his face. I lock eyes with him, and we both grin ear to ear. He doesn't have to say anything—it's a look that says *This is gonna be good.*

"We have the score for the University of Louisville," says the announcer from inside the arena, where the Cheer Division IA competition is coming to a close. "Our Division IA champions, with a 9.66."

Louisville has just won their fifth National title in a row. For the past four years they have edged out SFA by fractions of a point and left Daytona with the Grand Nationals trophy. To win Grands this year, SFA will need to beat a 9.66.

Doug's ears perk up as he hears Louisville's score. "The numbers are there. Yesterday, we got a 9.50 with a raw score of 9.70," he says. "The scores usually go up for finals. It's very possible we could win." He shakes his head. "Ahh, there's just so much anticipation right now."

Ashley Picard stands a few feet away in the shade. While the others had a flawless practice, hers was a little rough. "The first three Back Tucks I threw, I fell on my face," she says. "I finally landed one and I told myself no more until you go out there. I wanted to end on a good one."

Even though Jerrod sounded confident at the team meeting last night, he now seems tense. He yells at a cheerleader who has forgotten to put on an armband the squad wears in memory of a team member who died in a car crash years ago. Yvette grabs him by the arm. "Calm down," she says. She explains that the offending cheerleader is threatening to drop all of her stunts since people are being mean to her.

"I will break her," he says, shaking his head. Yvette meets his eyes, and he takes a deep breath. The cheerleader comes back with her armband. "Good hustle," he says to her. "Sorry, we're all stressing out."

Kali walks by me and picks up my right arm. She draws in curly handwriting the word *strength* on my wrist. "All the girls have to have it," she says. The other women around us sport the identical mark on their arms.

Trisha looks at the teammate who fell on her Full in preliminaries yesterday. "If you miss your Full today, I will ram this up your ass," she says, pointing to her shoe. The girl faintly smiles.

Sierra stands to the side of the group. Her blonde hair has gone several shades lighter in the past twenty-four hours—she dyed it yesterday, washing out the bleach just thirty minutes before the squad left for preliminaries. She stands, leaning on a metal bar, her hands clasped together. Her eyes are closed tight as she says a prayer.

Her boyfriend walks up beside her. She throws her arms around him—they hit just above his butt because of their height difference. He holds her there for a minute, as a cheerleader in green rolls by in a wheelchair, her leg propped up straight in front of her.

"Wichita State," calls an NCA staffer by the stage door. The Shockers place their bags in a pile and run past us. SFA tries to ignore them.

Wichita State will be the next to compete in Cheer Division 1, but SFA will not be able to watch. They'll be called to the stage door themselves in a few minutes. "I think it's an advantage not to see your competition," says Trisha. "It puts you in the mindset of performing to not lose instead of performing to win."

The squad gathers in a circle. James Brown, who has made no effort to camouflage his black eye, speaks. "Let's go out there and do our best. The audacity of them to think that they're gonna take a ring off my finger my senior year . . . ," he says, trailing off, his teddy bear face uncharacteristically hard. "Let's go out there and fucking *do* this."

Kali nods. "I am not even a little nervous right now," she says. "Everyone be confident—don't go in doubting anything. If you are nervous, keep it as far down as you can. I don't want to see any doubt right now."

Ashley takes a deep gulp and closes her eyes, trying to swallow her nerves.

"I don't want to hear any bitching or whining anymore," says Jerrod. "I don't care what's hurting—I will ice it for you at six o'clock."

Everyone laughs. The team members each throw a hand into the middle of the circle. "1-2-3, Strength," they shout at the top of their lungs as they break.

"Stephen F. Austin University," yells a woman in an NCA staff shirt. "You're on deck."

## "I've Got Chills."

Trisha, Doug, and I jog into the packed arena and push our way through the crowd to claim spots in the front corner of the stage. Every square inch of the bleachers is taken, and in the open area, hundreds of people have laid out beach towels to pad the ground as they watch. The entire arena smells like coconuts and suntan lotion, and almost every woman under the age of thirty is wearing a bikini. I feel horribly overdressed in my black shorts and bright purple top. The sky is perfectly clear, barely a cloud in sight as seagulls fly overhead.

The Wichita State team descends from the stage via a set of stairs. They are jubilant, a mass of excited energy as they wait under a projection screen for their score. "And now the score for Wichita State University," says the announcer, as the squad turns toward the screen. In bright red lettering, 9.60 flashes across it. "Our new leaders in Division 1 Cheer," says the announcer as the Shockers go crazy.

The SFA cheerleaders are backstage, so most likely can't hear the score. But it is good news. If they can just nail this routine, like I've seen them do so many times before, the Division 1 title is theirs. Heck, if they can get through with just one small deduction, they can still clear Louisville's score of 9.66 and win Grands. The Lumberjacks will be called to the stage any moment. I feel my heartbeat speed up. As I look at my wrist where Kali wrote *strength*, the letters are already feathering from my sweat.

Trisha stands directly in front of me, her front pressed against the stage. Doug is nestled among a cluster of SFA cheer alumni. Tyrone stands near them, screaming his head off.

"From Nacogdoches, Texas," calls the announcer. The SFA cheering section lets forth a surge of sound. "The Stephen F. Austin State University Lumberjacks."

"S! F! A! S! F! A! S! F! A!" the team jogs on stage chanting. The guys pound their fists toward the sun. Kali adjusts her uniform and waves to a friend she sees in the audience. Ashley gives the guy standing beside her five. They look down toward the ground, some shrugging their shoulders in anticipation.

"Go Kali!" someone yells, as she waves again.

"Yeah Samantha!"

"Come on Lumberjacks!"

Trisha stands silently, the noise scared out of her.

"We call this the drive for five," begins the digital voice as the women thrust out their right hands, fingers separated. They sail up and touch their toes, then spring backward into Back Tucks. Ashley lands on her feet and stumbles forward, but she does not touch the ground and get the team a deduction. I can practically feel her exhale from here.

In the front of the mat, five tumbler guys jump so high a basketball player could walk underneath them. They land and lurch backwards for Standing Fulls, their bodies thrashing around.

Behind them, Sierra steps into a basket toss and flies up, kicking a leg out and flipping back down to where James Brown and the rest of her spotters cradle her safely. Facing the back of the mat, she shuffles and whips into two back handsprings. She sails into a Full, landing front and center on the mat. This tumbling pass, called a Two to Full, is extremely hard, especially for women. After she lands it flawlessly, she shoots two imaginary guns at the audience with a wink. James Brown steps behind her.

Over the loudspeakers, the music shifts to Beyoncé, a remix that's sped up as fast as an Alvin and the Chipmunks song. "Baby, I swear it's déjà vu," she sings on hyper speed.

The five partner couples line up like a flock of geese, Sierra and James Brown leading the formation. The guys crouch down like they're ready to crush skulls in football and place their right arms on the small of their partners' backs. The women flip as they're powered into the air. The five One-Arm Rewinds all land perfectly.

"Yeah! Yeah!" yells Tyrone behind me, as the women kick their legs to their ears—airborne Rockettes. The women drop down to a cradle, landing in their partners' arms. They straighten their bodies as the guys spin them out over their shoulders. The women reach their arms toward the ground and step down from a handstand. Every milli-movement is in perfect unison.

"Yeah!" screams someone behind me. "Get it!"

Each woman stands about five feet in front of her partner. They handspring toward their partners, and the guys flick them to standing in their hands. The SFA cheering section goes wild.

The women stick out their chests and flash their arms under the letters SFA on the front of their uniforms. They continue to lean their chests forward as they bring their right legs behind them and reach over their heads for their shoes. Each woman pulls her body into a Scorpion, like five Cheerios suspended in the air. Sierra looks into the audience, smiling huge. She pulls her leg up as high as it will possibly go.

"She looks like she has no bones," someone near me says. Trisha still seems unable to speak. She pounds her hand on the wooden stage in front of her instead.

In the spaces between the partner couples, tumblers come flipping through, like streamers waving from the top of a Maypole. The women smile in their Scorpions and whip their bodies into straight lines as they Double Down, their curled hair spinning at the same angle. Their partners catch them in a cradle before returning them to the ground. "S! F! A!" the team yells, forming the letters with their bodies as they move into a new formation of four clumps. "Jacks!"

Four women load into baskets. Samantha and another woman in the back fly up first, their bodies twisting twice in perfect lines, ankles crossed. Kali and Sierra go up a second later, both of their bodies flying even higher and spinning even more quickly. All four women sail so high that they would come dangerously close to hitting the castle's stone arch if they were not on the platform in front of it.

The music changes again. It's time for their tumbling, and SFA boasts some of the top tumblers in the country. Guys crisscross the mat, one person tightly following after another, flipping, twisting, turning their bodies. Kali begins her Ball X Full tumbling pass. She runs with her arms toward the sky and bounds to the mat, rounding off and turning two handsprings. She curls her body into a tight ball in the air and flicks her legs out in a V, using the momentum as she snaps her legs together high to whip herself into a Full. She lands and pumps a triumphant fist in the air. "Yeah, Kali, yeah!" screams her friend in the audience.

Just as she lands, her brother starts his tumbling pass, crossing the mat in the other direction. His compact body disobeys gravity, a black crop of hair spinning around and around as he adds more tricks to his pass. He lands and turns to the audience, who let out a big bout of applause for him. Behind the cacophony of tumbling, Ashley and Samantha top two 2-1-1 pyramids.

"I've got chills," says an SFA alumnus behind me.

"My nipples are hard right now," says someone else.

"Yes!" says Trisha, letting out the first sound she's been able to make since her team walked on stage.

Six stunt couples line up across the mat. The women reach back and grab the wrists of their partners. They go up, hair flying out to the sides as they spin once and land in their partners' hands. The women bring their knees across their bodies, a hand on their hip, the other to their ear, as if they're pinups in a '50s magazine. They kick their knees behind them and stand in unwavering Arabesques.

The audience claps hard as the women Double Down. An alumna behind me in the SFA cheering section is screaming so loud that I know she will have laryngitis in the morning. Trisha pounds a fist against the stage. The elite stunt sequences were perfect, the tumbling amazing, the second stunt sequences flawless. The team has crossed the minute and a half mark, and Trisha begins to relax—all the team has left is their dance, an easier stunt sequence, and their final pyramid. "Come on!" she yells, as the squad moves in tightly toward the middle of the mat. Jay-Z's "Big Pimpin'" comes on with its lackadaisical riff.

"S! F! A!" they shout as the women in the front clap their hands together overhead and drop to their knees, another line following behind them a count later and staying a touch higher. The guys do the same movements while standing, forming three rows of cheerleaders at different heights. "You catch our drift!" they yell as each person leans forward clasps their hands together, and pulls as if playing an intense game of tug-of-war. "National Champs!" they scream as two women in the front roll back, their legs creating a frame around Sierra as she dances on her knees. "1, 2, 3, 4, Fif!" Sierra pushes her palm forward and counts with each finger.

A remix of Michael Jackson's "Smooth Criminal" comes on. Yvette has her turn front and center as her partner tosses her high in the air and she kicks out her legs and arms into an X. She lands and shimmies her shoulders with the rest of the women. They bend from the waist, their hair flipping over as they dance like short-circuited robots. Yvette comes through the center of the formation again, doing a scissor high kick—half kung-fu fighter, half chorus line.

The Wichita State cheerleaders have migrated to the right side of the stage. They look like they're caught in the headlights of a car about to run them over.

The SFA women fan out in a straight line for the final stunt sequence. All eight women jump high as their partners toss them. As they fly, they ball their knees to their chests and kick a leg up, grabbing their feet in a Heel Stretch position before they reach their partners' outstretched hands. Every single stunt lands perfectly.

Trisha jumps up and down. "Yeah! Yeah!" she screams, bringing her acrylic-nailed hands to her face.

The team gets into position for the pyramid. Journey pipes in through the speakers. "Don't stop believin'! Hold on to that feelin'!"

Ashley, Yvette, and Samantha pop up in the back of the SFA cluster, then to the left, then in front, where every flyer shoots up, hair whipping around their faces as they spin. Three women stay up in Shoulder Stands, Kali in the center. She puts one arm over the other, like Barbara Eden granting a wish in *I Dream of Jeannie*, and leans down. Yvette drifts up and lands on her forearms, as Sierra and a shadow on the left side catch Ashley and Samantha on top of their knees in 1-1-1s. Ashley and Samantha kick their inner legs up to meet Yvette's hands—the last two lines needed to complete the drawing of the house. They hold it for a second, the women making sassy faces. Yvette raises her eyebrows and opens her mouth into a huge O, as if she's trying to catch flies.

Jerrod, spotting the pyramid in the front, throws a fist up like Arsenio. SFA's first pyramid has hit. The Wichita State cheerleaders at the side of the stage have looks of fear on their faces.

Trisha claps so hard she could bruise her palms as she jumps up and down. "Yes! Yes! Yes!" she yells. There are less than ten seconds left in the routine and only one final move. Her squad has given the best performance of their lives, and the entire arena is electrified. People in the stands are on their feet, and people on the ground have edged onto their knees for a better look. Even on the balconies of the hotel overlooking the castle, people are going crazy for SFA.

On the stage, Yvette does a bird flip forward from the top of the pyramid, and Jerrod and James Brown catch her. Ashley and Samantha fall backwards, where bases step in to catch them. The middle layer of the pyramid stays in the air. Kali's base turns to the side so that she faces Sierra. A second woman to Kali's left does the same, turning out to the other direction. Kali kicks a leg up to Sierra's hands, her shadow doing the same thing to the left. Ashley and Samantha are tossed from the back of the formation, each of them landing on one of the outstretched thighs.

"Yeah!" yells Trisha. Doug jumps up and down. The final pyramid is 85 percent completed.

Jerrod sends Yvette up through the middle, between Kali and her shadow. The two women scoop their inner arms under Yvette's feet. Yvette throws her arms around Ashley and Samantha, three climbers who've made it to the top of a mountain.

And then it happens. Ashley slips closer to the center of the pyramid, falling to her knees on Kali's thigh. It starts a chain reaction. Sierra seems pulled off balance and Kali leans inwards, the whole right side of the pyramid sliding down. Ashley clings to Yvette in the middle and the two of them crumble, pulling Samantha with them, her legs flying out from under her. The three women fall slowly, like they're caught in quicksand and can't quite seem to find anything to hold onto to keep them from being sucked into the earth's core.

"Yea-oohh," says the audience, their excitement turning mid-scream into disappointment as Ashley, Yvette, and Samantha fall. Trisha cups her hand to her mouth.

On stage, Jerrod's eyes tear as he looks up and sees the three women falling. "No, God, no!" he yells and reaches up to catch them.

To the right, the Wichita State cheerleaders begin to cheer. A yellow flash of a Shocker jumps onstage so quickly that he is up there before the three women are even caught. He pumps his fist in the air, ignoring all rules of sportsmanship to bask in Goliath's fall. Other team members behind him pound the stage. "Yeah!" they yell, jumping and turning to hug each other.

Spotters catch Ashley, Yvette, and Samantha safely. The rest of the guys stay put, bracing the middle layer women so they don't fall, too.

Trisha whips around as if she's seen someone get shot. "Oh my God," she says quietly. "They just lost it." Her tears instantly begin to flow.

Silence. No one yells "Jacks!" as they normally do at the end of the routine. The team looks like they've just woken up from a nightmare as they walk offstage. Some of them are already in tears, others seem like they don't know what's happened. Jason's eyes fill with tears, and he balls his fist to his mouth to try to stop them. Yvette's always smiling face is pulled downwards. Ashley's eyes are open wide, in shock. She stands a few feet away from the others.

"We can't win this," one of the cheerleaders says. "There's no way."

An SFA alum pulls Trisha in toward his chest, giving her a place to cry in peace.

Jerrod cups his hands to his mouth. "It is *not* over yet," he yells, fire in his voice. The team gathers around him to the side of the stage, where they'll wait for their score. "It is *not* over. It is a small deduction. Everyone chill. *Strength*," he shouts at the devastated group. "We are SFA, we can still get the points. And if the Shockers beat us, we will hold our heads up high and congratulate them because they've been busting their asses for years, just like us. Champions don't just act like it when they win. If they win, we will go shake each one of their hands." Spit flies out of his mouth as he speaks.

By now former teammates and friends have made it to the circle. "It was perfect, the whole routine," says one blonde, doing her best to comfort her friends.

"Guys, that was badass," says a former tumbler.

"It's the best I've ever seen it," says someone else.

"God is on our side," says an alternate. "God is on our side."

Jerrod puts his arm around the squad members next to him. The team pulls into a twenty-five-person group hug—Yvette, Sierra, and Kali in the middle, the others around them like petals on a rose. They stand silently, still hugging as the next team takes the stage, not letting the pounding bass disturb them. They sway ever so slightly, together, blocking out the noise of Wichita State celebrating nearby.

Trisha walks over to the group and joins the outside of the hug. Black eyeliner and mascara are dotted under her eyes and cheeks. She sways with her cheerleaders, letting the togetherness comfort her.

"We now have the score for Stephen F. Austin State University," says the announcer, his pep totally unaffected by the pyramid's collapse. The team uncurls a little from the hug, their heads turning toward the screen behind them. A red number flashes up on the screen: 9.48.

Wichita State screams. A dreadlocked guy in a Shockers uniform knocks me over as he runs toward his team and jumps on his friends. "Yes!" one guy yells. "Finally!" They walk through the exit, two stone towers, going crazy.

The SFA squad is stunned. Ashley Picard doesn't move—she seems like she's sleepwalking, unaware of what's happening around her.

Near her, Kali wrings her wrist brace. "I've never felt a routine like that—it was perfect. Even when the pyramid was going up, I was like, 'Yeah!' I don't know what happened. In my head, I think that I'm Wonder Woman and that I can save anything," she says, tearing up. Samantha swoops in and hugs her tightly.

Jerrod steps back from the circle and claps, the others joining in. "We'll remember the experience we gained here this year," he says to his team. He leads them out of the castle, squeezing past other teams whose members reach out and pat them on the back as if to say *I'm so sorry* without words.

Jerrod continues around back of the stage, half of the squad still following him in a procession. In front of them, the Wichita State cheerleaders are being interviewed by Fox Sports Net. Jerrod waits until the red light on the camera goes off, and then he approaches the victorious team. "Good job," he says, shaking each person's hand. One of the women on the Wichita team begins wailing with tears of happiness as her family runs up to congratulate her.

The SFA cheerleaders walk away. A guy with arm muscles like a young Arnold Schwarzenegger heaves into sobs. His friend, another big guy on the squad, turns him around, and they hug like men, fists balled. "It's okay, man," his friend says as he cries. "It's okay."

At the sight of all these men bawling, tears pouring out of their eyes in direct contrast to the size of their bodies, I feel overwhelmed. My mouth feels like I've just eaten something sour. And then I realize—I'm crying, too.

On the other side of the castle, Sierra's brown eyes are as reflective as glass. She walks up to Ashley, who stands motionless, still stunned. "That was *your* fault," she says, pointing a finger in Ashley's face.

An SFA guy grabs Sierra. "I can't believe you would say that," he says, shaking her. "That's not LCLM." Sierra begins to cry.

Ashley doesn't move. Her eyes roll up into her head, and she falls toward the pavement. Her hand barely breaks her fall, and the side of her head bounces off the pavement. She's fainted. The guy who scolded Sierra quickly bends down and picks her up, rushing her tiny body to the white medical tent around the other side of the castle.

Where the majority of the team has congregated, no one has seen Ashley faint. They're still fuming about how Wichita State acted in the final seconds of their routine. "That guy jumping onstage was the most unsportsmanlike thing I've ever seen," says Michael Seitzer.

The University of Louisville's coach walks by the group and pats Doug on the back. "I'm sorry twice—once for the fall, and once for the other thing," he says, glancing at the Wichita State team nearby. "I've never seen anything like that. They're going to have to do something about that."

"They should get some kind of a deduction next year," says Doug.

"What can you do?" Kali whispers. "They haven't won in years. If I hadn't won in years and my rival dropped, I'd be excited, too."

"They hit the best routine of their life, and they still had to pray that we messed up," says Jerrod, still doing his best to keep the team's spirits up. "I hope you all realize how good you did."

The blonde, all-American-looking Shockers cheerleader who jumped onstage walks up to Doug, and the two talk quietly. The guy walks toward the team. "SFA, can I apologize to you?" he asks, addressing the whole group. "When I jumped onstage, it wasn't meant to disrespect you. It wasn't because you boggled, and I'm sorry if that's how it looked. I've been cheering in college for seven years and all I've ever wanted is just *one*. I hope you believe that. I'm sorry."

Several SFA cheerleaders offer their palms to shake his hand. One guy turns around, ignoring him. "Ahhh," he says, "I just hate this place."

About fifteen feet away, inside the medical tent, the athletic trainers are tending to Ashley. She is awake now, an oxygen mask on her face. They've pricked her finger to check her blood sugar. Trisha sits by her side, her arms wrapped around Ashley. "You worked your butt off on the mat," she whispers. "Things happen. It sucks that it happened today and to you, but you can't blame yourself." Ashley stays silent. A few minutes later, Trisha helps her walk out of the tent and up to her hotel room, where Trisha puts her to bed.

It's been less than an hour since the team's downfall. The Junior College Division is performing now, and several SFA cheerleaders have wandered back to the stage to watch the teams they cheered for before coming to SFA. Khris Franklin, an SFA cheer alumnus, stands near me. "After what happened today, none of the people on the mat will *ever* let it happen again," he says. "I'm just worried Ashley is gonna put the whole thing on herself." He looks over at a person wearing an SFA T-shirt listing all the years of victory—1994, 1997, 2000, 2001, 2003, 2004, 2005, and 2006. "You see that break in 2002? That was me—I dropped a stunt, and I put the loss all on myself. I never cheered again. Now I realize it was just a fluke."

Sierra walks up and stands beside us. She reaches out her short arms and gives Khris a hug. "I saw Ashley lean in to Kali and I thought, 'Save it!' but I couldn't get her foot like I did yesterday," she says. "I can't believe that we lost in the last second. I feel like we let you down."

He turns and looks her dead in the eye. "You didn't," he assures her. "You guys were phenomenal."

Sierra looks up at me. "I was mean to Ashley," she says. "I was on the side watching it fall—it's not like some gust of wind came along or her foot slipped. She pulled Yvette down. We told her so many times that if she feels like she's going to fall, lean in to me—don't pull on Yvette.

Literally, my heart stopped when I saw her going down. She just seemed la-di-da after, and I took it out on her. I feel bad. I apologized."

Nearby, Yvette screams for the junior college she cheered for two years ago. She is already tipsy—one of the teammates packed a bar's worth of drinks in their backpacks. "I knew any tiny little mistake and we were done," says Yvette behind her oversized sunglasses. "I knew as soon as we dropped that we had lost. The NCA is very political, and they want teams to come back to competition. For a team like Wichita State that never wins, eventually they won't come back. If we open the door with a mistake, there's no way they're going to give it to us again."

She pauses. "It just makes me sick to my stomach that people like that can win. The ring doesn't matter as much as the family, and I know that Wichita doesn't have the love and trust that we do. Everything happens for a reason and we'll all have to get over it," she says, cracking a devilish grin. "I'm gonna come back tonight not knowing what my room number is. I'm gonna come back tonight not knowing what my name is."

## "It's Like When Someone Dies."

It's the day after Nationals—a day informally known as Stuntfest, where hundreds of cheerleaders gather on the lawn outside the castle to throw stunts and hang out. The SFA cheerleaders meet Trisha in the hotel lobby. For the first time in days, her neck is bare. The necklace of championship rings has been dismantled, each shiny piece of silver and gold handed back to its rightful owner.

Trisha's face is sullen, but as the team approaches, she swings into coaching mode. "You are no longer covered by the school's insurance policy, so don't try stupid stuff," she says. "Don't grab a drink and go stunt. Be smart. None of the girls should hit the ground—I don't care if there's already another spotter there, there should be an SFA guy with every SFA girl."

Many of the squad members look severely hung over. Trisha glances at a guy whose eyes are as red as his T-shirt. "You are on your own until we leave early tomorrow morning," she says. "Do not be so incapacitated that someone has to carry you to the bus. It's not fun to ride eighteen hours with someone throwing up next to you."

Many people laugh. "Seriously," she says sharply. "And remember, we're not a snotty team. If someone asks you for help, give it to them. You all weren't born badass—someone helped you, so be that person for someone else."

The squad members split up, most of them heading outside to the lawn. Others go straight back upstairs to their rooms. As they leave, Trisha's face sinks. It doesn't seem like she's had a chance to process her own emotions. "The first thing you think is, 'If I was a good coach, they would have won,'" she says. "I know people are saying that—I had people before I was even hired say, 'Well, if she's coach, the program's going to die.' After a semester, they came around, but I know people will talk."

"Do you think what happened has anything to do with you being a new coach?" I ask her.

She shakes her head. "It can happen to *any* coach," she says. "Once they get out there on the mat, it's up to them. All you can do is sit there and hope."

"When they fell, did you think there was any chance they could still win?"

"No," she says. "Not only was it our big pyramid, but it was the ending. It takes away from the pyramid score and it takes away from the overall effect score because it's the last thing the judges see."

"Did you see the Wichita State cheerleader jump on the stage?" I ask her.

"I didn't. I kind of had tunnel vision at that point looking at my kids. Immediately, there were people crying on the mat. I was too busy thinking, 'I can't believe this is happening.'"

She pauses. "I was glad to see that when they came off the mat, there was no judgment. Ashley was devastated and people were hugging her just saying, 'It's okay. We'll be back next year and this won't happen again,'" Trisha says. "That goes along with LCLM."

She shakes her head, reddish hair swirling. "I need a nap," she says, proceeding to her room. She doesn't wake up for the rest of the day.

In a room down the hall, Ashley gets ready for Stuntfest. A pink polka-dotted suitcase sits by her bed, and on her bedside table is a photo of Bitsy in a pink frame. "I don't travel anywhere without her," says Ashley as she combs her thick brown hair. "I've already called the pet-sitter so many times."

We walk down the hall together. "How are you feeling?" I ask.

There's a moment of silence. "This is going to sound bad, but it's almost like when someone dies—you cry and cry about it until you can't cry anymore," she says. "It still stings, and it probably will for a long time."

"Do you remember how you felt waiting to go on yesterday?"

"Numb. My dad told me when I was little that if you relax your fingers, everything else will go with it. So I closed my eyes and went numb," she says. "As soon as the music turned on, it was like a spark ignited. After I landed my Tuck, I was on a high. We transitioned to the elite stunt sequence and rocked it."

"How did the first pyramid feel going up?" I ask.

"Amazing. I remember popping off and being like, 'This is it. We're going to hit this routine,'" she says. "I found out later that Samantha's side kind of bobbled, too. I thought it was just my side. I've been trying to piece it together in my head, because I know there's no way I could have fallen that bad just myself. There had to be something pulling the other side."

"Do you remember what was going on right before you fainted?"

"I remember them announcing our score," she says. "My peripheral vision got dark and I passed out cold. I passed out when I didn't get accepted to the college I wanted to go to, I passed out when my dog was injured—I just pass out when traumatic things happen."

We reach the stairs outside, and Ashley perks up a bit as she sees the lawn packed with people. All around, women pop up above the crowd, smiling as they mold their bodies into different forms in the air. The lawn is, fittingly, about the size of a football field. At the west end is the castle, its stone spires reaching into the blue sky. Along the north side is the Hilton Daytona Beach, a hotel with a faux balcony at each window. At the east end of the lawn is a phallic-looking clock tower. And on the south side is Daytona's boardwalk, the beach visible just over the railing, the horizon a simple line between blue and gray.

Ashley walks down the stairs, taking off an SFA T-shirt to reveal a white bikini that pops off of her tan skin. She sees a group of friends from an old team and is instantly enveloped by a group of guys, who take turns tossing her in the air.

There are no skirts on the lawn today—those have been packed away. The cheerleaders are now in practice clothes, and for the first time all week, cheerleaders mingle with people on other teams. Tigers stunt with Terrapins, Wolves with Sooners, Cowboys with Coyotes. It's so crowded on the lawn that it's hard to observe—everywhere I stand, I come within inches of being hit by someone going up or coming down.

I spot Yvette in the crowd wearing a terry-cloth tracksuit over a bright pink bikini. She holds a drink in her hand. "I don't stunt at Stuntfest," she says. "This is my spring break, damn it." She watches as the other women on the team go up, circles forming around them as people stop to see SFA in action.

Yvette takes a sip of her drink through a straw. "We're still the team that everyone wants to be on. I decided that I have to come back next year—I want to be a part of the team to win it back!" she enthuses, before disappearing into the mass of cheerleaders.

Behind me, Kali gawks at a group of women in hot pink shirts. The front reads: STUNT SLUTS. They turn around to show Kali the back. WE LIKE IT ON TOP. "That shirt is amazing, I have to get one," says Kali.

"I'll trade you for an SFA shirt," says one of them.

"Really? I'll run upstairs and get you one. Wait right here," says Kali, sprinting up to her room.

I make my way to a four-foot clearing, where Samantha and Tyrone practice a segment from their second-place UCA Partner Stunt routine. Tyrone's face drips sweat. "We're taking some steps down memory lane," says Samantha.

They try a One-Arm Rewind, Tyrone placing a hand on Samantha's lower back. She flips and he hurls her up, reaching his hands up to grab her feet. Samantha lands, and the tattoos on Tyrone's arm dance as his muscles shake. "Damn, I'm out of shape," says Tyrone. "It's been months of just chilling for me."

"I still love you, baby," says Samantha as she pops down.

Samantha spots a friend and runs to say a quick hello. "Man, I've missed this," says Tyrone.

"Have you figured out what you're doing next year?" I ask him.

"My mom just moved back to Oklahoma and we're going to see if she can handle herself," he says. "If she's good, I'm gonna come back to SFA. If I don't feel comfortable with that, I'm going to go to a community college near home. Everyone on the team understands—they know it's family first. That almost makes it harder—it would be a lot easier if these weren't people who meant a lot to me."

Samantha is hoping that Tyrone returns and that they can get another shot at a Partner Stunt Championship. "Tyrone and I have something special," she says. "We have a connection that I've never had with a partner. If he came back, I would be thrilled. But I'm not getting my heart set on it."

"But you'll definitely be back?" I ask.

"If Trisha takes me," she says. "Every flyer I know who is trying out has a Full, and mine still isn't consistent. It's whether Trisha wants a reliable Full or if she wants me." At the beginning of the year, Samantha was the girl close to getting cut, and even though she rose to become one of SFA's most badass stunters, she can't stop thinking of herself on the borderline. I tell her that I have a feeling Trisha will want her back.

"Move back, move back," a guy yells. He's clearing a long strip of grass where the tumblers can show off their skills. Michael Seitzer is one of the first to run down the strip, the crowd applauding as he contorts his body in midair. The guy tumbling behind him does an entire pass with a cigarette dangling from his lips.

At the top of the clearing I see Kali, proudly wearing her new shirt. She runs and throws her Ball X Full to a burst of cheers. She squeezes into the sidelines of the clearing, watching in awe as her brother does another killer pass. "Thanks to this team, I have my brother back," she says. "Now he's my best friend, my roommate, my teammate. LCLM brought us together."

"Does it feel weird that this is your last day as a college cheerleader?" I ask her.

She laughs. "I *thought* this would be my last year. But I figure I'm not in a wheelchair, I'm still building new skills, so I should keep going," she says. "I'm going to try out at Hawaii Pacific University for next year. Their new head coach is old LCLM. It's an opportunity that hit me in the face—a 100 percent full scholarship for a graduate program. I don't know what I'm going to grad school for, but I'll figure it out."

Near us, Sierra does a lap around the lawn in her green-and-blue-striped bikini, looking for James Brown. Her boyfriend, Adam, trails behind her. "I wish my stunt partner was here," she says wistfully. But he is nowhere to be found.

Sierra turns to her boyfriend. "You stunt with me," she says, pulling his arm. She raises a painted-on eyebrow like a puppy begging for a bone.

They start with a simple Liberty to get Adam warmed up. His face grits as he holds Sierra in the air—he's as tall as James Brown, but he's half as wide. They laugh as they try again and miss completely.

Three hours later, the crowd on the lawn has thinned, leaving a mess of beer cans and bottles on the grass. Sierra and Adam are still in the center of the lawn, now stunting as if they've been working together for years. Two women stand watching them as they nail a Handspring Up. "This girl is so good. She's *S-F-A*," one of them says, the admiration in her voice more appropriate for a senator. Even with just two people watching, Sierra jolts into performance mode.

The sun begins to set, winding a purple and pink pattern through the sky. A chill settles in from the ocean. Sierra and Adam throw a final Full-Up and walk back to the hotel, arms wrapped around each other. Sierra takes her phone and listens to her messages. "Oh my God!" she squeals. "My great-aunt just called—it's snowing in Texas!"

## "It's Like Four-and-a-Half Wins."

It's been a week and a half since the SFA Lumberjacks made the somber drive back from Daytona Beach. Trisha sits in her office among the trophies that crowd the room, this year's golden megaphone smaller than she would have liked.

Her phone rings. As she speaks to the person on the other end, her jaw drops a little more with each sentence. She hangs up, stunned. She turns on her computer, navigates to the NCA's website, and there, in black and white, is the confirmation that what she's just heard is true:

*After the conclusion of the 2007 NCA Collegiate Cheer Championship, Wichita State University (WSU) administration representatives notified NCA that its cheer squad competed with an ineligible performer in the Cheer Division 1.*

*Based on WSU's report and our subsequent investigation, NCA has determined that the WSU cheer squad did in fact violate NCA's competition eligibility requirements. Accordingly, the WSU cheer squad has been disqualified and WSU has agreed to forfeit the 2007 championship title and awards.*

*As a result of the foregoing, the 2007 championship title and first place honors for Cheer Division 1 will be awarded to Stephen F. Austin State University.*

Trisha jumps up from her seat and hurries down the hall to tell Doug and Michael Preston. "I have mixed emotions," she says, and it's obvious from their quiet reactions that they feel the same way. "While it's nice to have the win, it's not like we went on the stage and straight-up won. We didn't do our job."

Michael nods. "We should accept the title graciously," he says. "But we shouldn't make a big deal about it—no rings, no big public thing."

"And I want to make sure the squad knows not to hold it against anybody on the Wichita State team," says Trisha. "I don't want anyone to look down on them, because it was their leadership that failed them."

A grin crosses Doug's broad face. "It's kind of like four-and-a-half wins in a row," he jokes.

Trisha walks back to her office and types a long text message into her cell phone to send to the squad. The crux of it is this: "Wichita State forfeited their title, and we are now the National Champions. Congratulations!"

Sierra is one of the first to check her messages. "I was at the gas station when I heard. I started jumping up and down and screaming—I was so excited," says Sierra. "I have never heard of a team being disqualified for an ineligible member. You can't just grab someone off the street and say, 'Put on this uniform and go to Nationals with us.' "

Still, it's not the same sensation of victory that Sierra has gotten used to over the past eight years. "The best feeling is being down by the scoreboard and knowing you won," she says. "We didn't get that, so I can't quite experience the joy."

In three years, Sierra has attended three colleges. And next year, she will cheer for her fourth—the University of Texas at Arlington. "My friend just started as the head coach and my boyfriend's going to be the assistant coach," she explains. "I've always wanted to be on the best team, but I think I'm getting a little mature for that. This is a program that's just getting started, and I can help them build."

Sierra hopes that being on a less intense team will help her focus more on school. "Nacogdoches is a big party scene, and I don't know that I'm strong enough to avoid it," she says. Plus, in Arlington, she'll be closer to her mom, her grandparents, and her boyfriend.

At the beginning of the year, Sierra thought she had found her dream stunt partner, but even though they didn't come home from Daytona with a Partner Stunt trophy, Sierra hasn't given up on that goal. "Me and my boyfriend decided after we did so good at Stuntfest that we're going to practice all year and do the Partner Stunt Competition next year," she says. "We're gonna work out every day, so I can get real small and he can get really big. We've only stunted together five times and we're already really good."

James Brown is at work when he gets Trisha's text. "Honestly, I wasn't very excited," he says. "It doesn't mean we won—it just means we didn't lose."

James was sure that this would be his fourth and final year as a college cheerleader. But in the week since Nationals, he's changed his mind. "I just feel like I didn't do what I needed to do for the team this year. So I'm coming back," he says. He will, of course, be looking for a new stunt partner.

For Ashley, the news that Wichita State was disqualified came just a few days too late. In the week after Nationals she began binging and purging. Realizing she was on a downward spiral, she decided to go home to Boston. She left Nacogdoches four days ago, making arrangements with her professors to finish her finals and papers from afar.

"You know what's funny?" says Ashley. "When I heard we won, I was so pissed, I could have thrown punches at someone. I've been a complete wreck over losing, and I didn't have to go through that."

Earlier in the year, Ashley called herself a ringchaser. She's spent the past several years of her life hopping from school to school in hopes of winning a National Championship ring. "Initially, I was upset that in Trisha's message she said that she didn't think rings were necessary. It would be nice to show off some bling, bling," she sighs. "But the more I've thought about it, I don't want my ring to come from a technicality."

Like Sierra, Ashley will not come back to SFA next year. Instead, she plans to finish her degree at home. On the side, she's been offered a spot on the Boston Celtics cheerleading team. "It's actual stunting and you get $100 a game," she says. It's not a ring, but it is cheering for 18,000 fans on a regular basis.

Back in Texas, Yvette checks her cell phone, her eyes lighting up at the sight of Trisha's message. "I'd heard the rumor right after we got back, but I didn't say anything to anyone because I didn't want to jinx it," she says. "Karma's a bitch. I feel bad for them, but I truly believe that everything happens for a reason. It's like we were supposed to win."

Part of me can't help but think that she's right—that the universe had some kind of plan that went astray when the top layer of that pyramid came crashing down. No one in the NCA can remember a college team being stripped of their title, and it happens this year, to benefit this team who, until the final second of their routine, I thought had clenched it. It feels like something more than a coincidence.

While she thought she'd be retiring this year, Yvette has also changed her mind. "I told Trisha in Daytona that I was coming back because I didn't want to end on a loss," she says. "But now I want to do it for LCLM."

LCLM. For this team, the letters are everywhere—embroidered on their pillowcases, tattooed on their bodies, stitched into all of their gear. It can be used as a noun or an adjective, and it can justify almost any

346 | KATE TORGOVNICK

seemingly nonsensical action. It is their highest value, a religion of sorts. Its hold on them is so strong that cheerleaders from the early '90s still respond to the phrase.

But in the end, I have no idea what the letters mean. I've heard several theories from people, like myself, on the outskirts of the team: Lumberjack Cheerleaders Love Me; Love Comes Later, Man; Lumberjack Cheer Lifts Mountains. Some are convinced that the letters are phantom—that they don't stand for words at all. While several of the SFA cheerleaders happily explain that the letters DBAP stamped on their backpacks stand for "Don't Be a Pussy," none of them will reveal the meaning of LCLM. It's a mystery, a well-guarded secret that no one who hasn't worn the Lumberjack uniform can ever know.

# THE CHEERLEADER'S DICTIONARY

**AACCA** The American Association of Cheerleading Coaches and Administrators. The group responsible for setting rules and promoting safety.

**All-Girl** A division of cheerleading where teams are composed solely of women.

**All-Star** A type of cheerleading based around gyms rather than schools. It is focused on competition rather than supporting an athletic team.

**Arabesque** A stunt in which a flyer, held in the air, extends one leg directly behind her, lowering her chest parallel to the floor.

**Awesome** A stunt in which a base holds both of a flyer's feet in one hand.

**Base** A cheerleader, male or female, who lifts and holds flyers in the air.

**Basket Toss** A cheerleading move where a flyer is thrown high in the air by a group of bases and caught in the cradle of their arms.

**Bid Video** A recording created by college teams to secure an invitation to Nationals. Done in lieu of regional or qualifying competitions.

**Bloomers** Opaque underpants with heavy-duty elastic so that they do not budge while performing.

**Boring** A cheerleader who does not perform with energy. Characterized by a blank facial expression and a lack of style.

**Build** To climb and hoist to create a pyramid or stunt.

**Castle, the** The stage at NCA College Nationals, which has a medieval façade.

**Catch-On** A dance in which a leader begins a movement and the rest of the dancers or crowd repeats it. Common on Southern University campus.

**Clean** A cheerleading move performed with absolute precision.

**Cleat Chaser** A girl who goes after football players, baseball players, or other athletes. Used in a derogatory manner.

**Coed** A division of cheerleading where men and women compete together.

**Cowboy** To open your knees when you do a back tuck to the point where a horse could fit between them.

**Cradle** An interlocking of arms that allows a safe place for a flyer to be caught after a basket toss or stunt.

**Double Down** A difficult dismount from a stunt, in which a flyer twists two times before being caught in a cradle between her base and a spotter.

**Drop** When a base, or group of bases, fails to catch a flyer and she falls to the ground. Generally comes with a stiff punishment. See also, Eat Mat.

**Eat Mat** A severe drop where bases allow their flyer to fall face-first to the ground or mat. Generally comes with a stiff punishment.

**Elevator** A stunt in which two bases lift a flyer, each gripping one of her feet between two hands held at chest height.

**Extension** A stunt in which a base lifts a flyer, holding a foot in each hand and fully extending their arms.

**Facials** Winks, head bobs, open mouths, dropped jaws, surprised looks, and other expressions that can be seen from the back row of an arena.

**Flyer** A female cheerleader who is lifted into stunts and pyramids and thrown in basket tosses. Will generally be very small.

**Full** An elite tumbling move where a cheerleader flips while doing a full twist.

**Headcase** A cheerleader who constantly overthinks a move to the point where he or she can't make their body do it. See also, Mental.

**Heel Stretch** A stunt in which a flyer, held in the air, kicks a leg straight up and holds it in place.

**Helicopter** A stunt where three women, held off the ground, grip hands and are tossed high, spinning like a horizontal propeller.

**Herkie** A jump where a cheerleader reaches one leg forward and bends one back behind him or her. Also, the nickname of Lawrence Herkimer, one of the founding fathers of modern cheerleading.

**High V** A basic cheerleading position where the arms are held overhead and separated.

**Hit** To perform a cheerleading routine perfectly, where no stunts, pyramids, tumbling, or basket tosses fall. See also, Nail.

**LCLM** An acronym, like a fraternity's letters, that symbolizes Stephen F. Austin cheerleaders' bond. Exact meaning unknown.

**Liberty** A stunt in which a flyer, held in the air, lifts one knee and places her hands above her head in a high V. Possibly named because from afar, it looks like the Statue of Liberty holding a torch.

**Little Girl Syndrome** A condition whereby a small flyer relies on her base to do all the work in a stunt and doesn't jump hard or squeeze tight to get and keep herself in the air. Abbreviated LGS.

**Load in** When a cheerleader steps onto her bases' arms and steadies herself before a basket toss.

**Make the Castle** Southern cheerleaders' terminology for making it to the finals at NCA Nationals.

**Mat** The safety surface, generally 42 × 54 feet of blue foam, on which cheerleading is performed.

**Mat Room Talk** A cheerleading version of a "Come to Jesus" meeting. Common among SFA cheerleaders.

**Mental** A condition where a cheerleader has overthought a move to the point where he or she can't make their body do it. See also, Headcase.

**Middle Layer** The flyer, or group of flyers, who are in the middle row of a pyramid.

**Nationals** The showdown of teams from across the country that cheerleaders look forward to all year. Term is slightly deceiving because many cheerleading organizations hold their own nationals annually. See also, NCA and UCA.

**NCA** The National Cheerleaders Association, the original cheerleading organization founded by Lawrence Herkimer.

**NCAA** The National Collegiate Athletic Association. Does not currently oversee cheerleading.

**Oldhead** An alumnus or alumna of Southern University cheer who still spends a considerable amount of time watching and advising the team.

**One-Man** Also called a One-Man Walk-In. A stunt where a single base boosts a flyer overhead. A hallmark of the Memphis All-Girl squad.

**Pom-Poms** A ball of colored nylon, paper, or other material held by cheerleaders during sporting events.

**Pyramid** A cheerleading formation created by stacking bodies vertically, often by one person climbing or being thrown on top of others.

**Rewind** A difficult stunt where a flyer does a back flip as her base or bases hoist her into the air and catch her feet.

**Ringchaser** A cheerleader who switches colleges often, in hopes of winning a National Championship ring. Usually used in a derogatory manner.

**Scorpion** A stunt where a flyer held in the air brings a leg behind her and reaches back overhead to grab her foot, creating a circular body line.

**Sharp** Cheerleading moves performed with absolute precision.

**Shoulder Stand** A stunt where a flyer climbs or is tossed onto her base's shoulders.

**Spotter** A cheerleader who stands in the most effective place to prevent injuries.

**Standing Back Tuck** A tumbling move where a cheerleader bounds from standing into a back flip.

**Stunt** One of the basic building blocks of cheerleading. Any move where a base or group of bases lifts or tosses a flyer overhead to perform a trick in the air.

**Stunt Group** In All-Girl cheerleading, a flyer plus three bases (a main base, a side base, and a back spotter) who perform stunts together.

**Stunt Partner** A flyer and base pair who stunt together, often entering individual competitions.

**Squeeze** What a flyer must do to stabilize herself in the air. See also, Tight.

**Superman** A stunt where a base stands with his legs apart and brings his flyer between them before throwing her overhead. Name derived because the flyer's body is held parallel to the ground, resembling Superman in flight.

**Tick-Tock** A stunt where a cheerleader, held overhead, quickly switches legs, her base catching the new foot to keep her in the air.

**Tight** What a flyer must be in order to remain tossable and liftable. Attained by squeezing all muscles.

**Toe Touch** A jump where a cheerleader swings their legs in a split, touching their toes in the air.

**Toeing** When a flyer points her toes during a stunt, shifting her weight line and making the stunt hard to hold.

**Top Flyer** The flyer who is the point on a pyramid. Often the lightest member of a squad.

**Toss** When a base grips the waist of his or her flyer and throws her upwards as the flyer jumps. Often added in front of a stunt's name—Toss Awesome, Toss Liberty, etc.

**Tuck Check** Like walking a straight line or touching their nose, a test to make sure a cheerleader is not too inebriated.

**Tumbler** A cheerleader who specializes in gymnastics passes.

**Tunnel, the** Before performing at UCA Nationals, teams line up backstage in a narrow corridor of curtains.

**Two-a-days** Intense training where two practices are held in one day. Term adopted from football.

**UCA** The Universal Cheerleaders Association. Founded by Jeff Webb, it was the first organization to hold a national competition.

**1-1-1** A pyramid where a middle layer stands on a base's shoulders, and a top flyer is tossed to standing on her knee.

**2-1-1** A pyramid with two bases on the bottom, one person in the middle, and one on top. Forms an Eiffel Tower shape.

**2-2-1** A pyramid where two Shoulder Stands are side-by-side. A top flyer is tossed through the center and held in place.

# ACKNOWLEDGMENTS

IF THIS WERE AN Oscar acceptance speech, the get-off-the-stage music would start playing at the bottom of page one. But, what the heck—this is my first book and I want to thank everyone properly.

First off, extreme thanks to the members of the Stephen F. Austin Large Coed, the University of Memphis All-Girl, and the Southern University Varsity cheerleading squads for letting me into your lives. I wish this book could have been 2,000 pages long so that I had enough space to tell each and every one of your stories with the detail and care they deserve. You are all amazing people and astonishing athletes, and I wish you all the best. Special thanks to James Smith, Brad Patterson, Trisha O'Connor, Michael Preston, Carol Lloyd, and Frankie Conklin for agreeing to be part of this project. I have truly learned so much.

Thank you to Lawrence Herkimer, Jeff Webb, Dawn Calitri, Dean Oblonski, Bill Ahern, and everyone else at the NCA and the UCA who helped me with this project. Thank you for working so hard to make cheerleading what it is today. Thanks also to awesome mascotologist Roy Yarbrough.

There are two people who I want to thank for taking this project from a vague idea in my head to a completed, real book. To my agent extraordinaire, Laurie Abkemeier, from our first email exchange all the way through this project, you have been amazing. Thank you for all of your crisis control and encouragement. And Amanda Patten—I feel so honored to have had an editor as smart and enthusiastic as you are. Thank you for helping me boil down everything that happened this year to its most essential elements.

Tammy Tibbetts and Jen Trolio, thank you for your tireless research, transcribing, and fact checking. Gary Bogdon and Beth Fandal—your photos kick ass.

Halfway through, deep breath.

I have to send my love to all the Crucial Minutiaeteers. (Shameless plug: check out our blog at *www.crucialminutiae.com*.) You are all superstars and have helped me immensely in shaping this project and staying sane throughout the process. I want to give a special shout-out to Courtney Martin—you constantly inspire me and there is no way I would have said, "I think I'm gonna write a book," unless I'd seen you do it first. Joie Jager-Hyman, you are the best writing buddy around. Jennifer Gandin Le and Ethan Todras-Whitehill, long live the NYPL days. And Kimberlee Auerbach, your smile is worth a million words.

Jane Pratt, thank you for hiring me as your second assistant, which isn't nearly as *Devil Wears Prada* as it sounds, when I hadn't even graduated from college yet. You taught me so much about writing and creating stories. And a huge thank you to all my amazing friends at *Jane* over the years.

Jeff Gordinier, thank you for being my mentor. I'm 22 percent through that reading list you gave me, which is sort of an accomplishment. Bill Van Parys, thank you for dispensing sage advice along with a dirty joke. Warren St. John, I still can't believe that you responded to my random email, and thank you for all of your awesome advice. It's meant so much to me.

Being a teacher can be a thankless job. So thank you to all the tremendous teachers I've had over the years. Marcie Pachino, there is no way I would be a journalist today if it hadn't been for your guidance on the Jordan High School *Falcon's Cry*. Kelly Moore, I know you are out there somewhere inspiring the next wave of sociology majors.

Oh, and big ups to all current and past staffers of the *Falcon's Cry* and the *Barnard Bulletin*!

To all my amazing friends, thank you so much for your support and enthusiasm over the past two years. I wish I had the space to name each and every one of you, but I do want to give one special shout-out. Christina Rogers, your passion for journalism (and life) is contagious.

Last and by no means least, my family. Lizz, you are the best sister on the planet, and a darn good editor to boot. Dad, thank you for your encyclopedic knowledge of sports, and for the best last name ever. Mom, I still remember being a kid and hearing your writing group laughing in the living room. You are a tremendous writer, and I totally know where I got my talent. I feel so blessed to have the three of you just a 45-minute subway ride away.

# ABOUT THE AUTHOR

**KATE TORGOVNICK** writes for *The New York Times*, *Page Six Magazine*, Time.com, and *Glamour,* and her articles have also appeared in *Newsweek*, *New York Magazine*, *Sports Illustrated*, and *The International Herald Tribune*. Kate was formerly an associate editor at *Jane* magazine, where she interviewed bands galore and wrote the magazine's Prank column. She now lives in New York City, but grew up in North Carolina where she learned to complete a Rubik's Cube in less than two minutes. This book took just a little bit longer.

# CHEER!

## FOR DISCUSSION

### Part One: Tryouts

1. Cheerleading is one of the only sports where men and women compete together. Yet when asked about dating teammates, James Turner, captain of the Southern University cheer squad, says, "The girls on the squad are like my younger sisters. People always ask 'Are you holla-ing at 'em?' But I don't even look at them that way" (page 29). How do gender dynamics seem to play out on college cheerleading squads? Does dating a teammate have the same implications as dating a coworker? How could team romances affect the squad's overall chemistry? How do the cheerleaders in the book navigate this minefield?

2. In *Cheer!*, Torgovnick gives many reasons why, in the cheerleading world, all-girl teams are seen as secondary to coed teams—including that all-girl teams are associated with high school, and that all-girl squads typically cheer for less-attended sports like women's basketball and volleyball. Why do you think this hierarchy has developed? The University of Memphis All-Girl Tigers say that one of their objectives in creating new moves and trying coed stunts is to get all-girl cheerleading the respect it deserves. Is this a feminist undertaking?

3. During the tryouts at Stephen F. Austin University, Samantha—who is listed as five foot one—is nearly cut on account of her being "too tall." Do flyers need to be tiny, tiny, tiny to be good cheerleaders? What kinds of pressure do you think this puts on the women? Is this different than the fact that top football players are 250 to 300 pounds and that many basketball players are close to (if not over) seven feet tall?

4. While observing the Memphis tryouts, Torgovnick notes that of all the criteria the judges consider, "Look" carries the greatest amount of weight. Discuss cheerleading's emphasis on appearance. Is it a necessary evil and/or an inherent part of the sport? Is cheerleading capable of shaking this infatuation? Should it? What are some other subcultures that place such a high value on looking good?

## Part Two: Spirit Camps

5. When discussing the differences between male and female coaches, Sierra says, "Honestly, I was kind of worried about coming to SFA and having a guy coach." What factors contributed to her making this statement? Consider the case of Trisha replacing Brad. How significant is the sex of a coach in the world of cheerleading?

6. Safety is a primary concern of counselors at spirit camp, but consider this statement made by an announcer at the UCA camp Memphis attended: "Right now cheerleading attracts athletic people. Y'all are good-looking, all-American people. If they decide to ground you, they won't see the effects for five years.... Remember, a girl goes down and cheerleading will change." How do cheerleading's governing bodies approach the sport's built-in dangers? Do safety restrictions limit the sport? How do cheerleaders seem to interpret the risks inherent in their sport? Are they cavalier about the danger, or is their risk-taking admirable?

7. Southern University's status as one of the premier historically black college cheerleading teams is both a blessing and a curse. They routinely lack the necessary funds and numbers to compete with the better-funded, traditional powerhouses. At the same time, every time the team performs, Torgovnick notes, everybody stops what they're doing to "watch them intently." Why is competitive cheerleading so expensive? Should schools provide bigger budgets to cheerleading teams? And should attendance at Nationals require large sums of money?

8. Speaking candidly about steroid use in the sport, one cheerleader at camp says, "If they started drug testing . . . hoo boy." If steroid use is as prevalent as he says, why don't the major cheer organizations police it? Or should this responsibility fall on individual schools and coaches? How would open discussion about steroids change the cheerleading world? Why do you think athletes go to these extremes?

## Part Three: Football Season

9. Upon winning the intramural football championship at the University of Memphis, one member of the cheerleading team says, "This takes away every doubt people have that cheerleaders are athletes." This theme—cheerleaders reaffirming their status as athletes—recurs throughout Torgovnick's narrative. Do college cheerleaders seem to have an inferiority complex? Why do you think people tend to view cheerleading as just pom-poms, hair ribbons, and rhyming chants? Why is the common understanding of cheerleading so different from the reality?

10. Throughout SFA's chapters in *Cheer!* the letters LCLM come up over and over again. Why do the Lumberjack cheerleaders guard the meaning so vigorously? Consider the role these letters play in building a collective identity for a squad like SFA, where team members are recruited from across the country, versus at schools like Southern and Memphis, where cheerleaders tend to be local talent drawn to cheer for their love of the school.

11. Regarding friendships with noncheerleaders, Torgovnick quotes Sierra, "It's boring to me to talk to normal people." Is this sentiment consistent throughout all of the teams Torgovnick analyzes, or is it unique to SFA? How would you imagine "normal people" perceive the cheerleaders on campus? Consider what the Memphis cheerleaders have to say about preferring to date other athletes. Would they fit Sierra's definition of normal?

12. In Chapter 9, Torgovnick tells the story of Mary, who started using cocaine as a way to stay skinny for cheerleading. Discuss Mary's story. Ultimately, who is responsible for her spiraling out of control? Should coaches and advisors be expected to supervise and stop this sort of behavior? Can they? Considering all the body pressures on cheerleading, how can coaches, schools, and the major cheerleading organizations make sure that cheerleaders don't go to hazardous extremes—like developing eating disorders or using hard drugs—to keep their weight down?

13. Discussing Southern's failure to secure a paid bid to Nationals, one squad member says, "The system is not designed to entice a struggling historically black college team." Later, Coach James hypothesizes that "Talent is not the question, it's just the finances." Based on what you're reading, are these statements accurate? Analyze the racial undertones of Torgovnick's book. What role, if any, does race play in the world of competitive collegiate cheerleading?

## Part Four: Bid Videos

14. Before devoting an afternoon to community service at a retirement home, Casi mentions she might lose her job on account of missing so much work for cheer practice. Later, Kristen mentions missing a friend's wedding for a cheerleading commitment. Cheerleading, it seems, always takes precedence over the rest of a cheerleader's life. What other examples of this did you find in the book? In your opinion, do the benefits outweigh the sacrifices?

15. Even with safety training and precautions, injuries remain a constant part of cheerleading. One Memphis cheerleader quoted in the book almost seems proud of the sport's dangerous nature, because as Torgovnick points out, doing so "somehow legitimizes

her hard work." Yet despite the obvious risks and frequent injuries, few cheerleading teams have their own athletic trainers to deal with medical concerns. What would it take for this to change?

16. Compare the rapport between stunt partners Tyrone and Samantha with that of James Brown and Sierra. What are some of the major differences between how they treat each other and how they approach the sport? If you could partner with any of these athletes, who would it be, and why?

17. At the conclusion of section four, we learn Southern will not produce a bid video, essentially forgoing Nationals. The decision comes after several members leave the squad to focus on noncheerleading activities. One of them, Tiffany Jones, says, "It's a hard decision, but what I came here for was an education." Compare this sentiment to those of the SFA or Memphis cheerleaders. Can you imagine people on those squads making this statement?

## Part Five: Nationals

18. Going into Nationals, Kern was Memphis's savior. After the team's disappointing performance, though, she was sobbing alone, avoiding her teammates. Discuss Kern's swift fall from hero to zero. Does one person deserve responsibility for a failed routine? Consider the way her teammates treat her in response to her mistakes. Is their behavior justified?

19. How would you have reacted in Chapter 17, when Sierra falls during a basket toss and is rushed to the hospital? How does this injury affect the team? And what do you think of her drive to come back?

20. Talk about all of the obstacles faced by the Southern Jaguars, from the start of the season to the anticlimactic finale at the New Orleans Convention Center. Put yourself in their shoes. Considering all of the turmoil faced throughout the season, how/why do you think they never gave up? How does their experience at a relatively insignificant competition compare to those of the book's other teams who were able to compete at Nationals?

21. With the conclusion of each team's season, several members seem set on retiring early from the sport, even if they are not graduating. Torgovnick isn't entirely convinced. Why do you think so many cheerleaders feel this way at the end of the season? And why doesn't the author buy it? If you had to guess, which of these cheerleaders do you think came back for the 2007–2008 season? (E-mail Kate at cheerbook@gmail.com to find out the answer.)